P9-EEB-781

Kouzes and Posner have quite literally written the book on leadership. Not only that, but they're also generous and thorough enough to keep updating it, as our tumultuous times demand. This seventh edition of *The Leadership Challenge* is a masterpiece—informative, practical, and engaging. If you take these ideas to heart and apply the book's Five Practices assiduously, you will be well on your way to becoming a better leader. You will be well on your way to enriching the lives of others and making the organizations you care about better.

—**Amy C. Edmondson,** Professor, Harvard Business School; Author of *The Fearless Organization*

Did we really need a seventh edition of *The Leadership Challenge*? The answer is a resounding *yes*. This seminal book-series is more important than ever, far more important. The world is a mess. And the best way out, as I see it, is to better our organizations and the lives of their employees. The Five Practices that are the keystone of the book can without doubt trigger an internal revolution of organizational excellence—which can, collectively, give one hope, on a global scale, for a brighter future. Bravo, Jim and Barry.

—**Tom Peters,** bestselling business author and speaker

For years, the US Coast Guard Academy has relied upon the foundational principles set forth in *The Leadership Challenge* to develop the next generation of leaders of character who will serve the people of the United States. This exciting seventh edition draws upon conclusive research and is bursting with compelling, real-life examples to learn from and lead by; it's an indispensable resource for leaders at all levels who desire to make extraordinary things happen . . . in the workplace, at home, and in society. Jim Kouzes's and Barry Posner's 40-year collaboration in studying leaders, researching leadership, and leading brings us a masterful work designed to help people become the best leaders they can be. If you want to learn how to earn trust and respect as a leader others yearn to follow, let this book serve as your proven field guide.

—**Sandra Stosz,** Vice Admiral, USCG (ret.), trustee for the US Coast Guard Academy James M. Loy Institute for Leadership; Author of *Breaking Ice and Breaking Glass: Leading in Uncharted Waters*

This is a classic—one of the few books on leadership that's actually worth reading. *The Leadership Challenge* is more relevant than ever: a practical, evidence-based resource on how to mobilize people around a common goal.

—**Adam Grant,** #1 *New York Times* bestselling author of *Think Again* and host of the TED podcast WorkLife

I've been a student of leadership derived from my time in the military and a practitioner of the five practices of *The Leadership Challenge* for nearly 30 years. I have found that *The Leadership Challenge* is a call to action for any individual who wants to lead through inspiration and accomplish only what others dream of achieving. It's required reading for my leadership team and has been a foundational training platform for my management teams over the years. If you are looking for an *X* factor in results for yourself, your team, or your company, look no further and devour and apply the principles in this book!

—**Mark Leposky,** Executive Vice President, Global Operations, Callaway Golf

Jim and Barry's work has transformed our understanding of what constitutes leadership excellence over the last three-plus decades. This updated edition provides essential insights into what it takes to identify and develop stellar leaders now.

—**Sally Helgesen,** lead author, *How Women Rise*, author, *The Web of Inclusion*

I've been a fan—and follower—of *The Leadership Challenge* for almost 25 years, and the principles are as relevant today as they have ever been. In this leadership classic, Kouzes and Posner have identified and brought to life invaluable practices that are as insightful as they are practical.

—**Patrick Lencioni,** President, The Table Group; bestselling author of *The Five Dysfunctions of a Team and The Advantage*

I'm a raving fan of Jim Kouzes and Barry Posner. There are few, if any, folks in the leadership field better than the two of them. If you don't believe me, read the seventh edition of their classic book, *The Leadership Challenge*. With every edition they upgrade the content with new research and observations. It continues to be a must-read!

—**Ken Blanchard,** Co-Author of *The One Minute Manager* and *Simple Truths of Leadership*

It has been my experience that many companies underestimate the importance of leadership. In my opinion, leadership is the common ingredient in America's great companies. *The Leadership Challenge* and the Leadership Practices Inventory create a common language with which leaders can discuss both strategic and everyday issues in leading organizations and people. The characteristics of admired leaders alone set a standard for all executives to follow. *The Leadership Challenge*'s teachings played a strong role in our success.

—**Jim Kerr,** Executive Chairman, D.A. Davidson Companies

Kouzes and Posner boil down the concepts of excellent leadership into easy-to-apply principles. I share this book with my entire team of young professionals. It is my "go-to" resource and truly helps people grow in their careers.

—**Jacquelyn McCormick,** Chief of Staff to Berkeley Mayor Jesse Arreguin

Jim and Barry have done it again! An established classic in its field, *The Leadership Challenge* continues to provide valuable knowledge for today's fast-changing leadership dynamics. Filled with engaging case studies and updated research, this book is a must-read for anyone looking to improve their leadership, team, organization, or career.

—**Marshall Goldsmith,** Thinkers50 #1 Executive Coach; *New York Times* bestselling author of *The Earned Life*, *Triggers*, and *What Got You Here Won't Get You There.*

The five practices of exemplary leadership have stood the test of time, and this revised and updated edition shows why. In these volatile and uncertain times, the world needs more leaders to rise to the leadership challenge.

—**David Burkus,** Author of *Leading from Anywhere*

Leadership is everyone's business. *The Leadership Challenge* is essential reading for anyone who wants to be an exceptional leader. Jim and Barry believe that every challenge is an opportunity and provide actions you can take to ensure that you reach leadership success. They demonstrate how you can rise to every occasion to be the best leader you can be.

—**Elaine Biech,** 2022 ISA Thought Leader, Author, *Skills for Career Success, The New Business of Consulting*

In 2020 the working world leaped from in-person interaction to virtual meetings. The change confronted leaders with new challenges, yet leadership basics remained the same. Kouzes and Posner hit it head-on in their seventh edition of *The Leadership Challenge* by building on the foundation of their earlier editions with evidence-based guidance for navigating the new normal.

—**Jim Hancock,** President and Founder, San Francisco Sailing Science Center

Jim Kouzes and Barry Posner have once again provided leaders a great gift in the seventh edition of *The Leadership Challenge*. Truly tested over time, the Five Practices of Exemplary Leadership continue to guide leaders at all levels in making positive contributions around the world. This book is not only filled with captivating stories about what great leaders do but shares how they may go about developing themselves to make positive and remarkable differences with the individuals and organizations they encounter.

—**Brent Kondritz,** Executive Director, University of Dayton Center for Leadership

The Five Practices operating system is not some random set of rules but rather a well-researched framework. I experienced firsthand during these tough times how it made me a better leader.

—**Mainak Pal,** Senior Project Manager, Global Development, AGTEK Development Company, Inc.

The Five Practices are a timeless and all-encompassing operational leadership system. It is relevant during uncertain times like today and during settled times. It is practical, learnable, measurable, and effective. When put into practice, these skills have proven to be effective leadership tools and can bring out better leaders in all of us.

—**Maria Hirotsuka,** Senior Manager, Xilinx

When these practices are understood, adopted, and put into practice, anyone can become a better leader. This is not just a system but also a leadership guide. This guide serves as a resource for users to consult when faced with leadership challenges, turning difficulties into opportunities.

—**Rusty Stevenson,** Senior Contracting Officer, US Department of Veteran Affairs

The pandemic has added new variables and challenges to being a leader, but I have found that when I returned to The Five Practices for guidance and leadership, it helped me go a long way.

—**William Yuen,** Director, Western Digital

Applying The Five Practices has been a game-changer in the many challenges I have faced in the workplace. I encourage leaders at all levels to learn these practices to deal with any situation that calls for leadership.

—**Prashnath Thandavamuthy,** Director Portfolio Management & Strategy, Juniper Networks

By applying these five practices, we can all become better leaders in our workplaces, our homes, and our communities.

—**Jennifer Lee,** Senior Vice President, Provident Credit Union

Speaking from personal experience, The Five Practices is a very practical framework that focuses on developing and enhancing proven attributes that make leaders extraordinary. I have systematically executed this "operating system" during the last ~20 months in my organization and have seen a significant and continuing increase in team members' overall engagement, enthusiasm, ownership, and accountability.

—**Edwin Haghnazari,** Director, The Jackson Laboratory

Everyone can become a better leader by adopting The Five Practices of Exemplary Leadership model. This model is an operating system guiding rail to develop future leaders with promising results.

—**Hong Lu,** Manager, Cisco

That is what I love most about The Five Practices. It is not about here are steps to follow, once you do those steps you are done. It is about here are steps to follow, keep doing them over and over again and adapt and change as you find ways to do better and move forward.

—**David Mahal,** Senior Global Sales Director, Flex

# THE LEADERSHIP CHALLENGE

# THE LEADERSHIP CHALLENGE

**SEVENTH EDITION**

## How to Make Extraordinary Things Happen in Organizations

JAMES M. KOUZES

BARRY Z. POSNER

Published by John Wiley & Sons, Inc., Hoboken, New Jersey.
Published simultaneously in Canada.



For general information on our other products and services or for technical support, please contact our Customer Care Department within the United States at (800) 762-2974, outside the United States at (317) 572-3993 or fax (317) 572-4002.

Wiley also publishes its books in a variety of electronic formats. Some content that appears in print may not be available in electronic formats. For more information about Wiley products, visit our web site at www.wiley.com.

***Library of Congress Cataloging-in-Publication Data***

Names: Kouzes, James M., author. | Posner, Barry Z., author.
Title: The leadership challenge : how to make extraordinary things happen in organizations / James M. Kouzes, Barry Z. Posner.
Description: Seventh edition. | Hoboken, New Jersey : Jossey-Bass, [2023] | Includes index.
Identifiers: LCCN 2022029443 (print) | LCCN 2022029444 (ebook) | ISBN 9781119736127 (hardback) | ISBN 9781119736165 (adobe pdf) | ISBN 9781119736158 (epub)
Subjects: LCSH: Leadership. | Executive ability. | Management.
Classification: LCC HD57.7 .K68 2022 (print) | LCC HD57.7 (ebook) | DDC 658.4/092—dc23/eng/20220711
LC record available at https://lccn.loc.gov/2022029443
LC ebook record available at https://lccn.loc.gov/2022029444

Cover Design: Wiley
Cover Image: Lake Bachalpsee © aCZhou / Getty Images

SKY10061040_112823

# CONTENTS

**INTRODUCTION** ........ xv

**1 When Leaders Are at Their Best** ........ 1

*The Five Practices of Exemplary Leadership*

*The Five Practices Make a Difference*

*Leadership Is a Relationship*

*Putting It All Together: Credibility Is the Foundation*

## PRACTICE 1

**MODEL THE WAY** ........ 29

**2 Clarify Values** ........ 31

*Find Your Voice*

*Affirm Shared Values*

**3 Set the Example** ........ 59

*Live the Shared Values*

*Teach Others to Model the Values*

## PRACTICE 2

**INSPIRE A SHARED VISION** ........ 85

**4 Envision the Future** ........ 87

*Imagine the Possibilities*

*Identify a Common Purpose*

**5 Enlist Others** ........ 111

*Appeal to Common Ideals*

*Animate the Vision*

## PRACTICE 3

**CHALLENGE THE PROCESS** ........ 137

**6 Search for Opportunities** ........ 139

*Seize the Initiative*

*Exercise Outsight*

**7 Experiment and Take Risks** ........ 165

*Generate Small Wins*

*Learn from Experience*

# PRACTICE 4

**ENABLE OTHERS TO ACT** ........ 191

**8 Foster Collaboration** ........ 193

*Create a Climate of Trust*

*Facilitate Relationships*

**9 Strengthen Others** ........ 219

*Enhance Self-Determination*

*Develop Competence and Confidence*

# PRACTICE 5

**ENCOURAGE THE HEART** ........ 247

**10 Recognize Contributions** ........ 249

*Expect the Best*

*Personalize Recognition*

**11 Celebrate the Values and Victories** ........ 275

*Create a Spirit of Community*

*Be Personally Involved*

**12 Treat Challenge as an Opportunity** ........ 303

*Your Leadership Matters*

*Liberate the Leader Within Everyone*

*Everyone Can Learn to Lead*

*Become Your Best Self*
*You Won't Always Get It Right*
*Make Becoming a Better Leader a Daily Habit*
*Remember the Secret to Success in Life*

**Endnotes** .......... 325

**Acknowledgments** .......... 367

**About the Authors** .......... 371

**Index** .......... 375

**INTRODUCTION**

# Making Extraordinary Things Happen

**THE LEADERSHIP CHALLENGE** has always been about how people go about mobilizing others to want to make extraordinary things happen. It's about the behavioral practices used to transform values into actions, visions into realities, obstacles into innovations, separateness into solidarity, and risks into rewards. It's about leadership that creates the climate in which challenging opportunities open the door to remarkable successes.

The fundamental purpose of *The Leadership Challenge* is to assist people in furthering their abilities to lead others to greatness. Whether you're in the private sector or public, an employee or a volunteer, a manager or an individual contributor, a student, teacher, or parent, we have written this book to help you further develop your capacity to guide others to places they have never been before.

## What's New?

We've been researching the practices of exemplary leadership for over four decades, and every time we sit down to write a new edition of this book, people ask us, "What's new and what's different? How has leadership changed since you started your studies?" These are understandable questions, and there certainly have been some significant changes in the world since the previous edition.

The COVID-19 pandemic tops the list. It was nowhere on anyone's radar in 2017, but by 2020 it had effectively disrupted every person's everyday life. It has been a crisis like none other in our lifetime. COVID-19 immediately impacted how we lived, cared for our sick and elderly, shopped, ate, learned, worked, worshipped, and were entertained. Everyone became more and more anxious as the sick and dying overwhelmed hospitals, and healthcare workers labored to exhaustion. All but essential businesses and services shut down worldwide for months, then opened up and shut down again. All organizations, at the very least, had to alter the way they conducted their operations. Millions were out of work, and individuals and businesses had to be protected with government loans and payments. Adults stayed home to go to work, and kids stayed home to go to school. People's sense of belonging declined, and many felt the pain of isolation. People put on masks and stood socially distanced in lines outside stores with fingers crossed, hoping to find toilet paper on the shelves when they entered. Ships backed up in ports, and supply chains broke down. Politicians publicly squabbled about how best to respond, and misinformation spread virally. Civic discourse became quite uncivil.

Then in the middle of all this, the world watched in horror when in the United States a black man, George Floyd, was murdered at the hands of a policeman. "I can't breathe" became a rallying cry for those who had felt strangled for decades by injustice. Protests erupted, not just in the United States but in many cities around the world. Thousands of frustrated citizens filled the streets. Longstanding grievances grew in intensity, and the cultural and political divide expanded. Ideological differences became more intense. Trust and confidence in institutional leaders hit an all-time low, and they've not yet turned much around.

Moreover, in the United States, what had historically been a peaceful transition of power from one presidential administration to the next was disrupted by a violent demonstration. Thousands stormed the halls of Congress, hundreds fought with police, and many even threatened to abduct and kill elected officials. A contentious debate ensued over the presidential election outcome. The political divide expanded, and trust in institutions fell even more.

After years of mask-wearing, social distancing, and staying at home, vaccines helped ease restrictions, and people began to venture out and return to work. But then something else unheard of happened. Fueled by disillusionment, discontent, and disaffection, a sizeable number of people voluntarily decided not to go back to work, at least with their same employer. What became known as the "Great Resignation" (or the Great Reshuffle, Great Exploration, or Great Imagination) emerged as another variance in economic recovery and organizational commitment.

And just as it seemed the world was emerging from the pandemic, a global conflict erupted in Ukraine, threatening the peace and security of Europe and perhaps the entire world. Refugees in the millions fled their homes with little more than a suitcase of belongings to their names. Economic inflation, already emerging as a concern, expanded to a major worry as fuel prices skyrocketed.

Concerns over climate change intensified, especially among the younger generations. With out-of-control wildfires, hurricanes, flooding, and other natural disasters devasting communities across the globe, they expressed pessimism about the world they are inheriting and its impact on their future lives and livelihoods. The beginning of the third decade of this century seems to be defined by a pervasive uncertainty that challenges individuals, institutions, communities, and nations. It was becoming the zeitgeist of the period.[1]

Yet among the tragedy and hardships, discord and discontent, people and organizations pivoted. Delivery trucks filled the otherwise empty streets as people turned to online shopping. Homebound workers adapted to remote Zoom meetings, and kids adapted to virtual schooling.

Government and businesses, often competitors, collaborated to develop vaccines in record time. Restaurants found ways to meet the demand for takeout meals and outdoor dining. Streaming services filled the pipeline with on-demand content. Families learned to connect through video chats. Organizations brought diversity, equity, and inclusion to the forefront of their agendas and addressed inequities. Physical and mental health became priorities. At-home workouts became commonplace. People began to reassess the meaning of work. Some decided that they'd change the career path they had been traveling, and others demanded more flexibility from the workplace they'd chosen. People started to reimagine the way they worked and the way they lived.

We'll return to many of these issues, and others, in the chapters to come. We'll do it through stories that people have told us about their experiences, research from scholars who've studied this period, and data we've collected on how leaders behaved and the impact their actions have had on engagement and work performance.

Before we do, however, let's take a step back and reflect on something else we observed because *there's an even more important lesson* that has emerged in these last few years.

## Challenge Is the Opportunity for Greatness

*The Leadership Challenge* has its origins in a research project we began over forty years ago. We wanted to know what people did when they were at their "personal best" in leading others. These personal bests were experiences in which people set their individual leadership standards of excellence. They were, so to speak, their Olympic gold-medal-winning performances.

When we reviewed the Personal-Best Leadership Experience questionnaires we had received, it became evident that every single case involved some kind of challenge. The challenge might have been a natural disaster, a health crisis, a cutting-edge service, a groundbreaking piece of legislation, an invigorating campaign to get adolescents to join an environmental program, a revolutionary turnaround of a bureaucratic government program, a heartbreaking injury to a child, an initiative to become the first female team to ascend one of the world's tallest peaks, a local emergency project to feed first responders and frontline workers, the startup of a new plant, the launch of a new product, the creation of a new market, or the turnaround of a failing business. Whatever the situation, all the cases involved overcoming great adversity. When people talked about making extraordinary things happen, they spoke about encountering obstacles, resistance, naysayers, hardened attitudes, seemingly impossible odds, uncertainty, hardship, setbacks, or other adversities. In other words, *challenge was the common denominator.* It was the context in which people said they did their best.

Keep in mind that we didn't ask people to tell us about their challenges. We asked them to tell us about their Personal-Best Leadership Experiences. They could have written about more stable, predictable, or conventional situations. But they didn't. Easy, undemanding endeavors simply aren't associated with award-winning performances. What people chose to discuss were challenging times. We continue to this day to ask people around the world about their Personal-Best Leadership Experiences, and we continue to find the same thing. Challenge defines the context in which people perform at their best.

That is *the* critical lesson from reviewing thousands of Personal-Best Leadership Experiences over forty years. *Challenge is the crucible for leadership* and *the opportunity for greatness.* Challenge shapes us, and challenge opens doors.

Leaders absolutely must address the current issues they, their organizations, and their communities face today. That was true in the past, and it is true today, and it will be true into the future. Contemporary dilemmas, such as those with which we began this introduction, must be on the agenda. Equally true is that there will be other challenges ahead, perhaps even more daunting than those we face in these moments.

Leadership challenges never cease, and leadership opportunities will always be there for those who choose to greet them. That is precisely why, from the beginning, we titled this book *The Leadership* ***Challenge***.

The study of leadership is how people guide others through adversity, uncertainty, and turbulence; triumph against overwhelming odds; take initiative when there is inertia; and activate individuals and institutions in the face of stiff resistance. This book describes what leaders did under challenging circumstances and what you can do to put their leadership behaviors into practice and make a difference.

## An Evidence-Based, Best Practices Operating System

We persist in asking today the same fundamental question we asked in 1982 when we started our investigative journey into understanding exemplary leadership: What did you do when you were at your personal best as a leader? We've talked to people of all ages, spanning across educational levels and ethnicity, representing just about every type of organization there is, at all levels, in all functions, and from many different places around the world. Their stories, and the behaviors and actions they described, resulted in the discovery of The Five Practices of Exemplary Leadership® framework, an operating system for leadership. When leaders do their best, they engage in The Five Practices—they Model the Way, Inspire a Shared Vision, Challenge the Process, Enable Others to Act, and Encourage the Heart. In the following chapters, we go into depth about each of these leadership practices, both conceptually and practically.

*The Leadership Challenge* is evidence-based. We derived The Five Practices from rigorous research, and we illustrate them with examples from real people doing real things. With each new edition, we continue to update the stories, cases, and examples of exactly what real people do when they are at their best. Their names are real, as are their experiences and quotations. However, for two reasons, we do not mention their organizations. First, most people are not still connected with that organization or in the same position. Second, the cases and our focus are about what *individuals* do, and not about their organizations, functions, or positions.

With each edition of the book, we update the quantitative research—both our findings and those from other scholars around the globe. In this regard, the *Leadership Practices Inventory* (LPI)—the instrument we designed to measure how often people use The Five Practices and how their frequency makes a difference with their teams and organization—provides ongoing empirical data that supports the validity of this leadership operating system. The LPI assesses the frequency with which leaders demonstrate the behaviors associated with The Five Practices—from the individual leader's perspective and from the observations of their manager, direct reports, colleagues, and others. There are over five million respondents in the normative LPI database. Respondents answer additional questions regarding how they feel about their workplace and their leader. For example, they respond to questions about their commitment and motivational levels, how proud they are to tell others they work for this organization, and whether they would favorably recommend their current leader to others. They also provide demographic data about age, education, gender, ethnicity, tenure, function, industry, hierarchical position, organizational size, and nationality. This robust database allows us to produce statistical analyses that support our claim that leadership makes a difference.

Furthermore, with each new edition we get the chance to reiterate what's still essential, discard what's not, and add what's new. We also take the opportunity to contemporize the framework and freshen up the language and point of view so that the book is highly relevant to current circumstances and conditions. With experience, and more cases and data, we can also be more prescriptive about the best practices of leaders. The empirical analyses show that personal and professional outcomes are directly related to how frequently you engage in these leadership practices. It's not about your title, position, function, age, gender, educational level, country of origin, or any other demographic variable. It's about how you behave. We firmly believe that exemplary leadership is within the grasp of everyone and that the opportunities for leadership are boundless and boundary-less.

We expect that all of you reading this book face vexing issues that not only make leadership more urgent but also require you to be more conscious and conscientious about employing exemplary leadership practices and behaviors. Others are looking to you to help them figure out what they should be doing and how they can develop themselves to be leaders. You don't just owe it to yourself to become the best leader you can possibly be. You're even more responsible to others. You may not know it, but they're expecting you to do your best.

## A Field Guide for Leaders

Think of *The Leadership Challenge* as a field guide to take along on your leadership journey. Think of it as a manual you can consult when you want advice and counsel on how to make extraordinary things happen with your team or organization. We have designed the book to describe what leaders do, explain the fundamental principles that support these leadership practices, provide actual case examples of real people who demonstrate each practice, and offer specific recommendations on what you can do to make these practices your own and to continue your development as a leader.

In Chapter 1 we establish our point of view about leadership. Leadership is a set of skills and abilities that are learnable by anyone with the desire to learn and the persistence to practice them. We provide an overview of The Five Practices, summarize the findings from decades of empirical studies about what leaders do when they are at their best, and show that these leadership practices make a difference. We also remind you that a complete picture of leadership requires understanding that leadership is fundamentally a relationship, and hence it is important to understand and appreciate what people look for in an individual they would be *willing* to follow.

The ten chapters that follow describe the Ten Commitments of Leadership that people employ to make extraordinary things happen, and there are two chapters associated with each of The Five Practices. There are two essential behaviors associated with each of the Commitments.

We provide actual case examples of people who demonstrate each of the leadership practices, commitments, and essential behaviors. We also offer evidence from our research, and that of others, to support the concepts and how they are applied and prescribe specific recommendations on what you can do to make each practice your own, becoming the best leader you can be.

Each of these chapters ends with a set of actionable suggestions about what you need to do to make these leadership behaviors and practices an ongoing and natural part of your behavioral and attitudinal repertoire. Whether the focus is your own learning or the development of your constituents, you can take immediate action on every recommendation. They don't require a budget or approval from top management—or anyone else. They just require your personal commitment and discipline. Select at least one that you will do as soon as possible, if not immediately, to make the transition between learning and doing. In addition, we offer several suggestions to converse with the people around you about leadership. These conversations are opportunities to build and reinforce a culture of leadership and underscore how important it is to act and think like a leader.

In Chapter 12, we call on everyone to accept personal responsibility to be a role model for leadership. We continue to champion the view that leadership is everyone's business. The first place to look for leadership is within yourself. Accepting the leadership challenge requires reflection, practice, humility, and taking advantage of every opportunity to make a difference. We close, as we have in every edition, with this conclusion: Leadership is not an affair of the head. Leadership is an affair of the heart.

* * *

We recommend that you read Chapter 1 first, but after that, there is no sacred order to proceeding through the rest of this book. Go wherever your interests are. We wrote this material to support you in your leadership development. Just remember that each practice and commitment of leadership is essential. Although you might skip around in the book, you can't skip any of the fundamentals of leadership.

# The Leadership Challenge

Challenge is the opportunity for greatness, and the most significant contribution leaders make is not to today's bottom line; it is to the long-term development of people and institutions so they can adapt, change, prosper, and grow. Our ongoing aspiration is that this book contributes to the revitalization of organizations, the creation of new enterprises, the renewal of healthy communities, and greater respect and understanding in the world. We fervently hope that it enriches your life and that of your community and your family.

Leadership is important, not just in your career and within your organization, but in every sector, community, and country. We need more exemplary leaders, and we need them more than ever. So much extraordinary work needs to be done. We need leaders who can unite us and ignite us.

Meeting the leadership challenge is a personal—and a daily—opportunity available to everyone. We know that if you have the will and the way to lead, you can make extraordinary things happen. You supply the will. We'll do our best to supply the way.

James M. Kouzes
*Orinda, California*

Barry Z. Posner
*Berkeley, California*

# CHAPTER 1
# When Leaders Are at Their Best

*Leadership is ultimately about creating a way for people to contribute to making something extraordinary happen.*[1]
*Alan Keith*

**WITH LEADERSHIP,** as with most things in life, experience is often the teacher. We learn what to do by trying it ourselves or by watching others. The problem is that not all of what's done or observed is effective or appropriate behavior. When recommending to leaders what they should and should not do, it's imperative to base leadership practices on the best of what people do and observe—the actions that represent the highest standards of excellence.

That was our objective when we first began our leadership research in 1983. We wanted to answer a simple question: What do people do when they are at their personal best as leaders?

To answer this question, we developed the *Personal-Best Leadership Experience* questionnaire and started collecting case studies. These were stories about times when, in their perception, leaders set their individual standard of excellence. They could select a recent experience or one from their past. They could have been the official person-in-charge or have emerged as the informal leader. They could have held a paid position or been a volunteer, either in a workplace or nonwork setting. They could have been part of a corporation, agency, community group, professional association, sports team, or school. The timing and context were up to them; it just needed to be an experience they felt represented their best leadership performance.

The *Personal-Best Leadership Experience* questionnaire is 12 pages long, consisting of 38 open-ended questions, and generally requires one to two hours for reflection and expression. More than 550 of these *surveys* were collected initially, and that number today is well over 5,000. In addition, we have conducted hundreds of in-depth interviews on the same themes.

In those interviews and case studies, we asked questions such as: Where did your personal-best leadership experience occur? When did it take place? How long was it from start to finish? What kind of project or undertaking was it? What was your specific role in this project? What external or internal challenges did you face? What words best describe how you felt at the beginning of this experience? How would you describe your feelings during this experience? Who initiated this experience? What did you aspire to accomplish? Who was involved in this experience? What actions did you take to get people moving in the right direction? How did you overcome setbacks? What did you do to keep people motivated? What did you learn from this experience? What key lessons about leadership would you share with another person from this experience?

Wherever we look, we find examples of exemplary leadership. We have found them in for-profit firms and nonprofits, agriculture and mining, manufacturing and utilities, technology and financial services, education and healthcare, government and military, and arts and community services. These leaders have been in hierarchical positions, as well as nonmanagers, individual contributors, and volunteers. They have been young and old, women and men, and represent a broad range of organizations and functions as well as racial, ethnic, religious, and cultural groups.

Leaders reside in every city, country, and nation. And we find this diversity to be true to this day.

The inescapable conclusion from analyzing thousands of personal-best leadership experiences is that (a) *everyone has a personal-best leadership story to tell,* and (b) *leadership is an identifiable set of skills and abilities available to anyone.* These findings challenge the myths that leadership is something that you find only at the highest levels of organizations and society, that it's something reserved for only a handful of charismatic men and women, and that it's something that ordinary people can't learn.[2] The notion that only a few great people can lead others to greatness is just plain wrong.

From the stories we gathered in interviews and written cases, a pattern of leadership behavior emerged. There were common themes in what leaders did when performing at their best, which led us to formulate a behavioral framework of exemplary leadership. We subjected our qualitative findings to a series of empirical tests. In our initial quantitative study, we asked over 3,000 managers to assess the extent to which they used these leadership behaviors. Their direct reports were asked how often they had observed their leaders utilizing these leadership behaviors, and we also asked them questions about their level of motivation, team spirit, commitment, productivity, and other standard engagement measures. This research has continued over the years, with the creation and development of the Leadership Practices Inventory (LPI), amassing a database that currently includes over 4.6 million people from more than 120 different countries.

The consistent results over five decades validate the model and yield another inescapable conclusion: Leadership matters. The frequency with which people engage in these leadership behaviors directly relates to assessments of workgroup performance and leadership effectiveness. There is a direct, positive correlation between the answer from direct reports of how effective their leader is and their perception of how often that leader engages in the leadership behavior—and this correlation actually increased over the two years of unprecedented volatility, ambiguity, and uncertainty experienced during the pandemic. In other words, exemplary leadership matters even more during times of extreme challenge.

# The Five Practices of Exemplary Leadership

*Being a good leader is not something that casually occurs. It takes great thought, care, insight, commitment, and energy.*

*Mary Godwin*

The critical lesson we've learned from carefully reviewing thousands of personal-best leadership cases is that the actions people take to make extraordinary things happen are much more alike than they are different, regardless of context. We continue to find that individuals who guide others along pioneering journeys follow surprisingly similar paths irrespective of the times or settings. Though each experience was unique in its expression, there were identifiable behaviors and actions that made a difference. When making extraordinary things happen in organizations, leaders engage in what we call The Five Practices of Exemplary Leadership®:

- **Model the Way**
- **Inspire a Shared Vision**
- **Challenge the Process**
- **Enable Others to Act**
- **Encourage the Heart**

These practices are not the private property of the people we studied. Nor do they belong to a few select shining stars. Leadership is not about personality; it's about behavior. The Five Practices are available to anyone who accepts the leadership challenge—the challenge of guiding people and organizations to places they have never been before. It is the challenge of moving beyond the ordinary to the extraordinary.

The Five Practices framework is not an accident of a particular moment in history. It has passed the test of time. While the *context* of leadership has changed dramatically over the years, the *content* of leadership has not changed much at all. Leaders' fundamental behaviors and actions have remained essentially the same, and they are as relevant today as they were when we began our study of exemplary leadership. The truth of each personal-best leadership experience—multiplied thousands of times and substantiated empirically by millions of respondents and hundreds of scholars—establishes The Five Practices of Exemplary Leadership as an "operating system" for leaders everywhere.[3]

Let's briefly review each of The Five Practices and a few examples that illustrate how leaders across a wide range of settings and circumstances use them to make extraordinary things happen. When you explore The Five Practices in depth in Chapters 2 through 11, you'll find scores of additional illustrations from the real-life experiences of people who have taken the leadership challenge.

**Model the Way** Titles are granted, but it's your behavior that is followed and earns you respect. In his personal best, Vince Brown, deputy program manager for a large-scale military initiative, made it a point to "set an example of what I wanted from my team." This was essential, he reported, "to building trust with the team. Trust needs to be earned by example, and I made sure to do what I said I would do. I would never ask my team to do something I would not do myself." Similarly, in his personal best, leading an Army Ranger platoon, Brock Jas noted that "because my team saw that I was putting all I had into the job, when I asked them to do something extra, they responded in kind." Exemplary leaders know that if they want to gain commitment and achieve the highest standards, they must be models of the behavior they expect of others.

To effectively *Model the Way,* you must first be clear about your guiding principles. You must *clarify values by finding your voice.* The personal bests illustrate that to stand up for their beliefs, leaders must first have some solid beliefs upon which to stand. When you understand who you are and what you believe, you can act with integrity when giving voice to those values.

In her personal-best leadership experience, Arpana Tiwari, a senior manager with one of the world's largest e-commerce retailers, found that "the more I spoke with others about my values, the clearer they became for me." She realized, however, that her values weren't the only ones that mattered. Everyone on the team has principles that guide their actions, and each individual cherishes their values. However, leaders must *affirm the shared values* to which all group members must commit. This requires getting everyone involved and on the same page about the importance of certain values. Doing so, Arpana observed, "makes it relatively easy to model the values that everyone has agreed to." She realized that another benefit of shared values was that "it is also less difficult to confront people when they make decisions that are not aligned. When someone violates a value, leaders have to do or say something, or they run the risk of sending a message that this is not important." Eloquent speeches about common values aren't nearly enough. Deeds are far more important than words when constituents determine how serious leaders are about what they say. Words and deeds must be consistent. Exemplary leaders must also *set the example by aligning the shared values* of the group. Through their daily actions, they demonstrate their deep commitment to their and the organization's beliefs.

The personal-best projects were all distinguished by relentless effort, steadfastness, competence, and attention to detail. We were struck by how the actions leaders took to set an example were often simple things. They were about the power of spending time with someone, of working side by side with colleagues, of telling stories that made values come alive, of being highly visible during times of uncertainty, and of asking questions to get people to think about values and priorities. *Model the Way* is essentially about earning the right and the respect to lead through direct individual involvement and action. People first follow the person, then the plan.

In fact, 99 percent of direct reports who *always* observe their leader Model the Way would favorably recommend that individual to their colleagues as a good leader. Just being above the average frequency on this leadership practice gives a 28 percent bump in being recommended by direct reports as a good leader over those below the mean on Model the Way.

There's only a one in twenty-five likelihood of being assessed as an effective leader by direct reports for those leaders who seldom Model the Way.

**Inspire a Shared Vision** People describe their personal-best leadership experiences as times when they imagined an exciting and attractive future for their organizations. They had visions and dreams of what *could* be. They had absolute faith in their dreams, and they were confident in their abilities to make those extraordinary things happen. Every organization, every social movement, begins with a vision; it is the force that energizes the creation of the future.

Leaders *envision the future by imagining exciting and ennobling possibilities*. You need to make something happen, change the way things are, and create something that no one else has ever created before. Before starting any project, leaders need to have both a realistic sense of the past and a clear vision of what success should look like. Leaders draw upon the lessons from the history of their organizations, and they also communicate a unique and optimistic view of the future. As a product manager with a full-service HR solutions provider, Puja Banerjee realized in her personal-best leadership experience that "my responsibility is always to communicate the big picture and vision of the initiative to my team and all of our stakeholders" because people always need to know the "why" for what they are being asked to do.

Too many people think that it's the leader's job to develop the vision when the reality is that people want to be involved in this process. You can't command commitment; you have to inspire it. You have to *enlist others in a common vision by appealing to shared aspirations*. At every step of the project "from discovery, design, development and final launch," Puja made sure that she communicated "what was happening so that we were all working toward a shared vision and our deliverables were aligned to it." Leaders ensure that the people they work with can see how their work is meaningful and their contributions fit into the big picture. This grassroots approach is much more effective than preaching one person's perspective.

In these times of rapid change and uncertainty, people want to follow those who can see beyond today's difficulties and imagine a brighter tomorrow. To embrace the vision and make it their own, people have to see themselves as part of that vision and as able to contribute to its realization. Leaders forge unity of purpose by showing their constituents how the dream is a shared one and how it fulfills the common good.

When you express your enthusiasm and excitement for the vision, you ignite that same passion in others. When reflecting on her personal-best leadership experience, Amy Matson Drohan, a senior customer success manager, remarked, "You can't proselytize a vision that you don't full-heartedly believe." Ultimately, she said, "The leader's excitement shines through and convinces the team that the vision is worthy of their time and support."

The empirical data backs up Amy's observation. Only three out of every one hundred direct reports—whose observations about the frequency with which their leaders Inspire a Shared Vision places them in the bottom quintile—strongly believe that this leader is effective. In contrast, more than one out of two leaders in the top quintile of the Inspire a Shared Vision distribution are evaluated as effective leaders by their direct reports.

**Challenge the Process** Challenge is the crucible for greatness. Every personal-best leadership case involved a change from the status quo. Not one person achieved a personal best by keeping things the same. Regardless of the specifics, all personal bests involved overcoming adversity and embracing opportunities to grow, innovate, and improve. The importance of this discovery is underscored by the rating leaders receive from their constituents. Few direct reports—less than one in ten—would strongly recommend someone as a good leader who did not frequently challenge the process, probably because there is little opportunity to make a difference when their leader doesn't create a climate for innovation. More than four times that number strongly agree that they would recommend the leader who most frequently challenges the process.

What differentiates an ordinary team from an extraordinary team is how they react to challenges and setbacks. If you're proactive, you focus on preparing; and if you're reactive, you focus on repairing. Leaders don't sit idly by waiting for fate to smile upon them; they venture out.

Taking risks was what Srinath Thurthahalli Nagaraj recalled about his personal-best (and first) leadership experience in India with a multinational electronics contract manufacturer. "When things did not work as expected," Srinath explained, "we kept on experimenting and challenging one another's ideas. You have to make room for failure and, more importantly, the opportunity to learn from failure." By making something happen and learning from experiences, Srinath was able to keep the project moving forward.

Leaders are pioneers willing to step out into the unknown. However, they aren't likely to be the only creators or originators of new products, services, or processes. Innovations come more frequently from customers, clients, vendors, and people in the labs and on the front lines than from individuals in leadership roles. And sometimes, as we learned during the darkest days of COVID-19, dramatic external events can thrust individuals and organizations into radically new conditions that force them to think differently, create differently, and act differently. Innovation comes more from listening than telling and from constantly looking outside of yourself and your organization for new and innovative ideas, products, processes, and services. You need to *search for opportunities by seizing the initiative and by looking outward for innovative ways to improve.*

Because innovation and change involve *experimenting and taking risks*, the leaders' main contribution is to create a climate for discovery, recognizing good ideas, supporting those ideas, having the fortitude to challenge the system, and being willing to fail. It would be ridiculous to assert that those who fail over and over again succeed as leaders. Success in any endeavor isn't a process of simply buying enough lottery tickets. The key that unlocks the door to opportunity is *constantly generating small wins and learning from experience.* David Ojakian's fundraising experience with the Armenian General Benevolent Union (AGBU) illustrates the importance of this "small wins" approach.

The AGBU launched the Aid for Artsakh campaign in October 2020 to assist families uprooted by the Azeri attacks. As chair of his local "young professionals" chapter, David worked on the drive with the AGBU central office and many other chapters globally. He credits the campaign's success to breaking down the project into pieces, which helped make the large-scale humanitarian initiative more manageable and possible, "allowing each chapter the ability to tailor their approach with their community and not feel overwhelmed in the process." This small win process gave each chapter the ability to tailor their approach, so as to not feel overwhelmed. In this way, each chapter could determine the best way within their local communities to start bringing awareness about the situation in Artsakh, see what they could learn as they progressed, and share best practices with other individual chapters. Chapters of all sizes and experience levels found innovative ways to raise funds despite the challenges, and this was a significant boost to everyone's confidence in the project and their willingness to stay involved.

There's a strong correlation between the process of learning and the approach leaders take to making extraordinary things happen. Leaders are constantly learning from their errors and failures. Life is the leader's laboratory, and exemplary leaders use it to conduct as many experiments as possible. The best leaders are the best learners. They learn from their failures and their successes.

**Enable Others to Act** Grand dreams don't become significant realities through the actions of a single person. Achieving greatness requires a team effort. It requires solid trust and enduring relationships. It requires group collaboration and individual accountability. After reviewing thousands of personal-best cases, we found that a very simple way to determine whether someone is on the road to becoming a leader is the frequency with which they used the word "we." The word "we" was used nearly three to four times more often than the "I" when people spoke about their personal-best leadership experience. When reviewing his personal-best experience, Sushma Bhope, program manager of a pioneering Indian suppler of probiotic products, concluded that "no one could have done this alone. It was essential to be open to all ideas and give everyone a voice in the decision-making process. The one guiding principle on the project was that the team was larger than any individual on the team."

Leaders *foster collaboration by building trust and facilitating relationships*. This sense of teamwork goes far beyond a few direct reports or close confidants. You have to engage everyone who must make the project work—and in some way, all who must live with the results. As the need for more inclusiveness grows and work-from-anywhere becomes more common, exemplary leaders find creative ways to connect with more diverse constituents.

Leaders appreciate that constituents don't perform at their best or stick around for very long if they feel weak, dependent, or alienated. When you *strengthen others by increasing self-determination and developing competence,* they are more likely to give it their all and exceed their own expectations. Leaders make it possible for others to do good work. They know that when people feel a sense of personal power and ownership, they are significantly more likely to be engaged and produce exceptional results. Leaders work to make people feel strong, capable, and committed. Exemplary leaders don't hoard their power; they give it away so that others can excel.

Focusing on serving others' needs rather than one's own builds trust in a leader. The more people trust their leaders and each other, the more they take risks, make changes, and keep moving ahead. In his personal-best leadership experience, Ankur Jaiswal, program manager with a multinational technology company, explained how he "worked hard to promote a creative and supportive work environment, where team success came ahead of individual recognition, and this fostered trusting relationships with one another." He appreciated how important it was to "empower the people around me and enable them to lead and be successful." When people are trusted and have more information, along with discretion and authority, they're much more likely to use their energies to produce extraordinary results. The LPI data supports this assertion. It shows that the motivational levels of direct reports increase in direct proportion to the extent they indicate their leader provides them with the freedom to decide how best to do their work.

**Encourage the Heart** The climb to the top is arduous and steep. People become exhausted, frustrated, disenchanted, and are often tempted to give up. Genuine acts of caring uplift people's spirits and draw people forward. Anne Moser, senior vice president with a corporate dining company, learned how impactful those actions are during her personal-best leadership experience: "Celebrate and give the team and the individual members proper recognition. Acknowledging an accomplishment is a great way to demonstrate the value of their contributions. It builds their confidence, and they will want to help out even more on the next project."

Leaders *recognize contributions by showing appreciation for individual excellence.* It can be one-to-one or with many people. It can come from dramatic gestures or simple actions. It can come from informal channels, just as well as through the formal hierarchy. It's part of the leader's job to show appreciation for people's contributions and to create a culture of celebration. In the cases we collected, there were thousands of examples of individual recognition and group celebration—from handwritten thank-you notes to elaborate "This Is Your Life" ceremonies. Eakta Malik, senior clinical research associate with a global medical device company, realized that many people were not feeling sufficiently appreciated and lacked a sense of team cohesiveness. She organized and designed some opportunities "for the team to unwind, get to know each other on a personal level, and to create a spirit of a community." She publicly acknowledged her teammates' hard work, which, she explained, "really lightens up the mood. I used to think that having praise on a project looks better when it comes from a director/manager, but I learned that praising someone doesn't have to be connected with having a title."

Being a leader requires showing appreciation for people's contributions and creating a culture of *celebrating the values and victories by creating a spirit of community.* Recognition and celebration aren't about fun and games, though there is a lot of fun, and there are a lot of games when people encourage the hearts of their constituents. Encouragement is, curiously, serious business because it's how you visibly and behaviorally link rewards with performance. When done authentically and from the heart, celebrations and rituals build a strong sense of collective identity and community spirit that can carry a group through extraordinarily tough times. Bringing a team together after a critical milestone reinforces the fact that people accomplish more together than apart. Engaging one another outside of the work setting also increases personal connection, which builds trust, improves communication, and strengthens the bonds within the team.

Recognitions and celebrations need to be personal and personalized. "There's no way to fake it," is what Eddie Tai, project director with a global real estate developer, realized. In telling us about his experiences, he noted, "Encouraging the heart might very well be the hardest job of any leader because it requires the most honesty and sincerity."

Yet this leadership practice, he maintained, "can have the most significant and long-lasting impact on those it touches and inspires." It is altogether too easy to get caught up in getting things done and not taking the time to acknowledge people for their contributions. Don't expect your direct reports to recommend you to their peers as a good leader if you aren't encouraging the heart. The LPI data indicates that four times the number of direct reports who observe their leader as frequently encouraging the heart would favorably recommend them as a good leader, compared with those direct reports that indicate their leader seldom encourages the heart.

These five leadership practices—Model the Way, Inspire a Shared Vision, Challenge the Process, Enable Others to Act, and Encourage the Heart—provide an *operating system* for what people are doing as leaders when they are at their best. There's abundant empirical evidence that these leadership practices matter. Embedded within The Five Practices of Exemplary Leadership are essential behaviors that serve as the basis for becoming an exemplary leader. We call these the Ten Commitments of Exemplary Leadership and they, along with The Five Practices, are displayed in Table 1.

These Ten Commitments serve as the template for explaining, understanding, appreciating, and learning how leaders make extraordinary things happen in organizations. They define the actions you need to demonstrate and with which you need to be comfortable. Each of them is discussed in depth in Chapters 2 through 11. Hundreds of studies have reported that The Five Practices make a positive difference in the engagement and performance levels of people and organizations. We highlight this research in the next section. In subsequent chapters, we report on much more of the evidence supporting this leadership operating system.

## Table 1 The Five Practices and Ten Commitments of Exemplary Leadership

1. Clarify values by finding your voice and affirming shared values.
2. Set the example by aligning actions with shared values.

3. Envision the future by imagining exciting and ennobling possibilities.
4. Enlist others in a common vision by appealing to shared aspirations.

5. Search for opportunities by seizing the initiative and looking outward for innovative ways to improve.
6. Experiment and take risks by consistently generating small wins and learning from experience.

7. Foster collaboration by building trust and facilitating relationships.
8. Strengthen others by increasing self-determination and developing competence.

9. Recognize contributions by showing appreciation for individual excellence.
10. Celebrate the values and victories by creating a spirit of community.

# The Five Practices Make a Difference

Exemplary leadership behavior makes a profoundly positive difference in people's commitment and motivation, work performance, and to the success of their organizations. That's the definitive conclusion from analyzing responses from nearly five million respondents worldwide using the Leadership Practices Inventory (LPI) to assess how often leaders engage in The Five Practices of Exemplary Leadership.

The leader's direct reports complete the LPI indicating how frequently they observe their leader engaging in the specific behaviors associated with The Five Practices. In addition, they respond to ten questions regarding how engaged they are in the workplace. For example:

- How proud they are to tell others they work for this organization
- Their commitment to the organization's success
- Their willingness to work harder and for longer hours if the job demanded it
- How effective they are in their jobs
- How much they trust management
- The extent they feel valued
- The strength of their work group's team spirit

They also provide assessments about their leader's overall leadership effectiveness and job performance, whether they would recommend that individual to their colleagues as a good leader, the likelihood of this person derailing, and how well this person compares with other leaders with whom they have worked.

When examining the most engaged direct reports compared to those who are least engaged—that is, in the top 20 percent or bottom 20 percent of this distribution—there are clear differences in how frequently they indicate their leaders utilize The Five Practices. The data shows that leaders of the most engaged direct reports are seen by them as using The Five Practices over 50 percent more often than those experienced by the least engaged direct reports. Similarly, when direct reports are asked, "Where would you place this person as a leader relative to other leaders inside and outside your organization?" there are clear differences in their responses directly attributable to their leaders' use of The Five Practices, as shown in Figure 1. It is quite evident that you are very unlikely to be considered among the best leaders by your direct reports unless you frequently demonstrate The Five Practices.

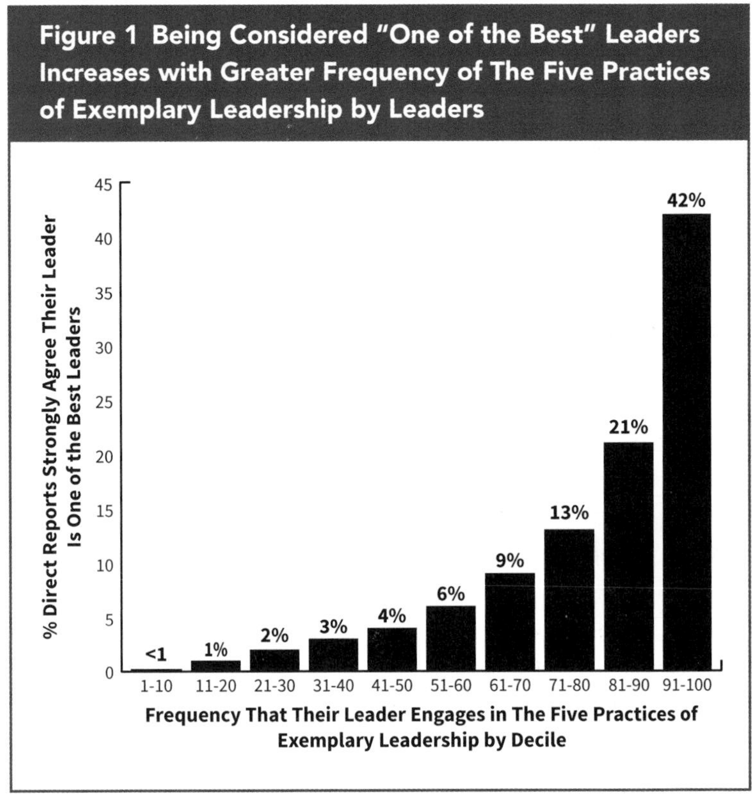


**Figure 1 Being Considered "One of the Best" Leaders Increases with Greater Frequency of The Five Practices of Exemplary Leadership by Leaders**

Multivariate analyses clearly show that how their leaders behave explains the extent to which their direct reports are engaged in the workplace. The alternative hypothesis is that demographic factors—individual characteristics like age, gender, educational level, length of service, and nationality—or that organizational factors—like function, hierarchical position, industry, and organizational size—are even more important in explaining why employees are engaged is simply not borne out by the data. All of these individual and organizational factors *combined* explain **nothing**—less than three-tenths of one percent—about why people are engaged. In contrast, leadership as measured by The Five Practices has over time consistently accounted for at least 33 percent, and in the past few years as much as 42 percent of the variance in engagement levels. No other variable or factor is as significant in explaining where people are in their level of engagement as is leadership. How leaders behave significantly influences people's engagement, and those behaviors are what make the difference regardless of who the direct reports are (e.g., age, gender, ethnicity, or education) or their circumstance (e.g., position, tenure, discipline, industry, or nationality).*

The empirical conclusion is that the more you utilize The Five Practices of Exemplary Leadership, the more likely it is that you'll have a positive influence on other people and your organization. If you want to impact people, organizations, and communities significantly, invest in learning the behaviors that enable you to become the very best leader you can be.

Furthermore, consider the findings on the financial impact of exemplary leadership. Researchers examined the financial performance of organizations over five years and compared those where constituents rated senior leaders as actively using The Five Practices with organizations

*Keep in mind that in the social sciences, we can't ever account for 100 percent of the variance (or explanation, as can generally be accounted for in the natural or physical sciences; e.g., two parts hydrogen and one part oxygen produce water). The unaccounted-for-variance is referred to as "noise" and results from errors associated with the measurement tools and the variability or lack of stability in the responses from humans.

whose leaders were significantly less engaged with The Five Practices. The bottom line: net income growth was nearly eighteen times higher, and stock price growth was nearly three times greater for those publicly traded organizations whose leadership more frequently engaged in The Five Practices than their counterparts.[4]

The Five Practices clearly make a difference. However, they paint only a partial portrait of what's going on. The complete picture requires an understanding and appreciation of what constituents expect from their leaders. Leadership is not granted; it is earned from the people you aspire to lead. They choose, day in and day out, whether they will follow and fully commit their talents, time, and energy. In the end, leaders don't decide who leads. Followers do. You can gain additional insights into what's important to your constituents by considering leadership from their standpoint. What do people look for in a leader? What do people want from someone whose direction they'd be willing to follow?

## Leadership Is a Relationship

*Leadership is in the eyes of other people.*
*It is they who proclaim you as a leader.*

*Carrie Gilstrap*

Another crucial truth that weaves throughout every situation and every leadership action is that personal-best leadership experiences are never stories about solo performances. Leaders never make extraordinary things happen all by themselves. Leadership, as we define it, is *the art of mobilizing others to want to struggle for shared aspirations*. Leadership is a relationship between those who aspire to lead and those who choose to follow. It's the *quality* of this relationship that matters most when making extraordinary things happen. A leader-constituent relationship characterized by fear and distrust will never produce anything of lasting value. A relationship characterized by mutual respect and confidence will overcome the greatest adversities and leave a legacy of significance.[5]

Exemplary leaders focus more on others than on themselves. Success in leadership, work, and life is—and has always been—a function of how well people work and play together. Success in leading is wholly dependent upon the capacity to build and sustain positive relationships. Any discussion of leadership must attend to the dynamics of this bond. Strategies, tactics, skills, and practices are empty without understanding the fundamental human aspirations that connect leaders and constituents.

Leadership is something you experience in an interaction with another human being. That experience varies from leader to leader, from constituent to constituent, and from day to day. No two leaders are exactly alike, no two constituent groups are exactly alike, and no two days in the life of leaders and constituents are exactly alike. Great leadership potential is discovered and unlocked when you seek to understand the desires and expectations of your constituents and when you act on them in ways that are congruent with their norms and image of what an exemplary leader is and does. What leaders say they do is one thing; what constituents say they want and how well leaders meet these expectations is another. John Gardner—founder of Common Cause, advisor to six U.S. presidents, and respected author and scholar—expressed it this way: "A loyal constituency is won when the people, consciously or unconsciously, judge the leader to be capable of solving their problems and meeting their needs, when the leader is seen as symbolizing their norms, and when their image of the leader (whether or not it corresponds to reality) is congruent with their inner environment of myth and legend."[6] Knowing what people want from their leaders is the only way to complete the picture of how leaders can build and sustain relationships that will make extraordinary things happen.

**What People Look for and Admire in Their Leaders** To better understand leadership as a relationship, we have investigated the expectations that people have of leaders. Over the years, we've examined responses from thousands of open-ended surveys about what people look for in a person they would be willing to follow.[7] Subsequent content analysis by several independent judges, followed by rounds of empirical analyses, resulted in a 20-item checklist called the *Characteristics of*

*Admired Leaders* (CAL) survey. Using CAL, we ask respondents to select the seven qualities, traits, or characteristics that they "most look for and admire in a leader, someone whose direction they would willingly follow." The key word in this statement is *willingly*. It's one thing to follow someone because you think you have to "or else," and it's another when you follow a leader because you *want to*.

Over 150,000 people around the globe have completed CAL, and we continuously collect responses and update the results. Remarkably, the findings have been quite consistent over the years, as the data in Table 1.2 show. There are some essential "character tests" individuals must pass before others are willing to grant them the designation of *leader*.

Although every characteristic receives votes, and therefore each is important to some people, what is most striking is that there continue to be four qualities that have always received the majority of votes. What people are looking for in a person whom they would *willingly* follow is someone who they believe is *honest*, *competent*, *inspiring*, and *forward-looking*. For all the dramatic changes in the world over these past four decades, what people look for has remained amazingly stable. Our analyses show that this is true across gender, ethnic background, educational levels, years of work experience, hierarchical position, industry, function, and nationality.[8] Despite all the changes over these past four decades in the world and workplace, whenever and wherever we have inquired about desirable leader attributes, the same qualities are selected most often.

Let's examine why each of these characteristics is essential for creating a sustainable relationship between those who aspire to lead and those who would be willing to follow. After that, we'll show how these characteristics reveal the foundation on which leaders must build that sustainable relationship.

***Honest*** In every survey administration, people select honesty more often than any other leadership characteristic. Overall, it emerges as the single most important factor in the leader-constituent relationship. The percentages vary, but the final ranking does not. First and foremost, people want a leader they perceive as being honest. This doesn't mean that every leader *is* honest, but people most want to see it.

## Table 1.2 Characteristics of Admired Leaders: Percentage of Respondents Selecting Each Characteristic[a]

| Characteristic | 1987 | 1995 | 2002 | 2007 | 2012 | 2017 | 2023 |
|---|---|---|---|---|---|---|---|
| Honest | 83 | 88 | 88 | 89 | 89 | 84 | 87 |
| Competent | 67 | 63 | 66 | 68 | 69 | 66 | 68 |
| Inspiring | 58 | 68 | 65 | 69 | 69 | 66 | 54 |
| Forward-looking | 62 | 75 | 71 | 71 | 71 | 62 | 53 |
| Dependable | 33 | 32 | 33 | 34 | 35 | 39 | 46 |
| Supportive | 32 | 41 | 35 | 35 | 35 | 37 | 45 |
| Intelligent | 43 | 40 | 47 | 48 | 45 | 47 | 41 |
| Broad-minded | 37 | 40 | 40 | 35 | 38 | 40 | 38 |
| Cooperative | 25 | 28 | 28 | 25 | 27 | 31 | 36 |
| Fair-minded | 40 | 49 | 42 | 39 | 37 | 35 | 36 |
| Ambitious | 21 | 13 | 17 | 16 | 21 | 28 | 33 |
| Straightforward | 34 | 33 | 34 | 36 | 32 | 32 | 30 |
| Caring | 26 | 23 | 20 | 22 | 21 | 23 | 29 |
| Loyal | 11 | 11 | 14 | 18 | 19 | 18 | 21 |
| Determined | 17 | 17 | 23 | 25 | 26 | 22 | 19 |
| Mature | 23 | 13 | 21 | 5 | 14 | 17 | 17 |
| Imaginative | 34 | 28 | 23 | 17 | 16 | 17 | 14 |
| Courageous | 27 | 29 | 20 | 25 | 22 | 22 | 13 |
| Self-controlled | 13 | 5 | 8 | 10 | 11 | 10 | 12 |
| Independent | 10 | 5 | 6 | 4 | 5 | 5 | 6 |

[a]Note: Since we asked people to select seven characteristics, the totals add up to more than 100 percent.

And you readily know what happens when you find out your leader has lied or been deceptive: both current and future motivational levels decline, often dramatically.

It's clear that if people anywhere are to follow someone willingly, they first want to be sure that the individual is worthy of their trust. They want to know that the person is truthful, ethical, and principled. When people talk to us about the qualities they admire in leaders, they often use "integrity" and "authentic" as synonyms for honesty. No matter what the setting, people want to be fully confident in their leaders, and this means they must believe that their leaders are individuals of authentic character and solid integrity.

***Competent*** To enlist in another's cause, people must believe that the person they are following is competent to guide them along the path to the future. They must see that person as capable and effective. If people doubt the leader's abilities, they're not readily going to enlist in the crusade. Studies point out that when people perceive their leader as incompetent, they reject the individual and that person's perspective.[9]

*Leadership competence* refers to the leader's track record and ability to get things done. This kind of competence inspires confidence—the leader can guide the entire organization in the direction in which it needs to go. When people talk about a competent leader, they aren't referring specifically to the leader's expertise in all of the core functions of the organization. People do need to believe that the person understands the company's current marketplace, operation, culture, and people. Still, they also know that as leaders move up in the organization's hierarchy, they can't be the most technically competent in every operational specialty. There's no expectation that a leader should be a super-human, all-seeing, all-knowing wizard. The type of competence demanded varies with the leader's position and the condition of the organization.

***Inspiring*** People expect their leaders to be excited, energetic, and positive about their prospects. A person who is enthusiastic and passionate about future possibilities conveys to others a stronger belief in those possibilities than someone who shows little or no emotion. People are most likely to believe what you are saying when they sense that *you* truly believe it. If a leader displays no passion for a cause, why should anyone else? Furthermore, being upbeat, positive, and optimistic offers people hope that the future can be brighter. This is crucial at any time, but in times of great uncertainty, leading with positive emotions is absolutely essential to moving people upward and forward.

You need more than a dream. A leader must be able to communicate that vision in ways that encourage others to sign on for the duration. People long to find some greater sense of purpose and worth in their day-to-day working lives. Although the enthusiasm, energy, and positive attitude of the leader may not change the content of work, they certainly can make the context more fulfilling. Whatever the circumstances, when leaders breathe life into dreams and aspirations, people are much more willing to enlist in a common cause.

***Forward-Looking*** People expect leaders to have a sense of direction and a concern for the future of the organization. After all, if the vision is simply same-old, same-old status quo, then what is the purpose of that leader anyway? Leaders are not content with things as they are today; they focus on how things should be better in the future and offer a path forward.

Whether you call that future a vision, a dream, a calling, a goal, a mission, or a personal agenda, the message is clear: leaders must know where they're going if they expect others to willingly join them on the journey. They have to have a point of view about the future envisioned for their organizations, and they need to be able to connect that point of view to the hopes and dreams of their constituents. You can't get yourself buried in the details and lose sight of the bigger picture. Leaders must have a destination in mind when asking others to join them on a journey into the unknown.

## Putting It All Together: Credibility Is the Foundation

These essential leadership characteristics, consistent over time and place, reveal a profound and crucial implication for leadership. It gets to the very essence of what enables leaders to attract and retain followers. In assessing the believability of sources of communication—whether news reporters, salespeople, physicians, or priests; whether business managers, military officers, politicians, or civic leaders—researchers typically evaluate them on three criteria: their perceived *trustworthiness,* their *expertise,* and their *dynamism.* The more highly people are rated on these dimensions, the more they are considered credible sources of information.[10] Honesty, competence, and being inspiring are clearly aligned with "source credibility."

Link the concept of source credibility with the data about admired leadership qualities, and the striking conclusion is that, more than anything, people want to follow leaders who are credible. *Credibility is the foundation of leadership*. Above all else, constituents must be able to believe in their leaders. They must believe that their leaders' word can be trusted and that they have the knowledge and skill to lead. Credibility is particularly significant when you consider that leaders ask people to join them on a journey to an unknown future. This is why being "forward-looking" is also an essential expectation of those who aspire to lead others. To willingly follow, constituents must believe that their leaders know where they're headed and have the competence to get them there.

The consistency and pervasiveness of these findings on the characteristics of admired leaders—people someone would willingly follow—results in **The Kouzes-Posner First Law of Leadership: If you don't believe in the messenger, you won't believe the message**. Before people determine what they think about what you are saying, they decide what they think of you.

Leaders must always be diligent in guarding their credibility. Your capacity to take strong stands, challenge the status quo, and move in new directions depends upon being highly credible. You can't take your credibility for granted. To believe in the exciting future possibilities leaders present, people must first believe in their leaders. If you are going to ask others to follow you to some uncertain future—a future that may not be realized in their lifetime—and if the journey will require sacrifice, then people must believe in you.

**Credibility Matters** You might reasonably wonder, "There are people who are in positions of power, and there are people who are enormously wealthy, yet people don't find them credible. Does credibility really matter? Does it make a difference?" These are sensible questions, and to answer them, we decided to ask the people whose responses matter the most—the leader's direct reports. Using a behavioral measure of credibility, we asked them to think about the extent to which their immediate manager exhibited credibility-enhancing behaviors.[11] The data revealed that when people perceive their *immediate manager* to have high credibility, they're significantly more likely to

- Be proud to tell others they're part of the organization.
- Feel a strong sense of team spirit.
- See their personal values as consistent with those of the organization.
- Feel attached and committed to the organization.
- Have a sense of ownership of the organization.

When people perceive their manager to have low credibility, on the other hand, they're significantly more likely to

- Produce only if carefully watched.
- Be motivated primarily by money.
- Say good things about the organization publicly but criticize it privately.
- Consider looking for another job if the organization experiences problems.
- Feel unsupported and unappreciated.

The significant impact of credibility on employee attitudes and behavior provides clear dictates for organizational leaders. Credibility makes a difference, and leaders must take it personally. Loyalty, commitment, energy, and productivity depend upon it.

Credibility goes far beyond employee attitudes. It also influences customer and investor loyalty. In an extensive study of the economic value of business loyalty, researchers find, "The center of gravity for business loyalty—whether it be the loyalty of customers, employees, investors, suppliers, or dealers—is the personal integrity of the senior leadership team and its ability to put its principles into practice."[12] Their findings underscore the importance of the First Law of Leadership.

**What Is Credibility Behaviorally?** How do you know credibility when you see it? We posed this question to tens of thousands of people around the globe. The answers we received were essentially the same, regardless of how they were phrased in one organization versus another or one country versus another. Here are some of the common expressions people use to describe how they know when people are credible:

- "They practice what they preach."
- "They walk the talk."
- "Their actions are consistent with their words."
- "They put their money where their mouth is."
- "They follow through on their promises."
- *"They do what they say they will do."*

The last is the most frequent response. When deciding whether a leader is believable, people first listen to the words, then observe the actions. They listen to the talk and then watch the walk. They listen to the promises of resources to support change initiatives, and then they wait to see if money and materials follow. They hear the pledge to deliver, and then they look for evidence that the commitments are met. A judgment of "credible" is handed down when words and deeds are consonant.

If people don't see consistency, they conclude that the leader is, at best, not serious, or, at worst, an outright hypocrite. If leaders espouse one set of values but personally practice another, people find them to be duplicitous. If their leaders practice what they preach, people are more willing to entrust them with their livelihood and even their lives. This realization leads to a straightforward prescription on the most significant way to establish credibility. It is **The Kouzes-Posner Second Law of Leadership: DWYSYWD: Do What You Say You Will Do.**

This commonsense definition of credibility corresponds directly to the first of The Five Practices of Exemplary Leadership identified in the personal-best leadership cases. DWYSYWD has two essential elements: *say* and *do*. To be credible in action, leaders must be clear about their beliefs and know what they stand for. That's the "say" part. Then they must put what they say into practice: they must act on their beliefs and "do."

## How Does Credibility Link to The Five Practices?

The practice of Model the Way relates directly to these two dimensions of people's behavioral definition of credibility. This practice includes being clear about a set of values and being an example of those values to others. This consistent living out of values is what it means to be authentic and is a behavioral way of demonstrating honesty and trustworthiness. People trust leaders when their deeds and words match—and when they trust their leaders, they more willingly follow.

To gain and sustain the moral authority to lead, it's essential to Model the Way. Because of this important connection between words and actions, we've chosen to start the discussion of The Five Practices with a thorough examination of the principles and behaviors that bring Model the Way to life.

# MODEL THE WAY

## PRACTICE 1

# MODEL THE WAY

- Clarify values by finding your voice and affirming shared values.
- Set the example by aligning actions with shared values.

# CHAPTER 2
# Clarify Values

*Having faith in my principles and beliefs*
*gave me the courage to navigate difficult situations.*
*Salil D. Amonkar*

**WHEN ALEX ANWAR** was hired as director of a new business unit for a medical equipment supplier, he faced resentment from many within the company because they felt he was too young and inexperienced to manage such a diverse group and product portfolio. Since many groups were siloed and polarized, a widespread question was whether he would be the kind of leader who would bring people together toward a common goal. Alex's first step was to communicate his values to the team. He circulated an email introducing himself, not as a manager, but as a fellow employee of the company charged with a difficult task. Instead of telling everyone what he wanted out of them, he clearly stated the values and performance criteria he demanded of himself every day. In communicating his value set, people were better prepared to understand his actions and the reasoning behind certain decisions; they could connect the outcome with a value—hard work, for example.

In an all-hands meeting later that week, Alex provided a few examples of cases where he exercised his core values of honesty and sincerity, discussing how he handled a particular problem with a customer. He took his constituents through the issue as though narrating a story. Alex subsequently used this storytelling style every time he made a case for how people should handle particular company situations. Making these lessons values-centered, personal, and relatable helped others understand and retain the intended lesson. As one of his direct reports explained: "Alex made his values understood through clearly communicating and providing contexts that would aid in their retention. He put all the values into his own words and thus gave us a clear idea about the kind of person he was."

The Personal-Best Leadership Experience cases are, at their core, stories of individuals who were clear about their values and understood how this clarity gave them the courage to navigate difficult situations and make tough choices. As Patrick O'Leary, a seasoned digital product manager, recalled, "Trusting in my values has served to guide me whenever obstacles appear, which instills a sense of confidence that I will persevere. When I haven't been clear about my values, my self-worth diminishes, and the quality of my work is adversely impacted." People expect that their leaders will speak out on matters of values and conscience. To speak out, however, you must have something to speak about. To stand up for your beliefs, you must know the beliefs you stand for. To do what you say, you must know what you want to say.

In beginning your leadership journey, you must commit to *Clarify Values*. Exemplary leaders know that it's essential to:

- **Find your voice**
- **Affirm shared values**

You must comprehend fully the deeply held values that drive you. You must freely and honestly choose those principles you will use to guide your decisions and actions. You must express your authentic self, genuinely communicating your beliefs in ways that uniquely represent who you are.

What's more, you must realize that leaders aren't just speaking for themselves when they talk about the values that guide actions and decisions. They must also make sure that everyone they lead agrees to a set of shared values and then hold them accountable to live those values and standards.

## Find Your Voice

*When I got this position, I had to figure out for myself, and within myself, what I thought was important and why.*

*Jason Ting*

Who are you? This is the first question your constituents want you to answer. Exemplary leadership does not come from the outside in. It comes from the inside out. Just imagine this scene. Someone walks into the room right now and announces to you and your colleagues, "Hi, I'm your new leader." At that very moment, right away, what do you want to know from this person? What are the questions that immediately pop into your mind? We've asked this question of many different groups, and their responses are almost always the same. People tell us they want to ask that new leader:

- What are your values?
- What do you like to do in your free time?
- What do you stand for and believe in?
- How do you make decisions?
- Why do you want to do this job?
- What qualifies you for this job?
- What do you believe (e.g., about this field, this time in

> history, how people should be treated, about family, health, wealth, etc.)?

Questions like these get to the heart of leadership. People always want to know some things about the person doing the leading—before becoming the people doing the following. They want to know what inspires you, what drives you, what informs your decisions, what gives you strength, what makes you who you are. They want to know about the person behind the role or position. At the start of her personal-best leadership journey, Sumaya Shakir, IT strategy director for a passenger railroad service, found that she needed "to question myself about what I stood for, what was important to me, what approaches I was going to follow, what I was going to communicate, and what my expectations were. I had to know and believe first within myself. There were so many things that came into my mind all at once, but I had to focus on the core values I wanted to represent."

Before you can become a credible leader—one who connects "what you say" with "what you do"—you first have to find your authentic voice, the most genuine expression of who you are. If you don't find your voice, you'll end up with a vocabulary that belongs to someone else, mouthing words written by some speechwriter or mimicking the language of some other leader who is nothing like you at all. If the words you speak are not your words but someone else's, you will not, in the long term, be able to be consistent in word and deed. You will not have the integrity to lead.

Consider how one constituent described his manager. It goes a long way toward explaining why this startup company never got off the ground:

> First, our manager never had an authentic voice, as he never had the courage to offer solutions or suggestions beyond what our three (never-agreeing) directors contributed to each decision. Often it felt like he acted as a simple conduit for mixed messages from above. . .without his personal voice defining a clear road for us to

> travel. This made it very difficult for the group to focus on a defined set of tasks connected to goals.
>
> Second, we had no specific organizational values to live by. Sure, we all knew the company's mission, but he never went beyond the ordinary in defining values for *our* business. Seemingly simple values went undefined and, as a result, were exploited by some team members.

As could have been predicted, this lack of clarity and consistency in values resulted in little internal cohesion and focus, and they failed to generate a favorable customer experience or positive business results.

In contrast, when Juliana Moreno-Ramirez was asked to be the new clinical research manager for a major university-based teaching hospital, her first step "was to look within myself and understand how I wanted to lead. More specifically, I needed to reflect on who I was and my values, finding my own voice and guiding principles because only then could I confidently lead this program." It took a while, she said, to "understand my values, because truthfully as an individual contributor, I never took the time to dissect them. Knowing that my decisions and actions would affect others brought a sense of responsibility to understand the kind of leader I wanted to be." Juliana felt that this was "probably the most critical step you can take to be an effective leader, finding a voice that represents clearly who you are. If you just put up an act, your team will see right through you and deem you unfit to lead them."

**Articulate Your Leadership Philosophy** To find your voice, you have to discover what you care about, what defines you, and what makes you who you are. You have to explore your inner self. You can only be authentic when you lead according to the principles that matter most to you. Otherwise, you're just putting on an act. When you fail to express your leadership philosophy in word and deed, you weaken your own and your team's engagement and effectiveness. Exemplary leaders know this. When we ask leaders to indicate how clear they are about their leadership philosophy, those who consider themselves at the top of this scale also rate their leadership effectiveness more than 128 percent higher than

**Figure 2.1 The Most Effective Leaders Have a Clear Philosophy of Leadership**

do those leaders who have indicated they are occasionally clear, at most, about their leadership philosophy. In addition, as you see in Figure 2.1, the leaders who are seen as most always clear about their leadership philosophy are evaluated substantially more highly as effective leaders by their direct reports than those leaders who lack clarity. Indeed, few direct reports consider their leaders effective unless they have a clear philosophy of leadership.

When Jared Smith became superintendent of a midwestern school district (K–12), he shared a document with the more than 250 staff members entitled "Leadership Principles & Core Values." He explains that "investing time to pinpoint my leadership principles has been hugely beneficial because it forces me to abide by these standards in my day-to-day operations." Jared looks for opportunities to share this document with staff and parents in a variety of settings, and this transparent approach, he says, is not only appreciated but "people find that we share many personal beliefs."[1] Ben Stevenson, an experienced facilities manager, framed his core values and posted them on the wall of his office as a reminder to himself and others of the values he holds most dear and operates by.

The evidence is clear. To be most effective, you must learn to find the voice that represents who you are. Leading others begins with leading yourself, and you can't do that until you're able to answer that fundamental question about who you are. When you have clarified your values and found your voice, you will also find the inner confidence necessary to take charge of your life.

**Let Your Values Guide You** After seven years of rigorous research, a landmark study of the observations from more than 100 CEOs and over 8,000 employees found that leaders who were clear about their values delivered as much as five times greater returns for their organizations than leaders of weak character.[2] This finding resonates with Courtney Ballagh, a sales supervisor for a fashion accessory store. "You find your voice by letting your values guide you and then sharing them with others," she told us. Courtney explained that when working in retail, "it is very common to get employees from different ethnic backgrounds, ages, educational levels, and varying degrees of commitment. But as long as you are honest, open, and willing to listen to their values, you will be able to find common ground." She described a situation where she was not initially getting along with Tracey, one of her underperforming associates. However, after clarifying her leadership values and beliefs, Courtney became more comfortable discussing them. She got together with Tracey, talked about her values, and invited Tracey to do the same.

> I helped Tracey express her reasons for what and why she worked for me and provided her the opportunity to talk to me about her values. These two steps were paramount in fixing our work relationship and leading to the team's future success. I've learned that not everyone you encounter in the workplace is going to think like you and

> approach problems in the same way—therefore, by affirming our shared values and finding each other's voices, we are able to communicate more effectively and build unparalleled levels of trust. The outcome of this situation was that my work relationship with Tracey became much stronger, and overall store productivity and morale increased.

A value is an enduring belief, which scholars routinely divide into two categories: means and ends. Leadership requires both.[3] In the context of our work, we use the term *values* to refer to here-and-now beliefs about how you should accomplish things—in other words, values that represent a *means* to an end. We use *vision*—discussed in Chapters 4 and 5—to refer to the long-term ends and values that leaders and constituents aspire to attain.

Values are your personal "bottom line." They influence every aspect of your life: for example, moral judgments, commitments to personal and organizational goals, and the way you respond to others. They serve as guides to action and set the parameters for the hundreds of decisions you make every day, consciously and subconsciously. They inform the priorities you set and the decisions you make. They tell you when to say yes and when to say no. They also help you explain the choices you make and why you make them. Being clear about your values enables you to perform better in difficult circumstances.[4] You seldom consider or act on options that run counter to your value system. If you do, it's with a sense of compliance rather than commitment. Without a doubt, in these chaotic times, a set of deeply held values allows leaders to focus and make choices among a plethora of competing theories, demands, and interests.

Seasoned executive Radha Basu explained how being clear about her values over her career allowed her to choose among competing demands, requests, and claims on her time and attention. "Knowing who I am and what's important to me," she told us, "gives me focus and enables me to keep juggling more balls in the air than I otherwise could. If you are clear about your values, and your actions are aligned, it makes all the hard work worth the effort."

Values are empowering. You can be much more in control of your life when you're clear about your values, as both Courtney and Radha found. Values are guides, supplying you with an internal compass by which to navigate the course of your daily life. The clearer you are about your values, the easier it is to commit to and stay on your chosen path. This kind of guidance is especially important in volatile and uncertain times. When daily challenges can throw you off course, it's crucial to have the means to tell which way is north, south, east, and west.

John Siegel, M.D., described the impact of speaking about his values during a discussion on restructuring the hospital's surgical department. At one point, the conversation veered off-track. It turned from worrying about residents' educational experience to how lazy the residents are, how they don't answer their pagers or have a vested interest in how the hospital runs or the quality of care delivered. John told us:

> In a calm, steady voice, I raised my hand and reminded everyone that our priority is to deliver excellent care for our patients. A restructuring plan that assured that our primary goal would allow an excellent learning experience for the residents. I added that it might even show them what it's like to care passionately about something like the quality of care and see the satisfaction we derive from providing it. Without saying it, I pushed the button in each of us, reminding us of the values we are living and the dream we all have for where we work.
>
> I had the least seniority of anyone, but I could say what I believed in—with confidence and strength that comes from that personal commitment to values—and they listened. The mood changed. We became constructively engaged again and eventually settled on a restructuring plan that would improve how our department works.

John's story is a reminder of how well values can keep you—and your colleagues—on course, especially when you become engaged in conflicts or controversies. Just reminding yourself of the most important principles often can refocus your attention on the things that truly matter. Rob Field's experience is similar. When he became the executive director of a

Black Arts Institution, it was faced with an unprecedented financial crisis and closure seemed unavoidable. To find the best solution, Rob began by examining his personal values and came to the realization that these matched and were at the core of the values upon which the organization had been founded. As a result of the clarity he gained about his personal values, he was able to connect to the historical values of the institution's founders. Rob recognized that these values were just as relevant today and could serve to unify the past with the present and build for the future. He shared these values at community meetings, church gatherings, and other community events. He spoke with passion and authenticity about these values, and his conviction resonated with a broader audience than he ever imagined. Social media picked up on this story, which resulted in a crowdfunding explosion, and he developed an international network of supporters and averted the financial crisis. Clarifying values was not only personally important but the process served to closely connect him with the organization and in turn provided a leadership philosophy both for himself and for the institution.

**Express Yourself** Leadership is an art, and just as with any other art form—whether it's painting, playing music, dancing, acting, or writing—leadership is a means of personal expression. To become a credible leader, you must learn to express yourself in ways that are uniquely your own. As author Anne Lamott tells would-be writers:

> And the truth of your experience can only come through in your own voice. If it is wrapped in someone else's voice, we readers are suspicious, as if you are dressed up in someone else's clothes. You cannot write out of someone else's big dark place; you can only write out of your own. Sometimes wearing someone else's style is very comforting, warm and pretty and bright, and it may loosen you up, tune you into the joys of language and rhythm and concern. But what you say will be an abstraction because it will not have sprung from direct experience; when you try to capture the truth of your experience in some other person's voice or on that person's terms,

you are removing yourself one step further from what you have seen and what you know.[5]

What's true for writers is just as true for leaders. You cannot lead through someone else's values or someone else's words. You cannot lead out of someone else's experience. You can only lead out of your own. Unless it's your style, your words, it's not you—it's just an act. People don't follow your position or your technique. They follow you. If you're not the genuine article, can you expect others to want to follow?

Raymond Yu found this out the hard way when he was, in his words, "demoted" from his management position because of a reorganization, which both frustrated him and lowered his self-esteem. "I never found my voice," he explained. With the benefit of time and reflection, Raymond realized that he had "walked down the wrong path. I had only been managing and not leading," he told us. Raymond had used his manager as a role model, with unintended consequences. "Rather than finding my voice, I parroted his and often used his name and authority to move projects along. In hindsight, I gave up my opportunities to lead by simply being a conduit for him." Appreciating that he didn't need to be in a management position to lead, Raymond vowed from then on to "find my voice based on my personal values so that I could become an exemplary leader."

Raymond's reflections are similar to what we learned from the artist and educator Jim LaSalandra. He shared his observation that "there are really three periods in an artist's life. In the first, we paint exterior landscapes. In the second, we paint interior landscapes. In the third, we paint ourselves. That's when you begin to have your own unique style." What applies to the art of painting applies just as well to the art of leadership.

When first learning to lead, you paint what you observe outside of yourself—the exterior landscape. You want to acquire tools and techniques that others have learned from their experience. People often return to this stage whenever they take on new and challenging roles for which their previous experience has not prepared them. Even though you realize that authenticity only comes when you find your authentic voice, sometimes, when you're first developing your talents, it can be helpful to copy someone else's work. It's not cheating to imitate someone else in the early stages. It can be beneficial to your learning. Author William Zinsser describes it this way:

> Never hesitate to imitate another writer. Imitation is a part of the creative process for anyone learning an art or a craft. Bach and Picasso didn't spring full-blown as Bach and Picasso; they needed models. Find the best writers in the fields that interest you and read their work aloud. Get their voice and their taste into your ear—their attitude toward language. Don't worry that by imitating them you'll lose your own voice and your own identity. Soon enough you will shed those skins and become who you are supposed to become.[6]

The same can be said for a leader's voice. It's useful to read, observe, and imitate the practices of leaders you admire. It's about learning the fundamentals. You'll discover over time what fits you and what does not. Like trying on a new suit of clothes, you'll realize that some things look ridiculous on you, and others bring out the best in you.

Somewhere along the way, however, you'll notice that your speech sounds mechanically rote, that your meetings are a dull routine, and that your interactions feel terribly sad and empty. You'll awaken to the frightening thought that the words aren't yours, that the vocabulary is someone else's, that the technique may be right out of the text, but it's not straight from the heart. This will be a turning point in your development. While you've invested so much time and energy in learning to do all the right things, you suddenly see that they're no longer serving you well. The methods seem hollow. You may even feel like a phony.

In these moments, you begin to stare into the darkness of your inner territory, and you begin to wonder what lies inside. You say to yourself, "I'm not someone else. I'm a unique human being. But who exactly am I? What is my voice?"

For aspiring leaders, this awakening initiates a period of intense exploration, a period of testing, and a period of invention. It's a time of going beyond technique, beyond training, beyond imitating the masters, and beyond taking the advice of others. When you surrender to it, and after exhausting experimentation and often painful suffering, there emerges from all those abstract strokes on the canvas an expression of self that is truly your own. You won't have to copy anyone else. You're able to recognize your own voice from the multitude of other voices ringing in your ears, and you find ways to express yourself in a singular style. You become the author of your own experience.

To exercise leadership, you've got to awaken to the fact that you don't have to copy someone else, you don't have to read a script written by someone else, and you don't have to wear someone else's style. Instead, you are free to choose what you want to express and the way you want to say it. You have a responsibility to your constituents to express yourself in an authentic manner, in a way that they would immediately recognize as yours. When you look at yourself in the mirror and ask, "Is this me?" you know that it is.

**Find Commitment Through Clarifying Values** Shandon Lee Fernandes, a former senior research officer in the consulate general of an Asian nation, told us that the first step in her personal-best leadership experience was getting in touch with her values and beliefs. She told us this was critical, "because only when leaders discover and clarify what they expect of themselves can they expect others to follow. Your ability to easily explain your actions and reasoning allows others to connect the values and the path they need to take in their actions. Intrinsic cohesion results in external alignment."

The results of our research strongly support Shandon's conclusions and further demonstrate how being clear about personal values makes a significant difference in how people behave in the workplace.[7] In a series of studies over time and across a range of organizations, we asked managers about the extent to which they were clear about their personal values, as well as the values of their organization. They also indicated their level of commitment to the organization—i.e., the extent to which they were likely to stick around and work hard.

The results, a classic two-by-two experimental paradigm, are shown in Figure 2.2. Quadrant 1 are those managers who are not very clear about their personal values or those of their organization. In quadrant 2 are those who are relatively clear about their organization's values but not very clear about their personal values. Found in quadrant 3 are those clear about both personal and organizational values, and in quadrant 4 are those managers clear about their personal values but not

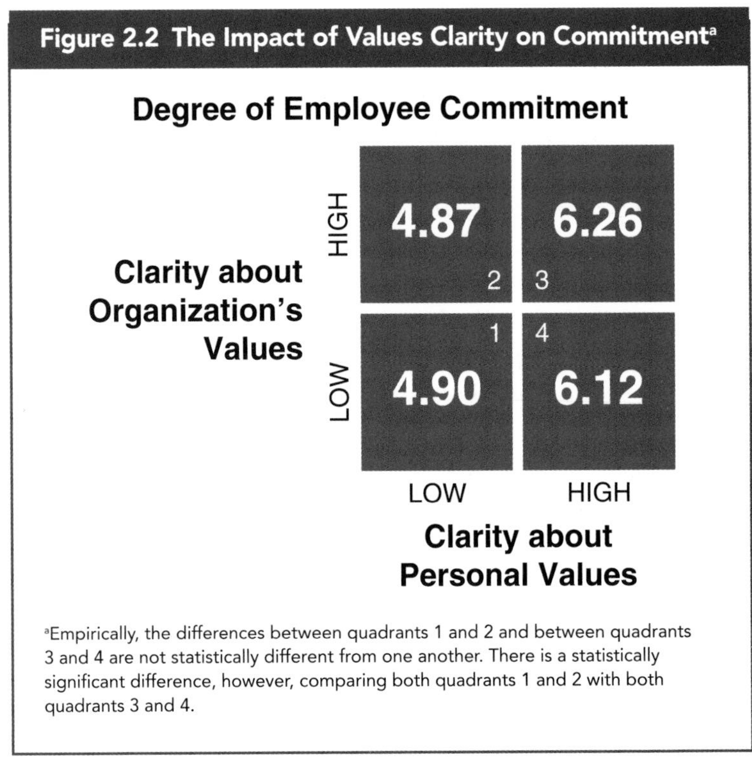


**Figure 2.2 The Impact of Values Clarity on Commitment[a]**

[a]Empirically, the differences between quadrants 1 and 2 and between quadrants 3 and 4 are not statistically different from one another. There is a statistically significant difference, however, comparing both quadrants 1 and 2 with both quadrants 3 and 4.

very clear about the organization's values. The average response scores of how *committed* these managers are to their organizations (on a scale of one to seven, with seven being the strongest) are displayed within each quadrant. Notice the pattern about which group is most committed based on knowing how clear they are about their personal and organizational values.

People who are clear about their personal values (quadrants 3 and 4) have significantly higher levels of commitment than either those who have heard the organizational litany but have never listened to their inner voice (quadrant 2) or the people who are not clear about both the organizational values as well as their own (quadrant 1). Even more revealing is that there are no statistically significant differences in commitment levels between quadrants 3 and 4.

In other words, personal values are what drive commitment. In our most recent replication of these studies, we found a similar pattern, with clarity of personal values being the route to increasing motivation and productivity. For example, there was a steady increase in how personally effective people viewed themselves in relationship to how clear they were about their personal values. This was also true in regard to responses to how valued people felt by their organization, the feeling that they were making a difference, and their pride in being with the organization.[8]

No matter their age, background, discipline, or function, the most talented people gravitate to organizations where they can look forward to going to work each day because their values "work" (they "fit") in that setting. The best employees are attracted to companies that align with who they are.[9] Julie Sedlock, senior vice president with a shopping mall–based retailer, echoes this observation: "I love to come to work here. I can't think of a day in twenty years that I didn't want to wake up and go to work." She explains that when you share the company's values, you "want to come to work, work hard, and achieve the goals that the organization has set."

Commitment is strongest when based on alignment with personal values. Researchers find that the values of an organization are motivating only to the extent that they reflect an individual's normative values.[10] People who are clearest about their values are better prepared to make choices based on principle—including deciding whether the principles of the organization fit with their own, and whether to join up and stay, or leave! In too many organizations, there is a considerable gap between what the organization says is valued and the degree that employees believe they can apply those values to their everyday work.[11]

## Affirm Shared Values

*The process of deciding on a common set of values was an extremely valuable unifying and clarifying experience.*

*Michael Lin*

As important as it is that you forthrightly articulate the principles for which you stand, it does not mean that your job is to get other people simply to comply with your beliefs. Just as your values drive your commitment, their own values drive the degree of their commitment. In becoming an exemplary leader, you have to transition from "what *I* believe" to "what *we* believe." People are most loyal and committed when they believe that their organization's values align with their personal values. The quality and accuracy of communication and the integrity of the decision-making process increase when people feel they share significant values with their colleagues. Leaders need to help guide people in finding that common ground. In her personal-best leadership experience, Joyce Tan experienced this firsthand. In her role as a legal operations analyst at a global biopharmaceutical company, she explained that because she and her "colleagues shared the same values and tried our best to abide by these principles, it made it easier to work together and accomplish our goals."

Discovering and affirming shared values build the foundation on which you create productive and genuine work relationships. While honoring the diversity of those around you, you will also need to stress the commonality within that diversity. That's the key role shared values play. They provide people with a common language for discussing goals and aspirations, problems and conflicts, and solutions and actions. When there's a clear and consistent understanding of guiding principles, conversations have an organizing theme around which everyone can rally. That generates positive energy, increases enthusiasm, and reduces tension. People have something in common to care about. Shared values act as an internal compass that enables people to function both independently and interdependently.

Exemplary leaders know that they can't get everyone to agree on everything. That's unrealistic and unnecessary. Moreover, to achieve it would negate the very advantages of inclusiveness. Nevertheless, leaders must build agreement around a few core values that everyone can pledge to uphold. To take unified action, people must have some common core of understanding. After all, if there's no agreement about values, then what exactly are the leader and everyone else going to model? And if disagreements over fundamental values continue, the result is intense conflict, false expectations, and diminished capacity. Leaders ensure that everyone becomes aligned and hold one another accountable to what "we" value by uncovering, affirming, and reinforcing shared values.

Michael Ryan, manager of systems integration for a cloud storage firm, told us that his company's core values were the glue that held his team together. To reinforce them, he included "value quizzes" in staff meetings—asking various team members to recall the company's values and provide examples of them at work. "We would then comment about our current project," he recalled, "and discuss how well these values were or were not being upheld and what to do about any misalignments." As Michael well understood, a leader's promise is an organization's promise—regardless of whether the organization is a team of two, an agency of two hundred, a school of two thousand, a company of twenty thousand, or a community of two hundred thousand. Without agreement about which promises will be kept, leaders, constituents, and organizations risk losing credibility. Shared values make a significant and positive difference in work attitudes and commitment.

Research confirms these experiences. Organizations with a strong corporate culture based on shared values outperformed other firms by a considerable margin. Their revenue and rate of job creation grow faster, and their profit performance and stock price are significantly higher.[12] For example, an internal analysis within a worldwide chain of coffeehouses showed a strong link between the performance of a given store and the percent of employees in that store who believed the company was living up to its values. There was "a very distinct market improvement in the store's comp performance [that is, same-store sales], controlling for all other variables when partners believe we're doing the right thing values-wise," making a significant difference to the bottom line.[13] Similar findings apply to public sector organizations. Within the most effective agencies and departments, there are strong agreements and intense feelings among employees and managers about the importance of their values and about how those values are best implemented.[14] A study examining the companies consistently appearing on the Fortune *100 Best*

*Companies to Work For* list revealed that their leaders conveyed an "authentic commitment" to values, made talking about them a priority, and took great pains to ensure that people learned about values from one another so that "their personnel shared a common interpretation of their organization's values."[15]

Periodically taking the organization's pulse to check for values clarity and consensus is well worthwhile. It renews commitment. It engages the team and organization in discussing, clarifying, revising, and recommitting to values most relevant to a changing constituency—for example, diversity, accessibility, sustainability, and flexibility. Real estate agent Cathy Wang told us how sharing her personal and work values creates a positive and productive climate because clients, lenders, escrow officers, and other parties understand her goals and what they can expect when they work with her. "I have found that sharing my values is very powerful," she said, "because when my values align with what the clients believe, a foundation of mutual trust is created, and that results in a smoother process with the demanding and sometimes tedious transactions." Richard Sasser, area manager with a diversified building company, keeps a white coffee mug on his desk on which he has written his seven values. When people ask him about the words on his coffee cup, Richard says that this provides "an opportunity to share my personal values and gets the other person to consider what matters most to them. In these conversations, we generally find ourselves in agreement about our shared values and the purpose behind what we are doing together."

Once people are clear about the leader's values, their own values, and shared values, they know the team's expectations and feel that they can count on others. Consequently, they can work more productively, be more innovative, manage higher levels of challenge, and better handle often-conflicting work–life balance issues.

**Shared Values Make a Difference** When leaders seek consensus around shared values, constituents are more positive and productive. People who report that their senior managers engage in dialogue regarding common values feel a significantly stronger sense of personal effectiveness than those individuals who feel that they're wasting energy trying to figure out what they're supposed to be doing.[16] That's the point. People tend to drift when they're unsure or confused about how they should be operating. The energy that goes into coping with, and possibly fighting about, incompatible values takes its toll on both personal effectiveness and organizational productivity. For example, studies have shown that in those organizations where leaders express innovation as one of their core values, they more consistently design, develop, and launch products.[17]

In our research, we've carefully examined the relationship between personal and organizational values.[18] The findings clearly reveal that when there's congruence between individual values and organizational values, there's a significant payoff for leaders and their organizations. For example, such congruence:

- Fosters strong feelings of personal effectiveness
- Enhances high levels of company loyalty
- Facilitates consensus about key organizational goals and stakeholders
- Encourages ethical behavior
- Promotes strong norms about working hard and caring
- Reduces levels of job stress and tension
- Builds pride in the company
- Increases understanding of job expectations
- Strengthens feelings of esprit de corps and teamwork

Studies show that high-performing companies align and enact their values throughout the organization, and that organizations with a strong corporate culture based on shared values outperform other firms by a huge margin.[19] For example, strong corporate culture organizations experience four times faster growth in revenue, their stock price grew twelve times faster, and profit performance was 750 percent higher. Studies of adaptive corporate cultures—organizations with consistent guiding values, a shared purpose, teamwork, innovation, and learning—showed similar powerful results. Compared with nonadaptive cultures, over a ten-year period, the organizations with strong values experienced nearly ten times the growth in net income and had three times the growth in stock price.[20]

Studies of public sector organizations also support the importance of shared values to organizational effectiveness.[21] Within successful agencies and departments, considerable agreement and intense feeling are found among employees and managers about the importance of their values and how they could implement those values. Periodically taking the organization's pulse regarding clarity and consensus of its values is well worthwhile. It renews commitment. It engages the institution in discussing values (such as diversity, accessibility, sustainability, and so on) that are most relevant to a changing constituency.

Is there some particular value or set of values that fuels organizational vitality? Consider this example of three electronics companies, each of which has a strong set of values.[22] The first company prides itself on technical innovation and has a culture dominated by engineering values; it informally encourages and rewards activities such as experimentation and risk-taking. The second company is much flashier; its important organizational values are associated with marketing, and the company gears itself toward providing outstanding customer service. The third company does things "by the numbers"; accounting standards dominate its key values, and energies are directed toward making the organization more efficient (by cutting costs, for example).

Each of these companies operates by a different set of values. All three compete in the same market, and all are successful, each with a different strategy and culture. It's apparent, then, that successful companies may have very different values—and that the specific set of values that serves one company may hurt another. Research on companies that are "built to last" supports this view. Compared with a like company in its industry, each high-performing organization had a very strong "core ideology" but didn't share the *same* core ideology.[23] The source of sustained competitive advantage for organizations begins with a values-based foundation on which management and leadership practices are built.

Although there may not be one best set of values, you can find some guidance from the research on central themes in the values of highly successful, strong-culture organizations.[24] There are three central themes in the values of these organizations—high performance standards, a caring attitude about people, and a sense of uniqueness and pride. *High-performance* values stress the commitment to excellence, *caring* values communicate how others are to be treated, and *uniqueness* values tell people inside and outside how the organization is different from all the others. These three common threads seem to be critical to weaving a values tapestry that leads to greatness.

**Give People Reasons to Care** Leaders who advocate values that aren't representative of the collective won't be able to mobilize people to act as one. There has to be a shared understanding of mutual expectations. Leaders must be able to gain consensus on a common cause and set of principles. They must be able to build and affirm a community of shared values.

Harmony among individual, group, and organizational values generates tremendous energy. It intensifies commitment, enthusiasm, and drive. People have reasons to care about their work, and because of that, they are more effective and satisfied, experiencing less stress and tension. As Courtney Ballagh recounted from her experience with her store's associates, "By getting to know each other on a personal level, we identified our shared values and gave each person a reason to care about more than just ourselves. Morale increased significantly, and the store functioned better as a whole." Most people believe that organizations, and their leaders, should be spending more time than they do talking about values with one another.[25] Courtney's experience reaffirms the research that when people believe that their values and the organization's values align, they are the most committed.

Conversations about values enable people to find more meaning in their work. When you converse with your team members about their values, and when you facilitate a values conversation among them, you are helping them to see how the work they do connects with who they are. You are helping them to make a much deeper connection to work than can ever be realized through discussions of tasks and rules. You are also creating a context where they can connect more deeply with each other.

These conversations renew commitment and reinforce feelings that everyone is on the same team, which is especially critical in geographically distributed and virtual workplaces. The resulting alignment enhances clarity about expectations. This transparency enriches people's ability to make choices, enables them to deal more effectively with difficult and stressful situations, and improves their understanding and appreciation of the options selected by others. When people care about the values, and when those values have meaning to them, they also care more about each other, their customers and clients, the work they do, and the organization.

**Forge Unity, Don't Force It** Questions such as "What are our basic principles?" and "What do we believe in?" are far from simple. Even with commonly identified values, there may be little agreement on the meaning of values statements. One study, for example, uncovered 185 different behavioral expectations about the value of integrity alone.[26] The lesson here is that leaders must engage their constituents in a dialogue about values. A common understanding of values emerges from a process, not a pronouncement. You cannot mandate unity; instead, you forge it by involving people in the process, making them feel that you are genuinely interested in their perspectives and that they can speak freely with you.

To be open to sharing their ideas and aspirations, they have to believe that you'll be caring and constructive in searching for common ground. It's not surprising that people who report that their managers engage in dialogue regarding values feel a significantly stronger sense of personal effectiveness than individuals who feel they have to struggle on their own to figure out what the priorities and principles are and how they're supposed to be behaving.

This is precisely what Michael Lin discovered when he became the technical support manager for a small wireless company. Although he felt that it was essential "to clarify my personal values from the onset, at the same time I needed to allow each of my fellow technical support engineers to express what individual values were important to them." He noted that it was not so important what the particular value was called or labeled but that everyone agreed on the importance and meaning of the values. One of his initial actions was to bring people together just for that purpose so that they could arrive at common and shared understandings of what their key priorities and values were and what these meant in action.

> The last thing I wanted them to feel was that my values were being imposed on them. So, each person talked about their own values, the reasoning behind them. In this fashion, we identified the common values that were important to us as a group. The fundamental values that the team and I felt were most important to model were honesty, responsibility, customer focus, and teamwork. This led us to draft a team credo: Do whatever it takes to satisfy the customer. The process of deciding on one common set of values was an extremely valuable unifying and clarifying experience.

No matter how extensive top management's support of shared values is, leaders can't impose their values on organizational members. Instead, they must be proactive in involving a wide range of people in creating shared values. Shared values are the result of listening, appreciating, building consensus, and practicing conflict resolution. For people to understand the values and agree with them, they must participate in the process. That means you need to provide opportunities for people to ask questions, clarify their own values, determine if they can live their values in the organization, and come to the decision about the fit between their own values and the values of the organization.

Someone who knows all about resolving conflict and building consensus around a unifying set of values is Pat Christen, president of a nonprofit organization that combines rigorous research with some very innovative solutions to improving the health and quality of life of young people with chronic illnesses. She found that shared values were critical guideposts when difficulties arose.

> All staff members have competencies that were really critical to our success, but they were often in conflict with one another in terms of what they felt appropriate. Our leadership role was to manage these tensions to bring out the best in everyone. It was an extraordinary challenge, but I believe that when you reach difficult crossroads in an organization, you go back to your core values. You constantly ask how you should be behaving and what path you should be taking to align your values with actions. The manner in which the staff rose to the occasion in producing such a high-quality product is a real testament to having a set of core values and using them to guide how you act and behave in the world.

A unified voice on values results from discovery and dialogue. Leaders must provide a chance for individuals to discuss what the values mean and how their personal beliefs and behaviors are influenced by what the organization stands for. Leaders must also be prepared to discuss values and expectations in recruiting, selecting, and orienting new members. Better to explore early the fit between person and organization than to have members find out at some key juncture that they're in violent disagreement over matters of principle.

This was precisely Charles Law's experience when assigned to launch a marketing campaign with a team of six colleagues of different ethnicities and business functions for a multinational financial services corporation. Progress was slow at the start due to frequent conflicts, as team members focused on their individual goals without considering the interests of others.

Charles saw that the team needed to agree on a shared set of values to function well. He noted that it was not so important what they called or labeled a particular value, but instead that everyone agreed on its importance and meaning. One of his initial actions was to bring people together to arrive at a common and shared understanding of their top priorities and values and what these looked like in action. He sat down and listened to each team member individually, then reported about everyone's opinions at their next group meeting. He encouraged open discussions and worked through any misunderstandings.

The last thing Charles wanted them to feel was that he was imposing his values on them, so each person talked about their personal values and the reasoning behind them. In this manner, they were able to identify the values that were important to the group. Charles explained:

> With a set of shared values, created with everyone's consent, everyone strived to work together as a team toward success. Shared values created a positive difference in work attitudes and performance. My action made my colleagues work harder, emphasized teamwork and respect for each other, and resulted in a better understanding of each other's capabilities to meet appropriately set mutual expectations.

Fervently shared values are much more than advertising slogans; they are strongly supported and broadly endorsed beliefs about what's important to the people who hold them. Everyone must be able to articulate the values and have common interpretations of how to practice those values. They must know how their values influence how they do their jobs and directly contribute to organizational success.

# TAKE ACTION:
## Clarify Values

The very first step on the journey to exemplary leadership is clarifying your values—discovering those fundamental beliefs that will guide your decisions and actions along the path to success and significance. That journey involves an exploration of the inner territory where your authentic voice resides. It's essential that you put yourself on this path because it's the only route to authenticity. Moreover, you must choose that path because your personal values drive your commitment to the organization and the purpose it serves. You can't do what you say if you don't know what you believe. Nor can you do what you say if you don't believe in what you're saying.

Although personal values clarity is essential for all leaders, it's not enough. That's because leaders don't just speak for themselves; they also speak for their constituents. There must be agreement on the values that everyone will commit to upholding. Shared values give people reasons for caring about what they do, making a significant and positive difference in work attitudes and performance. A common understanding of shared values emerges from a process, not a pronouncement. Unity comes about through dialogue and debate, followed by understanding and commitment. Leaders must hold themselves and others accountable to the set of values they share.

We suggest that you take these actions to *clarify values by finding your voice and affirming shared values*:

- Review your personal credo—the values or principles that you believe should guide your part of the organization.

Remember what we said about the importance of personal values clarity, so take the time to express them in your own voice; don't just copy the organization's values.

- If you haven't yet done so this year, review the vision and values of your organization. If you've never taken the time to compare your values to the organization's values, now is a perfect time. Reflect on the "fit" between your personal values and what the organization espouses. Are there any points of tension? If so, what can you do to resolve them?
- Ask your direct reports and other team members to write their personal credos and share them at team meetings. Have a conversation about the "fit" of personal values and organizational values. Are there any points of tension? What can be done to resolve them?

In addition, regular conversations about leadership will let people know it's something important to you, to the organization, and to them. In every interaction, you have the chance to direct people's attention to aspects of leadership that you think are important to focus on. Find opportunities to talk with others about these questions:

- What values and principles do you feel should guide our team's decisions and actions?
- Tell me something about yourself that will help me be more effective in my relationship with you.

# CHAPTER 3

# Set the Example

*The action that made the most difference*
*was setting a personal example.*
*Idan Bar-Sade*

**AS THE NEW** manager for a southwestern manufacturing plant, Steve Skarke realized that the management team had over many years discussed a vision of becoming a "World-Class Plant." They debated the defining characteristics of a world-class plant and agreed that a strong culture of safety and good housekeeping should be at the top of the list. Looking around, Steve could see that the housekeeping conditions did not meet this ideal. Whenever they had a pending customer visit, for example, Steve would have to remind everyone to make an extra effort to clean up. This included sending people out to pick up trash in the plant, the parking lot, and on the roads. He knew there had to be a way to make cleanliness part of their daily routine.

While offsite after lunch one day, Steve stopped at a hardware store, bought a two-gallon plastic bucket, and put the words "World-Class Plant" on its side. When he returned, he walked through the plant and started picking up trash. Soon his bucket was overflowing. He carried his bucket of trash through the main control room and, as everyone watched intently, emptied it into a trashcan. Then he walked out the other door, saying nothing. Word spread quickly that the plant manager was in the plant with a bucket, picking up trash.

Each time Steve ventured out with his bucket, he made sure that it would be visible. It didn't take long for more buckets to appear, with other managers going out into the plant to pick up trash each day, setting the example for all to follow. Soon, whenever Steve walked through the control room, operators would ask how much trash he found. He would walk by the supervisor's office when he had a full bucket and hold it up for inspection. The process that Steve started, by his hard-to-miss example, soon became the norm.

In addition to actual trash removal, Steve's actions started generating lots of discussion and new ideas about how they could make the job of cleaning the plant easier. To make debris collection easier, trashcans previously removed were placed back in central areas. The operations staff agreed to maintain them, and they came up with even more ideas to organize their work areas better. The maintenance technicians began carrying buckets to keep parts in and trash containers to make cleaning up quicker and easier. During this time, the plant launched a new program called "My Machine," whereby each operator was assigned a piece of equipment to keep clean and learn about its function to ensure proper operation.

"By simply deciding to venture out and start picking up trash," Steve told us, "I was modeling the way by aligning my actions with the shared value of having a clean plant. I made it personal for everyone. In a short time, many others were setting the same example."

Steve's story illustrates the second commitment of Model the Way—leaders *Set the Example.* They take every opportunity to show others by their example that they're deeply committed to the values and aspirations they espouse. No one will believe you're serious until they see you doing what you're asking of others. Either you lead by example, or you don't lead at all. Your actions provide evidence that you're personally committed. It's how you make your values tangible.

Being an exemplary leader requires you to live the values. You have to put into action what you and others stand for. You have to be the example for others to follow. And, because you're leading a group of people—not just leading yourself—you also have to make sure that the actions of your constituents are consistent with the shared values of the organization. An essential part of your job is to educate others on what the organization stands for, why they matter, and how they can authentically serve the organization. As the leader, you teach, coach, and guide others to align their actions with the shared values because you're held accountable for their actions, too, not just your own.

To *Set the Example,* you need to:

- **Live the shared values**
- **Teach others to model the values**

In practicing these essentials, you become an exemplary role model for what the organization stands for. You create a culture in which everyone commits to aligning themselves with shared values.

## Live the Shared Values

*Leading means you have to be a good example and live what you say. Only then can you persuade people honestly.*

*Tom Brack*

Leaders are their organizations' ambassadors of shared values. Their mission is to represent the values and standards to the rest of the world, and their moral obligation is to serve the values to the best of their abilities. People watch your every action, and they're determining if you're serious about what you say. You need to be conscious of your choices and the actions you take because they signal priorities that others use to conclude whether you're doing what you say.

The power of the leader's personal example can't be stressed enough. Researchers find that leaders who persist in attaining organizational goals, promote the organization to outsiders and insiders, and initiate constructive change in the workplace are much more likely to have direct reports who exhibit the same behaviors than leaders who don't set that kind of example. This effect is strongest when the leader is most visible to direct reports and considered a worthy role model.[1] Research on "behavioral integrity" demonstrates quite clearly that the alignment between a leader's words and deeds has a powerful impact on how much constituents trust the leader and on their subsequent performance levels.[2] Eighty-two percent of employees at high-performing organizations agree that their leaders consistently model values, while only 49 percent agree this is the case at all other organizations.[3] Clarifying the values and performance expectations you have for yourself communicates to constituents what you are likely to expect of them. Setting the example is how leaders embody shared values and teach others to model the values themselves.

Imani Williams has been a nurse for more than twenty years, and she is passionate about family—her own, the family of her team, and the family of patients they serve. A few months into the coronavirus pandemic, she was performing her rounds on patients and her staff in the intensive care unit. But because of COVID-19, there were no families on her rounds that day. Happening upon a staff nurse and physician who seemed to be in a serious conversation, she stopped and asked them both about their discussion and if there was anything she could do to help. The nurse explained that one of her patients needed to be put on a ventilator, and she was recommending that they first call the patient's home to speak with the family before the procedure. However, others wanted to perform the procedure quickly in order to move on to other patients (not unreasonable because the ICU was full of very sick people).

Imani knew what to do. She asked them if the patient would be okay for just another five minutes. They both agreed yes, the patient was stable. Imani called the patient's wife, who answered on the first ring, despite it being 6:00 a.m. She asked the wife to update the family and give them the chance to speak with their husband and father before he was placed on a ventilator. Learning about this intervention, the patient cried tears of thanks for the chance to talk with his wife and children before intubation. That conversation occurred because Imani was present, attentive, and clear in her and the organization's values about delivering patient and family-centered care. Acting upon these values, Imani also set an example to her staff by making decisions consistent with their shared values.

Later that day, Imani was contacted by a very grateful family. It turned out to be the last time they had the chance to speak with their father, as he died several hours later.

As shown in Figure 3, there's a consistent and dramatic relationship between the extent to which people trust their organization's management and the frequency that they find their leaders following through on promises and commitments. For those leaders reported by their direct reports as nearly always doing what they say they do, there is a one-to-one relationship between these two variables. People just do not trust those who don't keep their promises.

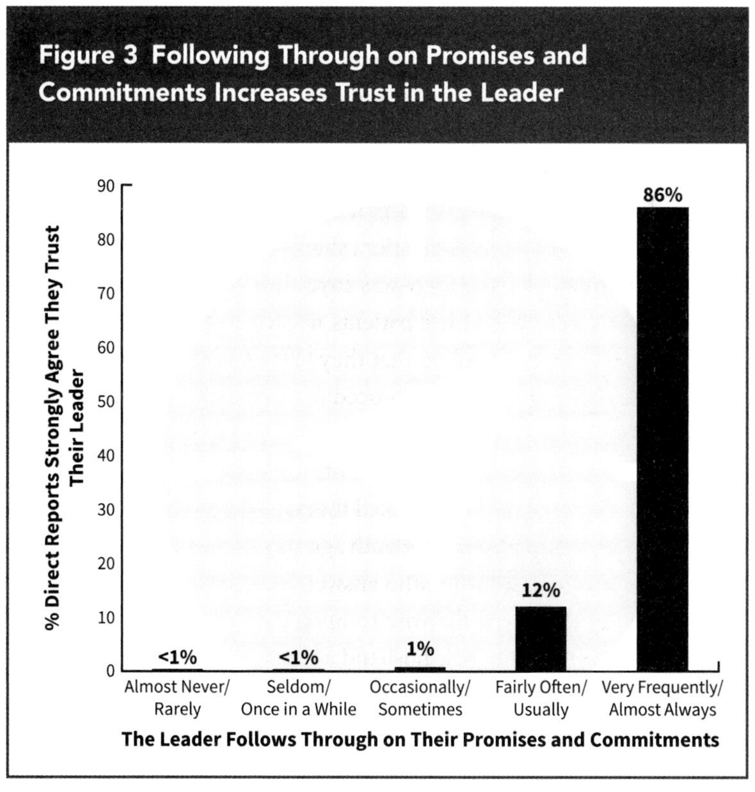


**Figure 3 Following Through on Promises and Commitments Increases Trust in the Leader**

Actions speak louder than words. The challenge is not to somehow find the best, jazziest, most profound, popular, or politically correct values, but to be faithful to those you profess. This is the challenge leaders face every day, ensuring that their values-in-use (actions) are consistent with their espoused values. In our studies, we've found that when at their best, leaders recognize that intentional modeling is essential to focus people's attention, energy, and efforts on the expected behaviors.

The four most significant signal-sending actions you can take to demonstrate that you live the values are: how you spend your time, what you pay attention to, the questions you ask, and your openness to feedback. These actions make visible and tangible your commitment to a shared way of being. Each provides the chance to show where you stand on matters of principle.[4]

**Spend Your Time and Attention Wisely** How you spend your time is the single clearest indicator to others of what's important to you. Spending time on what you say is important shows that you're putting your resources and energy behind your espoused values. Whatever those values are, they must show up on your calendar and meeting agendas if you want people to believe they are essential to you.

If you value service to others, for example, and say that store operators are important, you should be meeting with them in their locations. If you say that you're focused on customers (or clients, patients, students, voters, or parishioners), then you should be spending your time with them. If diversity, equity, and inclusion are critical, then make sure they are part of recruitment, selection, and retention efforts. If innovation is essential, you should be visiting the labs and participating in online open-source discussions. When you spend time doing the things you say you value, you earn the trust of others.

Brenda Aho, director of business development for a major regional distributing company, shared a good illustration of this point. Brenda's manager was supposed to leave on a week-long vacation, and his family showed up at the office to pick him up and head to the airport together. But before they arrived, Brenda told us, the organization received a complaint from one of their largest customers about the new installation program. Her manager had personally introduced the program to their customers during a luncheon kick-off. He got everyone excited about his vision of a white-glove type of service that was mission-critical to sales and told them that their participation and feedback were critical to making the program work. Unfortunately, the customer said that the new program was not helping their sales and was actually deterring people from buying due to poor follow-up, horrible response times, and lack of professionalism by the company's installation department.

At that moment, he was at a crossroads. He had promised to take his family on vacation, and he also had pledged to their customers that he was personally invested in this program and that its success relied on their feedback. He had to find a way to keep both his promises. He told his family to fly out ahead of him, and he would meet them after they resolved the customer's situation. After two days, following an intensive leadership team meeting, they straightened out the issues, and her manager then joined his family on vacation. His actions taught Brenda a powerful lesson.

He was able to win back the customer's confidence because he followed through on his promise to them, immediately acting on the feedback they provided and showing he was personally invested in the success of the program. He also mobilized his leadership team to struggle with him to rebuild this better model, just by his example of staying aligned to his values. He kept his word to their customers and his family.

Modeling the Way is what lends credibility to a leader's leadership. Without credibility, you are dead in the water, and people are not going to follow you if they don't believe in you.

Setting an example means making choices that are consistent with values, even when that is difficult and involves tradeoffs. It often means arriving early, staying late, working hard, and being there to show you care. It's about being the first to do something that everyone else should value. Whatever your values—family, teamwork, cleanliness, safety, service, fun, or something else—they have to show up in how you spend your time.

Leaders must set the standard for living in accordance with shared values. If you don't live the values, you will have little credibility when preaching them. Moreover, without credibility, the values become meaningless, no more than mere words in a script. Tyrone O'Neill, head of customer marketing for an Australian telecommunications company, took this understanding to heart and demonstrated how important it is to lead by example and how this enables others to live the values themselves.

Charged with the job of significantly improving customer retention and engagement, Tyrone realized that a fundamental change was needed in the psyche and operating habits of the organization, especially around the shared value of customer focus. However, people were already incredibly busy, and they weren't paying much attention to this new initiative. Accordingly, Tyrone turned his attention to changing people's behaviors, starting with his own. Everyone on the team who was not in a customer-facing role was assigned a list of customers to call to conduct a customer satisfaction survey.

Most everyone hated the phone calls at first, but Tyrone's actions helped change their perspective because he started calling and surveying customers himself—even after work hours. He would visit the call center and listen in on survey calls. He would discuss survey results with the call agents. He would go "mystery shopping" on the weekends to get a peek into what their frontline staff members were experiencing with customers on the ground. Then he would come back on Monday and share his reports with the team. As one of his constituents told us, "Tyrone led by example. He got into the trenches with us and did everything he could to get as close to as many customers as possible to know what they were thinking and feeling. The effect was that everyone wanted to get involved and mimic his behavior. Initially, we all had excuses for not making the calls or following through on other initiatives of the change program. But his personal crusade changed everything."

These experiences underscore the importance of a *Golden Rule* in leadership: only ask others to do something you are willing to do yourself. How leaders use their time shows others that they are serious about their dedication to the group, task, and shared values. You can't just talk the talk; you have to walk it, which often means rolling up your sleeves and being part of, not apart from, the action.

**Use Relevant Language** Try talking about an organization for a day without using the words *employee*, *manager*, *boss*, *supervisor*, *subordinate*, or *hierarchy*. You may find this exercise nearly impossible unless you've been part of organizations that use other terms—terms such as *associates*, *crew*, *cast members*, *team members*, *partners*, or even *constituents*. The corporate lexicon can easily trap people into a particular way of thinking about roles and relationships.[5]

Exemplary leaders understand and are attentive to language because they appreciate the power of words. Words don't just give voice to one's mindset and beliefs; they also evoke images of what people hope to create with others and how they expect people to behave. The words you choose to use are metaphors for concepts that define attitudes, behaviors, structures, and systems.[6] Gary Hamel, one of the world's most influential and iconoclastic business thinkers, points out that "the goals of management are usually described in words like 'efficiency,' 'advantage,' 'value,' 'superiority,' 'focus,' and 'differentiation.' Important as these objectives are, they lack the power to rouse human hearts . . . [and leaders] must find ways to infuse mundane business activities with deeper, soul-stirring ideals, such as honor, truth, love, justice, and beauty."[7]

You might think that language is merely semantics or a play on words, but the impact is quite the opposite. While simple in nature, the words you use are packed with meaning, creating imagery and communicating history, traditions, and beliefs. For example, Mark Linsky, who works with several nonprofit organizations, explains that there's a big difference, especially in working with volunteers, between providing feedback and offering constructive criticism. The former is "a gift," he says, and "focuses on facilitating learning, while the latter concentrates on an error and impairs learning because it makes the receiver defensive."

Language communicates a message beyond the literal meaning of your words and phrases, and researchers find that "a single word has the power to influence the expression of genes that regulate physical and emotional stress."[8] Positive words strengthen areas in the frontal lobes, promoting the brain's cognitive functioning and building resiliency. Conversely, hostile language and angry words send alarm signals to the brain as protection against any threats to survival and partially shut down the logic-and-reasoning centers in the brain.

The language and words leaders use affect their self-images and people's responses to what's going on around them. They help build the frame around people's views of the world, so it's essential to be mindful of your choice of words. Frames provide the context for thinking and talking about events and ideas and focus the listeners' attention on certain aspects of the subject. Frames influence how people view and interpret what's going on around them. For example, terms such as *boss-subordinate, top-down,* and *rank and file* put a hierarchical frame around a discussion about relationships in organizations. The words *colleagues, teammates,* and *partners* put a different, more collaborative frame around the same theme. Of course, you have to mean it when you say it. Calling someone a "partner" and then not treating them that way can backfire. "Watch your language" takes on an entirely new meaning from the times your teacher scolded you in school for using an inappropriate word. It's now about setting an example for others of how they need to think and act.

**Ask Purposeful Questions** When you ask questions, you send your constituents on mental journeys. Your questions choose the path that people will follow and focus their search for answers. The questions let people know what is top-of-mind for you. If you were to ask, for example, "What have you done today to partner with a colleague on getting the work done?" you are sending a signal about the importance of collaboration. On the other hand, if you were to ask, "What have you done today to reduce the costs of doing business?" you are sending a very different message. Both are legitimate questions, but they indicate very different priorities. Questions are one more tangible indicator of how serious you are about your espoused beliefs and direct attention to the values that deserve attention and energy.

Researchers point out that "questioning is a uniquely powerful tool" that promotes the exchange of ideas and fosters learning, promotes innovation, and builds rapport and trust.[9] A leader's questions highlight particular issues and concerns, and they send messages. They ask constituents to consider specific focus areas, such as operating costs, customer service, inclusion, quality, trust, or market share. Questions provide information about which values to attend to and how much energy should be devoted to them. They point people in a specific direction, and the first question you ask is an especially clear indicator of direction and priority.

When we examine how leaders make people aware of critical concerns or shifts in organizational focus, it is readily apparent that the leaders' questioning routine has a noticeable effect on the issues organizational members pay attention to. For instance, Gayle Mayville, area manager for a large public utility firm, told us about getting people to shift their concerns from revenue to customer satisfaction. In these efforts, she never let a day go by "without spreading the word that our customers are what we are in business for. I try to ask each account representative about what our customers are telling them about our services." The first questions in her staff meetings always focused on customer satisfaction.

Questions also develop people. They help people escape the trap of their mental models by broadening their perspectives and enlarging their responses by taking responsibility for their viewpoints. In addition, asking questions forces you to listen attentively to what people are saying. It demonstrates your respect for their ideas and opinions. If you are genuinely interested in what other people think, you need to ask their opinion, especially before giving your own. Asking what others think facilitates participation in whatever decision will ultimately be determined and consequently increases support for that decision.

Joshua Fradenburg was brought on to turn around a foundering sporting goods store, and he realized that every employee needed to contribute to coming up with ways to improve sales. For example, he asked each to go to the product wall and select which skis or snowboard they wanted. Then he had them pick out their bindings and boots. After giving them a few minutes to make their decisions, Josh asked them what they were thinking about when they were deciding. He asked them to close their eyes and envision what it would look like to use the new gear: "Feel the cold. Hear the wind whistle. Smell the fresh mountain air." His questions got them thinking about how most people made an emotional (rather than a technical) purchase decision. As all exemplary leaders do,

Josh used focused questions to reframe the staff's thinking and their approach to sales.

Think about the questions you typically ask in meetings, one-on-ones, telephone calls, and interviews. How do they help to clarify and gain commitment to shared values? What would you like each of your constituents to pay attention to each day? Be intentional and purposeful about the questions that you ask. When you are not around, what questions should others imagine you will ask them when you return? What evidence do you want to ask for that shows how people are making decisions consistent with values? Whatever your shared values are, come up with a routine set of questions that will get people to reflect on the shared values and what they have done each day to act on them.

**Seek Feedback** How can you know that you're doing what you say (the *behavioral* definition of credibility) if you never ask for feedback about your behavior? How can you expect to match your words and actions if you don't know how aligned others see them? Asking for feedback gives you a perspective about yourself that only others can see. With this insight, you have the opportunity to make improvements.

The feedback process strikes at a tension between two basic human needs: the need to learn and grow versus being accepted just the way you are.[10] Consequently, even what seems like a mild, gentle, or relatively harmless suggestion can leave a person feeling angry, anxious, poorly treated, or profoundly threatened. One major reason that most people, and especially those in leadership positions, aren't proactive in asking for feedback is their fear of feeling exposed—exposed as not being perfect, as not knowing everything, as lacking self-confidence, as not being as good at leadership as they should be, as not being up to the task.

Sarah Bjorkman, a healthcare construction leader, admitted that she initially felt uncomfortable and anxious when she received her feedback from the Leadership Practices Inventory. But when she

> thoroughly reviewed the report, had multiple conversations with my mentors about the data, and really started to dig into thoughts about how I could improve, I saw the feedback as more of a challenge than a setback. There is no way that this feedback could always

> be positive, and I had to remind myself that to be a good leader I constantly need to challenge myself and that requires feedback from people around me.

As Sarah realized, it takes a certain amount of courage to ask for feedback and there is simply no way to get around the fact that you can't grow as a leader without getting feedback. Researchers have found that people who seek out disconfirming feedback (contrary to their self-perceptions) perform better than those who only listen to people who see their positive qualities. "Being aware of your weaknesses and shortcomings," they say, "whether you like it or not, is critical to improvement."[11] These findings echo the experience of Hong Lu, manager of test engineering with a multinational high-technology firm, who told us how when she "took the initiative to ask for feedback from her peers and managers, much to my surprise, every discussion returned great results."

Throughout his career, soliciting feedback has been important to Seang Wee Lee, director of manufacturing product and component engineering for a flash data storage company: "I use feedback to further improve my leadership skills, identify shortfalls, and open up communications with the team. This promotes trust in my leadership and creates a climate of trust within the team and with me. I almost always learn about some things I can do to help develop each individual as well as the team and me." Leaders, like Seang, Sarah, and Hong, realize that although they may not always like the feedback, it is the only way they can know how they are doing as someone's leader. Seeking feedback makes a powerful statement about how everyone can be even better than they are today.

Self-reflection, the willingness to seek feedback, and the ability to engage in new behaviors based on this information are predictive of future success in managerial jobs.[12] However, the statement that consistently receives the lowest frequency rating, both from leaders as well as their constituents, on the Leadership Practices Inventory is "I ask for feedback on how my actions affect other people's performance." In other words, the behavior that leaders and their constituents consider to be the least frequently used is the behavior that most enables leaders to know how they're doing! You can't learn very much if you're unwilling to learn about the impact of your behavior on the performance of those around you. Researchers find that those rated the highest on their ability to ask for feedback had an overall rating on effectiveness that was more than four times higher than those who rated lowest in this regard.[13]

Being interested in information about how you are doing is characteristic of the best learners, and it's something all people, especially aspiring leaders, need to cultivate. "Focusing on asking for feedback and giving people a safe space and opportunity to provide feedback" was an area for growth that Amy Tomlinson identified as she took on responsibility for business development with a solar equipment startup. For example, she intentionally asked her new co-workers and manager questions like: "How do you think I could have made that meeting better? What advice do you have about what I could have provided or done better for you during the meeting?" Amy's experience was validated in a series of experiments where researchers found that "people received more effective input when they asked for advice rather than feedback."[14] Compared to those asked to give feedback, those asked to provide advice suggested 34 percent more areas for improvement and 56 percent more ways to improve. Feedback is too often associated with "being evaluated" and attends to what has already happened. When asked to provide "advice," people focus less on evaluation and more on offering suggestions about possible future actions.

Amy also noticed that framing the question more about the process than about herself led to "many sidebar 'deeper' conversations being initiated, co-workers fessing up about areas that were challenging them, healthy dialogues around possible solutions, and where assistance or encouragement would be welcomed." The more frequently feedback becomes part of everyday conversations, the easier it will be to hear and deal with it as constructive. The point is not to affix blame but to offer a way to exercise curiosity about what happened and what can be learned so that any problems, mistakes, misunderstandings, and the like are not repeated.

Of course, just because someone gives you feedback doesn't necessarily mean that they are right or a hundred percent accurate. Consider checking with other people to determine the reliability of any feedback you receive. After all, few people see you in your totality. Sometimes the feedback may be more about the sender than it is about the receiver. However, keep in mind that if you do not do anything with the feedback you receive, people will stop giving it to you.

## Teach Others to Model the Values

*Put the work in yourself*
*and others around you will emulate those qualities and*
*be encouraged to work hard and perform at their best.*
*Grace Castaneda*

You're not the sole role model in the organization. You have a responsibility to make sure that the promises that you and others have agreed on are being kept. People are watching how you hold others accountable for living the shared values and how you reconcile deviations from the chosen path. They're paying attention to what others say and do, and so should you. It's not just what *you* do that demonstrates consistency between word and deed. Signals are sent by every team member, partner, and colleague about what's valued. Therefore, you need to look for opportunities to teach not just by your example but also by taking on the role of teacher and coach.

U.S. Army General H. Norman Schwarzkopf was a master at creating moments to teach the importance of shared values. During his first day as a new division commander, one event illustrates how a leader can turn a chance encounter into a classroom. The morning after he arrived, he went out for a run. As he came upon the barracks area, a formation of troops raced by him, led by a guy who looked as if he belonged in the Olympics, and stretching back into the distance were the soldiers who hadn't been able to keep pace. He asked the company's captain what they were doing.

> "Sir, we've just completed our five-mile run."
>
> "That's terrific. But what about all those people back there?" I asked.
>
> "Sir, those are guys who couldn't keep up."
>
> "But you've run off and left them."

The captain gave him a puzzled look. "Think of it this way," Schwarzkopf said. "Suppose you're a new recruit. You come to your new unit, you're just out of basic training, and you're feeling great about being a soldier. But then you find out that your new unit does a lot more running than you're used to. And the very first day you're out with them, you run and you run until your legs give out and your lungs give out—but your unit keeps going and leaves you. What kind of unit cohesion does that build?" The light dawned on the captain's face. After suggesting ways for how he might reorganize the morning run so that nobody was ever left behind, Schwarzkopf jogged off, satisfied that he had just taught a young officer the importance of developing cohesion at every level.[15]

While many leaders might have passed up this chance encounter—after all, the morning run was mainly for exercise—Schwarzkopf recognized it as an opportune moment for the captain and the soldiers to learn an important lesson about group cohesion. All that was required was his clarity of belief and understanding that he needed to be alert to opportunities for teaching people about the importance of affirming shared values.

For direct reports, there's a very strong correlation between the frequency they indicate their leaders "make certain that people adhere to the principles and standards that have been agreed upon" and where they would place this leader compared with other leaders. Eighty-two percent of those leaders rated "among the best" by their direct reports very frequently or almost always engaged in this behavior. Similarly, 80 percent of direct reports who observe their leader very frequently or almost always build "a consensus around a common set of values" rate those leaders among the best they have ever worked with.

Exemplary leaders know that people learn lessons from how people handle unplanned as well as planned events on the schedule. They know that people learn from the stories circulating in the hallways, in the break room, in the cafeteria, on the retail floor, and on social media. Exemplary leaders know that what gets measured and reinforced is what gets done. If you're going to create a high-performance culture, you need to pay attention to bringing on board people who share the values held dear. To show others what you expect and ensure that they hold themselves accountable, you need to confront critical incidents, tell stories, and make sure that formal and informal systems reinforce the behaviors you want to be repeated.

**Confront Critical Incidents** You can't plan for everything. Even the most disciplined leaders can't stop the intrusion of the unexpected. Critical incidents—chance occurrences, particularly at a time of stress and challenge—are a natural part of every leader's life. They offer, however, significant moments of learning for leaders and their colleagues. Critical incidents present opportunities to teach important lessons about appropriate norms of behavior.

For example, Jennifer Tran, content manager at an online payments company, found out that being part of a team doesn't automatically mean that everyone has the same set of priorities. While working on a project that would significantly impact the way consumers pay for purchases, she discovered a serious problem with the documentation. The team's copy editor had already edited the documentation several times and was hesitant to step back and review it yet again. Jennifer pushed back, reminding her teammate about the possibility of not creating a "great user experience"—a core phrase for a shared value among all groups in their company. With that, the copy editor reconsidered, and Jennifer's team came up with a solution that satisfied everyone. "The fact that I stood up for this common value," Jennifer told us, "was instrumental in both mitigating potential conflict and encouraging greater team spirit." Jennifer saw in this situation not simply another problem to be dealt with but an opportune moment to remind her colleagues about the importance of living up to their shared values.

Having shared values may not always be sufficient to ensure that everyone's actions are aligned. There are critical moments when you have to act to put values squarely on the table and in front of others so that they can return to this common ground for working together. In the process, you make clear how shared values compel your actions. By standing up for values, you demonstrate that having shared values requires a mutual commitment to aligning words and deeds for everyone.

This is precisely what Emily Singh experienced when working through the merger of two business teams at a consumer goods manufacturer. She started by setting a tone of continuous communication with everyone involved, holding frequent meetings, encouraging open discussions, and making it safe for everyone to express their feelings about their work and the new team configuration. In building trust, she shared information and her own client experiences, soliciting feedback about others' experiences, and both seeking and incorporating their advice about handling client allocations. As one of her direct reports explained, "It would have been easy for her to play favorites, but she chose to do the right thing—her words and actions were consistent—and eventually that trickled down and made everyone believe that we were in it together."

Critical incidents offer the chance to improvise while still staying true to the script. Although they can't be explicitly planned, it's useful to keep in mind, as Jennifer and Emily did, that the way you handle these incidents—how you link actions and decisions to shared values—speaks volumes about what's important. Research clearly shows that behaviors modeling care and concern for others are contagious and have a ripple effect.[16] When you want people to be cooperative and helpful, be visible in doing that yourself. Better yet, make sure the entire team does, too.

**Tell Stories** Critical incidents create important teachable moments. They offer leaders the occasion in real-time to demonstrate what's valued and what's not. They become "stories" that are passed down, whether around the base (like Norman Schwarzkopf), around the department (like Jennifer Tran), across the company (like Emily Singh), or even from one generation to another, as demonstrated within most every family. Stories are another way that leaders pass on lessons about shared values and impress upon others the importance of being on the same page.

Stories are a powerful tool for teaching people what's important and what's not, what works and what doesn't, and what is and what could be.[17] Through stories, vital lessons are passed along about shared values and the seriousness in which they are taken. Paul Smith, former director of consumer and communications research for a multinational consumer goods corporation, and author of *Lead with a Story*, explains why telling stories is so important for leaders:

> You can't just order people to "be more creative" or to "get motivated" or to "start loving your job." The human brain doesn't work that way. But you can lead them there with a good story. You can't even successfully order people to "follow the rules" because nobody reads the rulebook. But people will read a good story about a guy who broke the rules and got fired, or a woman who followed the rules and got a raise. And that would be more effective than reading the rulebook anyway.[18]

Steve Denning learned firsthand how stories could change the course of an organization when he was the program director of knowledge management with a global financial development organization. After trying all the traditional ways of getting people to change their behavior, Steve found that simple stories were the most convincing way to communicate the essential messages within the organization. "Nothing else worked," Steve said. "Charts left listeners bemused. Prose remained unread. Dialogue was just too laborious and slow. Time after time, when faced with the task of persuading a group of managers or frontline staff in a large organization to get enthusiastic about a major change, I found that storytelling was the only thing that worked."[19]

In a business climate obsessed with PowerPoint presentations, complex graphs and charts, and lengthy reports, storytelling may seem to some like a soft way of getting the hard stuff done. It's anything but that; the data supports Paul's and Steve's experience with storytelling. Research shows that when leaders want to communicate standards, stories are a very powerful means of communication.[20] People more quickly and accurately remember stories—more than they recall corporate policy statements, data about performance, and even a story plus the data. Stories provide concrete advice and guidelines about how things are done and about what to expect in the organization.

## Formally Reinforce the Behaviors You Want Repeated

Measurement and feedback are absolutely essential to increasing efforts to improve performance. Score-keeping systems are essential to knowing how people are doing. You probably don't need much research to understand how measured performance subsequently affects behavior. You know about keeping score from the games and sports you've played. And it's not just the numbers themselves that are important. It's what you get points for. For instance, hockey was altered forever when the National Hockey League changed the rules so that players earned points for assists and not just for goals. With this change, team members started passing the puck to each other rather than always trying to be the one who put it into the net.

Using a simple score-keeping method, Brian Coleman turned around the lackluster manufacturing performance of a major carmaker in England. One of their strategies was having the workers indicate a defect by marking a tick on the outside of a car as it came down the line. Subsequently, when Brian asked the team where they should begin to make changes, they pointed to the area with the densest mass of ticks. That uncomplicated measuring device was a major factor in reducing the number of defects by over 70 percent and nearly doubling productivity in three months. The value placed on quality, the specific goal of reducing defects, and the scoring mechanism, in this case, all converged to produce results.

Research indicates clearly that measurement and feedback are essential to increased efforts to improve performance. Leaders can easily influence outcomes by providing the tools for measuring progress. For example, suppose the organization's performance-appraisal system fails to measure how well people perform against the standards of excellence set by organizational values. In that case, leaders can add clear performance measures that evaluate how well people are doing on these values (e.g., quality, customer service, innovation, respect for others, etc.). One highly innovative company, for example, measures turnover by division units every ninety days to make certain that each manager is paying attention to retention and providing a workplace that makes people want to stay. Likewise, building a team-oriented, collective feeling at a nationwide retailer is facilitated by knowing that the company tracks the number of tickets written by each salesperson. If someone writes a lot more than others in the store, this suggests possibly hogging the walk-in traffic, and that person gets appropriately counseled.

Rewards and recognition are also tangible means of reinforcing values (and we'll discuss recognition more thoroughly in Chapter 10). Keep in mind that what you choose to reinforce is what people will choose to value. You must stress the fundamental values important to building and sustaining the culture you want. For example, if innovation is a priority, you need to pay attention to assess whether risk-taking is rewarded or punished. Are positive or negative stories associated with innovative experiences?

Additionally, who is rewarded, promoted, and reprimanded and why are among the clearest ways leaders demonstrate their seriousness to a specific set of principles. With financial rewards, leaders literally "put their money where their mouths are" and put their hearts where their good intentions are with more personalized recognition. The same goes for all other support systems—incentives, recruitment, training, information, and the like. They all send signals about what is valued and what is not. These systems must be aligned with the shared values and standards that you're trying to instill in those you are working with. A leader may say teamwork is critical but permit individual performance to drive compensation. Or service quality is said to be vital, but it's seldom assessed. People will only take the values seriously when the practices and processes inside their organization are in sync with them.

**Use Informal Methods to Teach and Reinforce** You will be wise to also pay heed to the informal channels by which organizational messages are conveyed. Foremost among these are the symbols and artifacts of workday life. Sometimes symbols represent time-honored traditions. For example, the mission church adorns Santa Clara University's letterhead, signaling the institution's roots and credo. There are great benefits in linking your efforts, routines, and organizational issues to the history and traditions of your organization and community. When a new plant manager started calling people by their first names and introduced a dress code, these seemingly mundane actions created more personal relationships and a sense of professionalism. When drivers were given the keys to the company trucks, it was a tangible reminder that every employee was trusted to act responsibly.

Posters, pictures on walls, items on desks, sayings on coffee mugs, and buttons or pins on lapels can be much more than decorative items. Each of these artifacts serves as a *visible* reminder of some key organizational value. A name on a parking space often confers status, for example. But a new general manager demonstrated a commitment to egalitarianism and team spirit by announcing that names on the parking curbs would henceforth be ignored. Using a hot-air balloon to symbolize how the facilities department "uplifted people's spirits" is another example of how leaders consciously employ symbols to send messages.

When organizations make major changes, they often create new symbols and discard or destroy old artifacts in favor of the new. For example, when the president of a major financial services company wanted to signal a change in the company's portfolio and orientation, he called the senior management team together for a meeting whose theme was *Crossing the Chasm*. In keeping with the idea of stepping out of the known to create a new way of doing business, a speaker for the meeting was one of the engineers of San Francisco's Golden Gate Bridge. He made clear some of the challenges the engineers and workers had faced in building the bridge. At the conclusion of the meeting, the team boarded a bus to the bridge and saw with new eyes the challenges encountered in spanning the roiling stretch of water. By walking the bridge and crossing what had once been a chasm, team members together faced the idea of change. The walk became a lasting memory for the entire team. And to bring that lesson back to share with others in the company, everyone was given a miniature of the Golden Gate Bridge, engraved to commemorate the occasion.

Another example is the team logo that Santosh Prabhu's group used to capture the essence of their innovative medical device: "We replaced the filament inside a light bulb with our new implant. It symbolized that with this implant we are eliminating darkness and lighting up the lives of our patients. Instead of just surviving and waiting to die a slow death, they are now living their lives to the fullest." They used this logo in all their presentations and even created jackets with this logo that people proudly wore.

Architecture and the design of physical space can also send tangible messages about status, preferred ways of interacting, and the best way to get work done. However, they reflect leaders' messages only if consciously managed; otherwise, they replicate community standards and the preferences of architects and facilities planners. Consider workplace changes that took place before and accelerated after the coronavirus pandemic, including the elimination of private offices and assigned desks, open floor plans, smaller conference rooms, higher ceilings, and greater access to outdoor areas. Employees keep their personal belongings in a locker and their work materials in a rolling cart. They and the cart go wherever they are needed, based on the project at hand. One firm locked the elevators, leaving stairwells as the only way up and down, finding that this facilitated people not only seeing one another but also talking with one another more often in passing.

The critical point is that in the performing art of leadership, symbols, artifacts, and the design of space are a leader's props. They're necessary tools for making the message memorable and sustainable over time. Together with rituals, they're a means of teaching others about the vision and values.

## TAKE ACTION:
### Set the Example

One of the most challenging parts about being a leader is that you're always on stage. People are always watching you, talking about you, and testing your credibility. That's why setting the *right* example is so important and why it's essential to use all the tools you have available to do it.

Leaders send signals in a variety of ways, and constituents read them as indicators of what's okay and what's not okay to do. How you spend your time is the single best indicator of what's important to you. Time is a precious asset because once passed it is never recoverable. But if wisely invested, it can pay returns for years. The language you use and the questions you ask are other powerful ways to shape perceptions of what you value. You also need feedback to know if you're doing what you say or sending mixed messages.

Be mindful that it's not only what you do that matters. You are also measured by how consistent your constituents' actions are with the shared values, so you must teach others how to set an example. Critical incidents—those chance occurrences in the lives of all organizations—offer significant teachable moments. They offer you the opportunity to pass along lessons in real-time, not just in theory or the classroom. Often critical incidents become stories, and stories are among the most influential teaching tools you have. Remember that what you reinforce will be what receives the most attention. You have to keep score for people to know how they're doing and improve how they're doing it. You also must be rewarding the appropriate behavior if you expect people to repeat it.

We suggest you take these actions to *set the example by aligning actions with shared values*:

- Check your values–action alignment. For the next month, keep track of how you spend your time relative to each of your shared values. What percentage of your time is spent on each? Is this the proper balance? Given where your business is, are there values you should be devoting more time to right now?
- At the end of each day, ask yourself these three questions: What have I done today that demonstrated my personal commitment to our shared values? What have I done today that might have, even inadvertently, demonstrated a lack of commitment? What can I do tomorrow to make sure I set a good example?
- Ask a trusted colleague to give you advice about how you are doing on these three questions above.

Remember that repeated conversations about leadership will let people know it's something important to you, to the organization, and to them. Find opportunities to talk with others about these questions:

- What have you observed me doing in the last week to be a positive example for others?
- What's a behavior (or decision) that we've taken recently that demonstrates how our espoused values and actions are aligned? Is there another example of where we may have a possible misalignment?

# INSPIRE A SHARED VISION

## PRACTICE 2

# INSPIRE A SHARED VISION

- Envision the future by imagining exciting and ennobling possibilities.
- Enlist others in a common vision by appealing to shared aspirations.

# CHAPTER 4
# Envision the Future

*You begin with the end in mind,*
*by knowing what you dream about accomplishing,*
*and then figure out how to make it happen.*

*Jim Pitts*

**HAVING RECENTLY RETIRED** from a long career in public education, Diann Grimm was working as a curriculum developer for an early childhood education publisher. She brought a lot to the job, and though the work was important, it didn't feel personally meaningful. So, she asked herself a pivotal question: "What is *my* dream?" Wrestling inside herself to find an answer would set her on a new path: "I want to continue to foster education and learning, but to do so in an innovative way." But how was she going to make this dream a reality?

Diann had participated in many volunteer projects, most of them centered on early childhood education in developing countries. She felt especially called to Nepal, where she'd spent a summer working with Bhupendra (Bhupi) Ghimire, the executive director of Volunteers Initiative Nepal (VIN). Diann decided to reach out to her old friend to see if her aspirations and his might come together in ways that would be meaningful to both of them.

Her timing was serendipitous, as Bhupi was planning to bring VIN to Nepal's Okhaldhunga district. This underdeveloped area is far from tourist trails, and its residents, who depend on subsistence farming and bartering, had minimal infrastructure for education or any other public services. Within two weeks of Bhupi asking her, "Why don't you come to Nepal and help us do this?" Diann flew there, ready to make the most of this opportunity and eager to enact her and Bhupi's visions of a better future for Nepali children.

While the residents and local government were enthusiastic about starting a preschool, they were skeptical about how it could actually happen. Rather than Bhupi and Diann coming in to impose their vision, everyone in the community had to be involved and enlisted because the preschool would have great significance beyond itself. For example, it would make it possible for older siblings to start attending school because they wouldn't have to take care of their younger siblings. It also presented an opportunity for some of the district's women to make money outside of the home or to contribute to the community, as they would be the ones who would actually teach and volunteer in the schools. "This would be a true partnership among all parties," Diann told us, "and one that created a shared sense of purpose among the community." Their combined efforts have now led to the establishment of more than fifty classrooms in a number of Nepal's villages and districts, providing early childhood education to an average of nearly one thousand students annually.

Diann's vision has been realized in ways she never thought possible. "I had no idea where this would take me when I started," she said, "but I had a big dream and I just couldn't get it out of my head. Every setback was just a temporary obstacle to making it all happen. The reward is in the faces of the children and their parents, and in the realization that while I may never know these kids as adults, they will have a better chance to thrive as a result of our efforts." She also realized that her dream became a reality as a result of aligning with the hopes and aspirations of Bhupi, VIN, and the scores of teachers and villagers she works with.

The leaders we studied share with Diann the perspective that bringing meaning to life in the present by focusing on making life better in the future is essential to making extraordinary things happen. Leaders dream of what might be. Everyone at some time in their lives has had a glimpse of the future. You know, that time when you imagined running your own business, or that dream of traveling to an exotic place, or that bold idea for a game-changing new product, or that burning desire to get an advanced degree. Diann's story is not about one more ambitious person taking initiative in a crisis. Her story is about the connection between vision and action. When you feel passionate about the legacy you want to leave, about the kind of future world you want for yourself and others, then you are much more likely to step forward voluntarily. If people don't have the slightest clue about their hopes, dreams, and aspirations, then the chances that they will take the lead are significantly less. They may not even see the opportunity that's right in front of them.

All endeavors, big or small, begin in the mind's eye. They start with imagination and with the belief that what is merely an image today can one day be made real. In our research on personal-best leadership experiences, we found that people aspired to make something extraordinary happen. They imagined a better future as the result of their initiatives. Other scholars have confirmed our findings. In a study of the lives of ninety leaders, for example, researchers found that "to choose a direction, a leader must first have developed a mental image of a possible and desirable future state of the organization. This image, which we call a vision, may be as vague as a dream or as precise as a goal or mission statement. The critical point is that a vision articulates a realistic, credible, attractive future for the organization, a condition that is better in some important ways than what now exists."[1]

Call it what you will—vision, purpose, mission, legacy, dream, aspiration, calling, or personal agenda—the intent is the same. If you are going to be an exemplary leader, you have to be able to imagine a positive future, as Diann's story illustrates. We prefer the term *vision* because it is the most descriptive term for the ability that people described in their personal-best leadership experiences. Vision is a "see" word, and it evokes images and pictures. Visual metaphors are very common when people talk about their long-range aspirations. Vision also implies a future orientation, and it connotes a standard of excellence, an ideal. Vision implies a choice of values, and it also has the quality of uniqueness. A vision, therefore, is *an ideal and unique image of the future for the common good.*

Exemplary leaders are forward-looking—having a clear sense of the direction they want their team to take—and this quality is something constituents expect of those people they would willingly follow. But a vision doesn't belong only to the leader. It has to be a shared vision. Everyone has hopes, dreams, and aspirations and wants tomorrow to be better than today. Shared visions attract more people, sustain higher motivation levels, and withstand more challenges than visions exclusive to only a few. You have to make sure that what you see is also something others can see.

Leaders develop the capacity to *Envision the Future* for themselves and others by mastering these two essentials:

- **Imagine the possibilities**
- **Discover a common purpose**

You begin with the end in mind by finding a theme about what should be possible. Identifying a common purpose inspires people to want to make that vision a reality.

# Imagine the Possibilities

*The greatest achievement of the human brain is its ability to imagine objects and episodes that do not exist in the realm of the real, and it is this ability that allows us to think about the future.*

*Daniel Gilbert*

Leaders are dreamers. Leaders are idealists. Leaders are possibility thinkers. All ventures, big or small, begin with the belief that what is today only a yearning can be a reality in the future. It's this belief that sustains leaders and their constituents through difficult times. Turning exciting possibilities into an inspiring shared vision is essential to making extraordinary things happen.

However, knowing that vision is essential doesn't make one pop out of your head like a bright light bulb. When people first begin to exercise leadership, they typically don't have a clear vision of the future. And when we ask leaders to tell us where their visions come from, they often have great difficulty describing the process. When they do provide an answer, typically it's more about a feeling, a sense, a gut reaction, a hunch. After all, there's no map, or interstate highway, to the future.

What they do have—and what you, too, have—are concerns, desires, principles, hypotheses, propositions, arguments, hopes, and dreams—core concepts around which you organize your aspirations and subsequent actions. Visions are projections of your fundamental beliefs and assumptions about human nature, technology, economics, science, politics, art, ethics, and the like. Leaders often begin envisioning the future by discovering the "theme" that ties together these inner whisperings, much like composers find a musical theme from all the notes that swirl in their minds. Your central theme in life more than likely wasn't something that just occurred to you this morning. It's been there for a long time. You may not have ever explored your past for a persistent and repeating ideal, but if you were to examine the recurring theme in your life, what might you find?

What are your fundamental beliefs and assumptions about life and work that keep recurring in your life? What are the themes that keep repeating themselves? What are the social and charitable causes to which you contribute? What are the things that keep you up at night and the "I wish" statements that you find yourself repeating?

The answers to these questions don't come easy, and finding your vision, like finding your voice, is a process of self-exploration and self-creation. It's an intuitive, emotional process. What we've seen is that exemplary leaders have a passion for their projects, their causes, their programs, their subject matter, their technologies, their communities, their families—something other than their own fame and fortune. Your inner passion is an indicator of what you feel most deeply about and find worthwhile in and of itself. It's a clue to what is intrinsically rewarding to you. Leaders care about something much bigger than themselves. They care about making a difference and changing the status quo in some meaningful way. What do you care about most deeply? What do you wish for most often?

If you don't care deeply for and about something, then how can you expect others to feel any sense of conviction? How can you expect others to get jazzed if you're not energized and excited? How can you expect others to suffer through the inevitable long hours and hard work if you're not similarly inclined? However, when you express your passion through words and deeds, others are much more likely to catch it than if you keep it to yourself. Your emotions are contagious.

Visions are projections of fundamental beliefs and assumptions about human nature, technology, economics, science, politics, art, ethics, and the like. A vision of the future is much like a literary or musical theme. It's the paramount, persistent, and pervasive message you want to convey, the frequently recurring melody you want people to remember. Whenever repeated, it reminds the audience of the entire work. Every leader needs a theme, an orienting principle around which they can organize an entire movement. What's your central message? What's your recurring theme? What do you most want people to envision every time they think about the future?

To the questions of how often their leader "paints the big picture" and "describes a compelling image of what your future could be like," the data shows that those leaders who engage the most in these two behaviors have direct reports with the highest positive workplace attitude (PWA) scores. In fact, the highest frequency quintile compared with the lowest quintile have PWA scores that are 125 percent more favorable. Over 93 percent of the leaders who are viewed by their direct reports as most frequently "talking about future trends that will influence how our work gets done" are assessed as effective. Over 76 percent rate their leaders' job performance "among the best." These leadership behaviors are strongly associated with what direct reports indicate are their highest levels of motivation, commitment, and productivity.

Being able to envision the future is decidedly important. For many, however, compelling images of the future don't come easily—at first. Fortunately, there are ways you can heighten your capacity to imagine exciting possibilities and discover the central theme for your life and potentially the lives of others. Breakthroughs come when you *reflect* on your past, *attend* to the present, *prospect* the future, and *express* your passion.

**Reflect on Your Past** As contradictory as it might seem, you first need to look back into your past when aiming for the future. Looking backward before you stare straight ahead enables you to see farther into the future. Understanding the past can help you identify themes, patterns, and beliefs that both underscore why you care about certain ideals and explain why realizing those aspirations is a high priority for you.[2] This was precisely the lesson Megan Davidson learned when responsible for communications and data strategy at a global internet company. Based upon feedback she received from her colleagues on the Leadership Practices Inventory, Megan determined that "improving my ability to inspire a shared vision among co-workers would directly impact the success of my projects."

The first action was to identify her vision for the future of the projects she led by reflecting on her past. Since graduating college, Megan had held a new position in a different industry every two to three years. She had been a seventh-grade math teacher, managed clients ranging from nonprofit to engineering professionals, and worked at startups and large companies more than a hundred years old. She realized the common thread among these diverse experiences was "my fierce belief in the value of a 'customer focus.' I love improving the experience of students, users, customers, and the like, and I have sought out job opportunities that allow me to do so."

Your personal history is your traveling partner on every journey you take. It provides valuable guidance and informs the choices you must make. As historians John Seaman and George David Smith, partners at a history and archival services consulting firm, say, "The job of leaders, most would agree, is to inspire collective efforts and devise smart strategies for the future. History can be profitably employed on both fronts."[3] To lead with a sense of history, they maintain, is not being a slave to the past but recognizing that there are invaluable lessons to be learned by asking, "How did we get to the point we are today?" Michael Watkins, noted scholar on accelerating transitions, says that without a historical perspective, "you risk tearing down fences without knowing why they were put up. Armed with insight into the history, you may indeed find the fence is not needed and must go. Or you may find there is a good reason to leave it where it is."[4]

When you gaze first into your past, you realize how full your life has been, and you become more aware of all the possibilities that could lie ahead. Looking back enables you to understand better that the central recurring theme in your life has been there for a long time. Another benefit to looking back before looking ahead is that you gain a greater appreciation for how long it can take to fulfill your aspirations.

None of this is to say that the past *is* your future. That would be like driving while looking only in your rearview mirror. It's just that when you look deeply into your entire life's history, you understand things about yourself and your world that you cannot fully comprehend by looking at the future as a blank slate. It's difficult, if not impossible, to imagine going to a place you've never experienced, either actually or vicariously. Taking a journey into your past before exploring your future makes the trip much more meaningful and planning considerable more realistic.

**Attend to the Present** While the past is the prologue, the present is the opportunity. The past provides the knowledge and experience from which to draw, and the present offers the chance to apply it. The past is the source of light, while the present is the opening in the door through which the light can shine. Unfortunately, the daily pressures, the pace of change, the complexity of problems, and the turbulence in global markets can often hold people's minds hostage and make them think that they have neither the time nor the energy to be future-oriented. As counterintuitive as it might seem, creating the future involves being more attentive in the here-and-now. This means taking yourself off automatic pilot, stopping viewing the world through preestablished categories, and noticing what's happening around you. You have to *stop*, *look*, and *listen*. As a senior development manager in high technology, Amit Tolmare says he has learned that "to be able to envision the future, you have to understand the present. You have to listen to your team and feel their pain. Only when you understand the current challenges, will you be able to imagine a better tomorrow." To increase your ability to conceive of new and creative solutions to today's problems, you have to be present in the present.

Set aside some time each day to stop doing "stuff." Create some white space on your calendar. Remind yourself that your electronic devices have an off switch. Stop being in motion. Then start noticing more of what's going on around you right now. In *Leading the Revolution*, Gary Hamel, one of the world's most influential business thinkers, observed that many people don't appreciate and comprehend what's changing around them "because they're down at ground level, lost in the thicket of confusing, conflicting data." He says, "You have to make time to step back and ask yourself, 'What's the big story that cuts across all these little facts?'"[5]

Like Gary, the social forecaster John Naisbitt appreciated that "in the stream of time, the future is always with us. The directions and turns the world will take are embedded in the past and in the present. You often recognize them retrospectively, but our purpose is to anticipate what lies ahead."[6] Leaders peek behind the curtain to see what is hiding there. Look around your workplace and community. What do you see people doing now that they weren't doing a few years ago? How are people interacting when they are working virtually and not all in the same place at the same time? How do they feel about hybrid work, and what are the implications for change in your organization? What are the hot topics of conversation? What do people say is getting in the way of them doing their best? Listen as well to the weak signals. For example, what are people no longer talking about or paying attention to? Listen for things you've never heard before. What does all this tell you about where things are going? What's it telling you about what lies just around the corner?

To envision the future, you have to spot the trends and patterns and appreciate both the whole and the parts. You have to be able to see the forest *and* the trees. Imagine the future as a jigsaw puzzle. You see the pieces, and you begin to figure out how they fit together, one by one, into a whole. Similarly, with your vision, you need to rummage through the bits and bytes of data that accumulate daily and notice how they fit together into a picture of what's ahead. Envisioning the future is not about gazing into a fortune teller's crystal ball; it's about paying attention to the little things that are going on all around you and being able to recognize patterns that point to the future.

Consider Megan Davidson's experience again. After working on a few project teams, she saw that there were competing priorities, unclear roles, and responsibilities. Because she was able to listen and look around, Megan could "see" that some of the new communication tools had created information silos. What was needed were more clearly defined relationships between them.

**Prospect the Future** "One of the greatest gifts you can give others," Dan Schwab, director of training and development for a large nonprofit organization, told us, "is the understanding that they can think bigger things than they believe they can. What limits vision in an organization is nobody being willing to speak up for one. But once you do, there is a sort of avalanche or landslide factor; it just keeps rolling."

Darrell Klotzach's personal-best supports Dan's observations. Darrell was working at a small startup company that was developing software titles for young children. Everyone was quite keyed up about the project because, as Darrell explained, "there were endless possibilities. We all wanted to develop a high-quality game that children would find exciting to play, that they would play again and again, and would be an experience that they would learn from." Darrell said that he "kept people focused on the future, reminding people how much kids enjoyed what we were doing, and how much they would enjoy it when we were done. Without keeping an eye on the future, they might have become bogged down with some of the mundane day-to-day activities and become frustrated by some very difficult challenges."

Both Dan and Darrell appreciate how the leader's job is to keep people focused on the future so that they will be eager to meet the daily challenges, work through the inevitable conflicts, and persevere to the end. Ultimately, visions are about the future and come to fruition over different spans of time. It may take several years from the time you decide to climb a mountain until you reach the summit, or a decade to build a company, or a lifetime to repopulate a wildfire-ravaged forest, or generations to set a people free.

Keeping people energized in the present requires providing clarity about the future, especially in times of uncertainty and turmoil. Visions act like lenses, focusing unrefracted rays of light on the long-term destination. Visions enable everyone to clearly see why they should continue struggling to reach a promised ideal. Recall, for example, the last time you watched a PowerPoint presentation and imagine that the image was out of focus. How would you feel if you had to watch blurred, vague, and indistinct images? Most likely, you'd be frustrated, impatient, disappointed, angry, and even nauseous. You'd avoid the situation by looking away and paying attention to something else. The leader's job is to focus the projector so that everyone can see a bright and unobstructed pathway forward.

Leaders are their organization's "futures department," and even as you stop, look, and listen to messages in the present, you also need to raise your head and gaze out toward the horizon. Leadership requires you to spend considerable time reading, thinking, and talking about the long-term view, not only for your specific organization but also for the environments in which you're operating. This imperative intensifies with the scope and level of responsibility of your position.

You need to consider what you're going to do after the current problem, task, assignment, project, or program is completed. "What's next?" should be a question you are frequently asking. If you're not thinking about what's happening after the completion of your longest-term project, then you're thinking only as long term as everyone else is. In other words, you're redundant! The leader's job is to think about the next project, the one after that, and the one after that.

Researchers have shown how leaders who focus on the future attract followers more readily, induce more effort and intrinsic motivation from group members, promote group identification, mobilize collective action, and ultimately achieve better performance on individual and organizational outcome measures.[7] The future is where opportunity lies. You must spend time thinking about the future and become better at projecting ahead in time. Whether reading about trends, talking with futurists, listening to podcasts, or watching documentaries, developing a deep understanding of where things are going is a significant part of any leader's job. Your constituents expect it of you. You must spend more of today thinking more about tomorrow if your future will be an improvement over the present. And throughout the process of reflecting on your past, attending to the present, and prospecting for the future, you also need to keep in touch with what moves you, what you care about, where your passion is.

A note of caution, however. As scholar and researcher Adam Grant put it, "Predicting the future is hard. No one is right most of the time. But it's possible to be wrong less often." In looking at data from a forecasting tournament, Adam found that those who were more accurate at forecasting had the mindset of a scientist in contrast to those of what Adam called a preacher, prosecutor, or politician. They would treat their predictions as hypotheses to be tested rather than hard facts to be confirmed. They tended to be humbler about what they knew, open to challenging their own convictions, and curious in seeking out other ideas and people that might contradict what they thought. When thinking ahead, you need to think again. You need to look beyond your own beliefs and assumptions and consider other possible scenarios.[8]

**Express Your Passion** People have great difficulty imagining possibilities when they don't feel passionate about what they're doing. Envisioning the future requires you to connect with your deepest feelings. You must find something so important that you're willing to put in the time, suffer the inevitable setbacks, and make the necessary sacrifices. Without an intense desire, a grave concern, an all-consuming question, an urgent proposition, the fondest hope, or a cherished dream, you can't ignite the spark necessary to energize aspirations and actions. You have to step back and ask yourself, "What is my burning passion? What gets me up in the morning? What's grabbed hold of me and won't let go?"

Leaders want to do something significant, and accomplish something that no one else has yet achieved. What that something is—your sense of meaning and purpose—has to come from within. No one can impose a self-motivating vision on you. That's why, just as we said about values, you must first clarify your vision of the future before you can expect to enlist others in a shared vision. Research studies find that when you can imagine your "best possible self"—a time in the future when everything has gone well for you and you have realized your life dreams—you are much more intrinsically motivated and more likely to persist in challenging tasks.[9] You get emotional energy from this kind of exploration, and it's that drive that helps you to express your passion for what matters.

As you can see in Figure 4, the percentage of direct reports who strongly agree with the statement "Overall, this person is an effective leader" increases dramatically with the frequency they observe that this individual "speaks with a genuine conviction about the higher meaning and purpose of our work." People regard and respond most favorably to

**Figure 4 Speaking with Genuine Conviction about the Higher Meaning and Purpose of Work Raises Direct Reports' Assessments of Their Leaders' Effectiveness**

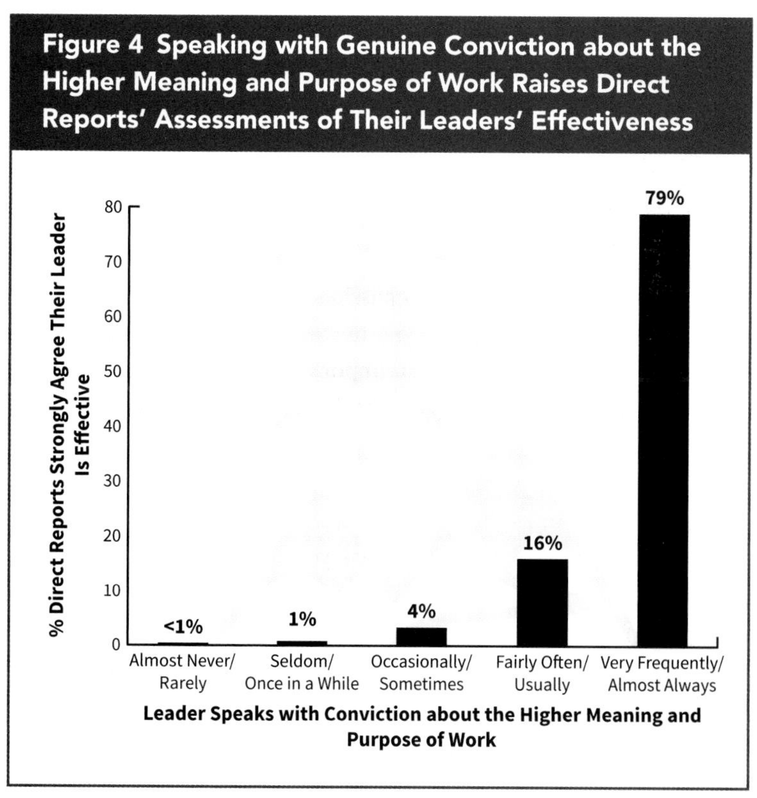

those leaders who regularly talk about the "why" of work and not just the "what" of work.

Feeling a strong sense of purpose—particularly one that benefits others and not just yourself—profoundly impacts performance and well-being. When organizations convey a strong sense of purpose, there is higher engagement and more robust financial performance than when people feel purpose is lacking. For example, students with a purpose in life rated their coursework as more meaningful than students who didn't have a purpose or had only extrinsic motivations, such as making more money. Furthermore, these students persisted longer when tasks were tedious and, consequently, achieved more in their courses.[10] In the workplace, people who believe their lives and jobs have meaning feel more connected to others, exhibit greater psychological well-being, are more creative and engaged in their work, and perform better in their jobs than those without a sense of meaning and purpose.[11]

Meaning and purpose matter whether you seek better grades, persistence in your efforts, greater personal well-being, or improved organizational performance. If you want to perform at your best, it's incumbent that you search inside yourself and discover what gives your work and life meaning and purpose. Research by the consulting firm Deloitte confirms that having a strong sense of purpose goes hand in hand with having clear values and beliefs.[12]

Your passion for something is the best indicator of what you find most worthwhile, and it's the clue to what you find intrinsically rewarding. For example, David Kretz, regional business manager with a global materials engineering company, realized in his personal-best leadership experience that "finding something you truly believe in" was the key to articulating a vision in the first place. Once you're in touch with this inner feeling, he says, then you can look and think "beyond the constraints of your current position and viewpoint into the future. This is how you connect your various tasks and team projects to how they help convert that feeling and vision into a reality."

When you feel your passion, as David did, you know you are on to something very meaningful. Your enthusiasm and drive spread to others. Finding something you strongly believe in is the key to articulating a vision in the first place. Once you're in touch with this inner feeling, you can look and think beyond the constraints of your current position and view the possibilities available in the future.

## Identify a Common Purpose

*You have to spend time with the team, listen to and work with them to understand their vision, values, and goals and how they become part of the organization's success.*

*Srinivasa Reddy Emani*

It is often assumed that leaders are solely responsible for being the visionaries. After all, if focusing on the future is what sets leaders apart, it's understandable that there would be this feeling that it's their job to embark alone on a vision quest to discover the future of their organization.

This is actually *not* what constituents expect. Yes, leaders are expected to be forward-looking, but they aren't supposed to impose their vision of the future on others. People don't want to attend solely to the *leader's* vision. They want to hear about how their own visions and aspirations will come true, their hopes and dreams fulfilled. They want to see themselves in the picture of the future that the leader is painting.[13] The critical task for leaders is inspiring a *shared* vision, not selling their own idiosyncratic view of the world. This requires finding common ground among all those people who implement the vision.

Paul Johnson, a vineyard manager, decided to bring his core team together and create a credo and vision statement. He said that "not only did we come together over why we were all there in the first place, but since then those core values and vision have been used to set our direction when things are uncertain." The values that Paul and his team developed became the foundation for creating a "guiding vision" for the organization. Paul admitted that he felt, at first, like he was giving up control of the business. Thoughts such as "what if their ideas are awful" and "will I get stuck with a direction I don't want to go" did enter his mind. However, once it was done, Paul said, "It was such a relief to have a group of people who were totally committed to the credo and vision statement because they were involved in its creation. Our team was now empowered to act, knowing that we have a constitution of sorts to rely upon."

Paul realized a fundamental truth that every leader must understand about enlisting others in a shared vision: nobody likes being told what to do or where to go, no matter how right it might be. People want to be a part of the vision development process. The vast majority of people are just like Paul's team members. They want to dream with their leaders, invent with them, and be involved in creating their futures.

This means you have to stop believing that visions come from the top down. You have to start engaging others in a collective dialogue about the future, not delivering a monologue. You can't mobilize people to travel willingly to places they don't want to go. No matter how grand the dream of an individual visionary, if others don't see in it the possibility of realizing their own hopes and desires, they won't follow willingly. You must show others how they, too, will be served by the long-term vision of the future, how their specific needs can be satisfied. The central task for leaders is inspiring a *shared* vision, not selling their personal view of the world. You need to imagine the end result and communicate your vision such that your constituents find a way to achieve their aspirations while attaining that result. This requires finding common ground among those who have to implement the vision.

**Listen Deeply to Others** Leaders need to know what is important to others. By knowing their constituents, listening to them, and taking their advice, leaders can give voice to their constituents' feelings. They're able to stand before others and say with assurance, "Here's what I heard you say that you want for yourselves. Here's how enlisting in a common cause will serve your needs and interests." In a sense, leaders hold up a mirror and reflect to their constituents what they say is what they most desire.

The outlines of any vision do not appear miraculously to leaders in the isolation of the organization's stratosphere. They come from interactions with employees on the manufacturing floor, in the lab, or in the cafeteria. They originate from conversations with customers in the retail stores. They live in the hallways, in meetings, and even in people's homes.

The best leaders are great listeners. They listen carefully to what other people have to say, how they feel, and what they want, value, and dream about. This sensitivity to others is no simple skill, and it is a genuinely precious human ability.[14] In making the transition from being a Navy submarine officer to marketing manager for a cloud-based software company, Jim Schwappach came to realize that "enlisting subordinates and other colleagues in defining the vision for the team pays off because the ideas that form the vision will be familiar to them and as a result it will be easier to get the buy-in that is essential for translating a single person's view to the rest of the team." Still, he couldn't accomplish this unilaterally.

> I began to actively and deeply listen to people. I started a collaborative, open environment so as to promote the free exchange of ideas. In turn, people began opening up with one another and actively talking about substantive improvements that they felt could be made to the organization as a whole.
>
> I started meeting individually with each of them, asking questions about what they thought were the key issues and best alternatives, and incorporating their feedback into our decisions. I asked people what they were proud of, what brought them to work every day, what management was doing well, and where they were blowing it. More importantly, once I asked the questions, I stopped and focused directly on the person answering. I found at first that some people were startled by the attention. After a few tries, though, the level of response and the value of those responses in contributing to defining a vision for our team grew immeasurably. I also began spending more time going out and visiting my employees' and colleagues' workspaces, and this increase in interaction allowed me to benefit from their varied perspectives and further enabled us to craft a vision that we can call our own.

Leaders find the common thread that weaves the fabric of human needs into a colorful tapestry. They develop a deep understanding of collective yearnings; they seek out the brewing consensus among those they would lead. They listen carefully for quiet whisperings and attend to subtle cues. They get a sense of what people want, what they value, and what they dream about. Sensitivity to others is no trivial skill; rather, it is a truly precious human ability. But it isn't complex: what's required is receptiveness to other people and a willingness to listen. As Jim discovered, it means getting out of the office into the field and spending time with people on the factory floor, in the showroom, warehouse, or back room. It means being acutely aware of the attitudes and feelings of others and the nuances of their communication.

Extraordinary things can happen when leaders listen—when they involve employees in identifying issues, hearing their frustrations and aspirations, and finding ways to respond with initiatives that address those concerns. Generating excitement in a workplace is possible when you pay attention to what people want and need. If you don't listen, you will quickly find yourself surrounded by people who have nothing to say, and that's never the truth.

**Make It a Cause for Commitment** People commit to causes, not to plans. How else do you explain why people volunteer to rebuild communities ravaged by a hurricane, ride a bike from San Francisco to Los Angeles to raise money to fight homelessness, rescue people from the rubble of a collapsed building after an earthquake, or toil 24/7 to create the next big thing when the probability of failure is very high? All of these experiences require investments of time, effort, and resources into something that may not be realized for many years, even decades, in the future. That kind of commitment into the future can only be made when people see these investments as significant and meaningful, tapping into deeper aspirations that go well beyond immediate gratification. To enlist others, exemplary leaders need to know what those aspirations are. Steve Coats, founder and managing partner of a Midwest-based leadership consulting firm, has found, "True leaders create a culture of great performance and meaningful work. They help people find pride in their work and make even lousy work (by many people's standards) enjoyable. Leaders make others feel important and needed."[15]

When you listen deeply, you find out what gives work meaning and people a sense of purpose. People stay with an organization, research finds, because they like their work and find it challenging, meaningful, and purposeful.[16] When you listen with sensitivity to the aspirations of others, you discover that there are some common themes that bring meaning to work and life:[17]

- *Integrity:* Pursuing values and goals congruent with their own
- *Purpose:* Making a significant difference in the lives of others
- *Challenge:* Doing innovative work
- *Growth:* Learning and developing professionally and personally
- *Belonging:* Engaging in close and positive relationships
- *Autonomy:* Determining the course of their own lives
- *Significance:* Feeling trusted and validated as persons

While interest in meaning and purpose has grown as Millennials have become the largest demographic group in the workplace, finding meaning is a universal desire among all generations and has been a topic of research and writing for decades. What people want has not changed very dramatically through the years,[18] and people have never voluntarily worked very hard or stuck around for long when what they do is trivial and unimportant.

There's more to work than making money. People want to do more than just exchange their labor for cash. People have a deep desire to make a difference. They want to know that they have done something on this earth, that there's a purpose to their existence. If you're going to lead others, you must put principles and purpose ahead of everything else. The larger mission is what *calls* everyone. The best organizational leaders address this human motivation by communicating the long-term significance of the organization's work. Sonja Shevelyov, human resources manager with a video content workflow management system company, found that there was "immense value in creating meaning to the work that is being asked of people. I've learned how important it is to take time to listen closely and connect with what is meaningful to others."

Almost 70 percent of employees reflected on their purpose during the COVID-19 pandemic, according to researchers. They found that those who said that they live their purpose at work were "six and a half times more likely to report higher resilience. They're four times more likely to report better health, six times more likely to want to stay at the company, and one and a half times more likely to go above and beyond to make their company successful."[19] Other research has found that about 30 percent of those who voluntarily left the workforce during the pandemic did so because of a lack of meaningful work. It was third on the list of reasons why they left. However, in listing the reasons why they would return to the workforce, meaningful work was the number-one reason overall.[20] It's clear from the data that leaders who want to attract and retain talent, especially during challenging times, must engage in deep conversations with others about what brings meaning to them, their work, and the workplace.

When people are part of something that elevates them to higher levels of motivation and morality, they feel energized and more committed; they feel that what they do matters. For example, researchers asked nearly 2,500 workers to analyze medical images for "objects of interest." One group was told that the work would be discarded, while the other was told that the objects were "cancerous tumor cells." Workers were paid for each image analyzed. The latter "meaning" group spent more time on each object, subsequently earning 10 percent less, on average, than the "discard" group and the quality of their work was substantially higher. After surveying over 20,000 workers around the world, analyzing fifty major companies, and conducting scores of experiments, researchers concluded that "why we work determines how well we work."[21]

**Look Forward in Times of Rapid Change** People often ask, "How can I have a vision of what's going to happen five or ten years from now, when I don't even know what's going to happen next week?" This question gets right to the heart of visions' role in people's lives. As the world becomes increasingly volatile, uncertain, complex, and ambiguous, visions are even more important to human survival and success than when times are calm, predictable, simple, and clear.

Think about it this way. Imagine you're driving along the Pacific Coast Highway heading south from San Francisco on a bright, sunny day. The hills are on your left, the ocean on your right. On some curves, the cliffs plunge several hundred feet to the water. You can see for miles and miles. You're cruising along at the speed limit, one hand on the wheel, sitting back, tunes blaring, and not a care in the world. You come around a bend in the road, and suddenly, without warning, there's a blanket of fog as thick as you've ever seen it. What do you do?

We've asked this question many times, and the responses are quite predictable. People say that they:

- "Slow way down."
- "Switch the headlights on."
- "Grip the steering wheel tightly with both hands."
- "Turn on the windshield wipers."
- "Sit up straight or even lean forward."
- "Turn the music off."

Then you go around the next curve in the road; the fog lifts, and it's clear again. What do you do now? You relax, sit back, speed up, turn off the lights and wipers, put the music back on, and enjoy the scenery.

This analogy illustrates the importance of clarity of vision. Are you able to go faster when it's foggy or when it's clear? How fast can you drive in the fog without risking your own or other people's lives? How comfortable are you riding in a car with someone else who drives fast in the fog? The answers are obvious, aren't they? You're better able to go fast when your vision is clear. You can better anticipate the switchbacks and bumps in the road when you can see ahead. There are times in your life, no doubt, when you find yourself driving in the fog, metaphorically speaking. When this happens, you get nervous and unsure of what's ahead.

A very important part of a leader's job is to clear away the fog so that people can see further ahead, anticipate what might be coming in their direction, and watch out for potential hazards along the road. Clear visions are meant to inspire hope—hope that despite the fog and stormy weather, despite the bumps in the road, despite the unexpected detours, and despite the occasional breakdowns the team will make it to its ideal and unique destination.[22]

As a marketing specialist with a semiconductor company, Kyle Harvey, and one of his colleagues, were given a huge project to create a video and articles about the wide range of products available. He set up a meeting with his co-worker to determine the direction they were going to take. "At the beginning it was really confusing," Kyle said. "She seemed uninterested in the project, and you could have said we were in the densest part of the fog. There was no vision for the project, and we really had no direction." After about two weeks, little had been accomplished, so Kyle called another meeting. However, this time before going into the meeting he developed a vision about how to approach the project:

> I knew that she was extremely artistic and enjoyed being creative, and I found ways to incorporate her talents and what she liked doing into the project. This jumpstarted her, and then we really got engaged; she began explaining how she wanted the video to look. The fog kept lifting, and the view ahead was becoming clearer.... After a month of work on the project, it finally seems like we have begun driving faster and left the fog behind.
>
> The fog analogy is especially strong for me in this case. I found that when our vision was unclear, we pulled off to the side of the road and did not continue to drive. However, after finding ways to motivate and inspire her, we were back on the road and moving through the fog. It was important to realize that the "shared vision" does not always come instantly or in the first meeting. The vision gets clearer the more people communicate and find ways to inspire each other.

Simply put, to become a leader you must be able to envision the future. The speed of change or the nature of the challenges doesn't alter this fundamental truth. People want to follow those who can see beyond today's problems and visualize a brighter tomorrow.

## TAKE ACTION:

## Envision the Future

The most important role of vision in organizational life is to give focus to human energy. To enable everyone to see more clearly what's ahead of them, you must have and convey an exciting, ennobling vision of the future. The path to clarity of vision begins with reflecting on the past, moves to attending to the present, and then goes to prospecting into the future. The guardrails along this path are your passions—what it is that you care about most deeply.

Although you have to be clear about your vision before you can expect others to follow, you can't authentically lead others to places they don't want to go. If the vision is to be attractive to more than a negligible few, it must appeal to all who have a stake in it. Only *shared* visions have the magnetic power to sustain commitment over time. Listen to the voices of all your constituents; listen to their hopes, dreams, and aspirations. Because a shared vision spans years and keeps everyone focused on the future, it has to be about more than the work at hand, a task, or a job. It has to be a cause, something meaningful, and something that makes a difference in people's lives. No matter what the size of your team or organization, a shared vision sets the agenda and gives direction and purpose to the enterprise.

Here are some suggestions on what you can do to *envision the future by imagining exciting and ennobling possibilities*:

- Five years from now, if you were bragging to someone about what you had accomplished in your current job,

(*continued*)

what would you say? How have you contributed to your job, your organization, your family, and your community? Record your responses.

- Reflect on your experiences, looking for the major themes in your life and what you find worthwhile.
- Deliver your vision speech to someone who will give you constructive feedback. Ask the person for advice on how imaginative, unique, and uplifting it is. Ask about how well it enables others to "see themselves in the picture" you have imagined.

Regular conversations about leadership will let people know it's something important to you, to the organization, and to them. In every interaction, you have the chance to direct people's attention to aspects of leadership that you think are important to focus on. Find opportunities to talk with others about these questions:

- Where do you see this organization in five years? Ten years? What will this place look like? Feel like? Be like to work in? What will it sound like when someone walks through doors? What will people be doing?
- When the longest-term project you are now working on has been completed, what will you be working on next?

# CHAPTER 5
# Enlist Others

*Leaders must communicate the vision in a way that attracts and excites members of the organization.*

*David Berlew*

**UPON ASSUMING COMMAND** of one of the U.S. Army's community hospitals, Colonel Eric B. Sones spent the first month observing and listening to employees. Early on he discovered that morale was low throughout the organization and outpatient satisfaction scores were dismal. Specifically, they were ranked twelfth out of fourteen hospitals in their region. He also learned that his hospital was on the cusp of being shut down or converted to a clinic.

It became quite evident to Eric that "an intentional, hospital-wide effort to reach employees needed to start immediately." He contacted his leadership team and told them he wanted everyone's input on where the organization needed to go. "We needed to come together as a team," Eric said. "There needed to be a purpose that the organization could strive toward—a common goal. They needed to be a part of something bigger than they were."

Eric didn't want to impose a top-down process. Instead, he scheduled an off-site retreat, asking each of his deputies to select two civilians and two military service members from their sections, half of whom should be relatively new and half senior in their tenure. Eric acted as the facilitator of the retreat because he wanted to "make sure everyone was heard and felt that they had a voice." After dividing the thirty-six participants into small groups, Eric asked the participants to look back ten years at the key events in the hospital, organize them into highs and lows, and reflect on the themes that played out in those moments. Eric then asked them to discuss three questions:

- What are the ideals that attract you to this organization?
- What are the higher-order values that give meaning and purpose to your life and work?
- Are you in this job to do something, or are you in this job for something to do? If you're here to do something, what is it?

Each group presented their summaries and together they searched for a common theme that flowed through all their conversations. The groups identified the recurring message of "strong teamwork through good and bad times." Eric asked each participant to explain what that phrase meant to them. The responses were different and at times filled with emotion as employees shared personal stories. As a closing exercise, Eric asked the group to come up with a "simple, meaningful, inspiring, and impactful vision statement" to express the central theme that ran through all the stories and keywords.

But the job still wasn't done. Everyone in the hospital needed to hear and understand the new vision and underlying values. Rather than delivering the shared vision himself, Eric had one civilian and one military representative speak during the hospital's upcoming town hall. The only instruction Eric gave was: "I want you to do the unveiling of our new vision statement. Tell the story of what we accomplished by explaining the *how*. This is not just the working group's vision but it is now our organization's vision. Create this new space for buy-in."

Eric credits this collaborative vision creation process with initiating an extraordinary transformation in the organization. Within nine months, they rose to number one in the region. These results were achieved because Eric understood and acted on a fundamental leadership truth. As he put it, "It is not my vision. It is really a shared vision."

In the personal-best leadership cases we collected, people talked about the need to get everyone on board with a vision and to *Enlist Others* in a dream, just as Eric did. They talked about communicating and building support for a unified direction in which to take the organization. These leaders knew that to make extraordinary things happen everyone had to believe fervently in and commit to a common purpose.

Part of enlisting others is building common ground on which everyone can stand. Equally important is the emotion that leaders express for the vision. Our research shows that in addition to expecting leaders to be forward-looking, constituents expect their leaders to be *inspiring*. People need vast reserves of energy and excitement to sustain commitment to a distant dream. Leaders are an important source of that energy. People won't follow someone who's only mildly enthusiastic about something. They only actively support those leaders who are *deeply* enthusiastic.

Whether you're trying to mobilize thousands of people in the community or one person in the workplace, to *Enlist Others* you must act on these two essentials:

- **Appeal to common ideals**
- **Animate the vision**

Enlisting others is all about igniting a passion for a purpose and moving people to persist against incredible odds. To make extraordinary things happen in organizations, you must go beyond reason, engaging the hearts and minds of your constituents. Start by understanding their strongest yearnings for something meaningful and significant.

## Appeal to Common Ideals

*You have to paint a powerfully compelling picture of the future for people to want to align with the vision.*

*Vicky Ngo-Roberti*

Leadership requires more than just having a vision, painting a picture of it, and selling your personal view of the world. You need to imagine the end result and communicate your vision of the future so that your constituents can see their ideals and aspirations included in that vision. They want to see themselves in the future that you are envisioning and this requires getting others on board who have to help implement the vision. People don't want to be told what to do or where to go, no matter how right it might be; they want to be part of the vision development process. As Santosh Prabhu, senior director with a global medical device company, explained in his personal-best leadership experience, "I always started with the big picture and vision for the organization. People always need to know the 'why' behind the vision." Their *why* was "about people living healthier and longer lives through the services that we provide." As he put together the strategy and plans, Santosh also solicited input from the broader cross-functional team so that they could see "how we are in this together and that I could not do this without them. It was not 'my' plans, but 'our' plans."

Visions are about hopes, dreams, and aspirations. They're declarations of a strong desire to achieve something ambitious. They're expressions of optimism. Can you imagine being able to enlist others in a cause by saying, "I'd like you to join me in doing the ordinary?" Not likely. Visions stretch people to imagine exciting possibilities, breakthrough programs, or revolutionary social change. However, grand aspirations such as these cannot be achieved until they are also shared by others you want to enlist.

You can't impose a vision on others. It has to be something that has meaning to them, not just to you. Leaders must foster conditions under which people will do things because they *want to*, not because they have to. Leaders create environments where team, department, program, or institutional visions and personal values intersect. For example, we found a strong correlation between the frequency with which direct reports indicated that their leader "shows others how their long-term interests can be realized by enlisting in a common vision" and their assessment of that leader's effectiveness. Similarly, the more direct reports indicated their leader being able to paint a "big picture" about what they aspired to accomplish, the more they expressed a stronger sense of team spirit within their group and organizational pride.

It's not enough for you to be clear about your vision and values; you must be attentive to those around you. Ask yourself who else must understand, accept, and commit to the vision. If you can't find alignment between what you care about and what others care about, you won't find a common purpose or succeed in changing the status quo. When reflecting on their personal-best leadership experiences, people frequently talked about the need to get buy-in from others on the vision. They explained how they had to communicate the purpose and build support for a unified direction. They knew that everyone had to commit to a common purpose. They understood that to get everyone on the same journey, they had to communicate *why* others should want to join in, what it would mean to them, and how it would benefit them. People will be reluctant to sign on if they can't see how their needs connect to the larger vision. But when they do, the team's ability to reach its potential soars.

Leaders talk about ideals. They express a desire to make dramatic changes in the business-as-usual environment. They reach for something grand, something magnificent, something never done before. Ideals reveal higher-order value preferences. They represent the paramount economic, technological, political, social, and aesthetic priorities. The ideals of world peace, freedom, justice, an exciting life, happiness, and self-respect, for example, are among the highest strivings of human existence. They're outcomes of the larger purpose that practical actions will enable people to attain over the long term. By focusing on ideals, people gain a sense of meaning and purpose from what they undertake. When you communicate your vision of the future to your constituents, you need to talk about how they're going to make a difference in the world and how they will have a positive impact on people and events. You need to speak to the higher meaning and purpose of work. You need to describe a compelling image of what the future could be like when people join in a common cause.[1] This is especially important in challenging and adverse times, such as a pandemic, economic distress, or global conflict.[2] A feeling that there's a shared purpose in moving forward gives relevance to the struggles in the present.[3]

**Connect to What's Meaningful to Others** Exemplary leaders don't impose their visions of the future; they liberate the vision that's already stirring in their constituents. They awaken dreams, breathe life into them, and arouse the belief that people can achieve something grand. What truly pulls people forward, especially in more challenging and volatile times, is the exciting possibility that what they are doing can make a profound difference in the lives of their families, friends, colleagues, customers, and communities. They want to know that what they do matters. Studies involving respondents from forty different countries (speaking sixteen different languages) found that connecting employees with purpose increased their levels of engagement and productivity.[4]

When Preethi Chandrasekhar was put in charge of a newly developed technical support center for a VOIP company, she understood that others would be looking to her for direction and setting standards. She quickly realized that to make the vision exciting and relevant to her team, she needed to make it meaningful. Preethi started by having informational sessions where she and the team members talked about the "big picture" and why their work matters. They discussed questions such as "What difference do we make for this company and our customers? How will our working together make a difference?"

Preethi asked the team to continue thinking about a vision and conducted a follow-up brainstorming session in which everyone shared their ideas and suggestions on what they needed to do to reduce call volume, improve customer wait times, and reduce the time reps spent on the telephone. Preethi recalled, "I could see the team was motivated, and each individual took it upon themselves to provide thoughtful insights on how we could improve the call center." But it was always important, she told us, "to keep focusing on the big picture while still concentrating on the details that would enable us to realize these aspirations."

While Preethi searched for a unique way for the team to articulate the meaning and significance of their work, what she discovered was that she could do something every day to keep people focused and excited about their vision. "All of us have the power within ourselves to accomplish whatever we desire," she told us, and she found ways each day to repeat this statement to the members of the call center in the context of achieving their shared vision. She made sure that each team member could repeat the vision, not just by rote but from the heart, and she showed how their individual and collective efforts could make a positive difference. "We put pride back in the workplace," Preethi observed. "We would be the envy of the company when it came to enjoying our work, basking in one another's accomplishments, and making our customers' lives not just easier but more productive. After all, what's better than being the geniuses who can answer other people's questions?"

In time, Preethi's message became a march. Everyone could connect with these ideas and aspirations. Each team member could easily see how they would talk to family and friends about the question "So, why do you work there?" Preethi lifted them from the humdrum mechanics associated with the call center—or any workplace for that matter—and reminded them about the nobility of what they accomplish.

The outcomes experienced by Preethi's staff are consistent with research findings on what occurs when people can connect the daily work that they do to a meaningful and transcendent purpose. For example, researchers followed the lives of nearly four hundred individuals for one month. Over this time period, participants completed a series of surveys about their activities, how easy or hard life was, and their attitudes toward money, relationships, time, and related variables. They were also asked how meaningful and happy their lives were.[5] The results showed that "when individuals adopt what we call a meaning mind-set—that is, they seek connections, give to others, and orient themselves to a larger purpose—clear benefits can result, including improved psychological well-being, more creativity, and enhanced work performance. Workers who find their jobs meaningful are more engaged and less likely to leave their current positions."[6] When you can make it clear to people that their work is making a difference, you strengthen their intrinsic motivation.

Similarly, our data reveals that direct reports give the highest effectiveness ratings to those leaders who are seen as most frequently showing people how enlisting in a common vision can help them achieve their long-term interests. In fact, there's a more than five-fold increase for these direct reports in comparison with the effectiveness ratings of those leaders who are rarely or seldom seen as engaging in this same leadership behavior, if at all. Researchers have shown that stressing the "why" to people, as in "Why are we doing this and why does this matter?" activates the brain's reward system and increases people's efforts and how they feel about what they are doing.[7] For example, consider the motivational difference between call center employees who see their purpose as helping people solve problems versus those who see their job as getting people off the phone as quickly as possible.

Leaders help people see that what they are doing is bigger than they are and bigger, even, than the business. Their work can be something noble. When these people go to bed at night, they can sleep a little easier knowing that others can live a better life because of what they did that day. As Figure 5 shows, the extent to which direct reports feel what they do matters systematically increases on the basis that their leaders are showing people how to realize their long-term interests by enlisting in a common vision. Similar relationships were found between this leadership behavior and direct reports feeling that the organization values their work and that they are effective in meeting the demands of their job.

Extensive research on employee engagement supports these findings. Researchers from the Great Places to Work Institute report, "When we ask employees in great workplaces to describe what it is like to work there, they begin to smile and talk about how they are excited to get to work, and then, at the end of the day, are surprised to discover that the day has already disappeared. . . . They share their belief that what they do matters in the organization—that their team or the organization would be less successful if it weren't for their efforts."[8] You have to make sure that the people on your team know that their work does, in fact, matter.

**Take Pride in Being Unique** Just like Santosh and Preethi, exemplary leaders also communicate what makes their constituents, workgroup, organization, product, or service singular and unequaled. Compelling visions differentiate, setting "us" apart from "them" in ways that attract and retain employees, volunteers, customers, clients, donors, and investors. Market researcher Doug Hall has found that "dramatically different" levels of *distinctiveness* in a new product or service increase the probability of success by over 350 percent. The same is true for a

Figure 5 Showing Others How Their Long-Term Interests Can Be Realized by Enlisting in a Common Vision Makes Direct Reports Feel That They Are Making a Difference

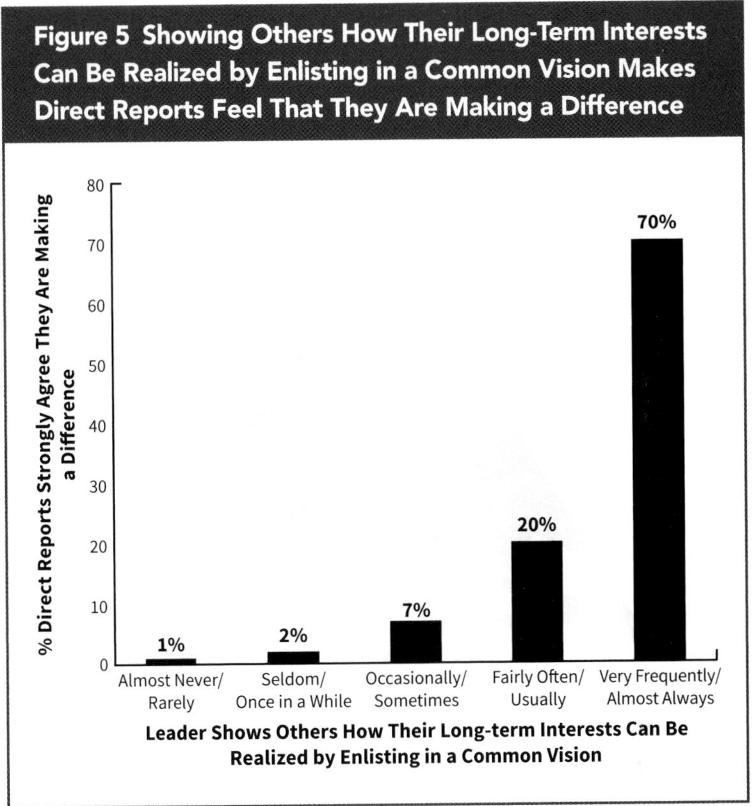


vision; the more unique it is, the higher the likelihood of getting people to buy in.[9]

There's no advantage in working for, buying from, or investing in an organization that does the same thing as the one across the street or down the hall. Saying, "Welcome to our company; we're just like everyone else," doesn't exactly make the spine tingle with excitement. When people understand how they're genuinely distinctive and how they stand out in the crowd, they're a lot more eager to sign up and invest their energies.

Uniqueness fosters pride, boosting the self-respect and self-esteem of everyone associated with the organization.[10] When people are proud to work for their organization and serve its purpose and feel that their work is meaningful, they become enthusiastic ambassadors to the outside world. Likewise, when customers and clients are proud to own your products or use your services, they are more loyal and likely to recruit and recommend their friends to do business with you. When members of the community are proud to have you as a neighbor, they're going to do everything they can to make you feel welcome and look out for your interests.

In leading a team of volunteers in a community bookstore, Azmeena Zaveri learned how important it is for people to take pride in being unique. The bookstore had been an iconic, celebrated, and cherished institution where people loved to gather, socialize, and learn. However, when Azmeena came on board, the bookstore was in survival mode. It was no longer providing a high standard of service, finances were in disarray, and there was little motivation for volunteers to go the extra mile. The reason for the decline, Azmeena told us, "was not because the team was incompetent or incapable of managing the tasks. A principal cause was the lack of vision and direction for the team. My goal was to inspire the team to bring the bookstore back to being the place where people loved to go, not just because of the great collection of books, but also for the inviting vibe and sense of community."

Azmeena coached people on ways to improve bookkeeping processes, discussed ways to better utilize the store's scarce resources, and reminded them how much the patrons relied on the bookstore as an important part of their lives. Throughout the process, she "emphasized how the institution was relying on them to survive and retain its significance to the community, and how they were in an honorable position not just to serve as a bookstore but be a community icon with an esteemed legacy."

Focusing on uniqueness makes it possible for smaller units within large organizations, or individual neighborhoods within big cities, to have their visions and still serve a larger, collective vision. Although every unit within a corporation, public agency, religious institution, school, or volunteer association must align with the overall organizational vision, each can express its unique purpose within the larger whole and highlight its most distinguishing qualities.

These days, though, with the latest and greatest available in a nanosecond at the touch of a key or screen, differentiation is increasingly difficult. Everything begins to look and sound alike. It's a sea of sameness out there. People become bored with things more quickly than ever before. Organizations, new and old, must work harder to distinguish themselves (and their products) from others around them. You need to be ever vigilant to ways in which you can be the beacon that cuts through the dense mist and steers people in the right direction.

**Align Your Dream with the People's Dream** In learning how to appeal to people's ideals, move their souls, and uplift their spirits—and your own—a classic example is the late Reverend Dr. Martin Luther King Jr.'s "I Have a Dream" speech. Replayed on the national holiday in the United States marking his birthday, it reminds young and old alike of the power of a clear and uplifting vision of the future.[11]

Imagine that you are there on that hot and humid day—August 28, 1963—when on the steps of the Lincoln Memorial in Washington, D.C., before a throng of 250,000, Martin Luther King Jr. proclaimed his dream to the world. Imagine that you're listening to Reverend King as thousands around you clap, applaud, and cry out. Pretend you're a reporter trying to understand why this speech is so powerful and how King moves so many people.[12]

Over the years, we've asked thousands of people to do just that: listen to his remarks and then tell us what they heard, how they felt, and why they thought this speech remains so moving even today. Following is a sampling of their observations.

- "He appealed to common interests."
- "He talked about traditional values of family, church, and country."
- "He used many images and word pictures that the audience was familiar with."
- "He mentioned things everyone could relate to, like family and children."

- "His references were credible. It's hard to argue against the Constitution or the Bible."
- "It was personal. He mentioned his own children, as well as struggling."
- "He included everybody: different parts of the country, all ages, genders, and major religions."
- "He used a lot of repetition: for example, saying 'I have a dream,' and 'Let freedom ring' several times."
- "While he talked about the same ideas many times, he did so in different ways."
- "He was positive and hopeful."
- "Although positive, he was realistic, not promising that it would be easy."
- "He shifted his focus from 'I' to 'we.'"
- "He spoke with emotion and passion. This was something he genuinely felt."

These reflections reveal the key to success in enlisting others. You need to speak about meaning and purpose to get others excited about your dream. You have to *show them* how to realize *their* dreams. You have to connect your message to their values, their aspirations, their experiences, and their lives. You have to illustrate that it's about them and their needs, not about you or the organization. You have to connect an inspiring vision of the future to the personal aspirations and passions of the people you are addressing.

Researchers underscore the importance of leaders using *image-based words* in communicating their visions: "Image-based words convey sensory information to paint a vivid picture of the future, one that employees can easily imagine witnessing. Along these lines, visions with image-based words are more consistent with the literal meaning of the word *vision*. When leaders include vivid images in their communications, they're transporting employees to the future by telling snippets of a compelling story—a story that captures events that have yet to unfold."[13] This is precisely what Martin Luther King Jr. did in describing people with well-defined attributes (such as children) and observable actions (such as sitting down at the table of brotherhood).

Image-based words inspire people. For instance, researchers tasked teams with developing a toy prototype. A vision communicated with image-based words ("our toys. . .will make wide-eyed kids laugh and proud parents smile") triggered higher performance than a vision with similar content but without visual wording ("our toys. . .will be enjoyed by all of our customers").[14] You need to frame abstract aspirations in terms of what the result will look, feel, and sound like. With these images, people begin to generate a level of passion and conviction about the vision that mirrors their leader's.

Using image-based language and creating a connection between personal aspirations and a shared vision is not only for leaders of social movements or product development teams. It applies equally to teams in workplaces like your own. Kent Christensen knew well his day-to-day responsibilities as a business analyst with a networking and communications organization. Still, he didn't see how his job fit into the larger scheme of things. However, this feeling changed at a town hall meeting when the vice president put up a slide with four letters: V-S-E-M, which stood for Vision, Strategy, Execution, and Metrics. The vice president described how this focus would enable the company to optimize customer outcomes, empower everyone in the organization, and provide a blueprint for action, stressing how everyone had a significant role to play and needed to work collaboratively within and across organizations. These remarks were powerful, and Kent maintained:

> They completely changed the way I did my job. This shared vision resonated with me and showed me the light when there was only darkness before. Coming out of the all-hands meeting, the vibe around the office was different. There was a buzz around people as everyone started to feel like they belonged. It looked as if everyone had a purpose. Having a vision helped managers and their teams to become inspired and committed to a shared goal.

By showing others how their work connects to a larger purpose, and by aligning individual aspirations with organizational ones, you can get people to see how they belong and inspire them to work together toward a common goal.

## Animate the Vision

*The vision has to appeal to people's head, heart, and hands.*

*Jan Pacas*

Part of motivating others is appealing to their ideals. Another part, as demonstrated by Martin Luther King's "I Have a Dream" speech and Kent's vice president, is enlivening the vision and breathing life into it. To enlist others, you need to help them *see* and *feel* how their interests and aspirations align with the vision. You need to paint a compelling picture of the future, one that enables constituents to experience what it would be like to live and work in an exciting and uplifting future. That's the only way they'll become sufficiently motivated internally to commit their energies to the vision's realization.

You would not be the first person to think, "But I'm not like Martin Luther King. I can't possibly do what he did. Besides, he was a preacher, and I'm not. His constituents were on a protest march, and mine are here to get a job done." Many people don't see themselves as personally uplifting, and most certainly don't get much encouragement for behaving this way in organizations. Despite the acknowledged potency of clearly communicated and compelling visions, our research finds people more uncomfortable with inspiring a shared vision than with any of the other four leadership practices. Most of their discomfort comes from having to express their emotions. Many people find it hard to do this, but don't be too quick to discount your capacity to do it.

People's perception of themselves as uninspiring is in sharp contrast to their performance when they talk about their personal-best leadership experiences or when they talk about their ideal futures. People are nearly always emotionally expressive when relating extraordinary achievements or major successes. When talking about intense desires for a better future, expressiveness tends to come naturally. And it doesn't matter what language people are speaking, because when they feel passionate about something, they let their emotions show.

Most people attribute something mystical to the process of being inspirational. They seem to see it as supernatural, as grace or charm bestowed on them—often referred to as charisma. This assumption inhibits people far more than any lack of natural talent for being inspirational. It's not necessary to be a charismatic person to inspire a shared vision. You have to *believe,* and you have to develop the skills to transmit your belief. Your passion is what brings the vision to life. If you're going to lead, you have to recognize that your enthusiasm and expressiveness are among the strongest allies in your efforts to generate commitment in others.

**Use Symbolic Language** When Janet (McTavish) MacIntyre became the new head of the intensive care unit/cardiac care unit at a Canadian hospital, she shared her intense passion for nursing, along with her extensive knowledge and accomplished skills. Janet wanted to fully engage her colleagues in the opening of this new state-of-the-art hospital and found some compelling ways to do that:

> I began by creating a logo with a slogan and choosing a mascot, one that identified with our Canadian roots and symbolized the journey we were on. An Inukshuk, built by the Inuit Natives across the Canadian Arctic, is a stone landmark that denotes a spiritual resting place along a migration route to food or shelter. Most importantly, it communicates that "you are on the path." That was us. We were on a path. We were on a journey.

The Inukshuk mascot was built with six stones: four representing the organization's corporate values of respect, caring, innovation, and accountability, and two additional stones reflecting the ICU/CCU's values.

A "passport" served as a creative education tool for getting everyone engaged—115 staff members in all, from nurses and respiratory therapists to business clerks and environmental aides. With so many diverse learning needs for the various disciplines, the passport provided a customized checklist, site map, and information that identified a path to working safely in the new environment. A mock patient setup room, called the "sandbox," gave the staff plenty of time to "play" (and practice, hands-on) with the new technology and equipment and lessen the anxiety on moving day.

The Inukshuk mascot, the passport, the map, and the sandbox were all ways that Janet brought the vision to life through evocative metaphors and symbols. Leaders, like Janet, embrace the power of symbolic language to communicate a shared identity and give life to visions. They use metaphors and analogies. They give examples, tell stories, and relate anecdotes. They draw word pictures, offer quotations, and recite slogans. They enable constituents to picture the possibilities—to hear them, sense them, and recognize them.

Studies have found that people use a metaphor every ten to twenty-five words, or about six metaphors a minute.[15] You can use metaphors explicitly and deliberately to influence others. Metaphors are everywhere—there are art metaphors, game and sports metaphors, war metaphors, science fiction metaphors, machine metaphors, and religious or spiritual metaphors. Metaphors influence what people think, what they invent, what they eat and drink, how they think, whom they vote for, and what they buy. When Amy Cole, a director of sales training and services with a software services company, was putting together her team, she spoke about "getting everyone on the bus." "I used the metaphor that we are a team traveling in a bus," because, she explained, "it is important that we all travel in the same direction."

The intriguing impact of language was vividly illustrated in an experiment in which researchers told participants they were playing either the Community Game or the Wall Street Game.[16] In both scenarios, people played the same game by the same rules; the only difference was that experimenters gave the same game two different names. Of those playing the Community Game, 70 percent started out playing cooperatively and continued to do so throughout. Of those told they were playing the Wall Street Game, just the opposite occurred: 70 percent did not cooperate, and the 30 percent who did cooperate stopped when they saw that others weren't cooperating. Again, remember: the name, not the game, was the only thing that was different!

Your ability to enlist others in a common vision of the future will be greatly enhanced by understanding the powerful effect these tools of language can have in shaping the way people envision their work and determine their actions. If one word can make a difference in how people work together, then you need to be clear about the words you choose when communicating the future you envision. If you want to recruit and retain employees and constituents, you need to be clear about the words that evoke the future states they desire. Words and phrases such as *diversity-equity-inclusion*, *purpose*, *meaningful work*, *emotional well-being*, *ethical leadership*, *civility*, *connection in a virtual workplace*, *flexibility*, and *positive culture* resonate with the newer generation of workers. Pay attention to the words. Make sure that the picture you paint of your shared vision evokes the culture you aspire to create.

**Create Images of the Future** Visions are images in the mind; they are impressions and representations. They become real when leaders express those images in concrete terms to their constituents. Just as architects make drawings and engineers build models, leaders find ways to express collective hopes for the future.

When talking about the future, people typically use terms such as *foresight*, *focus*, *forecasts*, *future scenarios*, *points of view*, and *perspectives*. What all these expressions have in common is that they are visual references. The word *vision* itself has at its root the verb "to see." Vision statements, then, are more like word pictures. They are *images* of the future. For people to share a vision, they have to be able to see it in the mind's eye.

In our workshops and classes, we often illustrate the power of images with this simple exercise. We ask people to shout out the first thing that comes to mind when they hear the words *Paris, France*. The replies that pop out—the Eiffel Tower, the Louvre, the Arc de Triomphe, the Seine, Notre Dame, delicious food, wine, and romance—are all images of real places and real sensations. No one calls out the square kilometers, population, or gross domestic product of Paris. Why? Because most of what we recall about memorable places or events are those things associated with our senses—sights, sounds, tastes, smells, tactile sensations, and feelings.[17]

To enlist others and inspire a shared vision, you must draw on that very natural mental process of creating images. When you speak about the future, you need to create pictures with words so that others form a mental image of what things will be like at the end of the journey. Although some people may have a more creative imagination than others, everyone can get other people to see places they've never been to before. You first have to vividly imagine the destination in your mind's eye, and then be willing to describe it so colorfully that others will see it and want to go there themselves.

Debbie Sharp, manager of employee learning and organization development for a community college district, paints a very vivid image in her vision statement:

> More than any other institution of higher education the community college is in the business of changing lives. We meet our students where they are and help them define and achieve their goals. As they fulfill their potentials, we help them shine!
>
> In days gone by, the lamplighter dutifully set about lighting the streetlamps as day faded to night. We in ELOD light the lamps of learning, chasing away the darkness of uncertainty and doubt for our customers.
>
> When asked why he is so committed to this repetitive, mundane task, the lamplighter replies, "I do it for the light I leave behind."
>
> As learning and development professionals, we too are lamplighters, creating conditions that nurture the spark of new ideas and perspectives. Through encouragement, thoughtful questioning, and provision of safe spaces for experimentation, we ignite innovative thinking and self-discovery in our learners.
>
> The light we leave behind illuminates the paths of those we touch, enabling them to spread their light throughout the college.

Getting people to see a common future does not require special powers. Just like Debbie, you possess this ability. You do it every time you take a vacation and share the photos with your friends. If you doubt your ability to paint word pictures, try this exercise: sit down with a few close friends and tell them about one of your favorite vacations. Describe the people you met, the sights and sounds of the places you visited, the smells and tastes of the food you ate. Show them the photos or videos if you have them. Observe their reactions—and your own. What do you and they experience? The answer is that people always report feeling energized and passionate. Those hearing about a place for the first time usually say something like, "After listening to you, I'd like to go there someday myself." Isn't that what you want your constituents to say when you describe your vision of the future?

**Practice Positive Communication** To foster team spirit, breed optimism, promote resilience, and renew faith and confidence, leaders look on the bright side and keep hope alive. They strengthen their constituents' belief that life's struggles will produce a more promising future. People seek to follow those who demonstrate an enthusiastic, genuine belief in the capacity of others, who strengthen people's will, who supply the means to achieve, and who express optimism for the future. Constituents want leaders who remain passionate despite obstacles and setbacks. In today's uncertain times, people desperately need leaders with a positive, confident, can-do approach. Naysayers only stop forward progress; they do not start it.

Consider the positive attitude and communication style that Joan Carter exhibited when she took over as general manager and executive chef at the Faculty Club, a café at a small private university. Before Joan's arrival, both membership and sales had been seriously declining, patrons were unhappy, and the staff was divided into factions.

Joan took all this in, but what she saw was a dusty diamond. "I saw a beautiful and historic building full of mission-era flavor and character that should be, could be, would be *the* place on campus." In her mind's eye, she saw the club bustling. She saw people chatting in this lovely setting and enjoying high-quality, appealing yet affordable meals. Joan could see a happy staff whose primary concern was customer satisfaction, a kitchen that produced a product far superior to "banquet food," and a catering staff that did whatever it took to make an event exceptional. She wasn't quite sure how the club had deteriorated to the extent it had, but that didn't matter. She decided to ignore the quick fix and set out to teach everyone how unique and wonderful the club could be.

Over the next two years, as she talked with customers and worked with her staff, she instilled a vision of the club as a place that celebrated good food and good company. As food and service quality improved, smiles became more prevalent among customers and staff, and sales began to rise—20 percent the first year and 30 percent again the next. When a senior university executive asked how she had managed to turn the finances around so quickly and dramatically, Joan responded, "You can't turn around numbers. The balance sheet is just a reflection of what's happening here, every day, in the restaurant. I just helped the staff realize what we're really all about. It was always here," she said, "only perhaps a little dusty, a little ignored, and a little unloved. I just helped them see it."

A positive approach to life broadens people's ideas about future possibilities, and these exciting opportunities build on each other. Being positive opens people up, consequently enabling them to see more options, making them more innovative. Individuals who enjoy more positivity are also better able to cope with adversity and are more resilient during times of high stress.[18] In contrast, researchers working with neural networks find that when people feel rebuffed or left out, the brain activates a site for registering physical pain.[19] When leaders threaten and demean people, use scare tactics, and focus exclusively on problems, they activate regions in the brains of their audience that make people want to avoid them. Moreover, people remember negative comments far more often, in more detail, and with more intensity than they do encouraging words. When pessimistic remarks become a preoccupation, people's brains lose mental efficiency.

**Express Your Emotions** In explaining why particular leaders have a magnetic effect, people often describe them as charismatic. However, *charisma* has become such an overused and misused term that it's almost useless as a descriptor of leaders. Being charismatic is neither a magical nor a spiritual quality, and like being "inspirational," it's mostly about how people behave.

Instead of defining charisma as a personality trait, social scientists have investigated what people are doing when others say they are charismatic.[20] They've found that individuals who are perceived to be charismatic are simply more animated than people who are not. They smile more, speak faster, pronounce words more clearly, and move their heads and bodies more often. They display more energy, express more enthusiasm, and convey more emotion than less captivating individuals.

Emotion also makes things more memorable. Because leaders want constituents to remember their messages, you need to be adding more emotional content to your words and actions. In addition, emotionally significant events have been shown to create the strongest and longest-lasting memories. No doubt you've experienced this yourself when something emotionally significant has happened to you—perhaps a severe trauma, such as an accident, or a joyful surprise, such as winning a contest.

The events don't even have to be real to be memorable. They can simply be stories that arouse emotions. For example, in an experiment, people were shown a series of twelve slides.[21] Accompanying the slide presentation was a story, one line for each slide. For one group, the narrative was quite boring; for the other, the narrative was emotionally moving. Participants didn't know when they watched the slides that they would be tested, but two weeks later, they returned and took an assessment of how well they remembered the details of each slide. Although the subjects in the two groups didn't differ in their memory of the first few and last few slides, they did differ significantly in the recollection of the slides in the middle. Those who had listened to the emotionally arousing narrative compared with the people who listened to the neutral story remembered details in those particular slides better.

Emotional arousal creates stronger memories, and you're more likely to remember the key messages when attached to something that triggers an emotional response.[22] People are hard-wired to pay more attention to stuff that excites them or scares them. Keep all this in mind the next time you deliver a PowerPoint presentation. It's not just the content that will make it stick; it's also how well you tap into people's emotions. Furthermore, giving people a concrete example is better than telling them about an abstract principle, which still leaves them on the outside looking in. For example, studies have shown that a story about a starving seven-year-old girl from Mali prompted people to donate more than twice as much money as the message that "food shortages in Malawi are affecting more than three million children in Zambia."[23]

Even better is getting people to experience the vision you are trying to explain and achieve. Louise Baxter is the executive director of an Australian charitable foundation dedicated to "brighten the lives" and "lift the spirits" of seriously ill and hospitalized children and their families. She developed a program that has everyone in the organization spending at least a half-day each quarter in one of their partner hospitals seeing first-hand the foundation's impact and experiencing how their personal aspirations connect to those of the organization. One data manager testified to how Louise has inspired everyone, no matter what work they do.

> I've never cared more about the outcome than I do in this job. I feel so totally responsible for what I have to actually do for the organization, and I can totally see the positive impact of my contribution to the overall good. I know that what I do will lead to the outcome, and it's an outcome that matters, and we can see the effect of what we do.

"By staying connected to our impact, we are inspired by our vision, and people don't get so bogged down by their daily tasks," Louise told us. They regularly experience the type of challenges that children and their families have in a way that they can never forget. This powerful program speaks volumes about how much more influential leaders can be when they tap into people's emotions rather than only telling them what to do or how to feel. People need to do more than conceptually understand the importance of their work.

The dramatic increase in the use of electronic technology also impacts the way people deliver messages. More and more people are turning to their digital devices and social media for information and connection.

Because people remember things that have high emotional content, social media can engage people more than do emails, memos, and PowerPoint presentations. It's no longer enough to write a good script; you also have to put on a good show. A word of caution, however. Whether it's social media or traditional media, positives attract and negatives repel. Even though negative social media messages often become more viral, if your intent is to attract others, you need to focus on the benefits.

Keep in mind that the content alone doesn't make the message stick; the key is how well you tap into people's emotions. To be motivated to change, people have to feel something. Thinking isn't nearly enough to get things moving. Expressing emotions helps do that.[24]

**Speak Genuinely** None of these suggestions about being more expressive will be of any value whatsoever if you don't sincerely believe in what you're saying. If the vision is someone else's and you don't own it, you'll have a tough time enlisting others. If you have trouble imagining yourself living the future described in the vision, you certainly will not be able to convince others that they ought to sign up for making it a reality. If you're not excited about the possibilities, you can't expect others to be. *The prerequisite for enlisting others in a shared vision is genuineness.*

When asked how she was able to lead the development team in creating a new family of microprocessors for a semiconductor company, Laila Razouk replied simply, "I believed. Believing is a very important part of the action. You have to have faith. If you don't have that, then you're lost even before you get started." It's easy to understand why people were eager to follow Laila:

> If I believe in something badly enough, and if I have the conviction, then I start picturing and envisioning how it will look if we did this or if we did that. By sharing these thoughts with other people, the excitement grows, and people become part of that picture. Without much effort—with energy, but not much effort—the magic starts to happen. People start to bounce ideas back and forth, they get involved, brainstorm, and share ideas. Then I know I don't have to worry about it.

How successful would this project have been if instead Laila had thought, "This project is overly ambitious and unlikely to be very successful. The person who thought this up doesn't understand the details. I'm doing this because it's my job, but I really think this project is a stupid idea!" For Laila, the net effect of speaking from the heart, as she explained, was that "by openly sharing what I saw, what I knew, and what I believed—not by dictating it, but by being willing to iterate and adjust things—I got other people involved."

The most believable people are the ones, like Laila, with a deep passion. The people who are the most fun to be around are those who are openly excited about the magic that can happen. People want to follow those who are upbeat, optimistic, and positive about the future. There's no one more determined than someone who believes fervently in an ideal. Are you that someone?

# TAKE ACTION:

## Enlist Others

Leaders appeal to common ideals. They connect others to what is most meaningful in the shared vision. They lift people to higher levels of motivation and continuously reinforce that they can make a difference. Exemplary leaders speak to what is unique and singular about the organization, making others feel proud to be a part of something extraordinary. Exemplary leaders understand that it's not their personal view of the future that's important; it's embracing the aspirations of their constituents that matters most.

To sustain visions, they must be compelling and memorable. Leaders must breathe life into visions; they animate them so that others can experience what it would be like to live and work in that ideal and unique future. They use a variety of modes of expression to make their abstract visions concrete. Leaders generate enthusiasm and excitement for the common vision through skillful use of metaphors, symbols, word pictures, positive language, and personal energy. Above all, leaders must be convinced of the value of the shared vision and communicate that genuine belief to others. They must believe in what they are saying. Authenticity is the acid test of conviction, and your constituents will willingly follow only when they believe that you believe.

To Inspire a Shared Vision, you must *enlist others in a common vision by appealing to shared aspirations*. Here are several suggestions for how to do this:

- Talk with your constituents and find out about their hopes, dreams, and aspirations for the future. How can

(*continued*)

you better relate your organization's vision to their personal aspirations?

- Be positive, upbeat, and energetic when talking about your organization's future, and make liberal use of metaphors, symbols, examples, and stories.
- Find ways to make conversations about the shared vision a part of regular meetings and conversations, virtual and in person. Insert the shared vision into emails and other written communication, post it on intranet sites, and work it into your speeches. The point is to increase the frequency with which you communicate the shared vision to others.

Repeated conversations about various aspects of leadership will let people know what you are thinking and why something is important to you, to the organization, and to them. Find opportunities to talk with others about these questions:

- It's five years from now and you're stopping by for a visit to this organization. What excites you most about what you see, hear, and feel?
- If you were to send a few scouts out ahead of this "wagon train" to see what's over the horizon, what would they come back and tell us?

# CHALLENGE THE PROCESS

## PRACTICE 3

# CHALLENGE THE PROCESS

- Search for opportunities by seizing the initiative and looking outward for innovative ways to improve.
- Experiment and take risks by consistently generating small wins and learning from experience.

# CHAPTER 6
# Search for Opportunities

*Leadership requires changing*
*the "business-as-usual" environment.*

*Joe J. Sparagna*

**JACQUELINE MAARTENSE BELIEVES** that "you can build a great company if the customer is the center of all we do." Jacqueline had the chance to demonstrate her commitment to this ideal boldly and quickly when she was appointed managing director of the United Kingdom division of a personal and small-business financial software company. That division had never been profitable, and she was given one year to turn it around. She "wasn't met with a warm fuzzy reception" when she informed everyone on her first day in the office that they would have an all-hands meeting about building partnerships with customers. When she looked around the room that morning, most everyone was slumped in their chairs, their folded arms telegraphing their skepticism and resistance.

> I asked the team to suspend judgment for one day. I invited them to be open to the possibility that we could turn the company profitable if we learned to listen to customers better than everyone else

> on the planet. I shared my belief that we will build products and programs right the first time, because collectively we will know what customers want. With that opening, I spent a half-day teaching people customer-contact techniques and how to gain insight from customer interactions.

By noon, she saw growing optimism, but there were still some grumpy people. That's when she handed out the customer phone list and challenged them to make calls to find out how they could make a difference in their customers' lives.

Magic took place that afternoon as they began to hear about what customers were experiencing and started to realize, "Wow, I can do something about this," or "Wow, I didn't know you felt that way." In many cases, the reports back from customers were wonderful, and it was just an opportunity for employees to hear about how great the company was. That in itself was inspiring.

Following the phone calls, the entire company broke into cross-functional groups to talk about what they had learned and the actions they needed to take to change the system and address specific customer problems. "By the end of the day," Jacqueline reported, "the place was on fire. After we regrouped to share our stories, the people who had been the most disgruntled were the ones who were now saying, 'Wow, I can't even imagine developing a product without doing this kind of thing on an ongoing basis.'"

The ideas generated that day about how to create customer delight became the fabric of their business plan and the beginning of a new way of doing business. To ensure that the momentum continued, over the next several months Jacqueline made a point to listen in on calls and to get on the phone herself every week so that everyone could know that she was calling customers. She spent lots of time with the customer service and technical support reps, continually asking them, "What did you learn about what we could do to make a difference in a customer's life today?" That question became a ritual, for herself and other company leaders, in their interactions with employees. Within seven months, the division became profitable for the first time in its history.

What Jacqueline did is what all exemplary leaders do. She looked outward, keeping up with changing trends and remaining sensitive to external realities. She convinced others to take seriously the challenges and opportunities that they faced. She served as a catalyst for change, challenging the way things were being done and convincing others that new practices needed to be incorporated to achieve greater levels of success.

Our analysis of the personal-best leadership cases revealed that the situations people chose to discuss were major changes that significantly impacted their organizations. The people in our study talked about times when they turned around losing operations, started up new plants, developed new products or services, installed untested procedures, renewed operations threatened with closing, or released the creative spirit trapped inside stifling bureaucratic systems. The cases continue to be about radical departures from the past, doing things that have never been done before, and going to places not yet discovered.

Change is the work of leaders. In today's world, business-as-usual thinking is unacceptable, and exemplary leaders know that they must transform the way things are being done. Delivering results beyond expectations can't be achieved with good intentions. People, processes, systems, and strategies all need to change. In addition, all change requires that leaders actively seek ways to make things better—to grow, innovate, and improve.

Exemplary leaders embrace the commitment to *Search for Opportunities* to ensure that extraordinary things happen. They make sure they engage in these two essentials:

- **Seize the initiative**
- **Exercise outsight**

Sometimes leaders shake things up, and other times they just harness the uncertainty surrounding them. Regardless, leaders make things happen. They actively rely on their outsight to seek innovative ideas from beyond the boundaries of familiar experience.

# Seize the Initiative

*You have to take initiative, dare to challenge the system, and find creative ways to do things.*

*Sunny Song*

When people recall their personal-best leadership experiences, they always think about times of challenge, turbulence, and adversity. Why? Because personal and business hardships have a way of making people come face to face with who they are and what they're capable of becoming. They test people. They test their values, desires, aspirations, capabilities, and capacities. They require innovative ways of dealing with novel and difficult situations. They also tend to bring out the best in people.

Meeting new challenges always requires things to be different than they currently exist. You can't respond with the same old solutions if you expect different results. You must change the status quo, which Larry Evans, as vice president of manufacturing, did in his personal-best leadership experience. In one year, his team reduced the time it took to completely build a computer from twenty-six weeks down to six. How? "Well, the first thing you've got to do," he said, "is challenge the process all the time."

This perspective is consistent with what researchers found in examining the human resource practices and organizational designs of innovation-producing organizations, seeking to learn both what fostered and what hindered innovation in corporations. Our studies and theirs were done independently of each other, in different regions and periods in time. We were studying leadership, and they were studying innovation. Yet we reached similar conclusions: *leadership is inextricably connected with the process of innovation,* of bringing new ideas, methods, or solutions into use. Innovation means change, and "change requires leadership. . .a 'prime mover' to push for implementation of strategic decisions."[1]

We did not prompt people to tell us about change. They could review any leadership experience. What people chose to discuss were the changes they made in response to the challenges they faced. Their electing to talk about times of change underscores the fact that leadership demands altering the business-as-usual environment. There is a clear connection between challenge and change, and there's a clear connection between challenge and being an effective leader. Amy Brooks, chief innovation officer for a major sports franchise, says that "every person, whether they are in charge of our broadcast or selling tickets or our social media platforms, has to think every day: How can I challenge the status quo and do something different."[2] Robin Selden, general manager of a European manufacturer of computer peripherals and software, told us how she "realized that my job as a leader was to make change each and every day." Our data backs up the importance of Amy and Robin's perspectives, illustrating that the more frequently leaders "challenge people to try out new and innovative ways to do their work," the more strongly their direct reports agree that they are committed to the organization's success and feel personally productive. Similarly, as Figure 6.1 illustrates, your direct reports are unlikely to recommend you as a good leader to their colleagues unless they see you frequently "taking initiative in anticipating and responding to change."

The study of leadership is the study of how people guide others through adversity, uncertainty, and other significant challenges. It's the study of those who triumph against overwhelming odds, who take initiative when there is inertia, who confront the established order, and who mobilize individuals and institutions in the face of stiff resistance. It's also the study of how people, in times of constancy and complacency, actively seek to disturb the status quo and awaken others to new possibilities. Leadership, challenge, and seizing the initiative are linked. Humdrum situations simply aren't associated with award-winning performances.

That's the attitude that Robin Donahue brought to the quality engineering team at a global healthcare company when tackling numerous nonconformance issues in their products. While the general area to be improved had been defined, the way they were going to reduce

Figure 6.1 The More Frequently Leaders Take Initiative and Respond to Change, the More Frequently Direct Reports Would Recommend Them as Good Leaders to Colleagues

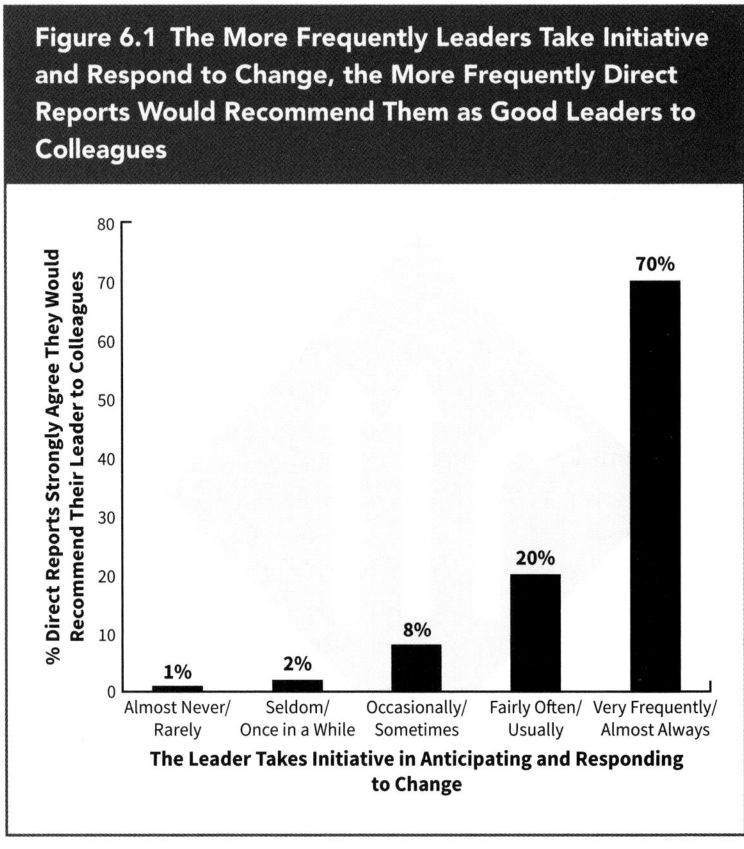


nonconformance rates, with a 20 percent target, was entirely up to them. Owning this objective, she and her colleagues felt they could challenge all parts of their existing systems, but they realized that this would be insufficient. They'd have to, in Robin's words, "think outside the box, not take any existing site practice as set in stone, and experiment with new ideas." They began by brainstorming "what would we change if anything was possible." They followed this up by benchmarking with other sites, both inside and outside their organization, to gain new perspectives on such issues. By year's end, they reduced the number of noncompliance reports by nearly triple their initial objective. Robin felt that being proactive, looking for things that could be improved, and being willing to look around (both internally and externally) for ideas "fostered a culture of inquisitiveness, innovation, and learning."

This experience reminded Robin that change is the business of leaders. "Having regulations doesn't mean you can't make changes," she said. "There are always ways to improve the process, and you should take them." The lesson for leaders is that you can't simply go through the motions when it comes to doing your job. Even if you're on the right track, you're likely to be run over if you just sit there. To do your best as a leader, you must seize the initiative to improve the way things are, and this necessarily requires change.

**Make Something Happen** Exemplary leaders understand that you don't get to a different place if you just keep doing the same things again and again. Getting out of routines and ruts requires treating every job and assignment as an adventure. This involves lifting up your head from what you are doing—instead of keeping your "nose to the grindstone"—and looking all around, investing your time and energy in finding out about other possibilities.

Joe Barsi's personal-best leadership experience involved reviving a branch office of a leading global logistics provider. To accomplish the revival, he had to change their business-as-usual environment. He got everyone on the team to adjust their perspectives and start focusing outward rather than inward. He urged them to spend time understanding customer requirements by getting out of the office gathering data and meeting face-to-face with them. This process resulted in many little decisions, such as extending office hours to make services available over a longer time period, conducting feedback sessions with their top customers, and analyzing their competition for best industry practices. Joe frequently asked his team, "How are we going to work together to improve this business? What will we have to be doing differently?" At the end of two years, net revenue increased by over 140 percent, and they went from being one of the lowest-performing offices in the company to a top-thirty branch.

As Joe's personal-best demonstrates, the highest performance levels come about when people work beyond their job description and see opportunities where others don't. Sure, some standard practices, policies, and procedures are critical to productivity and quality assurance. However, many are simply habitual and matters of tradition, as Emily Taylor, working in client services for a European global financial services firm, related in her personal-best leadership experience. She noticed how her manager had become so entrenched in a certain way of doing things that he "could not see, or did not want to see, how inefficient the current system was, and how disastrous the manual way of doing things would have been going forward." What she realized was "how important it is for leaders to be constantly on the lookout for opportunities for improvement, to identify and challenge systems that are not working well, and foster an environment where everyone is open to sharing new ideas."

As Emily recognized, new jobs and new assignments are ideal opportunities for asking probing questions and challenging how things get done. They are the times when you're expected to ask, "Why do we do this?" However, don't just ask this when you're new to the job. Make it a routine part of your leadership. Be proactive in asking questions that test people's assumptions, stimulate different ways of thinking, and open new avenues to explore. Asking questions is how you'll continuously uncover needed improvements, fostering innovation. Studies of business breakthroughs find that they often originated from someone asking questions about why a problem existed and how to tackle it.[3]

Leaders don't wait for permission or specific instructions before jumping in. They make something happen when they notice what isn't working, create a solution for the problem, gain buy-in from constituents, and implement the desired outcome. For example, Starbucks' Frappuccino came to market because one district manager, Dina Campion, was frustrated that her customers were going to competitors' stores for cold blended drinks. Starbucks didn't offer the product, and corporate declined many requests for the drink. Dina, however, saw an opportunity and was eager to experiment with it. She convinced a colleague in retail operations in Seattle to champion her cause, and he bought her a blender to experiment with formulations of the drink. They didn't ask for permission; they just took the initiative, made the product in one of Dina's stores, and tested it with her customers. As more and more people requested the product, the company became convinced to invest in the drink, and after several trials, brought it to the larger market. Frappuccino became the most successful new launch in company history.[4]

Research clearly shows that people who are most proactive are assessed by their immediate managers as more effective leaders.[5] Co-workers who evaluate their peers as being high on proactivity also consider them better leaders.[6] Similar results about the connection between proactivity and performance have been found among entrepreneurs, administrative staff, and even college students searching for jobs. Proactivity consistently produces better results than reactivity or inactivity.[7] Using cross-cultural samples, we've found that proactive managers score higher than average on the leadership practice of Challenge the Process, and this inclination is independent of both gender and national culture.[8] People perform better when they take charge of change. As is said in basketball, one hundred percent of the shots you *don't* take never go in the hoop.

The mantra of one leading sportswear company's founder, "It's perfect. Now make it better," inspires and informs everything that the business does. In the experience of Prashant Shukla, supply chain director, leaders "have a bias for action and inventiveness. They love to solve big challenges and keep progressing towards the desired outcome. They have no affiliation with the status quo and favor instituting changes that they believe will contribute positively to the organization's success." He finds that they "are *constantly looking to improve and innovate*."

Leaders, as Prashant observes, want to make something happen and are often frustrated by the "if it ain't broke, don't fix it" mentality. Wander around your workplace and look for things that don't seem right. Ask questions. Probe. When Phil Turner became the manager of a wire and cable factory, he spent a lot of time getting accustomed to the sounds and smells of the plant. At first, he couldn't tell one sound from another; it all seemed like indistinguishable noise. But soon he was able to hear the unique music of each machine, much as a conductor gets to know the instruments in an orchestra. Phil discovered that the machines used to spool the wire weren't running at full speed. When he asked why, people told him they didn't know how to fix them and were afraid they would wear down if the machines ran at capacity. Phil went quickly into action and began an employee training program that got the machines thriving and enabled the operators to fix them whenever they broke.

**Encourage Initiative in Others** Change requires leadership, and every person, down to the most junior member of the organization, can drive innovation and improvements in a team's processes. Azmeena Zaveri had seen how tradition, along with daily pressures and demands in the corporate workplace, could diminish innovation and responsiveness to new ideas. She admitted how easy it was to fall into this same trap when she worked with a group of volunteers for a local community center in northern California. She realized that she had become preoccupied with logistical and clerical tasks, "making sure that the increasingly monotonous activities were done correctly and predictably," and that she had not been sufficiently open to new ways of thinking.

To break out of this pattern, she created a new forum that met after every event to brainstorm how to do things better for the next event. In these forums, she invited the team to give their opinions and suggestions for improving their program and encouraged them to share what they might have read about or experienced at other events. She also created a digital diary for the team to pitch new ideas, get into the details of the ones they decided to try, and generate a log of what they've learned from those experiences. Azmeena and her team understand that not everything will be successful, but, as she says, "trying new things was necessary for the program to improve and stay relevant with ever-changing times."

Leaders seize the initiative themselves and encourage initiative in others. They want people to speak up, offer suggestions for improvement, and be straightforward with constructive criticism. The data shows that the more frequently direct reports indicated that their leaders "challenge people to try out new and innovative ways to do their work," the stronger were their feelings of accomplishment. Additionally, their belief that they were making a difference was heightened. Their responses to the question "Would you work harder and for longer hours if the job demanded it?" connected directly to the extent that they felt their leaders challenged them "to try out new and innovative ways to do their work." There was over a tenfold increase in motivational levels between those who indicated that their leaders very frequently challenged them to try out new and innovative ways to do their work compared with those whose leaders infrequently challenged them.

The empirical findings were similar when direct reports assessed how frequently they observed their leaders doing the same *themselves*—that is, "seeks out challenging opportunities that test their own skills and abilities." Their own levels of commitment, motivation, and productivity increased proportionally to how frequently they indicated their leaders challenging themselves. No surprise then that this leadership behavior was strongly related to the extent that direct reports viewed their leader as "one of the best" they had worked with, as shown in Figure 6.2.

When one engineer responded to his question about the project's feasibility with "It won't work," Stephen Ravizza found that everyone jumped on this refrain and sounded quite ready to accept defeat. As the project lead, he suggested that the team take another tack, and this time he asked: "What is working?" Posing this question, Stephen explained, stimulated new discussion. People slowly turned their cynicism into a positive outlook, concentrating their comments on the positive elements of the proposed project. Stephen then asked, "Suppose we could magically remove this particular obstacle—how will this help us?" Focusing on possibilities and not being hampered by limitations of conventional thinking gave birth to several new ideas on how to revive the project. People responded with new levels of creativity and imagination and decided that they could actually make the project successful.

You can create conditions so that your constituents will be ready and willing to seize the initiative in tumultuous as well as tranquil times. First, generate a can-do attitude by providing opportunities for people to gain mastery of a task one step at a time. Training is crucial to building people's ability and confidence to effectively respond to demanding situations. For example, when Aristotle Verdant, marketing project manager at a storage networking company, realized that his problems were not unique to his company, he persuaded his manager to

**Figure 6.2 Evaluations of Leaders' Job Performance Increases the More Frequently Their Direct Reports Indicate That Leaders Seek Opportunities to Challenge Themselves**

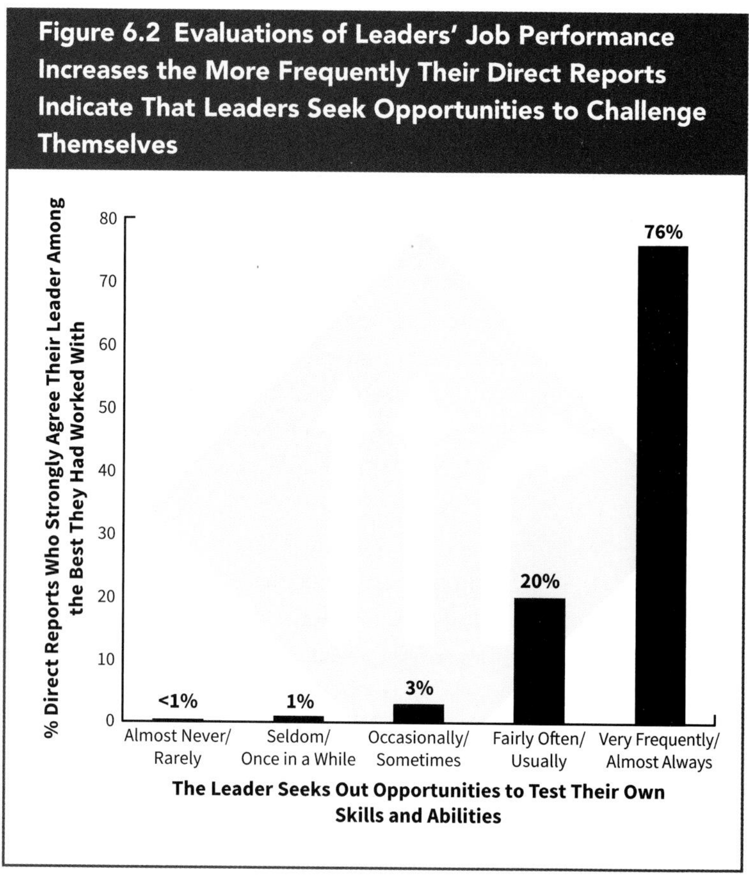


provide funds for specialized training for the team on the most current processes being utilized in the industry and outside of their company. As a result of the training, people could see that adopting new processes would be beneficial and productive, allowing the organization to manage better the uncertainties they were facing in their projects. However, before rolling out any new process applications, Aristotle told us, more work was needed.

> We needed to experiment with its effectiveness in our environment. The experiments would bring in practical learning, allow us

to course-correct as necessary, and manage better the change effort. The best way to achieve that in a controlled environment was to do pilot programs that were small in scope. Through these pilot projects, we monitored the progress as we advanced through different stages, identified the pitfalls, and used the solutions to continuously fine-tune the new process and customize it to our environment.

This experience also demonstrated that leaders find ways for people to stretch themselves. Set the bar incrementally higher but at a level at which people feel they can succeed. Raise it too high, and people will fail; if they fail too often, they'll quit trying. Raise the bar a bit at a time, and as more and more people eventually master the situation and build the self-confidence to continue, move the bar upward. Knowing how high to raise the bar also requires that you know the current capabilities of the people you lead. For some, a 5 to 10 percent increase in improvement may be too easy, but for others it may be too daunting.

You also foster initiative by providing access to role models, especially among peers, who successfully meet challenges. Our data strongly indicates that the more people observe their leaders as role models for taking initiative, testing skills and abilities, and learning from experience, the more favorable they feel about their workplaces. By observing exemplary behaviors, people can gain insights into the dynamic nature of the skill they are trying to acquire. Positive role models are necessary because it is nearly impossible for anyone to excel based upon a negative. You can most easily excel with a positive example. You can know a hundred things not to do, but if you don't know even one thing to do, then you can't perform very well at the task. Get people to focus on one or two skills they most want to learn and look for someone who's good at them to learn from and emulate. Connect people with role models from whom they can start learning and help them take the next steps of creating a mental picture of performing that same skill themselves and internalizing why it is important to develop that competency.

**Challenge with Purpose** Purpose is a tremendously powerful source of motivation, and people cannot persevere for very long without it.[9] Consequently, leaders don't challenge simply for challenge's sake. It's not about shaking things up just to keep people on their toes. Individuals who simply complain about how things are going, grumble about what's not working well, criticize new thoughts and thinking, or point out problems with the ideas of others without offering alternatives are neither challenging the process nor leading. Exemplary leaders challenge for meaning's sake and with the desire to take action for the better. Leaders challenge, usually with great passion, because they want people to live better lives. They fervently believe that the lives of all their stakeholders will be better when processes, products, services, systems, and relationships are continuously improved. But to be fully engaged in the challenge, people need to know why. Meaningfulness thrives when people understand their organization's purpose and the work they do. Making challenging work meaningful shows how the practices of Inspire a Shared Vision and Challenge the Process are inextricably linked. Struggling to achieve something over the long term is more sustainable when people can see how the vision meaningfully connects to the work they are doing in the present.

The strongest motivation to deal with life and work's challenges and uncertainties comes from *inside* people, not outside. It doesn't typically come from something others hold out in front as a carrot or stick.[10] The evidence from our research and studies by many others demonstrates that if people are going to do their best when challenged, they must be internally motivated. Their tasks or projects must be intrinsically engaging.

Researchers have challenged the assumption that giving people more money (for example, providing or increasing financial incentives) significantly improves performance. Current thinking is that contingent rewards (for instance, pay for performance) may be a losing proposition.[11] Studies provide convincing evidence that reliance on extrinsic motivators can actually lower performance and create a culture of divisiveness and selfishness, precisely because it diminishes an inner sense of purpose.[12] When it comes to excellence, it's definitely not "What gets rewarded gets done"; it's "What *is* rewarding gets done."

You can never pay people enough to care—to care about their products, services, communities, families, or even the bottom line. After all, why do people do so many things for nothing? Why do they volunteer to put out fires, raise money for worthy causes, or help others in need? Why do they risk their careers to start a new business or risk their security to change the social condition? Why do they risk their lives to save others or defend liberty? Extrinsic rewards certainly can't explain these actions. Similarly, what gets people through the tough times, the scary times, the times when they don't think they can get up in the morning or take another step?

Having a sense of purpose larger than yourself answers these questions. When Arlene Blum, who lead the first all-woman team to climb Annapurna I, the tenth-highest mountain in the world, is asked *why* people climb mountains, her response is much more than "because it is there." Arlene maintains that the dividing line that separates those who make a successful ascent from those who don't is believing that "what you're doing is meaningful. . .[and then]. . .you can cut through fear and exhaustion and take the next step."[13] The research is clear. Unless people can find meaning and purpose in their work, they are not likely to stick around very long or put in the effort required to make a difference. These feelings are particularly important for leaders to tap into during times of high uncertainty. Research on the "Great Attrition" that accompanied the pandemic provides further evidence to support the importance of meaning and purpose. People cited the need to find more meaningful work as one of their main reasons for voluntarily leaving their employer.[14]

When risk and complexity increase, people have a greater need for direction and guidance than when times are safer and simpler. People need a reason to keep on climbing, to keep on striving, to keep on struggling. That reason needs to be more than a short-term reward. It needs to be something more sustaining. When challenging people to grow, innovate, and improve, explain how it will benefit their colleagues, customers, families, and communities. Connect the challenge to the greater good. Give them a reason to care.

# Exercise Outsight

*People who get extraordinary things done are always out and about.*

*Ann Bowers*

On a visit to the rugged coast of northern California, we came across important advice for leaders. Printed at the top of a pamphlet describing a stretch of the Pacific Ocean was this warning: "Never turn your back on the ocean." The reason that you can't turn and look inland, to catch a view of the town, is because a rogue wave may come along when your back is turned and sweep you out to sea, as many an unsuspecting traveler has discovered. This warning holds sound advice for leaders as well. When you take your eyes off the external realities, turning inward to admire the beauty of your organization, the swirling waters of change may sweep you away.

So too with innovation. You must always scan the external realities. Innovation requires the use of outsight. The sibling of *insight* (the ability to apprehend the inner nature of things) is *outsight* (the awareness and understanding of outside forces). Outsight comes through openness. That's because researchers find that innovations come from just about anywhere.[15] According to a global study of CEOs, the most significant sources of innovative ideas are discovered outside the organization.[16] Sometimes ideas come from customers, sometimes from lead users, sometimes from suppliers, sometimes from business partners, and sometimes from the R&D labs of other organizations.

Leaders must always be actively looking for the fuzziest signs and intently listening to the weakest signals to anticipate the emergence of something new over the horizon. By keeping the doors open to the passage of ideas and information, you become knowledgeable about what is going on around you. Insight without outsight is like seeing with blinders on; you compromise your viewpoint, and you won't get a complete picture.

Consider Suk Yee Ho's comment about her manager, who had a great deal of experience in finance and accounting. While working for him, she said, he always asked her

> a ton of questions. How does XYZ work? What is the impact of this and that? What is your opinion on this? Initially, I found it strange that he would ask someone with less experience so many questions. Did he not know the answer? Was he unsure of himself? I soon realized what he was doing was exactly what a leader should be doing. He was exercising outsight—obtaining others' points of view to diversify his knowledge further and to see many different perspectives so he could have the best understanding possible. His current and future discussions and decision-making would only benefit from his continued inquiries.

**Look Outside of Your Experience** Like Suk Yee's manager, Anne Wong, director of digital marketing at a business data center and cloud computing security company, has always been open and insatiably curious about what's going on around her. She's known for asking lots of questions; one of her direct reports described her as "unrelenting in her questions until she completely understands whatever is being discussed." An important rationale for doing so, Anne says, "is always trying to clearly understand situations from other people's perspectives."

In shadowing senior executives, researchers discovered that the most successful ones were not waiting for information to come to them, but were out and about making themselves knowledgeable so that they could understand what to do next.[17] For example, they were checking the morning news, dropping by their colleagues' offices for a quick catch-up, walking the hallways or plant site, going to the cafeteria for coffee or lunch with peers, participating in informal gatherings and celebrations, attending training programs and conferences, and so on. One of their main preoccupations was "staying on top of what was happening within and around [their] organizations." They were vigilant in making sure they didn't find themselves in the position of asking after the fact: "How could this happen without me knowing?"

Leading by wandering about and asking questions allows leaders to look outside of their experiences and promotes external and internal dialogue about finding innovative opportunities. It also strongly influences the pride and loyalty people experience about their organizations, and their willingness to take that extra step to make their projects most successful. For example, our data reveals that the more people observe that their leader "actively searches for innovative ways to improve what we do" the greater the extent to which they feel they themselves are making a difference in the work they do.

Studies into how the brain processes information suggest that you need to bombard your brain with stuff you have never encountered to see things differently and creatively. Novelty is vital because the brain, evolved for efficiency, routinely takes perceptual shortcuts to save energy. Only by forcing yourself to break free of preexisting views can you get your brain to recategorize information. Moving beyond habitual thinking patterns is the starting point to imagining novel alternatives.[18]

The human mind is surprisingly adept at supporting its deep-seated ways of viewing the world while sifting out evidence to the contrary. McKinsey & Company researchers suggest that direct personal experience is the antidote: "Seeing and experiencing something firsthand can shake people up in ways that abstract discussions around conference room tables can't. It's therefore extremely beneficial to start creativity-building exercises or idea generation efforts outside the office, by engineering personal experiences that directly confront the participants' implicit or explicit assumptions."[19] You can't very well understand what's going on around you by simply sitting at your desk in the office or on the couch in your living room.

Courtney Ballagh realized the importance of outsight while employed as an assistant manager in a retail store where the sales team was not making its numbers. In retailing, as in many organizations, people often stick to one tactic that works for them until forced to change it.

> No one could think of ideas to bring to the table to change our style, so I had each associate pick two or three stores in the mall to observe. I wanted to inspire and challenge the team by getting them to pay close attention to how those associates were selling their products and bring back new ideas to share together. They went everywhere from the Gap, a mid-level nonaggressive brand focused on customer satisfaction, to Louis Vuitton, a commission-based luxury retailer that is all about making the sale. Once they all came back and gathered their information, they were able to think outside the box and see that what makes other people successful can work for them, too. These new selling techniques helped our team break out of their rut and get back on track.

As Courtney went on to explain: "If you only speak to those around you and do not go out of your way to see new perspectives, you will never come up with anything new. New things are challenging and exciting, and it takes going out of your comfort zone to see that."

Leaders understand that innovation requires more listening and greater communication than routine work. Successful innovations don't spring from the fifty-second floor of the headquarters building or the back offices of city hall. You need to establish relationships, network, make connections, and be out and about.

**Listen to and Promote Diverse Perspectives** Demand for change will come from both inside and outside your organization. If everything worked perfectly, there might not be any urgency to do things differently. But the truth is that if the aspirations are to get or be better, then some things will have to be done differently. Standard operating practices keep things going the way they are but are often not well suited for dealing with turbulence, uncertainty, pandemics, or mandates for better results.

In the beginning of his career as a financial analyst for an international financial services company, Luis Zaveleta told us how they trained him in the SOPs (standard operating procedures), which he was expected to follow. Some of his duties dealt with daily, weekly, and monthly reports that were suited to the use of SOP, "but the rest of my duties involved more creative thinking." As he gained experience and developed more managerial skills on the job, he began to question how the work was being done: "I started by asking the more experienced workers and my manager the reason behind the usage of the SOP to solve every problem within the department. I soon learned the reason of the heavy usage of SOPs was none other than the lack of alternatives. Every employee in the last ten years was taught how to do their jobs using the SOP and nobody ever thought to update it or even use a different method to solve a problem."

Luis went on to say that he felt "a leader needs to be brave enough to go against the tide in order to improve a process," he also realized that he needed to know the limitations of his knowledge and be open to exploring ideas and experiences from those around him. So he talked with his colleagues, co-workers, managers from different departments, and a few directors to get their input. What turned out to be the best advice, he said, came from an unlikely source, a co-worker who at the time was working as a teller for one of the local branches. "Knowing that ideas can come from anybody allows a leader never to miss an opportunity for innovation," Luis told us. "In my example, I asked everybody within the company about overcoming my challenge and I was open and receptive to ideas from outside my department." Luis's lesson applies to a host of other challenges and is especially relevant when the challenge is novel. During the COVID-19 pandemic, for example, people had to choose between following SOP and innovating. The normal way of doing business didn't work when organizations were locked down and employees worked from home. Leaders had to pivot and adopt entirely new ways of getting things done.

The receptivity to new ideas that Luis demonstrated is necessary for leaders to embrace to challenge the process effectively. You need to appreciate that one person may have a valid point of view about a problem, but individuals from different backgrounds can offer diverse views on the same problem. The extra information and varied perspectives can help you formulate better answers and improve outdated systems. Successful leaders need to encourage the sharing of information from all stakeholders, be receptive to different ideas no matter the source, and use the collective knowledge to develop an effective solution to any challenge. Significant developments in consumer tastes, employee expectations, and stakeholder needs can be missed or ignored without looking beyond current ways of doing business. Leaders must become more inclusive in their search for needs, trends, and opportunities to remain relevant and effective.

Researchers find that unless people actively encourage external communication and seek diverse points of view, they tend to interact with outsiders less and less frequently, and subsequently find themselves cut off from new ideas. Classic research studies examined the relationships between how long people worked together in a specific project area, their interpersonal oral communications, and technical performance.[20] They found that the higher-performing groups had significantly more communication with people outside their labs, whether with organizational units, such as marketing and manufacturing, or outside professional associations. Intriguingly, the groups that had been together for the longest time reported the least amount of external communications, which isolated them from technological advances and ideas from other organizational divisions.[21] The long-lived teams cut themselves off from the information they needed the most to come up with new ideas, thus reducing their performance over time. They'd been together so long, it appears, that they felt they didn't need to talk to outsiders; they were content just to speak to each other.

One reason that people are often afraid to ask around for advice and input from others is because they believe that doing so means, or at least implies, that they're incompetent or don't know something that they should. These fears are misplaced. Studies show that people perceive those who seek advice as more competent than those who do not seek advice and this belief is even stronger when the task is difficult than when it is easy.[22] You can enhance people's opinions about your competence by asking questions and seeking advice from those who know what they are talking about. For one thing, doing so makes that other person feel affirmed. Consequently, when you have a particularly perplexing problem, don't hesitate to talk about it with someone who has dealt with similar situations. There is a good chance they will think more of you afterward!

Open yourself up to new information by taking on multiple perspectives. For example, take the perspective of someone who frustrates or irritates you and consider what that person might have to teach you. Listen to learn, rather than to change their perspective. Furthermore, seek out the opinions of people beyond your comfort zone, folks you don't typically talk with. Another strategy is making associations through analogies; for example, forcing comparisons between your organization and another.[23] Consider how you might stir the imagination of your colleagues by discussing with them: "How would Google manage our data?" "How would FedEx redesign our logistics system?" "How would Toyota alter our production system?" "How would Sephora change our customer loyalty program?" or "How would Salesforce go about making us a 'best company' to work for?"

Asking questions and seeking the advice of others naturally leads to knowledge sharing across an organization. This inquisitiveness also strengthens interpersonal relationships. It is imperative that you listen to the world outside and ask good questions. You never know where a great idea will come from.

**Treat Every Job as an Adventure** When we asked people to tell us who initiated the projects described in their personal-best leadership experiences, we assumed that the majority would name themselves. That's not what we found. Someone other than the leader—usually the person's immediate manager—initiated more than half the cases. At first, this caught us by surprise, until we realized that people are assigned much of the work they do. That's just a fact of organizational life; few get to start everything they do from scratch. Whether the project is self-initiated or assigned is not the important variable. What matters is how those on the receiving end view the assignment. They could see it as just another job—a task to complete—or they could see it as an adventure—a possibility of making something extraordinary happen. Hands-down, exemplary leaders choose adventure.

It's not critical whether you find the challenges or they find you. What is important are the choices you make. What's important is the purpose you find for challenging the way things are. The question is this: When opportunity knocks, are you prepared? Are you ready to open the door, go outside, and pursue an opportunity? The real magic in sustainability, e-commerce, lean manufacturing, big data, social media marketing, agile development programs, hybrid work, and the like is mostly about a dedication to getting everyone involved in making routine work more challenging and more meaningful.

Even if you've been in your job for years, treat today as if it were your first day. Ask yourself, "If I were just starting this job, what would I do?" Begin doing those things now. Always stay alert to ways to improve your organization. Identify those projects that you've always wanted to undertake but never have. Ask your team members to do the same.

Be an adventurer, an explorer. Where in your organization have you not been? Where in the communities that you serve have you not been? Make plans to explore those places. Take a field trip to a factory, a warehouse, a distribution center, or a retail store. Visit with people in a function, department, location, or even client base that intrigues you. See how customers are treated when you become a "mystery shopper," or call your customer service department and learn how responsive they are, or consider taking on a job of someone on the frontlines to experience what it's like to do that job.

You don't have to be at the top of the organization to learn about what's going on around you. Be on the lookout for new ideas, wherever you are. If you're serious about promoting innovation and getting others to listen to people outside the unit, make gathering new ideas a personal priority. Encourage others to open their eyes and ears to the world outside the organization's boundaries. Collect ideas through focus groups, advisory boards, suggestion boxes, breakfast meetings, brainstorming sessions, customer evaluation forms, secret shoppers, mystery guests, visits to competitors, and the like. Online chat rooms are great venues for swapping ideas with those outside your field. Invite customers, suppliers, folks from other departments, and clients to your meetings to offer their suggestions on how your unit can improve.

Make idea-gathering part of your daily, weekly, and monthly schedule. Call three customers or clients who haven't used your services in a while or who have made recent purchases, and ask them why. Sure, there's email, but the human voice is better for this sort of thing. Work the front counter and ask people what they like and dislike about your organization. Shop at a competitor's store or, better yet, shop anonymously for one of your organization's products and see what the salespeople in the store say about it. Dial your workplace and listen to how people answer telephone calls and handle questions. Devote at least one-fourth of every weekly staff meeting to gather ideas for improving processes and technologies and developing new products and services.

These methods will keep your eyes and ears open to new ideas. You can never tell where or when you might find new ideas. Remain receptive and expose yourself to broader views. Be willing to hear, consider, and accept ideas from sources outside the company. If you never turn your back on what is happening outside the boundaries of your organization, the waves of change that roll in won't catch you by surprise.

## TAKE ACTION:
## Search for Opportunities

Leaders dedicated to making extraordinary things happen are open to receiving ideas from anyone and anywhere. They are adept at using their outsight to survey the landscape of technology, politics, economics, demographics, art, religion, and society in search of new ideas. They are prepared to search for opportunities to address the constant shifts in their environment. They seize the initiative and address the changes they see. Moreover, because they are proactive, they don't just ride the waves of change; they make the waves that others ride.

You don't have to change history, but you do have to change business-as-usual thinking. You have to be proactive, continually inviting and creating new initiatives. Be on the lookout for anything that lulls you or your colleagues into a false sense of security. Change, innovation, and leadership are nearly synonymous. This means that your focus is less on the routine operations and much more on the untested and untried. Keep in mind that the most innovative ideas are often not your own nor from your organization. They're elsewhere, and the best leaders look all around them for the places in which breakthrough ideas are hiding. They ask questions and seek advice. Exemplary leadership requires outsight, not just insight.

The quest for change is an adventure. It tests your will and your skill. It's tough, but it's also stimulating. Adversity introduces you to yourself. To get the best from yourself and others, you must understand what gives meaning and purpose to your work.

*(continued)*

To Challenge the Process, you must *search for opportunities by seizing the initiative and looking outward for innovative ways to improve*. You can apply this essential behavior by:

- Beginning each weekly meeting with your team with this question: "What action did you take last week to make your performance even better this week?"
- Volunteering for a tough assignment in your workplace or your community. Be proactive in looking for chances to stretch yourself and learn something.
- Shopping for ideas. Visit a local organization other than one like your own—anything from a restaurant to a machine shop to a hospital to an educational institution. Don't come back until you see one thing that the business does very well and that your organization could adapt.

In addition, use your interactions with others as an opportunity to talk with people and direct their attention to aspects of leadership that you think are important to focus on. Converse with them about these questions:

- If you were our strongest competitor, what would you do to put us out of business?
- What's one surprising fact or trend that you recently heard about or learned, and what are the implications for our business/organization?

## CHAPTER 7

# Experiment and Take Risks

*Leaders are not afraid to take risks*
*and step outside their comfort zones.*

*Chris Hintz*

**YOU NEVER KNOW** where or when the opportunity for leadership will arise. Indeed, this was the case for Jenna Wingate, zookeeper at a midwestern zoo and botanical garden. When one of her colleagues decided to create a local chapter of the American Association of Zoo Keepers (AAZK), Jenna was right beside her. They needed to recruit members from their fellow animal care workers, but they were also required to participate in the national organization's annual fundraising event, "Bowling for Rhinos." It was here that Jenna stepped up and provided leadership in helping her newly formed chapter make a measurable and lasting impact.

Jenna jumped into the fundraising event with great excitement, although she was neither a formal event planner nor an experienced fundraiser. With the number of nonprofit organizations seeking sponsorships and funding (almost all utilizing professional fundraisers), she knew her team's approach had to be distinctively different. "The whole thing was mostly a 'figure it out as you go' endeavor," Jenna explained. Her colleagues suggested several ideas for raising money and how to attract sponsors and donors. But they had no way of knowing in advance if any of them would work. For example, they decided to create different sponsorship levels—ranging from a company name and logo on a T-shirt to personalized tours with animals at the zoo. "We had no idea," Jenna said, "if we were appropriately matching the donation amount with the benefit. We just agreed to experiment, learn, and move forward."

They realized they had to do something other than simply send out generic email announcements and add postings on social media to promote the event. They organized happy hours for their colleagues, where people could socialize and talk with them about the importance of the fundraiser. Then, Jenna said, they would recruit volunteers, and "we would head out in small groups, literally cold-calling small businesses, restaurants, and 'mom-and-pops.' It was always scary and awkward asking for money but doing it in these small groups really helped us get after it."

Jenna and her colleagues tried a lot of things. Some ideas worked out, and some didn't. However, as she reflected, "We just learned from the mistakes and missteps and then tried something else. Although it is funny now, we learned from our first bake sale not to sell desserts outside in the summer heat of July. Icing melts."

Several risks were inherent in this first-time fundraising event, not the least of which was whether they could actually get people to donate, mainly because the chapter wasn't allowed to solicit from any of the zoo's current donors. Jenna looked outside the organization's philanthropic foundations and community benefactors. For example, she reached out to various contractors working at the zoo, who reached out to their subcontractors, who reached out to their friends. Another risk was how high to set their fundraising goal. In fact, the chapter president thought they were initially being too ambitious. And for Jenna herself, if this event was not successful, she worried about how she would be viewed in her day job with the zoo. Yet the potential payoff was always worth the risks because she felt their efforts were going to such a good cause.

Across the entire AAZK network, it usually took about six years for established chapters to hit $2,000 in funding for Bowling for Rhinos.

In their first year, Jenna's chapter raised $9,000, and within five years, through silent auctions, merchandise sales, and raffles, they increased this amount to $35,000. This was the largest contribution from any chapter, including those from much bigger zoos such as St. Louis, San Diego, and the Bronx. Much of this success occurred because of Jenna's genuinely new ways of thinking about what Bowling for Rhinos could be.

To achieve the extraordinary, you must be willing, like Jenna, to do things that have never been done before. You must take the initiative and then persevere. Leadership is not about maintaining the status quo or doing what everyone else is doing. Every Personal-Best Leadership Experience case speaks to the need to take risks with bold ideas. You can't achieve anything new or extraordinary by doing things the way you've always done them. You have to test unproven strategies. You have to break out of the norms that box you in, venture beyond the limitations you usually place on yourself and others, try new things, and take chances.

Leaders must take this one step further by getting others to join them on these adventures in uncertainty. It's one thing to set off alone into the unknown; it's entirely another to get others to follow you into the darkness. The difference between an exemplary leader and an individual risk-taker is that leaders create the conditions where people *want* to join in the adventure.

Leaders make risk safe. They turn experiments into learning opportunities. They don't define boldness as primarily go-for-broke, giant-leap projects. More often, they see change as starting small, using pilot projects, and gaining momentum. The vision may be grand and distant, but the way to reach it is by putting one foot in front of the other. These small, visible steps are more likely to win early victories and gain early supporters. Of course, when you experiment, not everything works out as intended. There are mistakes and false starts. However, what's critical is that leaders promote learning from and building upon these experiences.

Exemplary leaders commit to *Experiment and Take Risks*. They know that making extraordinary things happen requires that leaders

- **Generate small wins**
- **Learn from experience**

These essentials can help leaders transform challenge into an exploration, uncertainty into a sense of adventure, fear into resolve, and risk into reward. They are the keys to making progress that becomes unstoppable.

## Generate Small Wins

*We broke the project down into small pieces.*
*This helped to increase our focus, making sure that*
*everyone knew what their responsibility was.*

*Abey Mukkanachery*

An African proverb advises, "Never test the depth of the water with both feet." Wise counsel whenever you're trying something brand new. Leaders should dream big but start small, which is what Gary Jamieson did in personal-best leadership experience while at a multinational networking company:

> At the start of the project, there was this general belief that it could never be completed. It was important to prove to the team early in the project that it could be achieved. To do so, I structured the project so that key early milestones had significant and distinct deliverables that could be seen as clear achievements under difficult circumstances. Making these early milestones gave the team members confidence in their ability to deliver. I then ensured that intermediate milestones were announced as small achievements within the larger project and demonstrated the benefits of achieving the milestone. This helped to build not only excitement but also momentum.

To get people to do things they have never done before, you make progress incrementally. You move step by step, creating a sense of forward momentum by generating *small wins*. A small win is "a concrete, complete, implemented outcome of moderate importance."[1] It identifies a place to begin. Small wins make the project seem doable and within the parameters of existing skills and resources. They minimize the cost of trying and reduce the risks of failing. What's exciting about this process is that once people achieve a small win, it sets in motion natural forces that favor progress over setbacks. Planting one tree won't stop global warming, but planting one million trees can make a difference. It's that first tree that gets things started. While Google's "moonshot" factory is inspiring and ambitious and gets most of the publicity, the less-talked-about route to many of Google's innovations is small wins—the consistent, short-term, and incremental "roof shots" that make their products better year after year.[2] Similarly, when writing, if we thought about achievement as only setting a target of producing 90,000 words, it would make the project extremely daunting. Breaking it into chunks of 500 words, or two pages, and then achieving that in a few hours or a day makes it feel much more doable—and worth celebrating.

Figure 7.1 shows that the percentage of direct reports who strongly agree that their leader is effective increases dramatically with the extent to which they observe that individual utilizing the process of small wins by "identifying measurable milestones that keep projects moving forward." Key engagement factors for direct reports show similar relationships. For example, when their leaders are very frequently/almost always employing the process of small wins, nearly nine out of ten of their direct reports strongly agree that they are clear about what is expected of them, effective in meeting the demands of their jobs, and highly productive in their jobs.

The scientific community has always understood that major breakthroughs result from the work of hundreds of researchers, as countless contributions finally begin to add up to a solution. Its been shown that all the "little" improvements in technology, regardless of the industry, have contributed to a greater increase in organizational productivity than all the great inventors and their inventions.[3] Rapid prototyping, and plenty of it, brings higher-quality products more quickly to the marketplace.[4] In fact, studies across multiple occupations and disciplines generally find that people, when challenged, come up with more ideas than they initially give themselves credit for being able to do.[5]

**Figure 7.1 Using the Small-Wins Process Increases Leadership Effectiveness Ratings by Direct Reports**

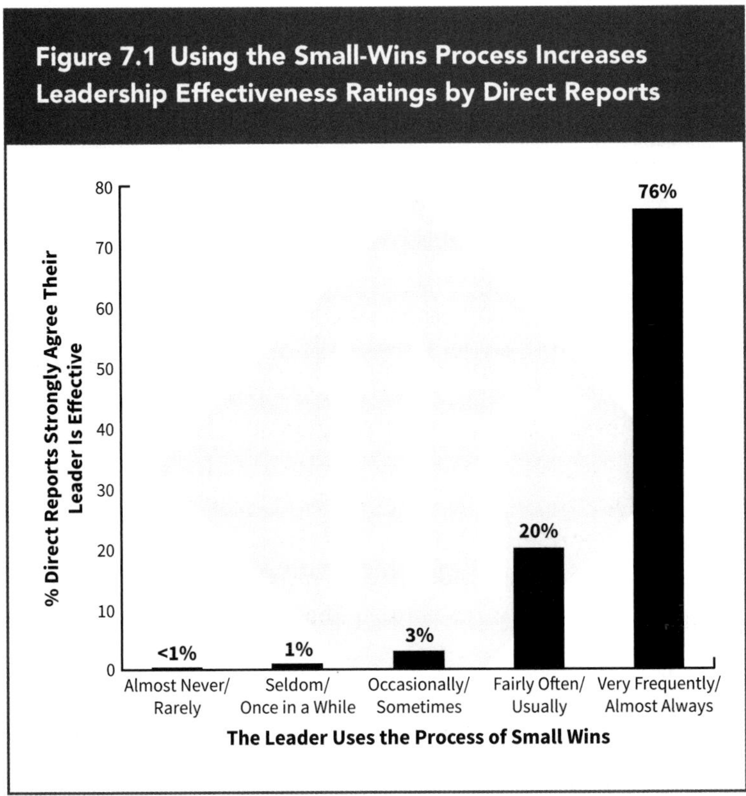


Extensive investigations demonstrate that the key to motivating performance is supporting progress in meaningful work. Big wins are great but relatively rare and small, incremental, and consistent steps forward have a significant impact on people's motivation. Researchers analyzed nearly 12,000 questionnaires and diary entrees from employees across seven companies and they found that "even when progress happens in small steps, a person's sense of forward movement toward an important goal can make all the difference between a great day and a terrible one."[6] Our data backs these results up, showing a positive relationship between the extent to which leaders "identify measurable milestones that keep projects moving forward" and the clarity around job expectations reported by their direct reports, as well as their levels of motivation and commitment to the success of their organization. When people don't feel overwhelmed by a task, their energy goes into getting the job done instead of wondering, "How will we ever solve that problem?"

In a similar vein, it is easier to do something small, then build up to something big. If your aspirations are to do something extraordinary, get started by doing some small things and set progressively larger targets as you move forward. Breaking initiatives into smaller wins was how Hong Lu, manager of test development engineering, said she "kept the team focused on what they could control in their work. It made it safe for people to experiment and take risks by promoting learning from experience, debriefing successes and failures, capturing lessons learned, and disseminating them broadly." Just as Gary and Hong did, ask yourself at the beginning of a big project, "What are the early milestones that have significant and distinct deliverables and will signal that we've made meaningful progress?" Communicate those clearly to your team and then celebrate your progress regularly. In finding all the small ways that people can succeed at doing things differently, exemplary leaders make people want to both be involved and stay involved.

**Build Psychological Hardiness** Problems presented too broadly or too expansively can appear daunting and suffocate people's capacity to conceive of what they can do in the future, let alone right now. Leaders face this dilemma because they want people to reach for great heights but not become fearful of falling. They want people to feel challenged but not overwhelmed, curious but not lost, excited but not stressed. Small wins consistently show up in personal-best leadership experiences as people use this process to generate enthusiasm, energy, and extraordinary performance despite difficult and stressful circumstances.

Psychologists have discovered that people who experience high degrees of stress and yet cope with it positively have a distinctive attitude, one they call "psychological hardiness."[7] Whether corporate managers, entrepreneurs, students, nurses, lawyers, or combat soldiers, people with high psychological hardiness are much more likely to cope with severe challenges and bounce back from failure than those with low hardiness.[8] Hardiness is a quality that people can learn and that leaders can support.

There are three critical factors to building psychological hardiness: *commitment, control,* and *challenge*. To turn adversity into an advantage, you first need to commit yourself to what's happening. You must become involved, engaged, and curious. You can't sit back and wait for something to happen. You also must take control of your life. You need to strive to influence what is going on. Even if it's unlikely that all your attempts will be successful, you can't sink into passivity. Finally, you need to view challenge as an opportunity to learn from negative and positive experiences.

The actions by Maureen Collins illustrate how the hardiness principles are applied when her team faced the severe emotional and physical health crises brought on by the COVID-19 pandemic. While the methodical and measured approaches of continuous improvement are common in healthcare organizations, not much was methodical or measured about the impact of COVID-19 on every nurse and every hospitalized patient and their family members. For example, while isolating patients was not a new procedure, isolation was much different during the pandemic. Because of the unknown transmission route and the highly contagious nature of the virus, maximum isolation was put into effect. Total isolation for patients meant no family and friends could visit a family member, and there was as little contact with nurses and the care team as necessary. That meant nurses were the closest to patients for the most prolonged periods during COVID-19. They instantly became the lifeline for the patient in providing life-sustaining care and, as surrogates for absent spouses, siblings, and children, a lifeline for soul-sustaining care. Maureen quickly realized that this new form of "isolation" must be addressed and remedied so that patients and families could still be connected during the scariest and most tragic time of their lives.

Maureen reminded her team that nurses care for the patient in the bed and those who love them who might not be physically present. The impact was significant because parents are part of the patient and healthcare team dyad. They play a critical role in infant and child support, security, safety, and care delivery. Parents not being present with their children created a psychosocial issue and a patient safety risk. This was intolerable to the team despite fears about the unknowns of COVID-19.

The nursing team identified the possibility of utilizing any device available that would offer visual connections to their patients. Options included iPads typically used for patient education, laptops used for medical record charting, and even the nursing staff's personal cell phones. Maureen listened intently to her team's suggestions, their thought process, and most importantly *why* they wanted to do it. Knowing this was bigger than just her unit, Maureen formally convened a task force, engaging her colleague from IT as their partner.

The entire hospital rallied in support of this task force. They knew their charge, were inspired by the opportunity to support patients and their families, and were appreciative of senior management's encouragement and approval. Committed to finding a solution, feeling in control of the problem, and up for the challenge, the task force created a virtual visitation and communication policy for all patients. The new approach included livestreaming, centralized device distribution, patient and family communication expectations, and the development of a communication champion for each clinical unit. The model was quickly recognized as a best practice exemplar and an interdepartmental model of excellence. The usually slow pace of change and innovation typical of this organization was nowhere in evidence.

As Maureen's experience demonstrates, your ability to cope with change and stress depends on your viewpoint. To start that new project and take that first step, you have to believe that you can influence the outcome. You have to be curious about whatever is happening and look for ways to learn every step of the way. With a hardy attitude, you can transform stressful events into positive opportunities for growth and renewal. What's more, you can help your team feel the same way.

**Break It Down and Accentuate Progress** Leaders appreciate that they have to break down big problems into small, doable actions. They also know that when initiating something new, they have to try many little things before they get it right. Not every innovation works, and the best way to ensure success is to experiment with many ideas, not just one or two big ones. Exemplary leaders help others see how breaking the journey down into measurable milestones moves them forward and promotes continued progress.

This is exactly how Venkat Dokiparthi led a technical development team in India. Improvements were needed in the product, and he asked the team to come up with ideas about how to go about it. Several weeks went by, with the only response being that this task was "beyond their scope." Venkat realized that he needed to break down the task and make it simple for members of the team to feel successful:

> I divided the task into a ten-week program and asked them to try the first week's assignment. The task for that week was now so clear to them, and so much within their capabilities, that they actually implemented it within three days. So I encouraged them to start on the following week's assignment. They showed considerable progress and in fact completed the entire implementation process in six weeks! Initiating incremental steps and encouraging small wins has really been the key to success of this task.

A small-wins approach fits especially well with the nature of work in volatile, uncertain, and complex times. Once you've set your sights, move forward incrementally. Provide orientation and training at the start. Make sure you include a few early successes. Assigning tasks that team members are unequipped to handle is like sending a group of novices to the top of the expert ski slope. Instead, let people start on the beginner's slope and work their way up to the advanced. Identify a doable project that people initially feel that they can accomplish with existing skills and resources.

That's just what Rayona Sharpnack did when she was coaching her eight-year-old daughter's softball team. On one of the first days of practice, she had everyone try to do some batting. She tossed a soft, spongy ball to the first girl, who was standing maybe 10 feet away. Rayona was throwing baby tosses, but the girl screamed and hid her head. So Rayona said, "Hey, no problem, Suzy. Go to the back of the line. That's fine. Betsy, you step up." But Betsy did the same thing—buried her head and screamed. Rayona realized that she needed to do something different. She went out to her car and retrieved some whiteboard markers from her briefcase. She used the markers to make smiley faces—red, black, blue, and green—on each ball. Now, when the kids looked at a ball, they would see a smiley face. She called the girls back over and told them, "Okay, we're going to play a different game. This time, your job is to name the color of the smiley face. That's all you have to do."

So they started all over again. Rayona tossed a ball by Suzy, who watched it all the way and said, "Red." Then Betsy went up and said, "Green." All the girls started yelling with excitement because they could identify the color of the smiley faces. Rayona said, "Okay. Now I want you to do the same thing, only this time I want you to hold the bat on your shoulder when the ball goes by." The same level of success. Excitement continued to build. The third time through, she asked them to touch the smiley face with the bat. In the girls' first game, they beat their opponents 27 to 1.[9]

Personal-best leadership experiences were achieved step by step, not in a single leap. While there is a very real human tendency to focus on the negative, you need to concentrate on progress—not on the gap between aspirations and reality, but on how much you have advanced. Negativity can quickly become pervasive and contagious, stifling performance. Appreciate that there are outside influences affecting the situation, many of which you had no control over. Reframe the outcome, emphasizing what people are accomplishing and learning.

Leaders who emphasize the positive are not just getting themselves and their constituents to learn and succeed in future undertakings. Research also shows that people who can maintain a positive outlook are more creative and innovative because they don't wallow in setbacks and disappointments. They continue to be open to new possibilities. On a personal level, they have lower rates of depression and cardiovascular disease and hence live longer.[10]

Exemplary leaders accept reality, but they do not readily accept defeat, nor do they become consumed by self-pity and grief. They regroup, reassess, and prepare to go forward.[11] They inspire others by sharing their determination to beat the odds. To turn setbacks into an advantage, you have to have a positive outlook and commit to learning from experience. By learning from experience and focusing on the positive, the same mistakes won't likely happen again, and you and your colleagues will be better prepared for the next challenge or opportunity.

## Learn from Experience

*We worked to understand the failure*
*and how to improve and prevent it in the future.*
*William Yuen*

Whenever you challenge the status quo, and experiment with innovative ways of doing things, you will sometimes fail. Despite how clearly you see challenge as an opportunity, how focused you can be, or how driven you are to succeed, there will be setbacks. When you engage in something new and different, you make mistakes. That's what experimentation is all about, and, as scientists know very well, there's a lot of trial and error involved in testing new concepts, new methods, and new practices.

According to their direct reports, the most effective leaders, as shown in Figure 7.2, are the ones who ask, "What can we learn when things don't go as expected?" rather than pointing fingers or assigning blame. The effectiveness ratings of their leaders increase dramatically with their use of this leadership behavior. In addition, the more leaders focus on learning from experience, the more their direct reports indicate that they are personally effective in their jobs. Less than three direct reports out of one hundred strongly agree that they are personally effective when their leader rarely asks, "What can we learn?" and that percentage is still less than 10 percent when their leaders only "sometimes" ask this question.

Additionally, nearly ten times the number of direct reports feel that the organization values their work when their leader frequently employs this leadership behavior than do those who report their leader rarely considers this question.

Figure 7.2 Asking "What Can We Learn?" Increases Direct Reports' Ratings of Their Leader's Effectiveness

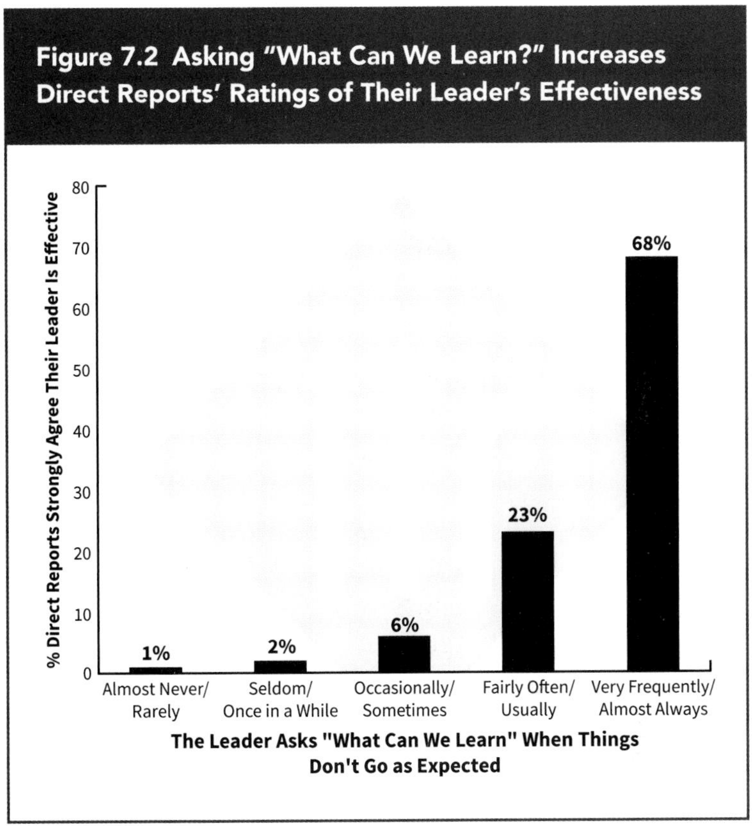


Repeatedly, people in our studies tell us how mistakes and failure have been crucial to their success, both personally and professionally. Without mistakes, they wouldn't know what they can and cannot do (at least at the moment). Without the occasional failure, respondents said, they would not have achieved their aspirations. It may seem paradoxical, but many echo the thought that the overall quality of work improves when people have a chance to fail. This was precisely the lesson from one high school ceramics teacher's experiment.

At the beginning of the semester, the teacher divided the students into two groups. The first group was told they could earn better grades by producing more pots (e.g., thirty for a B, forty for an A), regardless of the quality. The second group was told that their grades depended solely on the quality of the pots they produced. Not surprisingly, students in the first group got right to it, producing as many pots as possible, while the second group was quite careful and deliberate in how they went about making the best pots. The teacher was surprised to find that the students who made the most pots—those graded on quantity rather than quality—also made the best ones. It turned out that the practice of making lots of pots naturally resulted in better quality; for example, these students became more familiar with the intricacies of the kiln and how various firing positions affected the aesthetics of their products.[12]

In the ceramics teacher's experiment, the students who failed the most were the ones who succeeded the most, which is entirely consistent with other studies of the innovation process. For example, a study of NASA's space shuttle program employees concluded that they learned more from their failures than successes and retained those lessons more thoroughly in subsequent projects.[13] As this and other studies of the innovation process show, success does not breed success. It breeds failure. It is failure that breeds success. Failure is never the objective of any endeavor, of course. Success, however, always requires some amount of learning, and in turn, learning always involves miscalculations, mistakes, and errors.

**Be an Active Learner** Curious about the relationship between leadership and learning, we conducted a series of studies to determine if the range and depth of learning tactics affected leadership behavior. We investigated how engaged leaders were in learning, appreciating that people have various preferences regarding how they go about learning. We found that people most engaged in learning make the most frequent use of The Five Practices of Exemplary Leadership, regardless of their preferred learning style.[14] Leaders with a learning orientation are readier to embrace the ambiguity, complexity, and paradigm shifts that go along with experimentation and leadership.[15]

Consider what one leader we interviewed told us after taking his first skiing lesson. He reported to the instructor that after his lesson he had skied the rest of the day and hadn't fallen down once. He was stunned when the ski instructor replied, "Personally, I think you had a lousy day. If you're not falling, you're not learning." That ski instructor understood that if you can stand up on your skis all day long the first time out, you're doing only what you already know how to do, not pushing yourself to try anything new or more difficult. If your objective is to stay upright, you aren't going to improve yourself, because when you try to do something you don't know how to do, you'll fall. That's guaranteed, as anyone who has ever learned to ski knows very well.

When mistakes are made in the name of innovation, trying new things, or pushing one's limits, leaders don't look to blame or punish. Instead, they ask, "What can be learned from the experience?" Whether tracking your own performance or that of a new product, process, or service, these curves invariably show performance going down before it goes up. That's exactly the shape of learning curves: they go down before they go up. Learning doesn't take place in the absence of trial and error. Moreover, researchers find that allowing people an opportunity to experiment increases their motivational levels.[16] These studies support our data, which shows that the more frequently leaders challenge people to "try out new and innovative ways to do their work," the more willing direct reports indicate they are to "work harder and longer hours if the job demanded it."

We've discovered that leaders are simply great learners. They have, to begin with, a great sense of humility about their own sense of skills and abilities. Many leaders, despite what seems like objectively "extraordinary" achievements, are loath to attribute them to some extraordinary competency on their part. Think about who the most likely people in your organization are to voluntarily sign up and participate in leadership development programs. Chances are those people are already high, rather than low, on this set of abilities as demonstrated by their track record. Similarly, church services are populated not by sinners seeking redemption but by ordinary souls who know that life is full of struggles, temptations, and challenges.

The only way that people can learn is by doing things they've never done before. If you only do what you already know how to do, then you'll never learn anything new. Promoting learning requires developing a tolerance for error and a framework for forgiveness. One lesson high-tech executive Joe Hage took away from his personal-best was that "learning requires tolerating people who make mistakes, and it requires tolerating some inefficiencies and failures. Learning requires letting people try things they've never done before; things that they probably won't be all that good at the first time around." Showing others that you are interested in their learning means accepting the necessary tradeoff between gaining proficiency and achieving results.

Learning is the master skill, and it is an important predictor of future success in new and different managerial jobs. When you fully engage in learning—when you throw yourself wholeheartedly into experimenting, reflecting, reading, or receiving coaching—you are going to experience the thrill of improvement and the taste of success. More is more when it comes to learning. Exemplary leaders approach each new and unfamiliar experience with a willingness to learn and an appreciation for the importance of learning, as well as the recognition that learning inevitably involves making some mistakes. Baseball's home run champion Hank Aaron shared this same perspective: "My motto was always to keep swinging. Whether I was in a slump or feeling badly or having trouble off the field, the only thing to do was keep swinging."[17] *Harry Potter* author J. K. Rowling's viewpoint is similar: "It is impossible to live without failing at something, unless you live so cautiously that you might as well not have lived at all, in which case you have failed by default."[18] Studies of entrepreneurs find that those who tried and subsequently abandoned self-employment (or the entrepreneurial life) do better financially than salaried employees who don't have this "failure" experience in their career portfolio.[19]

You need to heed these lessons. History will not judge you harshly for your failures if you learn from them, but it will be unkind if you fail to try, if you stop swinging, or live too cautiously. Those who have left the most lasting legacies are those who have made mistakes, failed, but then tried again. That final try makes all the difference. Regardless of the field, there is no success without the possibility of failure.[20]

Building your capacity to be an active learner begins with what psychologists refer to as having a *growth mindset,* which "is based on the belief that your basic qualities are things you can cultivate through your efforts." This viewpoint contrasts with a *fixed mindset,* which assumes "that your qualities are carved in stone."[21] Individuals with a growth mindset believe that people can learn to be better leaders. Those with a fixed mindset think that leaders are born, not made, and that no amount of training will make you any better than you naturally or already are. Studies have shown that individuals with a fixed mindset working on simulated business problems give up more quickly and perform more poorly than those with a growth mindset. The same applies to kids in school, athletes on the playing field, teachers in the classroom, and even partners in relationships.[22] In our studies, those with a growth mindset were more willing than those with a fixed mindset to embrace challenges, persist when facing obstacles, and sustain efforts even when confronted with resistance. Believing that people can change and grow, growth-minded individuals were willing to foster innovation and focus on learning from setbacks. They displayed a propensity to support experimentation by others. In contrast, people with a fixed mindset tend to avoid challenging situations and are generally not interested in opening themselves up to feedback of any sort.[23] Your mindset, more than your skill set, makes the critical difference in deciding whether to take on challenging situations.

To develop a growth mindset and to nourish it in others, you need to embrace the notion that challenge is the catalyst for learning. When you encounter setbacks—and there will be many—you must persist. You must realize that your effort, and that of others, is your means of gaining mastery. Neither raw talent nor good fortune leads to becoming the best; hard work is what gets you there.[24] When you believe that you can continuously learn, you will. Only those who believe that they can get better will make the effort to do so.

**Create a Climate for Learning** It's an interesting paradox that for people to take a risk, they first must feel safe. Fear inhibits risk-taking, stepping outside the boundaries, and challenging authority. Fear also impedes judgment, limits creativity, and hampers problem-solving. People need to feel a sense of "psychological safety" if they are going to freely speak up, ask probing questions, challenge convention, and offer contrary views. Without feeling sufficiently safe, people will be unwilling, even unable, to experiment, take risks, and learn.[25] Researchers find that only three in ten employees strongly agree that their opinions count at work and they calculate that doubling this ratio would result in significantly less turnover and higher productivity.[26]

The concept of "psychological safety" is not a personality factor but rather a workplace characteristic.[27] Psychological safety exists in an environment where mutual trust and respect nurtures candor and a sense of obligation to communicate when there are disagreements, as well as opportunities. It exists where people believe that if they make a mistake, or ask for help, their colleagues will not think less of them, pick them apart, ridicule or punish them. Without these feelings, people will be reluctant to venture outside of their comfort zones, share information, or even ask for help. People will remain silent even when they believe they have something to say that has the potential to add value.

Studies of top performers strongly indicate that a supportive environment is required if people are to become the best they can be. One study involving more than 20,000 people around the world indicated that when they felt safe, there was a 347 percent increase in the probability of highly engaged employees, a 154 percent increase in great work, and a 33 percent decrease in moderate to severe burnout.[28] When high-quality relationships exist in the workplace, people engage in more learning behaviors. A climate that supports collaborative action is going to be more hospitable to the development of leaders than one that is internally competitive and focuses on a winner-take-all approach to selecting and promoting people.

The notion that "mistakes are few in great workplaces" is a myth. The best workplaces have *more*, not fewer, mistakes; and the reason for this is because people feel more secure and safe in taking ownership and responsibility for their mistakes.[29] For example, in looking at the performance of nursing units, studies have found that the units with the best relationships between leaders and co-workers reported the greatest number of mistakes (e.g., drug treatment errors). This was not because they were less effective; instead, in these units people were more willing to acknowledge a mistake when it happened and then figure out how to ensure that same mistake never again occurred.[30] Mistakes are the pathway to great ideas and innovation, and with the support of their leader, people are set up to learn (rather than set up to fail) from experimenting and venturing outside of their comfort zones.

Organizations serious about creating a climate for learning provide a variety of systematic opportunities to do so. These include formal and informal opportunities for development such as classroom-based learning programs, online learning options, external seminars, and mentoring and coaching. Rotational job assignments or special projects also challenge people to develop themselves. The corporate culture research and education company O. C. Tanner Institute finds, for example, that one of the six essential elements that define a thriving culture is the opportunity to experience personal and professional growth.[31]

In addition, organizations that encourage learning and innovation provide time for working on projects outside of formal responsibilities. Such environments nurture curiosity, an essential antecedent to thinking "outside the box." Studies reveal that being curious prepares the brain for learning. It makes learning a more gratifying experience by stimulating the brain circuits associated with reward and pleasure.[32] Having a strong sense of curiosity regarding what's happening around you is often the antecedent to sensing and understanding what's to come next.

Think about how you can have "curiosity conversations" with people inside and outside your organizational setting. You can begin with something like this: "I've always been curious about how you ended up as a [whatever that position or profession is], and I was wondering if you'd be willing to spend twenty minutes talking to me about what it took to get where you are and what the key turning points in your career were."[33] In that conversation, you can ask about a big challenge they faced in their careers, why they do something in a particular way, how they handled a tough leadership situation, or came up with a specific idea. There is no fixed set of questions. You have to tailor them to the person and situation, but questions, sparked by curiosity and with an underlying interest in learning, always get the conversation started.

Likewise, in your conversations with colleagues and in team meetings, ask questions that invite participation, especially from specific people who might not otherwise speak up (perhaps due to structural or cultural reasons). In asking questions, you create a space for other people to contribute their thinking. This conveys your interest in their perspective and respect for their opinions. Show a genuine interest in what others are saying by asking them to tell you more about their thinking and experiences: "Can you say more about that?" or "Can you give an example?" Show appreciation rather than judgment for people taking risks; for example, say, "Thank you for speaking up about this matter or option." Another strategy is to ask questions in a way that addresses what might be motivating people's reluctant silence and possible defensiveness. For example, don't ask, "What mistakes did people notice when we did XYZ?" Instead, consider reframing the question: "Did we do everything as well as we could have when we did XYZ?" Test for consensus rather than assuming that silence means agreement. Ask, "Who has a different perspective?" or "What might we not be taking into account?"

Creating a climate conducive to learning involves helping people to think realistically about what risk means to them.[34] Advances in brain imaging technology prove that people's brains are wired to overestimate risk, exaggerate its consequences, and underestimate their ability to handle it. Accordingly, fears about what people don't want to happen drive their choices more often than a commitment to what they wish to see; that is, they act to minimize potential losses rather than optimize wins. The personal-best leadership experience of Ryan Diemer, merchandise-planning manager with an online specialty retailer, affirms this viewpoint: "Taking risks is never easy and sometimes scary." However, he realized, "Taking risks is necessary because it requires you and those you are working with to challenge not only what you are working on but how you work. Sometimes the risks pay off and sometimes they do not, but what is always true is that if you do not take a risk, you won't get any gain." Nothing ventured, nothing gained!

People know that they don't always get it right the first time they try something and that learning new things can be a bit scary. They don't want to embarrass themselves in front of peers or look stupid in front of their managers. To create a climate for learning, you have to make it safe for others to be curious, ask questions, try, and fail with the ultimate objective of learning and growing from their experiences.

**Strengthen Resilience and Grit** Resilience, grit, and hardiness are mental, not physical, states. They have to do with how you view stress, disruption, uncertainly, ambiguity, and change in your life. People have overcome severe hardships throughout human history not because of physical prowess but because of "mental toughness." It takes determination and strength to deal with the adversities of life and leadership. You can't let the setbacks get you down or allow roadblocks to get in your way. You can't become overly discouraged when things don't go according to plan. You can't give up when resistance builds, or the competition gets stiff. Nor can you let other tempting new projects divert your interest or distract your focus. What's critical is how you respond to and cope with the inevitable mistakes, setbacks, failures, and accompanying stresses associated with leadership. It is more about bouncing forward than simply bouncing back. Researchers have found that highly resilient employees miss fewer workdays, report higher job satisfaction, stay on the job longer, and are in better health than those unable to cope effectively with stress caused by challenge and uncertainty.[35]

During the height of the 2020 coronavirus pandemic lockdown, it was evident that those who handled the crisis the best were examples of how resilient individuals respond to adversity.[36] They were able to maintain hope and find meaning and a larger purpose in the various individual changes required despite the unfortunate pain, loss, and suffering. They made a personal commitment to do something, even something very small, to take control of what they could. They volunteered to help others, shifted their small businesses to serve a need for food or equipment, picked up groceries for the most vulnerable, or found ways to express appreciation to caregivers and first responders.

A student of leadership throughout his career, basketball Hall-of-Famer and sports executive Pat Williams notes that the greatest leaders in history all faced tremendous obstacles and that they all should have given up about thirty times.[37] But they didn't. They had, according to Pat, "what Walt Disney called 'stick-to-it-ivity.' They've all battled through horribly tough times, and the reason we admire these leaders was because they didn't quit." In his fifty-plus years as a sports executive, Pat has had his fair share of wins and losses, and says, "I wouldn't be where I am today if I had not taken advantage of the disappointments and the setbacks. . . . Through those setbacks I've learned more, and made more advances, than through the good times."

Resilience is the capacity Pat describes—that ability to recover quickly from setbacks and continue to pursue a vision of the future—and similar to what psychologists call *grit*, which is "perseverance and passion for long-term goals."[38] Showing grit involves setting goals, being obsessed with an idea or project, maintaining focus, sticking with things that take a long time to complete, overcoming setbacks, and the like. Whether with kids in school, cadets in the military, working professionals, artists, academics, or others, there is convincing evidence that people with the most grit are the most likely to achieve positive outcomes. The more grit you demonstrate, the better you do.[39]

Resilience and grit can be developed and strengthened, much like hardiness and growth mindsets. According to researchers, people who don't give up have "a habit of interpreting setbacks as temporary, local, and changeable."[40] When a failure or setback occurs, they don't obsess with blaming themselves or the people working on the project. Instead, they consider situational circumstances that contributed to the failure and adopt the perspective that this particular situation is likely to be temporary, not permanent, emphasizing that a failure or setback is a problem in this one instance and not in every case. Even in times of high stress and extreme adversity, resilient people remain committed to moving forward by believing that what has happened will not be permanent and that they can do something about the outcome.

Breed a growth mindset when reaching milestones by attributing these wins to the hard work and effort of the individuals in the group. Convey a belief that many more victories are at hand and be optimistic that good fortune will be with your team for a long time. Bolster resilience by assigning tasks that are challenging but within people's skill level, focusing on rewards rather than punishments, and encouraging people to see change as full of possibilities.

Promote a sense of humility among your colleagues, and within team meetings, by focusing time and attention on what can be learned rather than simply on what didn't work and who might be to blame. Be willing to acknowledge your own fallibility and shortcomings. In her personal-best leadership experience, Dawn McCale, vice president of sales for an information technology company, found that at the onset of a new project, everyone was bogged down with negativity and a throng of "what-if's." She realized that "this was not getting us anywhere, and I steered the conversation and problem-solving approach to a positive vision around the possibilities of what we could do."

The Personal-Best Leadership Experience cases all involved change and stressful events in the lives of leaders, and nearly everyone described the experience in terms consistent with the conditions for psychological hardiness, resilience, and grit. They experienced commitment rather than alienation, control rather than powerlessness, and challenge rather than threat. They had passion. They were gritty and they persevered. They didn't give up despite the failures and setbacks. They showed that, even in the toughest of times, people can experience meaningfulness and mastery. They can overcome great odds, make progress, and change the way things are.

## TAKE ACTION

### Experiment and Take Risks

Change is the work of leaders. It's what they do. They are always looking for ways to improve, grow, and innovate. They know that the way things are done today won't get people to the tomorrow they envision, so they experiment, tinker, and shake things up. They ask, "Where can we experiment, and how can we improve?"

However, change can overwhelm, frighten, and immobilize some people. Exemplary leaders believe, and get others to believe, that change is a challenge they can successfully address and that individuals can control their life and influence outcomes. They make sure that everyone clearly understands the meaning and purpose of change, and they create a strong sense of commitment to the mission.

Using small wins to get things moving in the right direction, they break tasks down and set short-term goals. Taking a small-bets approach (e.g., setting up experiments, beta tests, pilot projects) gets people started, makes progress imaginable, builds commitment, and creates momentum.

Whenever you try new things, big or small, stuff happens that wasn't expected and, inevitably, mistakes and even failures occur. You never get it right the first time—and may not on the second or third try, either, which is why exemplary leaders create a climate that's conducive to learning. This means not punishing people for experimentation and risk-taking, and ensuring that people feel safe enough to learn from their experiences and pass those lessons forward. The truth is that the best leaders are the best learners. You need a growth mindset, believing that improvements happen when everyone puts in the effort to learn. You also need to create a learning climate—one in which people feel trusted, are encouraged to persist despite the odds, share successes and failures, adopt continuous improvement as the routine way of doing things, and have opportunities to view and interact with positive role models.

To Challenge the Process, you must *experiment and take risks by constantly generating small wins and learning from experience.* To move in this direction, take these actions:

- Reward risk-takers. Praise them. Award them prizes. Give them the opportunity to talk about their experiences and share the lessons they've learned.
- Identify a couple of successful people in your organization who excel at Challenging the Process. Interview them about what they think are the ingredients for innovation and experimentation. Act upon the insights gained.
- Hold a meeting with employees and ask them what really annoys them about the organization. Commit to making changes in three of the most frequently mentioned items that are hindering productivity and success.

In every interaction, you have the chance to direct people's attention to aspects of leadership that you think are important. Find opportunities to converse with others about these questions:

- When have you felt it wasn't safe to speak up, ask difficult questions, offer new ideas, or raise concerns? What was going on that made you feel that way? How can we make it safer around here to take a risk and learn from our mistakes?
- What's one mistake you made recently or action you wish could be a "do-over"? What did you learn from this experience?

# ENABLE OTHERS TO ACT

## PRACTICE 4

# ENABLE OTHERS TO ACT

- Foster collaboration by building trust and facilitating relationships.
- Strengthen others by increasing self-determination and developing competence.

# CHAPTER 8

# Foster Collaboration

*To be successful, teams must adopt a www.com (we will win) mindset, and not an imm.com (I, me, myself) mindset.*

*Lily Cheng*

**JILL CLEVELAND TOLD** us that her first order of business when she became a program manager for a multinational technology firm was "to learn how to trust my employees. After being responsible only for myself for so long, it was very difficult to have to relinquish control. But I understood that for my employees, and thus myself, to be successful, I needed to learn to develop a cohesive and collaborative team, beginning with trust as the framework." This is a crucial realization for all leaders.

Jill recognized that she needed to give her constituents the tools to succeed and trust them to get their work completed. She began by creating an environment in which people felt comfortable asking questions: "I felt that if I provided a climate where everyone felt safe to make mistakes that they would be better prepared to learn from those mistakes. I wanted people to know that the only stupid question was the one not asked." Jill explained that she also recognized "that leaders can't gain the respect of their team without instilling a sense of confidence within their employees and allowing them the freedom to come to their own conclusions."

She opened up lines of communication within her team by supporting face-to-face interactions. She set aside dedicated time to talk with each person—in addition to any daily interactions or telephone conversations—about mutual expectations and progress on key objectives. This provided an opportunity for people to raise questions or concerns and reinforced her commitment to her constituents and their continued growth. Jill also made sure that her employees developed working relationships with others outside of their department:

> I wanted to avoid becoming a bottleneck for information. In the past, I remembered how extremely helpless I felt when asked to complete a task when I knew I was missing some important piece of information, and I thought some previous managers had kept me in the dark to bolster their sense of self-importance. This type of situation definitely did not foster collaboration within a team and, in fact, only prompted distrust. I think the only way for our team to succeed is if we tap into every available source of information and attack problems and situations together.

This meant ensuring that people were given ownership of their projects and responsible for determining what to do and then executing. "The best way for me to give power to other people," Jill said, "is to allow creativity and freedom to explore new ideas and ways of thinking. I have to relinquish control and let my employees be responsible for their own jobs." Jill made certain she provided "the necessary training and support" before she let go but felt that "I had to let go of some responsibility and let my employees either succeed or fail at some particular task. They had to know that although I would always be there for support and guidance, they were ultimately responsible for the outcome and quality of work."

She also acknowledged people's areas of expertise, especially those outside of their immediate team, because "employees feel empowered when they feel important, especially in the eyes of others." She made it a point to recognize people for their work because "knowing that your work doesn't go unnoticed builds accountability as well as pride."

Jill appreciated that another crucial foundation for collaboration was cooperative goals. She saw to it that employees knew, for example, "what they were doing, why they were doing it, and for whom they were doing it. We had to see ourselves as part of a whole, not some individual cog in a wheel." To create a climate of collaboration, leaders understand that they need to build the team around a common purpose and mutual respect and determine what the group needs to do their work. Just as Jill did, leaders put trust and team relationships on their agenda; they don't leave these to chance but make them high priorities.

As Jill's experience demonstrates, leadership is not a solo act. It's a team effort, and how leaders act to build relationships and facilitate collaboration makes a difference in how people behave.[1] When talking about personal bests and the leaders they admire, people speak passionately about teamwork and cooperation as the interpersonal route to success, especially when conditions are challenging and urgent. Leaders from all professions and economic sectors around the globe consistently appreciate that "You can't do it alone."

Extraordinary performance isn't possible unless there's a strong sense of shared creation and shared responsibility. Exemplary leaders commit to *Foster Collaboration* by engaging in these essentials:

- **Create a climate of trust**
- **Facilitate relationships**

Collaboration is a critical competency for achieving and sustaining high performance. As organizations become increasingly diverse and dispersed, physically and globally, collaborative skills are essential to navigating the conflicting interests and natural tensions. Our empirical research shows that leaders who spend the most time and energy developing cooperative relationships among the people they work with are viewed by their direct reports as the most effective. In turn, those direct reports have the highest levels of engagement. Trust is a prime ingredient in building collaboration and promoting relationships for people to work together cooperatively.

# Create a Climate of Trust

*Trust was developed by building relationships, having open communications, involving team members in planning and decision making, providing training, and ensuring ownership of the project tasks.*

*Abdu-Quddus Mulla*

Trust is the central issue in human relationships. Without trust, you cannot lead. Without trust, you can't get people to believe in you or each other. Individuals who are unable to trust others fail to become leaders precisely because they can't bear to be dependent on the words and works of others. They end up doing all the work themselves or supervising work so closely that they become micromanagers. Their lack of trust in others results in others not trusting them. To build and sustain social connections, trust must be reciprocal and reciprocated. Trust is not just what's in your head; it's also what's in your heart.

For much of his career as a benefits consultant, Matthew Watson's default stance was that "trust is earned and not automatically given, but I had presented few opportunities for others to earn it." Then the pandemic came along, and he found that he had "no choice but to depend on the capabilities and knowledge of my teammates, and it became clear that I should have been doing so all along. Collaboration is key for effective working and personal relationships. Trust is essential for true collaboration, and as a leader, you need to be the first to extend that trust."

Matt saw this realization play out in other parts of his organization. For example, because of the initial pandemic quarantine, many at his firm were forced into a "work from home" situation. It was immediately apparent that the director was uncomfortable with this arrangement. She had managed her team for years by connecting with them on almost an hourly basis in the office, but now she was forced to allow her team to resolve their issues in real time. They experimented with possible solutions, often working with the clients themselves to resolve their problems.

The director was amazed by this new "triage" methodology as issues that at one time may have gone up and down the chain were now resolved often in one call. Her team would bring success stories back to the larger group, and everyone gained from each of these positive interactions. While it took the pandemic for her to see it, the trust she showed and the resulting collaborations made her entire team stronger and resulted in better outcomes for clients.

**Invest in Trust** Studies demonstrate that trust strongly predicts personal, team, and organizational performance.[2] The most trusting people are more likely to be happy and psychologically adjusted than are those who view the world with suspicion and distrust.[3] Those perceived as trusting are sought out more as friends, more frequently listened to, and subsequently more influential. Drawing from 112 studies representing over 7,700 teams, researchers found that the extent to which team members trust one another made a substantive difference in the team's performance.[4] Ernst & Young's survey of nearly 10,000 full-time workers in Brazil, China, Germany, India, Mexico, Japan, the UK, and the United States concluded that "trust is the cornerstone for creating a workplace where employees are engaged, productive, and continually innovating."[5]

Trust has also played a role in how well individuals and communities have fared during the COVID-19 pandemic. In a large-scale study analyzing data from 149 countries, researchers found that "social and institutional trust are the only main determinants of subjective well-being that show a strong carry-forward into success in fighting COVID-19."[6] This same finding has also been true for other crises such as floods, earthquakes, storms, and accidents. In other words, trust is a major factor in the health and well-being of people during adverse and difficult times. Building trust in remote-work environments is especially grounded in "emotional trust," the belief that employees have that their leaders care about them and their concerns.[7]

In addition, trusted companies significantly outperform their counterparts in achieving key business goals—including customer loyalty and retention, competitive market position, ethical behavior and actions, predictable business and financial results, and profit growth.[8] For example, the stock price performance over six years of trustworthy public companies is routinely 1.3 times that of the S&P 500, and the return to investors was nearly 28 percent in a year.[9] In the UK, outsourcing contracts that were managed based on trust, rather than on specific agreements and penalties, were shown to add as much as 40 percent more value to the contract.[10] The variable of "trust" comprises two-thirds of the criteria for *Fortune* magazine's listing of the 100 Best Companies to Work For. These companies consistently outperform their peers on financial performance measures and have fewer incidents of absenteeism, on-the-job injuries, voluntary turnover, and so on.[11] Furthermore, nearly two-thirds of people surveyed around the world indicated that they had decided not to purchase from a company they did not trust.[12]

When trust is the norm—that is, when each team member trusts the others—decisions are made efficiently and swiftly, innovation is higher, and profitability increases. In a role-playing exercise, business executives were given identical facts about a difficult manufacturing-marketing policy decision and then asked as a group to solve a problem related to that information. Half of the groups were briefed to expect trustworthy behavior ("You have learned from your past experiences that you can trust the other members of top management and can openly express feelings and differences with them"); the other half were told to expect untrustworthy behavior. After thirty minutes of discussion, everyone completed a brief questionnaire about their experiences.[13]

Those who were told that their role-playing colleagues could be trusted reported their dialogue and decisions to be significantly more positive than the low-trust group members on every factor measured. The members of the high-trust groups were more open about feelings, experienced greater clarity about the group's fundamental problems and goals, and searched more for alternative courses of action. They also reported higher levels of mutual influence on outcomes, satisfaction with the meeting, motivation to implement decisions, and closeness as a management team because of the meeting.

In the low-trust groups, genuine attempts to be open and honest were ignored or distorted. The managers who experienced rejection responded in kind: "What a bunch of turkeys. I was trying to be honest with them, but they wouldn't cooperate. If I had my way, I would have fired the entire group." The responses from their team were no less hostile: "I was sick of working with you—and we had only been together for ten minutes." Not surprisingly, more than two-thirds of the participants in the low-trust groups said that they would seriously consider looking for another position.[14]

Keep in mind that this was a *simulation*. These real-life executives responded as they did because they had been *told* that they couldn't trust their role-playing colleagues. It shows that trust, or distrust, can come with a mere suggestion—and in mere minutes. When asked after this simulation to think about what factors might have accounted for the differences between the outcomes and feelings reported by the various groups, not one person perceived that trust had been the determining variable.

When you create a climate of trust, you create an environment that allows people to contribute freely and innovate. You nurture an open exchange of ideas and an honest discussion of issues. You motivate people to go beyond compliance and inspire them to reach for the best in themselves. You foster the belief that people can rely on you to do what's in everyone's best interests. To get these kinds of results, you have to ante up first in the game of trust; you have to listen and learn from others and share information and resources with others. Trust comes first; following comes second.

**Be the First to Trust** Building trust is a process that begins when someone (either you or the other party) is willing to risk being the first to open up, show vulnerability, and let go of control. Leaders must go first. If you want the high levels of performance that come with trust and collaboration, you have to demonstrate your trust in others before asking them to trust you.

Going first can be a scary proposition. You're taking a chance. You're betting that others won't betray your confidence and that they'll take good care of the information you communicate and the feelings you share. You're risking that others won't take advantage of you and that you can rely on them to do what's right. This requires considerable self-confidence, but the payoff is enormous.

Trust is contagious. When you trust others, they are much more likely to trust you. However, understand that distrust is equally contagious if you choose not to trust. If you exhibit distrust, others will hesitate to place their trust in you. It's up to you to set the example and be willing to overcome the need for invulnerability. As Keni Thomas reflected on his experience as a U.S. Army Ranger, "Trust doesn't come issued; it's earned."[15]

Self-disclosure is one way that you go first. Whether your work setting is remote or in-person, letting others know what you stand for, what you value, what you want, what you hope for, and what you're willing (and not willing) to do reveals information about yourself. You can't be sure that other people will appreciate your candor, agree with your aspirations, or interpret your words and actions in the way you intend. But once you take the risk of being open, others are more likely to take a similar risk and work toward mutual understanding.

This is precisely what Masood Fakharzadeh experienced when assembling an offshore product development team as part of his personal-best leadership experience. "Early on," he said, "I asked everyone for their help. I told them that this is the first time that I'm leading such a project, and I needed their help and expertise to make the project successful. I wanted to show them that I had full trust in them by asking them to help me." Demonstrating his trust in them, Masood said, "resulted in people opening up and sharing lots of information. This got them fully engaged, and they took ownership."

Trust can't be forced. If someone refuses to understand you, viewing you as neither well-intentioned nor competent, there may be little you can do to change their perceptions and behavior. However, keep in mind that placing trust in others is the safer bet with most people most of the time. Humans are hardwired to trust, and without it would be unable to function effectively in the world.[16]

**Show Concern for Others** With the outbreak of the COVID-19 pandemic, Sean McLaughlin, vice president of news content for a national media company, realized he had to radically change the frequency, format, content, and purpose of calls with his nationwide team of news directors. The old routine of a once-a-year in-person meeting and twice-a-year conference calls could not possibly be enough to enable team members to do their best work, so Sean started checking in with everyone twice a week through video calling. The impact on Sean and the team was powerful.

Because the calls came from his home, they took on a more casual and personal tone. As Sean reflected, "We shared a lot more than before. Everyone was just more comfortable." Additionally, because he *saw* team members on video, he could more clearly observe that many were fatigued and sense their feeling overwhelmed and anxious. "Many times, I saw people who looked as if they were simply beat up and needed help," Sean said. "I would immediately turn around and reach out to them. I had never done that before."

Sean experienced first-hand how important it was to listen and be in tune with the emotional states of others, and he was reminded about how much the little things matter. "I would frequently tell people 'Thank you, I am here for you, I understand how you are feeling.' I could see the relief in them. It was as if they suddenly felt less isolated, less alone." Since those first months of the pandemic, Sean has continued the calls, regardless of the frequency of his field visits, because as he summed it up: "You really do need to know how people are doing."

Sean learned that showing concern for others and attending to their needs is central to enabling others to act, especially in stressful times. The concern you show for others is also one of the clearest and most unambiguous signals of your trustworthiness. When others know you will put their interests ahead of your own, they won't hesitate to trust you.[17] People need to see this in your actions—listening, paying attention to their ideas and concerns, helping them solve their problems, and being open to their influence. When you show your openness to their needs and your interest in their concerns, people will be more open to yours, which was precisely the lesson Sean had learned. Sean's actions illustrate how trust can be built and sustained even when people are working remotely. He increased his personal connections with people, intentionally looking for signs of how people were feeling and reaching out whenever he noticed that people might be experiencing difficulties.

By increasing the frequency of calls and consciously attending to how others were feeling, Sean also demonstrated the power of actively listening, a critical skill in showing concern for others. Consider the relationship we found between the extent to which direct reports indicate that their leader actively listens to diverse points of view and how they feel about their workplace. Nearly nine out of ten direct reports who agree or strongly agree that their leader almost always listens describe themselves as having a "strong sense of team spirit." Only one in fifty feels intense team spirit when they report their leader as seldom actively listening to diverse viewpoints. The findings for how direct reports evaluate their levels of motivation and productivity are also directly correlated with how frequently they gauge their leader's actively listening.

When people believe that you have their interests at heart—that you care about them—they're more likely to be open to your influence. It is also true that the more people feel you listen to them and understand their feelings and perspectives, the more favorable they will feel about their relationship with you. The data confirms that the frequency of listening is directly related to the extent that direct reports feel their leaders have the best interests of others at heart and are interested in their personal and professional development. In addition, as shown in Figure 8.1, there is a solid relationship between actively listening on the part of their leader and the extent to which direct reports feel valued by their organization.

Genuine active listening involves more than simply paying attention. The best listeners, according to a study involving nearly 3,500 participants in a coaching skills development program, did much more than remain silent while the other person talked. They demonstrated that they were listening by asking questions that "promoted discovery and insight."[18] Listening requires more than just hearing the other person's words. It means being engaged in a way that makes the conversation a positive experience, causing the person to whom you are listening to feel supported and valued. Showing appreciation for another's unique viewpoint demonstrates respect for them and their ideas. Being sensitive to what others are going through creates bonds that make accepting one another's guidance and advice easier.

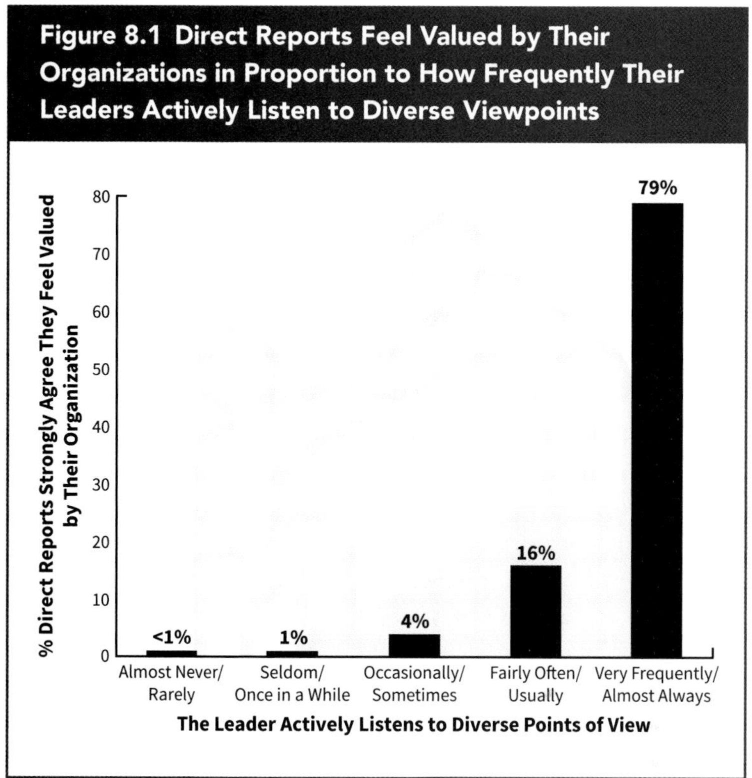


**Figure 8.1 Direct Reports Feel Valued by Their Organizations in Proportion to How Frequently Their Leaders Actively Listen to Diverse Viewpoints**

Studies have shown that there was a 40 percent increase in overall performance for those leaders who had mastered listening and responding with empathy. Empathy has been called the cornerstone of smart leadership because it "is not just about seeing things from another's perspective. The real competitive advantage of the human worker will be their capacity to create relationships, which means empathy will count more than experience."[19] In a study involving over 15,000 leaders from more than 300 organizations across 20 industries and 18 countries, empathy was found as the most critical driver of overall performance.[20] Leaders rated by their direct reports as engaging in "behaviors that signal empathic emotion" are perceived as better managers by their own managers[21] and they also experience greater subjective well-being.[22] Showing interest in others, being sensitive to their problems, and conveying compassion increases the abilities of both leaders' and their constituents' capacities to do their jobs.

Demonstrating empathy also goes a long way in building trust.[23] This is precisely the lesson Andy Cheng, worldwide product marketing manager for a global technology company, said he would share with others based on his personal-best leadership experience: "Empathy is critical. You have to understand how others feel and determine what you can do to help others to be successful. I want to be remembered for how I served my team and not as the one being served." When people believe that you have their interests at heart—that you care about them—they're more likely to be open to your influence, and when you act on your understanding of their needs and interests, showing compassion, you make a significant difference in the lives of others.

**Share Knowledge and Information** Competence is a vital component of trust and confidence in a leader. As we discussed earlier, our studies have demonstrated that people expect their leaders to know what they're talking about and what they're doing. Demonstrate your competence by sharing what you know, encouraging others to do the same, and connecting team members to valuable resources and people. Leaders who are knowledge builders set the example for how team members should behave toward each other. As a result, team members' trust in one another and the leader increases, along with their performance.

Darrell Klotzbach, engineering manager with a multinational computer software company, models the value of collaboration by sharing information and teaching techniques that he knows about and others don't. He connects people in his area with those outside that he believes they could learn from. He also spends time, in his words, "wandering around the shop floor so that I could pick up informal pieces of information that would be valuable for the team to know." He brings this news back and shares it during meetings so that everyone can be as informed and as up-to-date as he is about what is going on.

With a new hire right out of college, Darrell realized that the work would be overwhelming at the start, so he paced her adjustment into the role. For example, when he assigned her tasks, he did not tell her specifically what to do, but instead he provided direction by sharing a vision of the goal of the work:

> I gave her the freedom to act how she saw fit. The main requirement was, if she got stuck, she should come to me rather than continue to be stuck, and we would work it out. In addition, I had her join me in meetings with the teams I was supporting so she could see what was being requested and how I, but eventually we, would handle these.

Sharing your experience, knowledge, and information goes a long way in building trust and demonstrating your interest in the well-being of others. Divya Pari was somewhat anxious when she accepted a position with one of India's central banking institutions. Her fears were put to rest by the leadership actions of her new manager, beginning with how she was greeted on her first day:

> She congratulated me for landing the position and inquired about how I was feeling in this new place and role, whether the accommodation provided was comfortable, about my aspirations, interests, etc. She assured me that language would not be a problem, and indeed my co-workers communicated in English while speaking to me. She shared various aspects of the division's work and information on critical issues facing the division. The friendly interaction, sharing of information, concern for my problems and for my comfortable transition to the new role in the division, generated trust in me and I immediately felt positive and optimistic about my work. It also helped me open up, which in turn generated trust with my boss.

Divya's experience and Darrell's actions illustrate that facilitating relationships is how leaders build a climate of trust within the team. As Divya told us, "It proves that showing concern for people's problems and aspirations and intently listening generates trust and fosters collaboration." The fact that trust among team members goes up when people share knowledge and information—and the fact that performance increases as a result—underscores how important it is for leaders to stay focused on the needs of their team. If you show a willingness to trust others with information (both personal and professional), constituents will be more inclined to overcome any doubts they might have about sharing information. However, if you display a reluctance to trust and withhold information yourself—or if you're overly concerned about protecting your turf and keeping things to yourself—you'll dampen both their trust and performance. Managers who create distrustful environments tend to adopt self-protective postures. They're directive and hold tight to the reins of power. Those who work for such managers are likely to reciprocate the distrust by withholding and distorting information.[24] This reinforces why it's crucial for you to go first in sharing information.

## Facilitate Relationships

*We didn't need heroes; we needed people to work together and show how we can make things happen when we work as one team.*

*Maria Hirotsuka*

People work together most effectively when they trust one another. Asking for help and sharing information then come naturally and setting a common goal becomes almost intuitive, as Siobhan Pickett learned in her personal-best leadership experience. She was relatively new to this electrical and electronic manufacturing company and the first woman in a significant product development leadership position. She was taking over a project that was already several months behind schedule. Turning this situation around, she explained, "required, among many things, making sure that everyone saw how they were interconnected with one another, and that our success would not be the result of any one person or group's efforts, especially in the short-term, but because we were able to work together with an end goal in our collective sight. We prioritized deliverables to the group over other more individual responsibilities."

Siobhan facilitated relationships among her team members. Although she conducted weekly meetings to keep herself and the team informed, no one waited around for a meeting to address particular issues. When problems arose, people looked around and found those who would be best able to resolve them, then allowed and expected those individuals to explore solutions and bring forward their own recommendations. Siobhan kept the team focused on working together to identify the best solution and ways to prevent problems from recurring in the future.

Collaboration happens when people appreciate that they need each other to succeed. A sense of interdependence—a condition wherein everyone knows that they cannot succeed unless everyone else succeeds or can be more effective by coordinating their efforts rather than working alone—is a significant precursor to cooperative behavior and collaboration. Leon Perepelitsky, senior software engineer, observed that the main reason project teams around the globe were able to work together so smoothly was their appreciation that they could accomplish more by working together than they could by working alone. Because the team members were all experienced engineers, he explained:

> They can often come up with the solution for the problem by themselves. However, we found out over the years that if we involved the entire group, we could benefit more than twofold. First, the quality of the solution would be much higher, more long-term, and less error-prone. Second, the entire group would know what the rest of the group is doing and be on the lookout for ways to help—knowing that others are doing the same thing on their behalf.

Without a feeling that "we're all in this together," it's nearly impossible to create the conditions for positive teamwork. This feeling of "working together" doesn't require people to be in the same workplace location. Leon's constituents worked in different regions of the world, yet they knew they could reach out to each other and look for ways to be of help. To create these conditions, leaders need to develop cooperative goals and roles, support norms of reciprocity, structure projects to promote joint efforts, and maintain durable social connections.

**Develop Cooperative Goals and Roles** No one person can single-handedly educate a child, build a quality car, make a movie, create a world-class guest experience, connect a customer to the cloud, or eradicate a disease. The most essential ingredient in every collective achievement is a common goal. A focus on a collective purpose binds people into cooperative efforts and creates a sense of *inter*dependence. If you want individuals or groups to work cooperatively, you have to give them a good reason to do so, such as a goal that can be accomplished only by working together.

As the business development director for an Irish semiconductor intellectual property company, John Doyle needed to ensure that team members assumed ownership of their tasks, took responsibility for meeting their schedules, and, most importantly, knew that they were members of a team that had the same end goal in mind. John told us how he did it:

> I made sure that each team member depended on the other and that success could only be achieved through cooperation and teamwork. Each individual was completely informed in terms of feedback from customers, and they were completely aware of the financial impact the program was going to make to the overall company. In effect, this helped to create a buzz about being a part of this team.
>
> I also made certain that each team member realized how important his or her part was to the overall success of the program. I ensured that the team had the visibility to understand the impact they were making not only to the success of the program but to the overall success of the company. Finally, I focused the team on what we were doing that was special and differentiated us from other projects in the past. In the end, we were all striving toward the same common goal.

Like other exemplary leaders we studied, John realized that keeping individuals focused on a common goal promoted a stronger sense of teamwork than emphasizing individual objectives. For cooperation to succeed, roles must be designed so that every person's contributions to the final outcome are both additive and cumulative. Individuals must clearly understand that the team fails unless they each contribute whatever they can. It doesn't work for two people in a fishing boat to say to each other, "Your side of the boat is sinking, but my side looks just fine."

The data shows quite clearly that leaders who do not develop cooperative relationships among people they work with are simply not evaluated as effective leaders by their direct reports, as shown in Figure 8.2. Over nine in ten direct reports who indicate that their leaders very frequently or almost always develop cooperative relationships categorize their leader "among the best" compared with other leaders they have worked with. Leaders who most frequently develop cooperative relationships also have

**Figure 8.2 Leaders Who Develop Cooperative Relationships Among People Are Rated by Their Direct Reports as Among the Best They Work With**

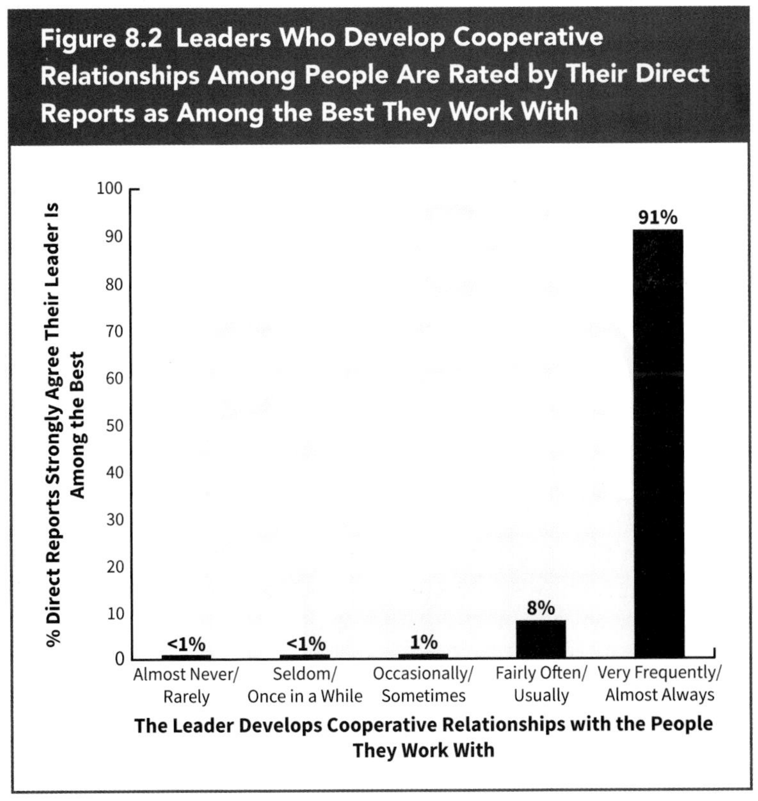

direct reports who indicate the strongest levels of commitment to the long-term success of the organization.

**Support Norms of Reciprocity** In any effective long-term relationship, there must be a sense of reciprocity. If one party always gives and the other always takes, the one who gives will feel taken advantage of, and the one who takes will feel superior. In such a climate, cooperation is virtually impossible. The power of reciprocity has been dramatically demonstrated in a series of studies involving the Prisoner's Dilemma paradigm.[25] The dilemma is this: two parties (individuals or groups) confront a series of situations in which they must decide whether to cooperate. They don't know in advance what the other party will do. There are two basic strategies—cooperate or compete—and four possible outcomes based on the players' choices: win-lose, lose-win, lose-lose, and win-win.

The maximum *individual* payoff comes when the first player selects an uncooperative strategy and the second player chooses to cooperate in good faith. In this "I win, but you lose" approach, one party gains at the other's expense. If both parties choose not to cooperate and attempt to maximize individual payoffs, then both lose. If both parties choose to cooperate, both of them win, though the individual payoff for a cooperative move in the short run is less than for a competitive one.

Scientists from around the world were invited to submit their strategies for winning in a computer simulation of this test of win-win versus win-lose strategies. The conclusion: "Amazingly enough, the winner was the simplest of all strategies submitted: cooperate on the first move and then do whatever the other player did on the previous move. This strategy succeeded by eliciting cooperation from others, not by defeating them."[26] Simply put, people who reciprocate are more likely to be successful than those who try to maximize individual advantage.

The dilemmas that are successfully solved by this strategy are by no means restricted to theoretical research. Similar predicaments arise every day: What price might I pay if I try to maximize my own personal gain? Should I give up a little for the sake of others? Will others take advantage of me if I'm cooperative? Reciprocity turns out to be the most successful approach for such daily decisions, because it demonstrates both a willingness to be cooperative as well as an unwillingness to be taken advantage of. As a long-term strategy, reciprocity minimizes the risk of escalation: If people know that you'll respond in kind, why would they start trouble? If people know that you'll reciprocate, they know that the best way to deal with you is to cooperate and become recipients of your cooperation. It's less stressful to work with others when you understand how they behave in response—especially in regard to your own behavior.[27]

The norm of generalized reciprocity has been shown as "so fundamental to civilized life that all prominent moral codes contain some equivalent of the Golden Rule."[28] Reciprocity leads to predictability and stability in relationships. Treat people as you'd like them to treat you, and it's likely that they'll repay you many times over, which was precisely Florian Bennhold's experience after accepting a position with an energy policy consulting business run by Wilson Rickerson: "Wilson built our relationship on trust. He made clear that he was willing to take the first step. After a few hours, he invited me to work on a project with him, and he immediately started sharing his contacts with me, mainly through direct introductions. I remember telling my wife how excited I was to work with him because I felt that he trusted my abilities." The payoff was abundant: "I knew that because of Wilson's trust, support, and the way he made me feel, I performed better than I ever expected." What's more, said Florian: "I felt compelled to reciprocate Wilson's trust."

Once you help others succeed, acknowledge their accomplishments, and let them shine, they'll never forget it. The "reciprocity norm" comes into play, and people are more than willing to return the favor and do what they can to make you successful. Whether the rewards of cooperation are tangible or intangible, when people understand that they will be better off by cooperating, they're inclined to recognize the legitimacy of others' interests in an effort to promote their own welfare.

**Structure Projects to Promote Joint Effort** Many people who grow up in Westernized countries that emphasize individualistic or competitive achievement perceive that they'll do better if everyone is rewarded solely based on their individual accomplishments. Empirically, that's not the case. In a world trying to do more with less, competitive strategies lose to strategies that promote collaboration.[29]

The motivation for working diligently on one's job, while keeping in mind the overall common objective, is reinforced when the end result gets rewarded and not merely individual efforts. Most profit-sharing plans, for example, are based on meeting the company's goals and not just those of separate independent units or departments. Certainly, each individual within the group has a distinct role, but on world-class teams, everyone knows that they are unlikely to achieve the group's goal if they only do their separate parts well. After all, if you could do it alone, why would you need a team?

The power of making sure that individuals understand that working together means "working *together*" was indelibly imparted to Jim Vesterman on his very first day in the Marine Corps when he and his fellow recruits learned to make their beds.[30] As Jim recounted, "When the drill instructor begins counting, you've got three minutes to make the bed—hospital corners and the proverbial quarter bounce. When you're done, you're told to get back in a line. The goal is to have every bed in the platoon made." Initially, Jim was quite proud of himself. He made his bed quickly, and when three minutes were up only about ten men had finished. But the drill instructors weren't handing out any congratulations. Everyone's bed had to be made, and that hadn't happened. The drill continued, with Jim ripping off the sheets again, and again, and again. Finally, one of the drill instructors looked Jim in the eye and said, "Your bunkmate isn't done. What are you doing?" At that moment Jim realized that making every bed wasn't just about his solo efforts to make his own. He then teamed up with his bunkmate, and together they were able to make their beds about twice as fast as they did individually.

Still, not everyone was finishing within the time limit. Finally, Jim realized, "Okay, when we're done, we've got to go help the bed next to us, and the bed down from that, and so on. I went from thinking, 'I'll hand my bunkmate a pillow, but I'm not going to make the bed for him' to making beds for anyone who needed help." Jim experienced an epiphany: you can't be successful without helping the people around you.

Scholars have shown that organizations filled with "givers"—those who help others—are consistently more effective than those loaded with "takers." Knowing about the amount of help people are willing to give one another is a highly accurate predictor of the team's effectiveness.[31] For example, in a series of studies, teams were rewarded for being the highest-performing team as a whole, prompting members to work together as givers, whereas a taker-culture was prompted in teams in which the rewards went to the highest-performing individual within each team. While the competitive teams finished their tasks faster than the cooperative teams, they were less accurate because members withheld critical information from each other.[32]

To boost the accuracy of the competitive teams, the researchers next had them complete a second task under the cooperative reward structure—that is, rewarding the entire team for high performance. The result this time? Accuracy didn't go up, and speed dropped because people struggled to transition from competition to cooperation—that is, shifting from taking to giving. It seems that once people had experienced their colleagues as competitors, they couldn't trust them. Completing even a single task under a structure that rewarded taking created win-lose mindsets, which persisted even after removing the structure.

Joint efforts reinforce the importance of working collaboratively and helping out one another. Figuring out how to take as much as possible from others, while contributing as little as possible, has the opposite effect. You have to make sure that the long-term benefits of joint efforts are greater than the short-term benefits of working alone or competing with others. You need to get people to realize that by working together they can complete the project faster than by thinking about any short-term (or individual) victories resulting from doing their own thing, complaining, blaming, or competing with others for scarce resources.

**Maintain Durable Social Connections** The critical currency in this VUCA (volatile, uncertain, complex, and ambiguous) world is *social capital*—the collective value of the people you know and what you will do for each other. When social connections are strong and numerous, there's more trust, reciprocity, information flow, collective action, and elevated well-being. Having strong social relationships is the best predictor of human happiness, trumping wealth, income, and material possessions, and those who fail to achieve this most basic need experience loneliness, anxiety, depression, low self-esteem, obesity, and anger.[33] Leaders find substantive ways to connect people with one another, as well as with others outside the boundary of their group or team.

The COVID-19 pandemic underscored the importance of social connections. While nearly everyone around the world was ordered to maintain "physical distance," the yearning for social connection increased. People invented all kinds of ways to continue to interact with their fellow human beings. There was seemingly no end to the creative ways that people invented to stay connected to each other virtually or in person, even in the worst moments of the crisis.

The most well-connected people are typically those who get involved in activities outside of their immediate job function or discipline. Find ways you can interact with people from a wide range of units, departments, projects, and professions. While specialization has its benefits, from a leadership perspective you don't want to dig yourself into a hole. If your connections are only in your specialty, you will be less influential than if your connections cross a lot of boundaries. When it comes to social connections, there's a payoff in mining deep and wide.

Greater connectedness can also be fostered when you and your team have enough confidence in one another's relationships to ask for help when needed. The impulse to give help when requested is generally a powerful, automatic, and emotional response formed early in life. Because people underestimate by nearly 50 percent the likelihood of receiving a positive response when requesting assistance,[34] many opportunities are lost. For example, prospective friends and clients go uncontacted, and chances to increase connectedness are squandered. Saying no when someone asks for help comes with the social cost of being seen as uncaring, unreasonable, insensitive, and even cruel. By contrast, saying yes is a positive and rewarding experience, and agreeing to help or cooperate strengthens the bond of connectedness between people. When you make someone else happy, you feel good about yourself, and this interaction strengthens connectedness. Feeling a sense of connection with someone else makes you more likely to volunteer your assistance. For example, onlookers most predisposed to help emergency victims are those who feel they share something in common with them.

Getting people to feel connected to those they are working with enhances well-being and fosters a greater commitment to colleagues. Research documents that high-quality connections contribute to people flourishing, resulting in better health, higher cognitive functioning, broader thinking, and stronger resilience.[35] Individuals with high-quality relationships also have a better sense of whom to trust and not trust. They are more open, they more fully understand themselves and the viewpoints of others.

Are *virtual* connections a good way to foster collaboration and build trust? There is no question that virtual connections are prolific and often necessary. In a global economy, no organization could function if people had to fly halfway around the world to exchange information, make decisions, or resolve disputes. Proof of this is also found with the exponential growth in virtual communications during the global COVID-19 pandemic, and that demand led to the development of new apps and platforms to meet the need. With a large percentage of people now working remotely and only going into an office intermittently, virtual connections represent a significant portion of the medium through which people communicate, learn, and conduct business.

That said, the stroke of a key, the click of a mouse, or the switch of a video doesn't get you the same results as an in-person conversation does. In an era that is becoming more and more dependent on virtual connections, there's a temptation to believe that such connections automatically lead to better relationships and greater trust. Unfortunately, virtual trust is much more difficult to build and maintain than trust developed in person. Even among Gen Z employees, who make up 20 percent of today's workforce, 72 percent indicate they prefer face-to-face communication at work.[36]

Virtual trust, like virtual reality, is still one step removed from the real thing. Human beings are social animals; it is their nature to want to interact face to face. Bits and bytes and pixilated images make for a very fragile social foundation. As handy as virtual tools such as e-mail, voice mail, apps, and texts are for staying in touch, they are no substitute for positive face-to-face interactions.[37] If you mainly know your group members virtually, you probably do not know them well enough to trust them with extremely important matters. This may sound heretical in a world driving itself more and more to depend on electronic connections, but you have to figure out how to combine and balance the benefits of technology with the social imperative of human contact. Data and information may be virtually shared, but ensuring understanding, sensitivity, knowledge, equity, inclusion, and action online or at a distance are matters still to be worked out.

To cement your social capital, you must intensify the durable nature of relationships. When people expect their interactions to continue and like being in the relationship, they are much more likely to cooperate in the here and now. When they know they'll run into one another at some event, continue to serve on a project team for several years, or participate in a subsequent task force together, they are more likely to be considerate of others. Whether in-person or remote, knowing that you have to deal with someone again—whether tomorrow, next week, or in the foreseeable future—ensures that you will not easily forget how you've treated one another. When interactions are likely to be frequent, the consequences of today's actions on tomorrow's dealings are that much more pronounced. In the end, enduring relationships, more than one-time or short-term ones, provide incentives to find ways to work together cooperatively to ensure mutual success in the future.

## TAKE ACTION:
## Foster Collaboration

"You can't do it alone" is the mantra of exemplary leaders—and for good reason. You can't make extraordinary things happen by yourself. Collaboration is what enables organizations, communities, and even virtual classrooms to function effectively. Sustain collaboration by creating a climate of trust and by facilitating effective long-term relationships among your constituents. Promote a sense of mutual dependence—the feeling that everyone in the group knows they need the others to succeed. Without that sense of "we're all in this together," it's impossible to keep effective teamwork going, stimulating people to look out for one another and do what they can to make the whole team successful.

Trust is the lifeblood of collaboration. To create and sustain the conditions for long-lasting connections, you have to trust others, they have to trust you, and they have to trust each other. Without trust, you cannot lead or make extraordinary things happen. Share information and knowledge freely with your constituents, show that you understand their needs and interests, open up to their influence, make wise use of their abilities and expertise, and, most of all, demonstrate that you trust them before you ask them to trust you.

The challenge in facilitating relationships is making sure people recognize how much they need one another to excel—how truly interdependent they are. Cooperative goals and roles contribute to a sense of collective purpose. The best incentive for people to work to achieve shared goals is knowing that you and others will reciprocate, helping them in return. Help begets help, just as trust begets trust. By supporting norms of reciprocity and structuring

*(continued)*

projects to reward joint efforts, you enable people to understand that it's in their best interest to cooperate. Get people interacting and encourage face-to-face interactions as often as possible to reinforce the durability of relationships.

We suggest that you foster collaboration by taking these actions to *build trust and facilitate relationships*:

- Increase both the quantity and quality of informal interactions among people who need to work more effectively together.
- Make sure that you use "we" at least three times as often as you use "I." You can't do it alone. "We" is an inclusive word that signals a commitment to teamwork and collaboration.
- Be open to admitting that matters don't always go as expected and focus your attention on making sure that the lessons from experience are widely shared. Never shoot the messenger.

In addition, regular conversations about leadership will let people know it's important. Use the opportunity in every interaction to direct people's attention to aspects of leadership that you think are important to focus on. Find opportunities to talk with others about these questions:

- To get extraordinary things done, what can be done to better connect you with those with whom you need to collaborate?
- What are we doing to ensure that people around here feel included and are involved in decisions that affect the way they do their work?

# CHAPTER 9
# Strengthen Others

*I emphasized that no one in the group was smarter or better than anyone else, and the key was to share knowledge and information rather than hoard it.*

*Sanjay Bali*

**EXEMPLARY LEADERS PROVIDE** people with the latitude and flexibility needed to take initiative. It is equally important for leaders to provide structure and clear guidelines as they encourage self-determination in their teams. Before people can feel comfortable and confident stretching themselves, they must feel competent in their abilities and roles. Otherwise, people will feel overwhelmed and disabled and tend to play it safe rather than taking any chances.

This is what Sydney-based Anthony Panuccio realized in his role as senior director of support and services in Asia Pacific for a global security software company. Too many people in his division were uncertain about how to perform their tasks and fulfill their roles effectively. To overcome this, Anthony undertook a year-long initiative called "Back to Basics." They looked at all of their operational processes and started systematically documenting what needed to be done. They developed a "playbook" around four major job roles, which broke down what team members needed to achieve daily, weekly, monthly, quarterly, and annually. Doing so provided a framework around what needed to be delivered, why, and how.

When asked if the playbook made people feel micromanaged, Anthony explained that they intended to cover just the basics. "After that," he told us, "comes a great deal of trust and latitude in the way people need to behave and are empowered to drive the right outcomes while managing the account." As Anthony points out, this happens with almost every single request that a customer makes because no two people whom you deal with are the same:

> We have to trust our people to interpret what's required and make sensible decisions around which actions to take next—you can't prescribe that at all. They need to be tuned into what's right and which decisions to make. Otherwise, managers will be micromanaging every single incident we get on a daily basis, which is counterproductive and demoralizing for the team.

One of his team members also addressed this issue when he assured us that he didn't feel micromanaged or abandoned under Anthony's leadership. "Anthony's great at finding that middle ground," he said. "I've really thrived under that style because I've been left alone to make improvements. At the same time, he'll still look at my work and ask, 'Have you thought about this?' So we have a continuous conversation about what I'm doing. He'll make tweaks and guide me through in the direction I need to go." Another team member told us that Anthony's able to get people to perform at their best because "he helps them understand what their goal is and provides them with the tools necessary to be successful."

Anthony acknowledged that he sometimes feels uneasy about letting go. He explained:

> Sometimes as a leader, you feel that if you don't have your eyes on it, then the outcomes are not going to be achieved. But I've learned to trust in the capabilities of the people I delegate to. I've learned to relinquish control and allow people to create something that I may not even realize they're capable of creating. And when I've done that,

> I've discovered that my team really has the capability of driving some excellent outcomes and developing processes and tools that are now being used worldwide.

Once leaders, like Anthony, appreciate that they can't accomplish anything extraordinary all by themselves, they start to understand the benefit of relinquishing control. They provide people with more opportunities to develop their talents and make decisions that matter. When team members feel they have the competence and confidence to take advantage of their leader's trust and support, they take initiative and responsibility, looking for ways to improve organizational performance without being asked. The data indicates that those people who report to leaders who are seen as very frequently or almost always ensuring that "people grow in their jobs by learning new skills and developing themselves" have engagement scores that are 66 percent higher than do the direct reports of leaders who are viewed as rarely engaging in this leadership behavior.

Anthony's experience illustrates how exemplary leaders make a commitment to *Strengthen Others*. They enable people to take ownership of and responsibility for their group's success by enhancing their competence and confidence in their abilities, listening to their ideas and acting on them, involving them in important decisions, and acknowledging and giving credit for their contributions.

Creating a climate in which people are engaged fully and feel in control of their own lives is at the heart of strengthening others. Exemplary leaders build an environment that develops people's abilities and bolsters their self-confidence to perform their tasks. In a climate of competence and confidence, people don't hesitate to hold themselves personally accountable for results, feel profound ownership for their achievements, and do all they can to make extraordinary things happen.

To Strengthen Others, exemplary leaders engage in two essentials. They

- **Enhance self-determination**
- **Develop competence and confidence**

Leaders significantly increase people's belief in their ability to make a difference. They move from being *in control* to *giving over control* to others, becoming their coach and mentor. They further develop existing talents, help learn new skills, and provide the institutional supports required for ongoing growth and change. In the final analysis, leaders turn their constituents into leaders.

## Enhance Self-Determination

*He shared his power with us, which led to an increased ability and desire to execute. Given more opportunities to be self-directed and make real decisions, we began to gain this incredible new sense of competence and confidence.*

*Casey Mork*

Leaders accept and act on this paradox of power: you become more powerful when you give your power away. Long before *empowerment* entered the mainstream vocabulary, exemplary leaders understood how important it was for their constituents to feel strong, capable, and efficacious. People who feel weak, incompetent, and insignificant will consistently underperform; they are disengaged, hoping to flee the organization at the first opportunity.

Individuals who are not confident about their power, regardless of their organizational position or place, tend to hoard whatever shreds of influence they have. Powerless managers tend to adopt petty and dictatorial styles. Powerlessness also creates organizational systems in which political skills are essential, and "covering your backside" and "passing the buck" are the preferred modes of handling interdepartmental differences.[1]

Over the past forty years, we've asked thousands of people to tell us about their own experiences of feeling powerless and powerful. Think about actions or situations that have made you feel powerless, weak, or insignificant, like a pawn in someone else's chess game. Are they similar

**Representative Actions and Conditions That People Report Make Them Feel POWERLESS**

- "No one was interested in, listened to, or paid attention to my opinion or questions."
- "I had no input into an important decision that affected how I did my work."
- "My boss strongly argued with me in front of my colleagues, referring to me and my ideas in unflattering ways."
- "My decisions were not supported, even though management said they would back me up."
- "Someone else took or received credit for my hard work and results."
- "Information essential to my work was withheld, and/or I was out of the information loop."
- "I was given responsibility but no authority to hold others accountable."

to what others have reported about the actions and conditions that made them feel powerless?

Now think about what it's like when you feel powerful—strong, efficacious, like the creator of your own experience. Are your recollections similar to what others recall about the actions and conditions that made them feel that they mattered and made a difference?

**Representative Actions and Conditions That People Report Make Them Feel POWERFUL**

- "All the important information and data were shared with me."
- "I was able to exercise discretion about how we would handle a situation."
- "I made decisions about key aspects of the project."
- "The organization invested resources in helping me to learn."
- "Management publicly expressed great confidence in my ability."
- "The supervisor told others about the great work I was doing."
- "My manager took the time to let me know how I was doing and where I could be improving."

As you examine what people say about powerless and powerful times, there is one clear and consistent message: *feeling powerful—literally, feeling "able"—comes from a profound sense of being in control of your life.* People everywhere share this fundamental need. When people feel able to determine their own destiny, when they believe they can mobilize the resources and support necessary to complete a task, they will persist in their efforts to achieve. However, when people feel controlled by others, when they believe that they lack support or resources, they naturally show little commitment to excel. Even though you may comply, you are disengaged and realize how much more you could contribute if you were given the opportunity.

In strengthening others, leaders show they believe that people are sufficiently smart and capable of figuring things out on their own. For Kinjal Shah, a software engineering leader with a startup organization in the digital cash solution space, the lesson from his personal-best leadership experience was that leadership was "not about having more power, but about empowering and enabling others around you to be leaders. People feel more empowered when they have decision-making power that could make real impact." Kinjal expected every team member to give their input in developing new software, and if they had questions or concerns, they were fully addressed before moving forward with the program. Taking these actions served two purposes, Kinjal noted, "because everyone's input is considered, they feel empowered, and everyone is aware of what is happening in other parts of the organization, and they have a say in how it gets developed." As a result, he found that "team members feel more responsible for the system as a whole. And, since people feel powerful, they are willing to take on leadership responsibilities in other parts of the organization as the opportunities present themselves." Research has shown that employees who have the most influence on how they do their work are, on average, both more productive and happier with their lives.[2]

Exemplary leaders, like Kinjal, give their power away by enhancing their constituents' self-determination based on the core principles of choice, discretion, and personal accountability. They appreciate how leadership actions that increase others' sense of self-determination and confidence make them more powerful and significantly enhance the energy and commitment they willingly put forward.[3]

**Provide Choices** Although he was just starting his career with a Chinese-based international trading company, John Zhang told us that what stood out for him in his personal-best leadership experience was how his "manager listened carefully to me and then *asked me what I thought* we should do." After presenting several alternatives, the manager asked John again what he thought should be done and said, "It's your decision." After talking some more about the options, John recommended a particular strategy, and "he backed me up completely, and I subsequently did everything I could to ensure our success. There was no way I was going to let us not be successful." Choice, as demonstrated in John's case, builds commitment.

The ability to make choices is essential to feeling freedom. When people perceive they don't have any choices they feel trapped, and like rats in a maze when left with no alternatives, they typically stop moving, and eventually shut down. By providing people with genuine autonomy, leaders can reduce the sense of powerlessness and increase the willingness to engage their capabilities more fully. Researchers have shown that the perception of increased choice activates reward-related circuits in the brain, making people feel more at ease, and enhancing their willingness to experiment and venture outside of their comfort zones.[4] High-performing organizations are composed of people willing to work beyond their job descriptions, and this results from their having the latitude to make choices about the work they do and how they do it.

In our studies, we ask people about the extent to which their leader "gives people a great deal of freedom and choice in deciding how to do their work," and we examine how this leadership behavior affects their attitudes about the workplace. The results in Figure 9.1 show that only 1 percent of direct reports strongly agree that they feel proud to tell others they work for their organization when their leader "almost never or rarely" gives them much freedom and choice. This sentiment improves very little even when the leader "occasionally or sometimes" engages in this leadership behavior. The dramatic shift in pride occurs (rising to 77 percent) when people report that their leader provides freedom and choice "very frequently to almost always." The shape of this relationship is similar to that computed for such outcomes as feelings of team spirit, commitment, motivation, and productivity by direct reports as a function of feeling freedom and choice in deciding how to do their work. For example, over 95 percent of direct reports indicate a strong sense of team spirit when their leaders provide discretion at least "fairly often," and the same percentage holds true in people feeling that they are making a difference.

Evaluations by direct reports of the overall effectiveness of their leader are also dramatically related to how frequently that leader provides people freedom and choice. Eighty-two percent of the leaders who most frequently engage in this leadership behavior are assessed as effective leaders by their direct reports and would be recommended as such to their colleagues. For the leaders at the bottom of this leadership behavior

Figure 9.1 Pride About Their Organization Increases When Direct Reports Feel They Have Freedom and Choice in Deciding How to Do Their Work

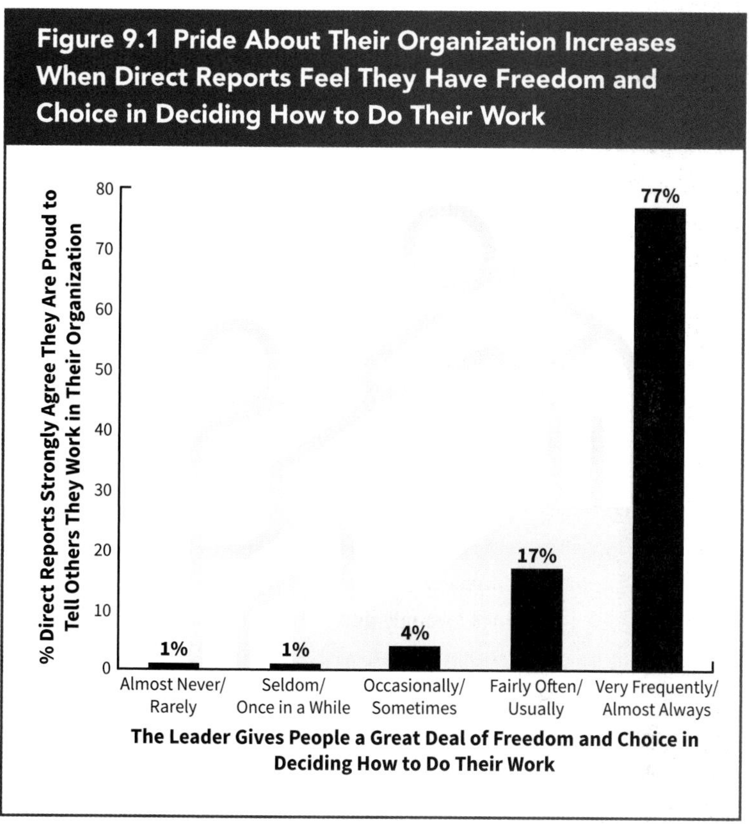


frequency distribution, less than 1 percent of their direct reports would rate or recommend them as effective leaders.

People can't learn to think for themselves, take initiative, and be self-directed if leaders always tell them what to do and how to do it. Without the opportunity to exercise some degree of choice, they are ill-prepared and handcuffed when needing to respond to a situation with a customer or colleagues who behave in ways that aren't in the script. If they have to ask the "boss" what to do—even when they think they know what needs to be done and feel they could do it—then the entire organization slows down. The most effective leaders give people the chance to use their best judgment in applying their knowledge and skills. This necessitates that, as their leader, you've prepared them to make these choices and that you've educated them in the guiding principles and standards of the organization.

Giving people choices and letting them make decisions on their own makes it quite difficult for them to blame "the company" (or management) when things don't go their way or when they don't like how things are going. After all, if they don't like the way something is done, they can do something about it. By providing choices, you enable people to take initiative and responsibility; in essence, they lead themselves.

**Structure Jobs to Offer Latitude** For people to feel in control, latitude needs to be designed into people's work. People need to be able to take nonroutine action, exercise independent judgment, and make decisions that affect how they do their work without having to check with someone else.[5] Liberated from a standard set of rules, procedures, or schedules allows people to be creative and take initiative and responsibility. People have more options (flexibility and discretion) when their jobs and work are broadly defined. Narrow job categories confine choices. The COVID-19 pandemic forced many organizations, large and small, in all sectors and functions, to provide people—especially those in frontline and midlevel positions—with greater latitude and discretion. The restructuring allowed people more freedom of movement to get things done. The same is true when people can more often work from anywhere.

Consider how you can get rid of multiple managerial layers and sign-offs. Those requirements are disabling and wasteful of time, money, talent, and motivation, and they also turn off customers. Responsive service and extra employee efforts emerge when people have the necessary leeway to meet customer needs and sufficient authority to serve customer wants. To feel in control of their own work lives (back to feeling "powerful"), people need to be able to engage in nonroutine action, exercise independent judgment, and make decisions that affect how they do their work, without having to check with someone else. Consider these two retail experiences that a colleague related, which illustrates how latitude in a job can either frustrate or delight a customer and impact revenue.

> I wandered into the "Alpha" men's store at the local galleria. I needed some new slacks for work. After trying several on, I selected one that was on sale for about 60 percent off the regular price. Excited about my selection, I headed to the checkout counter. The cashier scanned the tag and informed me that these pants were not on sale. I pointed out that the tag had a sales amount written on it, but the cashier said there was nothing that could be done because the computer was not showing a sales discount. I insisted it was on the sales rack, that it wasn't my fault that someone didn't update the computer, and that I felt entitled to the sales price. The cashier finally relented and picked up the phone to call the manager "upstairs." I don't know precisely what the conversation entailed, but approximately 15 minutes later, and with great embarrassment, the cashier was finally permitted to give me the price indicated on the tag.
>
> Not too long after this experience, I needed to buy a dress shirt and a new suit, but this time around I headed to "Beta" men's store. Again, I gravitated toward the sales rack and selected a shirt. When I went to check out, the sales associate informed me that it had been incorrectly placed on the wrong rack. Before I could say a word, however, this person indicated that this wasn't a problem and honored the discount advertised on the sales rack. I was quite pleased. As a result, I decided that I would just go ahead and look for the suit I needed right then and there. I purchased one that was not on sale, and the total transaction ended up being a substantial amount.

The fundamental difference between these two experiences is that employees in the Beta organization were trusted and given the latitude to use their judgment. However, employees at the Alpha organization were viewed merely as cogs in some machine, neither trusted nor respected for their common sense. These ideas don't just apply to frontline retail personnel. For example, researchers find a positive relationship between decision authority ("meaningful discretion") for city and county government managers and their overall performance.[6]

Only adaptive individuals and organizations will thrive in today's dynamic global environment. Leaders must support more and more individual discretion to meet the changing demands of customers, clients, suppliers, and other stakeholders, which increases the requirement to use and expand people's talents and experience. As the following example from Grace Chan illustrates, the payoff is greater performance.

Program manager for a large semiconductor chip manufacturer, Grace led a complex project requiring support from parties in Japan and the United States and input across several levels of management, functional partners, and suppliers. It was essential that job and specification requirements weren't so narrowly defined that people didn't have any room to maneuver. She made sure people had some latitude with their own choices and decisions and the chance to move across disciplines and boundaries. Grace empowered team members to claim ownership of various parts of the program, and as the owner of their respective areas, they were held accountable for the outcome. She insisted on "providing some leeway to the suppliers, for example, on terms which were critical to them, and in turn, we gained headroom on other terms essential to our business model. In the end, both parties were satisfied with the terms and conditions, and there were absolutely no hard feelings." This personal-best leadership experience reinforced her viewpoint that "empowering and strengthening all the members of the team to do their best really motivates them to strive for optimal results." Accountability is strengthened when people feel trusted and are given the latitude to use their judgment, resulting in both higher satisfaction and profitability.

**Foster Accountability** Leaders understand that the power to choose rests on the willingness to be held accountable; the more freedom of choice people have, the more personal responsibility they must accept. And, as Grace's experience demonstrated, the more people believe that everyone else is taking responsibility for their parts of the job—and has the competence to do it—the more trusting and the more cooperative they're going to be. It's also true that people will be more confident in doing their part when they believe others will do theirs. This interconnectedness between choice and accountability is increasingly important in a virtually connected global workplace.

In experiments to examine the impact of what's called "the IKEA effect"—coming to value something more as a result of being involved in creating it—researchers have found that when people participate in tasks and are able to see them through to completion, they prize them more and are more willing to take on additional tasks than if they were not self-made, were tossed out after completion, or were never completed. Accountability, in other words, is higher when people have a direct hand in creating and completing something.[7]

If you ask people if they wash a rental car before returning it, they will probably laugh and think this is a crazy question. "Of course not," they'll say, and the reason they give is that they don't own that car; they know the rental company will take responsibility for washing the car after they return it. Ask those same people if they ever wash their own car or get it cleaned at a local carwash, and most everyone will answer affirmatively. Why? Because it's their car, they own it. Using this analogy, it is apparent that when people feel they own something and it's theirs, they will care for it. However, when people feel they're only renting it, they are unlikely to treat it with the same care they would if they owned it. Similarly, when they don't have any line of sight to who will use the car next, they feel very little accountability for their actions.

How many people in your organization can justify not taking responsibility for something because it's not theirs? How many are just "renting" their workspaces? Those who feel this way are disengaged and may have quietly quit on the job. While people may not own their work in the formal or legal sense of the word, research indicates that when they feel psychological ownership, they are significantly more likely to be committed to their organizations.[8] Exemplary leaders have to create an environment in which others feel a sense of psychological ownership if they are going to make extraordinary things happen.

In Andy Gere's personal-best leadership experience, he was challenged to transform a fragmented, feuding group at a major metropolitan water treatment facility into a cohesive, cooperative team. He began by making the operators accountable. Andy gave them the authority to make plant process changes, including plant shutdowns, without first checking with a supervisor. "It took them a while," Andy admitted, "to get used to the idea that as licensed water treatment plant operators, they not only had the authority but the responsibility to optimize the plant processes to the best of their ability, all the time." He made the operators own the new procedures by letting them establish their specific intergroup work rules (such as the protocol for deciding when to turn on a creek intake after a storm) rather than dictating them from management. Similarly, the operators developed working rules, relationship rules, and getting-along rules that moved them beyond years of rivalry, grudges, and sour relationships.

Accountability was pushed by reminding the operators to "focus on the problem, not the person." And making each operator accountable was critical to the success of Andy's initiative, as he explained, "asking the operators to write their own mission statements and goals gave them a new sense of purpose and created an opportunity for them to see an end product that went beyond the end of their shift. They could see how they were interconnected and how by working together they could accomplish more than by working alone." Pointing out individuals' success in the presence of their peers was one of the ways that Andy reinforced who was accountable for what. This strengthened team members' existing feelings of personal capability, and Andy found that it "helped them to recognize just how competent their counterparts in other areas were."

When people take personal responsibility and are held accountable for their actions, their colleagues are much more inclined to want to work with them. They are more motivated to cooperate in general. Individual accountability is a critical element of every collaborative effort. Everyone must do their part for a group to function effectively.

Some believe that teams and other cooperative endeavors minimize individual accountability. They argue that if people are encouraged to work collectively, they'll take less responsibility for their actions than if they are encouraged to compete or do things independently. There is little evidence to support this viewpoint when teams have shared goals.[9] While it's true that some people become social loafers when working in groups, slacking off while others do their jobs for them, this doesn't last for long because their colleagues quickly tire of carrying the extra load. Either the slacker steps up to the responsibility, or the team wants that person removed.

Enhancing self-determination means giving people control over their lives, and it means you have to provide them something substantive to control and be accountable for. You can foster individual accountability in many ways: by ensuring that everyone, no matter the task, has a customer; by increasing spending authority, removing or reducing unnecessary approval steps; and by providing greater freedom of access, vertically and horizontally, inside and outside the organization.

You can't forget to provide the necessary resources (e.g., materials, capital, time, people, and information) for people to perform autonomously. There's nothing more disempowering than to have lots of responsibility for doing something but nothing with which to do it. In addition, increasing someone's sphere of influence should be relevant to the organization's pressing concerns and core technology. Choosing the color of the paint for the hallways may be a place to start, but you should prepare to give people influence over more substantive issues as time goes on.

## Develop Competence and Confidence

*I trained them, gave them the tools they needed, and let them run on their own. Giving them the space and latitude to do their work gave them the confidence to do what hadn't been done before.*

*Brenda Aho*

Choice, latitude, and accountability fuel people's sense of powerfulness and control over their lives. However, as necessary as enhancing self-determination is, it's insufficient. Without the knowledge, skills, information, and resources to do a job expertly, and without feeling competent to execute the required tasks, people feel overwhelmed and powerless. Even if they have the resources and skills, there may be times when people don't have confidence that they're allowed to use their abilities or that they'll be backed up if things don't go as well as expected. There also may be times when people just lack the self-confidence to do what they know needs to be done.

Developing competence and building confidence are essential to delivering on the organization's promises and maintaining the credibility of leaders and team members. To make extraordinary things happen, you must invest in strengthening people's capacity and resolve, which is especially critical during times of great uncertainty and significant change.

Think about a time when the challenge you faced was greater than your skills. How did you feel? Like most people, you probably felt anxious, nervous, scared, and the like. Now think of a time when your level of skill was greater than the level of challenge in the job. How did you feel? Bored and apathetic is most likely. No one does their best work when they're either anxious or bored. The best work is accomplished when the challenge people face is just slightly greater than their current skill level. That's when they feel stretched but not stressed out. This is the feeling of being "in the flow"—when people feel that they are fully immersed in an activity, experiencing energized focus, full involvement, and enjoyment in the process of the activity. They are confident that their skills match the level of challenge, even though it might be difficult and a bit of a stretch.[10] In a ten-year longitudinal study, managers reported being approximately five times more productive when they achieved flow.[11]

Although flow is not possible with every single task in every situation, it characterizes peak performances. Exemplary leaders strive to create the conditions that make flow possible. That means they continuously assess their constituents' capacity to perform given the challenges they face. Such assessment requires attention to each person's willpower and skills. On a long-term project for a European information technology services and consulting company that Srini Rajamani was responsible for, he implemented a policy of job rotation every four months. Along with this, he set up weekly "lunch and learn" sessions, where everyone had an opportunity, regardless of their level and role, to present their core job function and best practices they had learned to the rest of the team in an informal setting. Srini explained that this meant:

> When a person got rotated into a new role, they already had a decent understanding of what they needed to do and were not fully lost. Over time, this built great resiliency within the team. As a collective unit, they could handle most situations that they came across with no single point of failure. In addition, on a personal front, it brought people closer together because they clearly understood what challenges the person next to them was going through. As people grew in their roles, they rotated completely out of our team into much bigger roles in the organization.

The data backs up Srini's experience, as shown in Figure 9.2. The more leaders are seen by their direct reports to be taking actions that "ensure that people grow in their jobs by learning new skills and developing themselves," the more direct reports feel a sense of team spirit. Similar relationships exist between building people's competence and how this positively increases their feelings of making a difference, as well as feeling personally valued.

**Educate and Share Information** People can't do what they don't know how to do. Therefore, increasing latitude and discretion requires a corresponding increase in training and development. People who aren't sure how to perform critical tasks or are fearful of making mistakes will be reluctant to exercise their judgment. Studies of companies deemed "great workplaces" conclude that "ensuring that employees are given the training they need and involving them in decisions that impact their work creates both competence and commitment." Furthermore, the research points out that these organizations "understand that as the business continues to grow, they will need employees who can readily step into tomorrow's jobs rather than having them develop necessary skills on the fly, hiring from the outside, or simply losing market opportunity."[12]

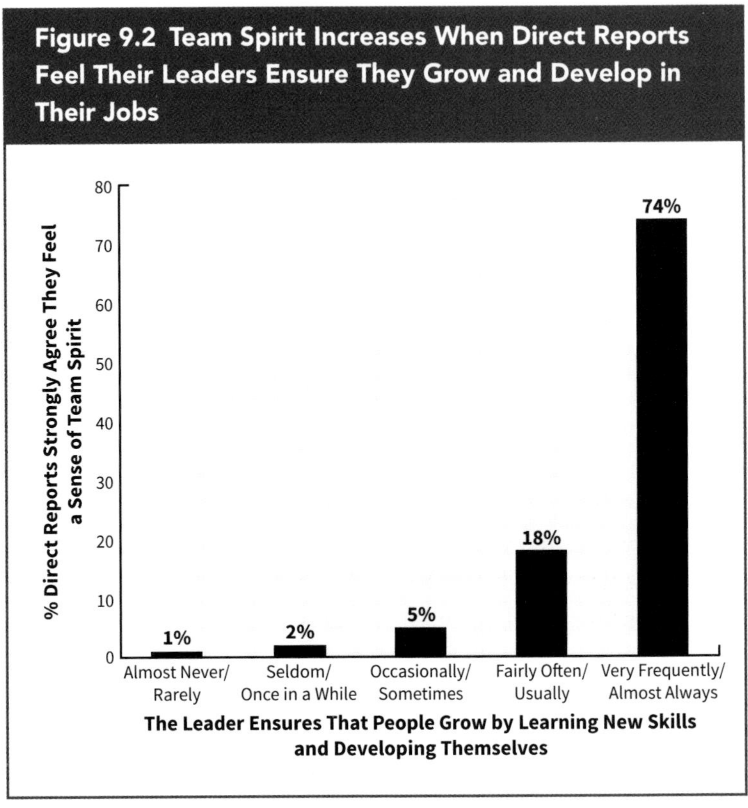


Celia Hodson inherited a very small staff when she took over an Australian program that helped local leaders set up, manage, fund, and lead successful social ventures. She worked with Fiona, who was very shy and had a real fear of speaking in public. Fiona was happy to distribute the name badges at events, but that was it. She even feigned illnesses to get out of speaking engagements. Celia asked Fiona, "How can we get you speaking in public?" Then she just edged Fiona toward it very gently. Fiona spoke with a small group, then a slightly larger group, and then another slightly larger group. In under a year, Celia told us that Fiona was standing on a platform presenting business awards to a large crowd.

Afterward, Fiona came up to Celia and said, "Oh, my gosh, I can't believe I did it!"

Like Celia, exemplary leaders enable people to see that they can improve, develop their skills, and do more than they thought possible. They ask questions like: "How do I support you to do what you're doing even better?" "To get you where you want to be, what are the skills you need to develop?" "What are the challenges that together we've got to push you through to get you to be incredible in that vision?" Or as Celia would exclaim, "What do you need from me so that you can completely rock at what you're doing?"

Strengthening others requires up-front investments in initiatives that develop people's competencies and foster their confidence. Such investments produce profits. Studies find that those companies that spend above-average amounts on training have a higher return on their investment than companies that are below-average spenders. The former also enjoy higher levels of employee involvement and commitment, better standards of customer service, along with a greater understanding of, and alignment with, company visions and values.[13] Furthermore, studies report that 40 percent of employees who report receiving poor training leave their positions within the first year. The lack of skills training and development is cited as the determining factor in their leaving.[14]

Sharing information is another important educational tactic. This factor showed up prominently on the list of what made people feel powerful and made them feel powerless when absent. Silicon Valley author and global strategist Nilofer Merchant echoes this observation: "Everyone is better off when they know why decisions are made with as much accuracy as possible. It gives them an understanding of what matters and provides information on which to base the trade-offs being made constantly at every level. When reasons behind decisions are not shared, the decisions seem arbitrary and possibly self-serving."[15] This is what Erika Long experienced when she brought her e-commerce team together, explaining their challenges and opportunities, outlining the tasks that needed to be completed, the projects she wanted the team to take on, and the expectations of upper management. Erika went on to say:

> Managers often think that withholding information will help the team be more focused, or perhaps it has to do with wanting the power for themselves. However, I found that sharing information fosters collaboration and communication among the team. Getting everyone on "the same page" not only helped them feel like they were important and valued members of the team, but it also actually helped the work process. The more information they had, the more they understood why they were doing what they were doing, and the more "bought-in" to the team's overall goal they were.

Making people smarter is the job of every leader. In today's world, if your constituents aren't growing and learning in their jobs, they're highly likely to leave and find better opportunities elsewhere.

**Organize Work to Build Competence** People can't act like owners and provide leadership if they lack a fundamental understanding of how the organization operates. To fully comprehend critical organizational issues and tasks, they need to be able to answer such questions as "Who are our most valuable customers, clients, suppliers, and stakeholders?" "How are we perceived in the marketplace?" "How do we measure success?" "What has our track record been over the past five years?" "What new products or services will we initiate in the next six months?" If your constituents can't answer critical questions like these, how can they work together to transform shared values and common purposes into reality? How can they know how their performance affects other teams, units, divisions, and ultimately the success of the entire enterprise or endeavor? How can they feel very strong or capable if they don't know the answers to the same questions every "owner" or CEO would know?[16]

When Raj Limaye joined one of India's premier skill development training centers as deputy manager, his group was feeling neither very competent nor successful. To deal with these sentiments, he immediately implemented regular meetings with new themes and new chairs each week and made a concerted effort to get everyone present to share their ideas. He met with each person and asked them what they wanted to do in their jobs. While their answers were not all the same, Raj made sure that he found challenging extensions to the tasks they were performing and added variety to each job:

> I tried removing unnecessary routine tasks wherever possible, and, if not, then these were rotated. In six months, we had reduced the routine tasks to a minimum, as everyone shared ideas about how to improve these tasks or find alternatives. We helped everyone become more competent by creating a learning climate where people needed to look beyond their own job descriptions and organizational boundaries. People were assigned important tasks, and I made them accountable at the same time.

Like Raj, exemplary leaders carefully look at what constituents are doing in their jobs and figure out where and how their tasks and positions could be enriched. They provide sufficient information so that members have an owner's perspective in making decisions, fostering greater competence, and enhancing self-confidence. They organize assignments so that people feel that their work is relevant to the pressing concerns of the business. Find opportunities to involve your team on task forces, committees, teams, and problem-solving groups dealing with critical functions and issues. Engage them in programs, meetings, and decisions that directly impact their job performance. Actions such as these build competence and promote a sense of ownership and accountability.

**Foster Self-Confidence** Even if people know how to do something, a lack of confidence may stop them from doing it. Strengthening others is an essential step in a psychological process that affects the intrinsic need for self-determination. People have an internal need to influence other people and life's events, to experience some sense of order and stability in their lives. Feeling confident that they can adequately cope with events, situations, and people prepares them to exercise leadership. Without sufficient self-confidence, people lack the conviction to take on tough challenges. The lack of self-confidence manifests itself in feelings of helplessness, powerlessness, crippling self-doubt, and eventual burnout. By building people's belief in themselves, you are bolstering their inner strength to forge ahead in uncharted terrain, make tough choices, face opposition, and the like because they believe in their skills and decision-making abilities.

Self-confidence affects people's performance. In a classic study, researchers told one group of managers that decision-making was a skill developed through practice: the more one worked at it, the more capable one became. Researchers informed another group of managers that decision-making reflected their basic intellectual aptitude: the greater one's underlying cognitive capacities, the better their decision-making ability. Working with a simulated organization, both groups of managers dealt with a series of production orders requiring various staffing decisions and the establishment of different performance targets. When faced with demanding performance standards, those managers who believed that decision-making was an acquirable skill continued to set challenging goals for themselves, used good problem-solving strategies, and fostered organizational productivity. Their counterparts, who thought that decision-making ability was latent (that is, you either have it or you don't), lost confidence in themselves over time as they encountered difficulties. They lowered their aspirations for the organization, their problem solving deteriorated, and organizational productivity declined.[17]

In a related set of studies, researchers told managers either that people are easily changeable, or that "work habits of employees are not that easily changeable, even by good guidance. Small changes do not necessarily improve overall outcomes." Those managers with the confidence that they could influence organizational outcomes through their actions maintained a higher level of performance than those who felt that they could do little to change things.[18] Still another study, involving entry-level accountants, found that those with the highest self-confidence were rated ten months later by their supervisors as having the best job performance. Their level of self-confidence was a stronger predictor of job performance than the actual level of skill or training they had received before being hired.[19] In applying these same concepts to teenagers, researchers found that in national field hockey championship competitions in Turkey, those with the strongest self-confidence were the most highly motivated, as evidenced, for example, by their intensive practice routines.[20]

These studies document what experience underscores: having confidence and believing in your ability to handle the job, no matter how difficult, are essential to promoting and sustaining consistent effort. By communicating to constituents that you also believe they can be successful, you help them extend themselves and persevere through challenging circumstances. This is what Celia Hodson told her staff, who had been told what to do and experienced little autonomy in the past. "Everyone fundamentally wants to be a valuable contributor to the team," Celia explained. "If I can get them to see that they can be, and do that authentically, then they develop the confidence to be their best selves. So I help them to gain a vision of who they could be." Her instructions to the team were to "proceed until apprehended." This meant, Celia said, that "you're willing to just have a go. Keep going. Ask yourself, 'What's the worst that can happen?' We needed that gutsy mentality of just moving forward until there was nowhere else to go. And the team really bought into that. They found their inner strength."

**Coach and Mentor** Although it's true that exemplary leaders communicate their confidence in others, you can't just tell people they can do something if they actually can't. Leaders need to provide coaching and mentoring, because no one ever got to be the best without constructive feedback, probing questions, and active teaching by people they respect.[21] One very large insurance company found that their employees were eight times more engaged when they evaluated their leaders as effective coaches. These employees demonstrated improved capacity, efficiency, and commitment, and they felt strongly supported by the company.[22]

Developing their staff is the competency most frequently found among those at the top of their field. In a three-year study of the impact of training, high-improvement learners were four times more likely to have had coaching conversations with their managers than individuals who showed little or no improvement.[23] This means that improvement isn't merely about the training; it's the coaching associated with it.

Exemplary leaders make themselves available to offer advice and counsel as people apply what they have learned in educational settings to real-time situations.

Brian Baker, family-practice physician and colonel in the U.S. Army, understood how important it is for leaders to coach. Upon his arrival as the base hospital commander, he was informed that this was the "most problematic hospital in the army." The staff was immensely talented, but their morale was dismal. They followed rigid institutional rules, and conflicts between doctors and nurses were routine. There was neither vision nor camaraderie—only fear and hostility. However, under Brian's leadership, the hospital came "within inches" of receiving an exemplary rating from their accreditation organization within two years—all without a single change in personnel.

What Brian did do was coach. He listened, mentored, and fundamentally changed the culture and the decision-making process. Restoring his staff's sense of self-confidence was the first challenge. To that end, Brian held a series of meetings in rapid succession designed to allow him to meet and communicate openly with all his constituents. No supervisor was allowed at these meetings because he wanted to ensure open and honest discussion. Brian promised that he would take no direct action as a result of the meetings, nor would he discuss what was said with anyone. He explained his philosophy of participatory and supportive (versus directive) management. These meetings set a tone of openness, genuine concern, and trust that was essential to ultimately restoring people's belief in their ability to succeed.

From Brian's perspective, his leadership challenge was just a matter of educating an already very bright and capable staff that wasn't fulfilling their potential. He explained that he wasn't here to tell people what to do but to make sure they understood what needed to be done and how to do it:

> You can't just tell them to go out and do a monumental task if you aren't sure they really know what exactly needs to be done. So you ask lots of questions to guide their thinking—you ask, "How are you going to do this and such"—but you never assume control of the is-

> sue. They own it, not you. You coach and you mentor, but you make them decide and act. If it's their plan, they're more likely to make it happen. I helped add what I consider the most important ingredient: mutual respect and a feeling of togetherness. After that, everything just came together.

When at their best, leaders never take control away from others. Like Brian, they leave it to their constituents to make decisions and assume responsibility for them. When leaders coach, educate, enhance self-determination, and otherwise share power, they're demonstrating deep trust in and respect for others' abilities. When leaders help others grow and develop, that assistance is reciprocated. People who feel capable of influencing their leaders are more strongly attached to them and more committed to effectively carrying out their responsibilities. They own their jobs. Good coaches and mentors understand that strengthening others requires paying attention and believing that people are smart enough to figure things out for themselves when allowed to make choices and provided with support and coaching. Exemplary leaders stretch people to grow and develop their capabilities and they provide them with opportunities to hone and enhance their skills in challenging assignments.

The success of every organization is a shared responsibility. As we said in Chapter 8, you can't do it alone. You need a competent and confident team, and the team needs a competent and confident coach. While you're at it, think about getting a coach yourself. There's no better way to model the behavior you expect from others than by doing it yourself.

# TAKE ACTION:
## Strengthen Others

Strengthening others is essentially the process of turning everyone into leaders—making people capable of acting on their own initiative. Create a virtuous cycle by extending more power and responsibility to others as they respond successfully. Leaders strengthen others when they make it possible to exercise choice and discretion, design options and alternatives to how work and service are conducted, and foster accountability and responsibility that compel action.

Leaders develop in others the competence, as well as the confidence, to act and to excel. They make sure that constituents have the necessary data and information to understand how the organization operates, gets results, makes money, and does good work. They invest in people's continuing competence, and they coach them on how to put what they know into practice, stretching and supporting them to do more than they might have imagined possible. Exemplary leaders help people think on their own and actively coach people to be at their best.

To Enable Others to Act, you must *strengthen others by increasing their self-determination and developing competence.* To accomplish this, we suggest you take the following actions:

- Take every opportunity to build people's capacity. Before you begin an interaction with someone, ask yourself, "What can I do in this encounter so that the other person leaves feeling more capable than when we started?" At the end of the encounter, ask yourself if you think the other person left feeling more or less capable. If you believe you made them feel less capable, rewind and do it again.

- Increase people's budgets and signature authority. When people are entrusted with greater financial responsibility, they feel more ownership and control of their work.
- Find ways to ensure that people are included in the decision-making process on matters affecting their work. Reach out to diverse and possibly underrepresented constituencies so that decisions are deemed inclusive and equitable.

Have ongoing conversations with your constituents about leadership so that they know it's important to you, to them, and to the organization. Seek out opportunities to talk with others about these questions:

- How well have we done in making people feel a sense of belonging in our workplace? What would be the advantages of having more diversity of backgrounds and perspectives on our team? Are you feeling that our processes and programs are impartial, fair, and provide equal possible outcomes for everyone?
- Are there recent actions or decisions that we have made that caused people to feel unimportant and not valued? If so, what can we do to make sure that doesn't happen again?

# ENCOURAGE THE HEART

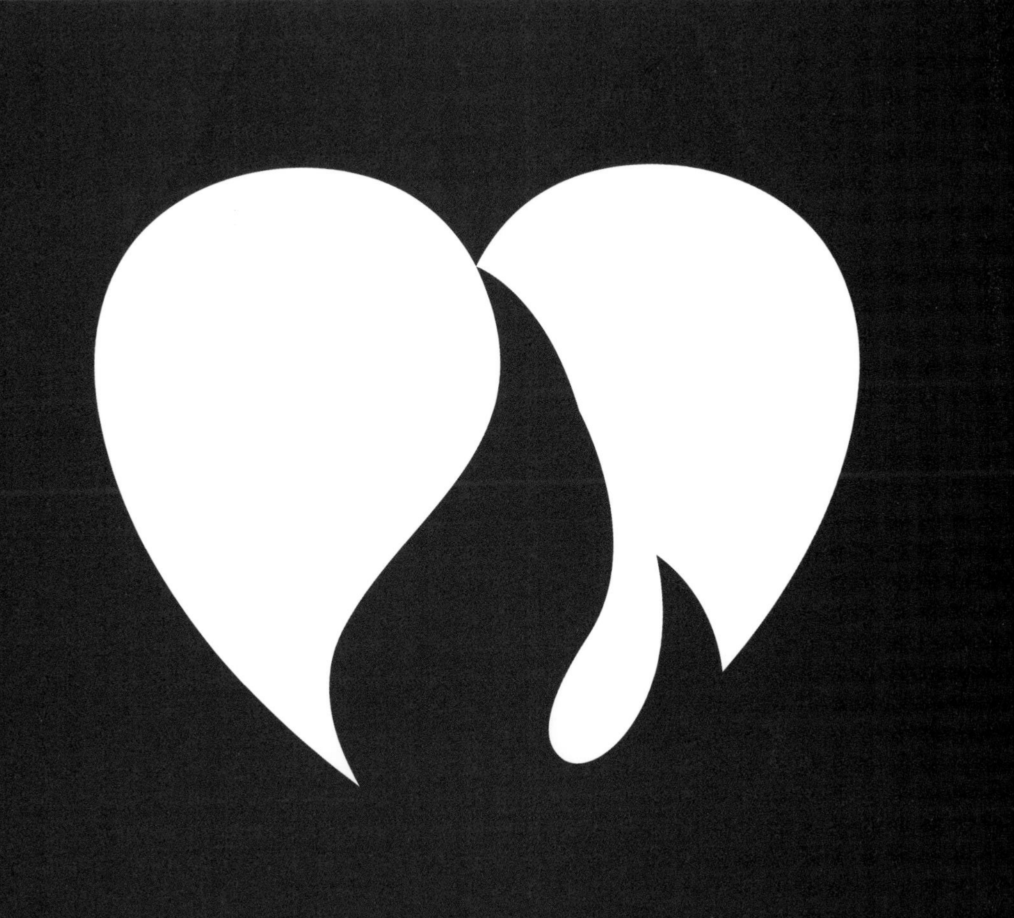

# PRACTICE 5

# ENCOURAGE THE HEART

- Recognize contributions by showing appreciation for individual excellence.
- Celebrate the values and victories by creating a spirit of community.

# CHAPTER 10

# Recognize Contributions

*People value being appreciated for their contributions. Recognition does not have to be elaborate, just genuine.*

*Alfonso Rivera*

**ALMOST MIDWAY THROUGH** her career, then as a general manager with a financial services firm, Joan Nicolo found that encouraging the heart remained particularly challenging. She was uncomfortable praising people in public. Yet she knew her direct reports deserved and needed to be acknowledged for their work. Being a conscientious person and knowing that recognizing others for their contributions was a critical leadership skill, she started asking herself what was holding her back. On the surface, it seemed such a simple task. So what was the big deal?

After considerable soul-searching, she came up with some theories. She was afraid that others would think she was playing favorites if she praised one person. She also felt that praising and encouraging activities took too much time. It was just another item for her to add to an already burgeoning list of responsibilities. Recognition, she worried, was for those sensitive (i.e., touchy-feely, warm-and-fuzzy) types, not for serious and performance-oriented managers. And, maybe, providing recognition would unduly play into stereotypes of women, but not her male counterparts, as "nurturing." However, the more she thought about it, the more she realized that her associates deserved to be recognized, and it was high time for her to come to terms with her resistance to it. She determined to give it a try.

Shortly after that, during a presentation, she made a special point of publicly thanking people for fostering a collaborative spirit in their projects. And it felt great—both to her and to others! She said, "I found that my spirit was lifted. They felt appreciated, and I felt that they had received the credit they deserved."

Joan felt vulnerable opening herself up like that to thank the group. But she knew that she'd established a human connection with her colleagues that hadn't been there before and would prove highly beneficial in the months ahead. Communication was more open after that, and she felt far less guarded. This was a real turning point for her.

In the weeks ahead, she brought much more of herself to her work relationships, and people responded with a new level of enthusiasm for her leadership. Indeed, she began to see her coworkers in a different light. She could focus on getting the job done and enjoy a human bond with everyone around her. Contrary to her worst fears, nobody got jealous when she praised one person or another, and the time it took to show her appreciation was well worth it. Coming to work in the morning, she felt more energetic than ever, and when she went home in the evening, she increasingly felt deep satisfaction with what she'd accomplished. At first, it wasn't clear how these changes would affect productivity. Would they translate into anything that would benefit the company? In a short time, she saw that this new way of relating brought her group together as never before, fueling an esprit de corps that spurred everyone on to give their personal best whenever an extraordinary effort was required.

Like other leaders we talked with, Joan came to understand that recognition is about acknowledging good results and reinforcing positive performance. It's about shaping an environment in which everyone's contributions are noticed and appreciated. Too many managers make the mistake of thinking that getting results is all there is to the job. Your real job is to get results in a way that makes your organization a great place to work—a place where people enjoy coming to work instead of just taking orders and hitting this month's numbers.

In our personal-best case studies, it was not unusual for people to report working intensely over long hours. Under these circumstances, some people may be tempted to give up. To persist for months at such a pace, people need encouragement. Literally, they need the heart to continue with the journey. One crucial way leaders give heart to others is by recognizing individual contributions. When participants in our workshops and seminars summarize the key leadership practices that make a difference in getting extraordinary things done, recognizing people's contributions is on just about every list. Recognition is even more essential in remote environments because you can't easily provide "on-the-spot" acknowledgment. Recognition helps to maintain a positive working culture and is also an important driver of productivity. Employee surveys have consistently shown that "having a caring boss" is rated even higher in importance than salary.[1] You show you care by sharing your appreciation for individual excellence.

Like Joan, exemplary leaders know how important it is to connect with the people around them, not take anyone for granted, and appreciate folks for who they are and what they do. All exemplary leaders make the commitment to *Recognize Contributions*. They do it because people need encouragement to function at their best and persist over time when the hours are long, the work is hard, and the task is daunting. Getting to the finish line of any demanding journey requires energy and commitment. People need emotional fuel to replenish their spirits.

To *Recognize Contributions*, you need to utilize these two essentials:

- **Expect the best**
- **Personalize recognition**

Putting these essentials into practice uplifts people's spirits and arouses the internal drive to strive. You stimulate their efforts to reach for higher levels of performance and aspire to be faithful to the visions and values of the organization. You help people find the courage to do things they have never done before.

## Expect the Best

*Through your actions, show them that they are capable of a lot more than they think they are.*

*Angelique Fahy*

Belief in people's abilities is essential to making extraordinary things happen. Exemplary leaders elicit high performance because they firmly *believe in* their constituents' abilities to achieve even the most challenging goals. When we ask people to describe exemplary leaders, they consistently talk about people who bring out the best in them, have their best interests at heart, and want them to be as successful as possible. Leading others requires having high expectations about what people can accomplish and treating them in ways that bolster their self-confidence, thereby making it possible for them to achieve more than they initially imagined.

Social psychologists refer to this as the "Pygmalion Effect," from the Greek myth about Pygmalion, a sculptor who carved a statue of a beautiful woman, fell in love with it, and appealed to the goddess Aphrodite to bring it to life; Aphrodite granted his prayers. Leaders play Pygmalion-like roles in developing their constituents. Research on self-fulfilling prophecies provides ample evidence that people act in ways that are consistent with others' expectations.[2] When you expect people to fail, they probably will. If you expect them to succeed, they probably will.

This truth was amply illustrated by Anita Lim's experience with her manager at a multinational chain of coffeehouses, whom she described as "warm, welcoming, and encouraging of all her team members." That manager, Anita told us, "believed that we all had the potential to do great things and so always expected the best of us. She made sure to take the time to sit with us and walk us through our business opportunities and weaknesses so that we could better tackle the problems at hand. She knew what it was like to be in our shoes and understood the challenges we faced on a daily basis."

Positive expectations profoundly influence your constituents' aspirations and, often unconsciously, how you behave toward them. You broadcast your beliefs about people in ways you may not even be aware. You give off cues that say to people either "I know you can do it" or "There's no way you'll ever be able to do that." You can't realize the highest level of performance unless you let people know in word and deed that you are confident that they can attain it. You can dramatically improve others' performance when you care deeply for them and have an abiding faith in their capacities, when you nurture, support, and encourage people in whom you believe. In a series of studies, psychologists showed that by starting with the statement, "I'm giving you these comments because I have very high expectations, and I know that you can reach them," the feedback they provided proved to be 40 percent more effective in subsequently changing targeted behaviors.[3] In describing the high expectations that her leader had in her, Carol Schweizer told us, "I think you always rise to expectations. If somebody thinks you can't do something, you can't do it. But when they ask me around here to do some things I've never done before, I think, gosh, I can try it. I bet I could do that. And I can."

The levels of motivation, commitment, team spirit, and productivity reported by direct reports are significantly associated with the extent to which their leaders "make it a point to let people know about their confidence in their abilities." As shown in Figure 10.1, what goes around comes around because there is a direct relationship between the extent that direct reports trust their leaders and how often they observe them sharing their confidence in people's abilities. Given this finding, it is not surprising to note that more than four out of five direct reports who indicate that their leader very frequently or almost always acts this way categorize their leader as "among the best" they have ever worked with.

**Figure 10.1 Expressing Confidence in People's Abilities Increases the Trust They Have in Their Leaders**

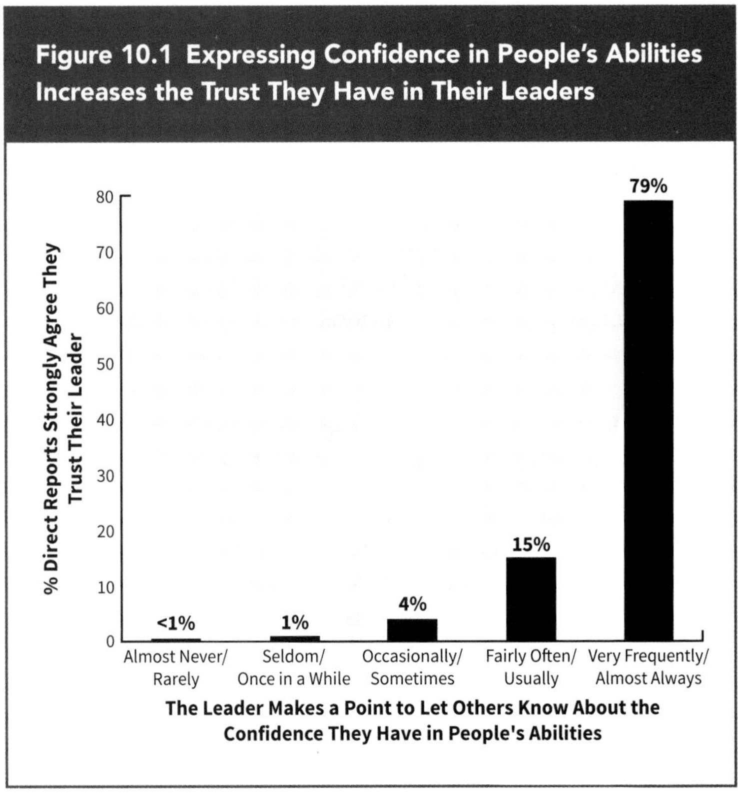


**Show Them You Believe** Leaders' positive expectations aren't fluff.[4] They're not just about keeping a positive outlook or getting others psyched up. The expectations you hold as a leader provide the framework into which people fit their realities. They shape how you behave toward others and how they behave on the task. Maybe you can't turn a marble statue into a real person, but you can draw out the highest potential of your constituents, which is consistent with the experience of the project team at a large telecommunications company that Patti Kozlovsky was leading. She described how she let team members know that she thought they could do the job, and she trusted their judgment to find the information and extract what was needed in a timely manner. When reviewing information team members were contributing in their group meetings, she made a conscious effort to thank members for what they had contributed rather than commenting on what had not been done.

The result was much less tension in the group, and team members felt as though everyone was participating to their fullest capacity. Patti found that instead of sniping at each other over what was not done, people generally supported one another, let their colleagues know what they had found, and shared resources and ideas about where others might find critical data. She noted:

> It was also interesting that team members were genuinely interested in what others had discovered and how that connected with the information they had gathered. Because the team had confidence in each other's abilities, this strengthened our respect for one another and made it easy to incorporate multiple perspectives into our final product. This experience taught me that people live up to our expectations. If you express confidence in their abilities, they will put their heart into whatever project is on the table.

To be most effective, you have to make sure that people feel they belong, are accepted and valued, and have the skills and inner resources needed to succeed. Recognizing people for the value they bring to the organization not only helps them perform better in their jobs but enables them to deal with adversity and challenges. Barbara Wang, when working in one of the largest and fastest-growing social sector organizations in China, wasn't initially very confident when asked to prepare her organization's business plan, but her manager helped her believe in herself. He told her that he had been watching the way she worked for the past few months and that if he had any doubts, he would not have assigned the project to her. "His belief in my skills and talent was what made me believe that I could handle the project on my own and made me psychologically stronger and motivated me to go ahead with a positive attitude. He brought out the best in me by expecting the best and showing me that belief. He believed that I was already a winner."

The manager acted toward Barbara as if she were a winner. For example, whenever she had any slight problems or doubts, her manager was supportive and reassuring, answering her questions and identifying methods for improvement. "This made me feel respected," she told us, and "encouraged me to do better rather than sulking about the fact that my work was not up to the standards he was expecting."

Believing in others is a potent force in propelling higher levels of performance. If you want your constituents to have a winning attitude, you need to act like Patti's and Barbara's leaders. Show that you believe your constituents are already winners. It's not that they will be winners someday; they are winners right now! When you believe that people are winners, you behave in ways that communicate that they are precisely that—not just in your words, but also through tone of voice, posture, gestures, and facial expressions. No yelling, frowning, cajoling, making fun, or putting them down in front of others. Instead, it's about being friendly, positive, supportive, and encouraging. Offer positive reinforcement, share lots of information, listen deeply to their input, provide sufficient resources to do their jobs, give them increasingly challenging assignments, and lend your support and assistance.

It's a virtuous circle: you believe in your constituents' abilities; your favorable expectations cause you to be more positive in your actions; and those encouraging behaviors produce better results, reinforcing your belief that people can do it. As people see that they are capable of extraordinary performance, another virtuous circle begins; they develop that expectation of themselves.

**Be Clear about the Goals and the Rules** Positive expectations are necessary to generate high performance, but that level of performance isn't sustainable unless people are clear about the ground rules and expected outcomes.[5] When you were a kid, you might have read Lewis Carroll's *Alice's Adventures in Wonderland*. Do you remember the croquet match? The flamingos were the mallets, the playing-card soldiers were the wickets, and the hedgehogs were the balls. Everyone kept moving, and the rules kept changing all the time. There was no way of knowing how to play the game or what it took to win. You don't have to fall down the rabbit hole to understand how Alice felt.

Sachin Gad, program director with a high-technology company, recalled learning how essential it is to be clear about what you're trying to accomplish and how to achieve it, especially when the going gets tough. Faced with a situation where timelines were challenging and kept changing—where documentation was unclear, and the customer's requirements were considered "unrealistic"—not surprisingly, morale and motivation on the project team were low. Sachin spent considerable time listening to everyone involved, held sales responsible for realistically managing customer expectations, and worked with others to set clear guidelines that addressed conflicting resource requirements. At the same time, he systematically tracked achievement and identified and recognized high performers. Over the course of a single year, the situation improved significantly, with employee satisfaction ratings improving by over 34 percent and attrition falling by 55 percent.

Believing that people can succeed is essential, but if you want people to give their all, to put their hearts and minds into their work, you must also make sure that they are clear about what they are supposed to be doing. You need to clarify what the expected outcomes look like and make sure that some consistent norms govern how the game is played and points are scored.

Goals and values provide people with standards that concentrate their efforts. Goals are typically short-term, while values (or principles) are more enduring. Values and principles serve as the basis for goals. They're your standards of excellence, your highest aspirations, and they define the arena in which you must set goals and metrics. Values mediate the path of action. Goals release the energy.

The ideal state—on the job, in sports, and in life generally—is often called "flow." Flow experiences, as described in Chapter 9, are those times when you feel pure enjoyment and effortlessness in what you do. To experience flow, you need to have clear goals. Goals help you concentrate and avoid distractions. Goals give intention and meaning to your actions; they provide a purpose for doing what you do. Action without goals, at least in an organizational context, is just busywork. It's a waste of precious time and energy.

Goals provide a context for recognition. They give people something to strive for, something meaningful to attain—for example, coming in first, breaking a record, and setting a new standard of excellence. Goals enhance the significance of recognition because the acknowledgment is for something a person accomplishes or exemplifies. While it's vital to affirm the worth of every one of your constituents, recognition is most meaningful when you reward appropriate behaviors and the achievement of something everyone knows is highly desirable.

Goals focus people's attention on shared values and standards. They help people keep their eyes on the vision. They help keep people on track. Goals enable people to choose the kinds of actions they need to take, know when they are making progress, and see when they need to course correct. They help people put their phones in do-not-disturb mode, appropriately schedule their time, and focus their attention on what matters most.

**Provide and Seek Feedback** People need to know if they're making progress toward the goal or simply marking time. Their motivation to perform a task increases only when they have a challenging goal *and* receive feedback on their progress.[6] Goals without feedback, or feedback without goals, have little effect on people's motivation and willingness to put discretionary effort into the task. Just announcing that the goal is to reach the summit is not enough to get people to put forth more or greater efforts. People need timely information about where they are on the mountain, the resources that have been consumed, and supplies that are still available. They need to know about optional routes, the expected terrain ahead, and forecasted weather conditions. With the end goal in mind and sufficient feedback, people can take initiative, self-correct, determine what support they need, and how they might assist others.

Eddie Tai was responsible for the recruiting, training, career development, promotion, and retention of project engineers and interns for a full-service general contracting company. Giving regular feedback, he found, "helps people self-correct and understand their respective role in the bigger picture. Setting goals without feedback on achievement and performance toward these goals is woefully incomplete." And what do his constituents say about this? One told us, "Receiving feedback is the most important thing in my growth because without knowing where I am, how can I plan where I need to go?" She went on to say, "I also enjoy getting feedback when I make a mistake because I take note and try to improve for the next time. Without making mistakes it is hard to learn, and without a colleague who can point out your mistakes they can sometimes be overlooked and not corrected."

Feedback is at the center of any learning process, and self-confidence diminishes without feedback. Researchers told participants in a study on creative problem-solving that their efforts would be compared with how well hundreds of others had done on the same task. They subsequently received praise, criticism, or no feedback on their performance. Those who heard nothing about how well they did suffered as great a blow to their self-confidence as those criticized, with only those who received positive feedback improving on their initial performance.[7] Saying nothing about a person's performance doesn't help anyone—not the performer, not the leader, not the organization. People hunger for feedback. They prefer to know how they are doing, and no news has the same negative impact as bad news. In fact, people actually would prefer to hear bad news rather than no news at all. As another of Eddie Tai's constituents said, "It sharpens people's skills when they get feedback. I believe the more you know about your performance and how you are doing, the better. It lets me know what I need to work on."

Learning, as this constituent noted, doesn't happen without feedback—it's the only way to know whether you're getting close to your goal and whether you're executing properly. Feedback can be embarrassing, even painful. While most people realize intellectually that feedback is a necessary component of self-reflection and growth, they are often reluctant to make themselves open to it. They want to look good more than they want to get good! Researchers consistently point out that the development of expertise or mastery requires one to receive constructive, even critical, feedback.[8] Even Akansha Sharma, as an HR director with several high-technology startup firms, admitted, "Receiving feedback is never easy, but acknowledging and accepting the feedback provided to me was the first step to becoming a better leader."

You should avoid serving a "feedback sandwich," a traditional technique for giving feedback where you put a slice of praise on the top and bottom and stick the meat of any criticism in between. The data, researchers note, indicates that the "feedback sandwich doesn't taste as good as it looks." Making feedback more constructive begins by explaining why you are giving the feedback. People are more open to criticism when they believe it's intended to help them and you show that you care personally about their well-being and performance. Second, because negative feedback can make people feel inferior, consider leveling the playing field by sharing how feedback has been helpful in your career. Most importantly, find out if the person wants your feedback; once they take ownership of this decision, they're less defensive about whatever you have to offer.[9] Framing feedback in this manner goes a long way toward transforming feedback into guidance, which is what most people hunger for.[10]

Feedback and guidance are vital to every self-correcting system and essential to the growth and development of leaders. Openness to feedback, especially negative feedback, is characteristic of the best learners, and it's something all leaders, especially aspiring ones, need to cultivate. Remaining open to feedback was Hilary Hall's key lesson from her personal-best leadership experience when she was on an audit team with a multinational conglomerate: "It can be somewhat of a painful and embarrassing experience to admit that there are parts of us that are unflattering, but it is a necessary component of self-reflection and growth." She appreciated how "becoming a great leader takes practice and the willingness to view oneself with a critical eye."

When leaders provide a clear sense of direction and feedback along the way, they encourage people to reach inside and do their best. Information about goals and progress toward those goals strongly influences people's abilities to learn and to achieve, and also applies to leaders themselves.[11] Encouragement is more personal and positive than other forms of feedback, and it's more likely to accomplish something that other forms cannot: strengthening trust between leaders and their constituents. Encouragement, in this sense, is the highest form of feedback.

# Personalize Recognition

*Not every person works the same or is triggered by the same incentive. Get to know every single person on your team and find out what it is that they desire.*

*Jeremy Moser*

One of the more common complaints about recognition is that it's far too often highly predictable, mundane, and impersonal. A one-size-fits-all approach to recognition feels insincere, forced, and thoughtless. Bureaucratic and routine recognition, along with most incentive systems, doesn't make anyone very excited. Over time, these can even increase cynicism and damage credibility. Moreover, generalized statements of encouragement fail to generate a significant effect because no one is very certain about either to whom the comments are directed or for what particular actions.

Personalizing recognition is precisely what makes it genuine. That genuineness comes from actually knowing people on a personal level and sincerely caring about them. "If you can't recognize something specific," Nathalie McNeil, HR director for a global pharmaceutical company, contends, "you're not paying attention. And good leaders pay attention. They know their people. When you truly know someone, not only do you recognize them for things they've done, but you also do it in a way that they personally value because it's relevant to what they care about." Recognition that is not personalized is often discounted and quickly forgotten. Over time it can even increase cynicism about the company's values and damage credibility.

Maurice Chan provided personal testimony to the necessity of personalizing recognition when he told us about his experience working as an engineer in a multinational telecommunications company. The Hong Kong branch adapted an incentive scheme from headquarters to reward staff achievements, which he received most every year. He would get an email telling him that he had won the award and that a small amount of money had been deposited into his bank account. He noted that "no one would come to your cube and talk to you about what you had achieved. It made the incentive scheme just like a 'bureaucratic procedure'. It didn't make me or anyone else very excited about getting the reward." Similarly, Alexey Astafev recalled, when he was working for a national railways system, he was called into the department head's office and silently handed a "Merit Citation" and a bonus certificate. "I don't even remember how much the bonus was," Alexey noted, "probably because the way I was rewarded was neither 'personalized' nor 'visible,' and it had no big impact on my performance." The lesson from such experiences, Alexey observed, is:

> In order to encourage people to do their best, you should be able to recognize their achievements and make them feel trusted and valued. It has to be personal, precise, and visible. Even if it is a great reward, if you don't give it out right—or get it right—it will be forgotten soon without achieving the purpose of bringing out the best in people. On the other hand, even a small appraisal such as a "thank you" tailored and meant specifically to you, can inspire people to great performance.

The most consistent response when people tell us about their *most meaningful recognition* is that it was *personal*, and because of that, it felt special. That's why it's so crucial for leaders to pay attention to the likes and dislikes of every individual. You get a lot more emotional bang for your buck when you make recognition and rewards personal. "A sincere word of thanks from the right person at the right time can mean more to an employee than a raise, a formal award, or a whole wall of certificates and plaques," writes Bob Nelson in *1001 Ways to Reward Employees*.[12] As he points out, "Part of the power of such rewards comes from the knowledge that someone took the time to notice the achievement, seek out the employee responsible, and personally deliver praise in a timely manner." When it comes to encouraging the heart, personalizing recognition pays off. Bob's perspective is supported by research involving over 1.7 million employees from small, midsized, and large companies, which found that personal recognition was the most common theme in response to questions about what would encourage them to produce better more often. Employees who receive recognition at work, compared to those who don't, are over two times more likely to believe promotions are fair, innovation is embraced, and people are more willing to go the extra mile.[13]

**Get to Know Constituents** Amy Lai, a demand analyst for a wireless technology company, realized that to give credit where credit is due one has to make certain, as Natalie, Maurice, and Alexey's experiences demonstrated, that you know your audience. Sometimes certain individuals may prefer private acknowledgments while some others may thrive on the attention from public tributes. She found that in being more specific, direct, and deliberate in showing her appreciation, people "are more likely to respond more quickly to my requests, and others are more likely to open up to me about problems they face. If nothing else, it is always a great way to build lasting relationships with the people you work with."

To deliver the appropriate type of recognition, you need to learn about the motivations of the people around you. Luis Zavaleta recalled one manager he worked for at a multinational financial services company who was simply not interested in getting to know the people on his team. As a result, Luis explained, that manager relied solely upon financial means for encouragement, which had the opposite effect from what he doubtlessly intended:

> Most members of the team viewed the financial reward that we received from our manager with indifference. We would get anonymous bonuses attached to our paychecks without any warning or knowledge of where it came from or the reason behind the reward. The lack of immediate acknowledgment for our work left people unhappy with management. The lack of feedback left most members unable to determine if they were doing a good job, which further decreased morale and productivity.

Because the manager was not interested in learning about the goals or needs of his constituents, Luis told us, "this lack of care led to a decrease in satisfaction and retention levels."

As Luis's story illustrates, you first have to get to know your constituents to make recognition personally meaningful. If you're going to personalize recognition and make it feel genuinely special, you'll have to look past the organizational diagrams and roles people play and see the person inside. You need to get to know who your constituents are, how they feel, and what they think. You need to repeatedly walk the halls and plant floors, regularly meet with small groups, and frequently hit the road for visits with associates, key suppliers, and customers. And when people are working from anywhere, you must find ways to connect virtually and have private conversations about recent wins or check social media to see what colleagues are "liking" or giving "thumbs up" for.

Paying attention, personalizing recognition, and creatively and actively appreciating others increase their trust in you. This kind of relationship is even more critical as workforces are becoming increasingly global, diverse, and often virtual. Daniela Maeder, section head in a European governmental agency, put it this way: "Organizational diagrams don't matter at all. Be sure to treat employees as human beings and not as functional workers." If you're going to personalize recognition and make it feel genuinely special, you will have to look past the roles people play and see the person inside. You must get to know your constituents, how they feel, and what they think. And they want to get to know who you are as well.

You have to get close to people if you're going to find out what motivates them, what they like and don't like, and what kinds of recognition they most appreciate. Yet managerial myth says that leaders shouldn't get too close to their constituents, that they can't be friends with people at work. Let's set this myth aside.[14]

Over a five-year period, researchers observed groups of friends and groups of acquaintances (people who knew each other only vaguely) performing motor-skill and decision-making tasks. The results were unequivocal. The groups composed of friends completed, on average, more than three times as many projects as the groups made up of acquaintances. Regarding decision-making assignments, groups of friends were 20 percent more effective than groups of acquaintances.[15] There is an important caveat, however. Friends have to be strongly committed to the group's goals. If not, then friends may not do better. This is precisely why we said earlier that it is necessary for leaders to be clear about standards and to create a condition of shared goals and values. When it comes to performance, commitment to standards and good relations between people go together. Furthermore, employees who report having a friendly relationship with their manager are two and a half times more satisfied with their jobs.[16] People are more willing to follow someone they feel knows who they are and what they need. Feeling a connection with others motivates them to work harder because people don't like to disappoint or let down individuals they consider friends. People also stick around longer at their companies when they feel they have friends at their workplace.

Remember, it's all about relationship, and relationships are predicated on trust. An open door is a physical demonstration of a willingness to let others in, and so is an open heart. To become fully trusted, you must be open to others. This means disclosing things about yourself in order to build the basis for a relationship. This means telling others the same things you'd like to know about them—talking about your hopes and dreams, your family and friends, your interests and pursuits.

Certainly, disclosing information about yourself can be risky. You can't be certain that other people will like you, appreciate your candor, agree with your aspirations, buy into your plans, or interpret your words and actions in the way you intend. But by demonstrating the willingness to take such risks, you encourage others to take similar risks—and thereby take the first steps necessary to build *mutual* trust as the foundation for any relationship.

**Be Creative About Appreciations** As a technical lead and senior software engineer, Anu Yamunan had to find out what was special for each of her constituents in order to get close to them. Armed with this information, she was able to be imaginative and creative in her approach to recognizing and incentivizing people. As she told us:

> People love to do what they are recognized for, and they won't come to work with enthusiasm if they expect to be criticized, punished, or ignored. As a leader, I try to find out what my constituents

> care about. The rewards can then be used to reinforce outstanding performance. Some people in my team crave being recognized; others appreciate one-on-one time with senior leadership; some relish the opportunity to be in control of an aspect of their work; others care about bonuses or gifts.

Leaders can't rely exclusively on the organization's formal reward system, which offers only a limited range of options. After all, promotions and raises are scarce resources, and it would be wrong to assume that individuals respond only to money. Although salary increases or bonuses are certainly valued, individual needs for appreciation and rewards include much more than cash.[17]

Blaze Silberman echoes the importance of creativity and makes the additional point that "in order to make meaningful recognition, it has to be genuine and relevant to the people involved." As the new manager of a sales team, he discovered that his salespeople didn't feel respected, experienced helplessness, and had a common belief that they were "treated like dogs." He also learned, quite ironically, that everyone had some positive connection to their family's dog or wanted to buy a puppy. Given these themes, a few weeks later, he told us:

> I began my team meeting by holding up a rawhide dog bone that I had spray-painted with gold paint. I explained how I had thought about all of their feedback and that everything they said was valid, and therefore, let's go ahead and treat ourselves like dogs. I designed two giant poster boards with little paper dog bone cutouts for a point system of rewards for the simple activities we needed to succeed—like making a phone call, booking a first meeting, leaving a voicemail, sending twenty prospecting emails by Wednesday, and so on. In addition, I created a point trade-in system for silly rewards. I had specifically listened to each person's hobbies, likes, and dislikes and chose one item that tied directly to each person's interests.
>
> It was fun to have each person explain to the others why their "dinky" reward was chosen. The person with the most little bones could opt to save up and possess the Golden Bone for the week. That

> prize came with other powers—full autonomy to set the agenda for our weekly team meeting, delegating their end-of-week pipeline cleanup to a person of their choosing, deciding where and what we would eat for lunch, and so on.

The entire "cost" of the rewards—including the toy, a can of spray paint, and some poster boards—was under forty dollars, but according to Blaze, "the payoff in morale, confidence, and energy was tremendous." After three quarters of earning their bones, this team produced the highest revenue attainment percentage of the six West Coast teams, earned an MVP award for Top Performance across more than fifty sales reps in the division, and received recognition for closing the largest transaction. This last accomplishment, said Blaze: "was closed by the same sales rep who told me in our first meeting that he was considering giving up and quitting by the end of the month and to expect nothing from him."

People do respond to all kinds of rewards. Verbal recognition of performance in front of one's peers and visible awards, such as certificates, plaques, and other tangible gifts, are potent symbols of accomplishment. That's why you see them hanging in cubicles in the office or sitting on the bookshelves at home. They are almost unlimited in their application. In difficult and challenging circumstances, sometimes all people need is to be supported and propped up. This can be as simple as asking people how they are feeling or taking them out for a cup of coffee. Putting a bit of time aside to acknowledge their extra efforts makes a big difference to how people feel. The data shows that when it comes to being recognized, those leaders who do so most *creatively* are seen by their direct reports as most effective, in contrast to less than one in ten direct reports who indicate that their leader is effective when this person seldom demonstrates creativity in providing recognition.

Spontaneous and unexpected rewards are often more meaningful than the expected formal ones. "The form of recognition that has the most positive influence on us, and that should be used most often, is on-the-spot recognition," says Sonia Clark, vice president of human resources for several high-technology startups. "When something really terrific happens, I comment on it right away and to anyone who might be close enough to hear." Similarly, Anita Lin told us about how her regional manager would show up in person to congratulate a store when it had a week with great results. She would deliver awards at their quarterly managers' meetings to those store managers who had proven themselves to have gone above and beyond in their duties. Anita said that she did "not base these awards on sales quotas alone. Rather, she found ways to reward people for stepping outside the box. For example, there were awards for most improved, most supportive, and even most courageous. When presenting these awards, she would accompany them with a personalized speech for the recipient and highlight all the achievements this individual had made in their time with the company."

Recognition is most effective when it is highly specific and given soon after the appropriate behavior. One of the most important benefits of being out and about as a leader is that you can personally observe people doing things right and then recognize them either on the spot or at the next public gathering. As Anu Yamunan maintains, "Whatever it is that motivates my team members, I try to give the rewards at the time of the achievement, not three or four months later. I also make the connection between the reward and the performance as direct, clear, and explicit as possible."

In workplaces that are mostly remote, this is more challenging but equally applicable. For example, in virtual meetings, create opportunities for people to share something they or others did that went above and beyond in service of an organizational value. Immediately after someone shares a story, thank them for the example and praise those who exhibited excellence.

Relying solely upon an organization's formal reward system typically results in a poor job of linking rewards to performance. In many organizations, the time lag between performance and recognition generally is too long to make recognition meaningful. For example, a global study involving more than 1,000 organizations in over 150 countries found that more than one out of three employees had to wait more than three months to get feedback from their managers.[18]

Furthermore, formal reward systems are often monetary, and while it is true that money may get people to do a job, it doesn't get them to do particularly outstanding work.[19] Your options are also quite limited if you rely exclusively on the organization's formal reward system. The truth is that people respond to all kinds of informal recognition and rewards, which is the beauty of being creative and personalizing them. We've seen people give out stuffed giraffes, rainbow-striped zebra posters, mugs with team photos, crystal apples, classic car rides, and hundreds of other imaginative expressions of appreciation. We've seen recognition done verbally and nonverbally, elaborately and modestly. There are no limits to kindness and consideration.[20]

It's important to understand that genuine recognition does not have to include anything tangible. Exemplary leaders make extensive use of intrinsic rewards—rewards built into the work itself, including such factors as a sense of accomplishment, a chance to be creative, and the challenge of the work—all directly tied to an individual's effort. These rewards are far more important than salary and fringe benefits in improving job satisfaction, commitment, retention, and performance.[21]

Being creative in your use of incentives boils down to being considerate. The techniques you use are less important than your genuine expression of caring. People appreciate knowing that you have their best interests at heart, and they are more caring about what they are doing as a result. When you genuinely care, even the smallest of gestures reap huge rewards.

**Be Appreciative** Researchers indicate that if employees receive four or more "touchpoints" of positive feedback in a quarter, retention rates increase to 96 percent over the next year.[22] However, too many managers struggle with showing appreciation, with less than 20 percent of employees reporting that their supervisor expresses appreciation "more than occasionally."[23] Not enough people show their appreciation by making good use of the most powerful but inexpensive two-word recognition: "thank-you." Tsung-Chieh (T.C.) Lin, project manager for a British commercial and defense electronics company, pointed out that "sometimes a 'thank you' is more important than a big victory party." He recalled with great fondness how he felt when one of his managers "simply stopped by my office frequently and gave me praise on what a good job I had done.

Furthermore, he called me to show appreciation when I worked late in the evening or on the weekend."

While managing the customer service support team for a multinational personal care corporation, Olivia Lai recalled how it clearly mattered to her constituents when she said, "Thank you" or "I really appreciate your help." "You should see the smile that it generates," she said. "It gives them a warm feeling knowing that their work was welcomed and recognized by others." Olivia understands that it's not just about achieving financial results and delivering on annual objectives. It's also about creating a winning team through trust and a personal connection. It includes extending a simple pat on the back, a handshake, a smile, and a "Thank you for your hard work."

Both Olivia and T.C. give personal testimony to what researchers have discovered: personal congratulations rank at the top of the most powerful nonfinancial motivators identified by employees.[24] Few basic needs are more important than being noticed, recognized, and appreciated for one's efforts. Surveys reveal that the clear majority of people (81 percent) indicate that they'd be more willing to work harder if they had an appreciative manager, and 70 percent report they would feel better about themselves and their efforts if their manager thanked them more regularly. More than three out of every four employees who quit their jobs cite a lack of appreciation as a key reason.[25]

Extraordinary achievements bloom more readily in climates marked with a high volume of appreciative comments. Research shows that performance recognition significantly impacts employee engagement at a rate of more than two to one. The same research finds that employees who receive strong recognition are more innovative, generating two times more ideas per month than those who aren't recognized very well.[26] Kevin Jiang, senior product engineer for a computer game company, reported in his Personal-Best Leadership Experience that he "always sent out appreciative emails to team members for achieving each milestone. I pointed out each individual contributor during project meetings and bolded their names in meeting minutes. I ensured that their managers were in the same email loop so that upper-level management could know that those people did a great job."

Our data clearly showed the importance of leaders, like Kevin, making it a point to "praise people for a job well done," given the impact of this leadership behavior on their direct reports. We found that only about one in fifty direct reports strongly agreed that they felt a sense of pride in their organization, were motivated to work hard for their organization, or were committed to the organization's long-term success when they indicated that their leader rarely praised people. You need to set an example in this regard, as researchers have found that members of top-performing teams provide at least three and as many as six times the number of positive comments for every negative one they make. Medium-performing teams average about twice as many positive comments as negative ones, but the average for the low-performing teams is almost three negative comments for every positive one.[27]

It is always worth the time to recognize someone's hard work and contributions. All too often, people forget to extend a hand, a smile, or a simple thank-you. People naturally feel a little frustrated and unappreciated when their manager or even a colleague takes them for granted. Sometimes they overlook this because people are under the pressure of deadlines, and the mandate to deliver on time overtakes expressing gratitude. However, it's critical that you stick around for that extra moment to say thanks.

Expressing your thanks also has another, more personal benefit. People who practice gratitude, compared to those who do not, are healthier, more optimistic, more positive, and better able to cope with stress. They are also more alert, more energized, more resilient, more willing to offer support to others, more generous, and more likely to make progress toward meaningful goals.[28] The wonderful thing about expressing gratitude and providing recognition is that they aren't hard to do, and you don't need to be on a particular hierarchical perch to dispense them. They cost you next to nothing and yet pay daily dividends. You can't ask for a better investment than that.

Being appreciative and providing personalized recognition come down to being thoughtful. It requires being authentic and sincerely caring about others. It means knowing enough about another person to answer these two questions: "What could I do to make this a memorable experience so that this individual always remembers how important their contributions are?" And "What would make my comment or action special and unique for this person?"

## TAKE ACTION:

### Recognize Contributions

Exemplary leaders have positive expectations of themselves and their constituents. They expect the best of people and create self-fulfilling prophecies about how ordinary people can produce extraordinary actions and results. Exemplary leaders' goals and standards are unambiguous, helping people focus on what needs doing. They provide clear feedback and reinforcement. Maintaining a positive outlook and providing motivating feedback stimulates, rekindles, and focuses people's energies and drive.

Exemplary leaders recognize and reward what individuals do to contribute to the vision and values. They express their appreciation far beyond the limits of the organization's formal systems. They enjoy being spontaneous and creative in saying thank you. Personalizing recognition requires knowing what's appropriate individually and culturally. Although recognizing someone's efforts may be uncomfortable or embarrassing at first, it begins by making a personal connection with each person. Learn from many small and often casual acts of appreciation what works for each of your constituents and how best to personalize recognition.

To Encourage the Heart, we suggest you take these actions to *recognize contributions by showing appreciation for individual excellence*:

- Wander around your work areas for the express purpose of finding people doing things that exemplify the organization's vision, values, and standards. Find a way to recognize those people on the spot.
- Regularly tell positive stories in public about people in your organization who exemplify the vision and values in action. Positive storytelling is not only a very effective way of showing appreciation, it's also a way of saying, "Here's a positive example of the behaviors we're looking for."
- Record a note in your mobile phone, PDA, or paper planner to recognize each of your direct reports at least once a week. That's what the research shows people need to be most highly engaged in their work.

In every interaction, you have the chance to direct people's attention to aspects of leadership that you think are important to focus on. Regular conversations about leadership will let people know it's something important. Find opportunities to talk with others about these questions:

- How effective have we been in creating a culture in which peers recognize each other? What are some positive examples of this, and how can we publicize them throughout the organization?
- Are there ways to be more intentional about noticing people who are doing "the right thing"—that is, showing commitment to shared values—and making sure their actions are visible to the rest of the team and organization?

# CHAPTER 11
# Celebrate the Values and Victories

*Ceremonies, celebrations, and rituals are not about the event. They're about touching the hearts and souls of every employee.*

*Victoria Sandvig*

**TO SOME, A** corporate celebration may seem like a wasteful distraction. You can almost hear the critics say in Scrooge-like voices, "We haven't got time for fun and games. After all, this is a business." But exemplary leaders and their organizations understand that one of the most significant contributors to a strong and resilient workforce—and one that can get extraordinary things done—is a culture that strengthens pride and makes people feel valued for their contributions.

"Celebrations at the organizational level play a critical role for us," Jennifer Ernst, director of business development with a research and development company, told us as she described their annual recognition event and why it was so important:

> As people entered the auditorium, they knew it wasn't a typical meeting. Lights on the walls gave the look of theatrical sconces;

> twenty-foot-high graphics of Oscar-like images framed the screen, and the sound of an orchestra warming up percolated through the audio system. Then the event started. The room went dark, a garish fanfare sounded, a spotlight hit the curtain, and our president, a quiet and understated man in most public appearances, strode out in a tux. The room exploded with laughter; the release of tension, pent up since a year-end layoff, was tangible. The laughter continued when, for the first award, he proclaimed, "The envelope please." As the presenting manager walked to the stage, a member of the administrative staff, wearing a floor-length black gown and dripping with jewelry, delivered an oversized envelope on a golden platter.
>
> For each award, senior managers told rich and personal stories about the research and its impact before calling individuals to the stage. Other lab members carried award plaques onto the stage, again on golden platters. When the recipients came down, triumphant music played in the background. Interspersed between the awards for major accomplishments were videos marked "special recognition," awards given for values such as exemplary service, "chipping-in," citizenship, and spirit. Each video featured people from different parts of the organization sharing how the award recipient had impacted them and expressing appreciation. By the end of the one-hour event, the room was on fire, creating a buzz that lasted for weeks.

Why was this so powerful? Certainly, the theatrics assured it would be memorable. Stories were crucial in recalling the accomplishments (and sacrifices), showing how the honorees modeled best practices. By stepping outside their comfort zones, the organization's leaders personally demonstrated that their expressions of respect and recognition were genuine. Between the on-stage volunteers, the presenters, and the people in the videos, nearly one-fourth of the workplace was actively visible in providing recognition to their peers. Finally, the messages of this event resonated with broadly held values of the organization—the senior managers' stories kept the scientific values at the forefront while the other elements of the event connected to the sense of community within the company.

Exemplary leaders know that promoting a culture of celebration fuels the sense of unity and mission essential for retaining and motivating today's workforce. Besides, who wants to work for a place with no ritual or ceremony—a boring place that neither remembers nor celebrates anything? David Campbell, a pioneer in leadership assessment, said it well: "A leader who ignores or impedes organizational ceremonies and considers them as frivolous or 'not cost-effective' is ignoring the rhythms of history and our collective conditioning. [Celebrations] are the punctuation marks that make sense of the passage of time; without them, there are no beginnings and endings. Life becomes an endless series of Wednesdays."[1]

What leaders like David and Jennifer know from their experience is confirmed in our research. Celebrations provide an essential opportunity to cement the lessons learned from accomplishments and strengthen relationships between people that promote future achievements. Performance improves when leaders bring people together to rejoice in their achievements and reinforce their shared principles. If leaders are to effectively *Celebrate the Values and Victories,* they must master these essentials:

- **Create a spirit of community**
- **Be personally involved**

When leaders bring people together, rejoice in collective successes, and directly display their gratitude, they reinforce the essence of community. Being personally involved makes it clear that everyone is committed to making extraordinary things happen.

## Create a Spirit of Community

*If you can create a community that supports itself, you can really achieve wonderful things.*

*Keith Sonberg*

Too many organizations operate as if social gatherings were a nuisance. They aren't. Human beings are social animals—hardwired to connect with others.[2] People are meant to do things together, form communities, and demonstrate a common bond.

When social connections are strong and numerous, there's more trust, reciprocity, information flow, collective action, and happiness—and, by the way, greater wealth.[3] Some of the fastest-growing and most successful businesses these days are evidence of the need for social connection. Facebook, YouTube, WhatsApp, Instagram, Messenger, Tik Tok, QQ, WeChat, Snapchat, and Twitter are only a few of the social networking sites with over one hundred million users.[4] Researchers have found that "social networking site users have more friends and more close friends" than nonusers.[5] Social capital is as significant a source of success and happiness as physical and intellectual capital.

Corporate celebrations are among the best ways to capitalize on the need to connect, socialize, and create a feeling of community. Research on corporate celebrations has found that they "infuse life with passion and purpose. . . . They bond people together and connect us to shared values and myths. Ceremonies and rituals create community, fusing individual souls with the corporate spirit. When everything is going well, these occasions allow us to revel in our glory. When times are tough, ceremonies draw us together, kindling hope and faith that better times lie ahead."[6] Moreover, scientists find that celebrating stimulates a feel-good chemical in the brain (dopamine) and strengthens the sense of connection that people have with one another.[7]

With celebrations, leaders create a sense of team spirit, building and maintaining the social support necessary to thrive, especially in stressful and uncertain times. The challenge, as Sebastian Molina, senior program manager with an aerospace company, explained is that in "the fast-paced environment and 'new normal' world we work in today, it can be all too easy to get caught up in the craziness and not take the time to celebrate. Yet it's when things are the most hectic and the workload is the heaviest that people need to come together and hear that they are appreciated for all the hard work they do."

Sometimes celebrations can be elaborate, but more often, they are about connecting everyday actions and events to the values of the organization and the accomplishments of the team. This was precisely Emma Van Sant's experience as a senior marketing manager. "It's important to remember that you can start small," Emma told us. "Something as simple as starting a meeting by checking in with everyone personally before diving into the agenda and work items can have a big impact. I think it's also important to note that celebrating others doesn't need to be a big formal affair. There are ways to celebrate others in a less formal capacity that will lift morale and create a sense of community and appreciation."

Exemplary leaders seldom let an opportunity pass to make sure that constituents know why they're there and how they should act in service of that purpose. This connective power is most evident in sports, because when a team performs at its best, every player and coach, even all the people in the stands, experience great joy. One of our leadership development workshop participants explained what this looked like in practice. His sales vice president used regular monthly conference calls with the entire sales organization to shine the spotlight on people who have been given "Standing Ovations." These were individuals whom peers had nominated for their contributions or achievements. Monthly sales calls featured the recipient's photo and a summary of accomplishments, and meeting time was reserved to highlight and congratulate their "heroic efforts." In addition, the vice president followed up with all the individual nominators and thanked them for taking the time to share their feedback. This public, enthusiastic, and heartfelt recognition went a long way in making both the recipients and bystanders feel that they were valued and built a positive, empowering community. Actions like these are especially important these days when seven in ten Americans wish they received more recognition. Even more (83 percent) readily admit they could do more to recognize others.[8]

Whether they're to honor an individual, group, or organizational achievement—or to encourage team learning and relationship building—celebrations, ceremonies, and similar events offer leaders the perfect opportunity to explicitly communicate and reinforce the actions and behaviors that are important in realizing shared values and common goals. Exemplary leaders know that promoting a culture of celebration fuels the sense of unity essential for retaining and motivating today's workforce.

**Celebrate Accomplishments in Public** As noted in Chapter 10, individual recognition increases the recipient's sense of worth and improves performance. Public celebrations also have this effect, and they add other lasting benefits for individuals and organizations that private individual recognition can't accomplish. MT Vu, program analyst with a multinational aerospace, defense, and technology company, illustrated these benefits when she shared her experience receiving an Operational Excellence Award for her contribution to a new business proposal: "The award was presented in front of all my peers and management. I felt a great sense of pride and fulfillment. This encouraged me to continue to perform well to show my peers and management that the award represented my values." Not only did she say that this public acknowledgment energized her, but it revalidated to others that great performance will be recognized. In one field experiment, when thank-you cards were publicly awarded to the top three performers in small work groups, researchers found that performance increased not just for the top performers who received the recognition, but for all members of the group. Observing colleagues receiving recognition can induce people to step up their own performance.[9]

Public events are opportunities to highlight actual examples of what it means to "do what we say we will do." When the spotlight shines on certain people and others tell stories about what they did, those individuals become role models. They visibly represent how the organization would like everyone to behave and concretely demonstrate that it is possible to do so. Public celebrations of accomplishment also build commitment, both among the individuals recognized and those in the audience. When you communicate to individuals, "Keep up the good work; it's appreciated," you are also saying to the larger group, "Here are people just like you who exemplify what we stand for and believe in. You can do this. You too can make a significant contribution to our success."

Jan Pacas, Australia's general manager for a European global construction and building industry company, understood that celebrations strengthen the sense of community, helping to ensure that people feel that they belong to something greater than themselves and that they are working together toward a common cause. In particular, he wanted to make sure that people knew it wasn't just the sales force that was responsible for top-level results. There were also many people in support functions who contributed to the company's success.

To ensure that these behind-the-scenes folks did not go unnoticed, Jan introduced peer-nominated awards for people in non-managerial roles who had demonstrated outstanding customer focus. Anyone in the company could submit a nomination along with a story to support their nomination. The Executive Management Team would review the submission to make sure that the candidates consistently lived the company's values. The first of these awards were given out at the gala dinner, and there was an air of excitement as Jan read the list of recipients. No one knew until that moment who would be walking up on stage, and it was inspiring to see 250 people give a standing ovation to those who exemplified the company's shared values. The announcement of the winners was, according to Jan, "the pièce de résistance to an overall great two-day event. However, it was not about the prize, although the prize was very exciting. It was the feeling that you had been selected by your peers for something very, very special that you had achieved. It made everybody proud being a winner of this, and at the same time it cemented our 'high expectations/high rewards' culture with all staff."

The data shows that the frequency with which leaders publicly recognize people who exemplify commitment to shared values correlates significantly with the extent to which their direct reports feel the organization values their work and they are making a difference. Like the one Jan described, public ceremonies serve as a collective reminder of why people remain with an organization and of the values and visions they share. By making celebrations a public part of organizational life, leaders create a sense of community. Building community helps ensure that people feel that they belong to something greater than themselves and work together toward a common cause. Celebrations serve to strengthen the bond of teamwork and trust.

Jerry Lukach, plant manager for a small factory making patio doors, explained ceremonies' impact on his facility. He said they "break down barriers, particularly between departments, and remove people from their cast roles at the plant and cause them to relate to each other in new manners." He told us that celebrations do not solve problems, "but a celebrative atmosphere washes away some of the stress and bitterness that surrounds those problems. The positive atmosphere at the plant makes people more positive about managing day-to-day challenges of working in a manufacturing facility."

These observances add excitement or drama to the organization's rites and rituals and make things even more memorable and lasting. Everything about a ceremony or celebration should be matched to its purposes. From the setting to the speeches, from the music to the mood, every little detail can impact the lasting influence of the event. For organizational values to have an impact, leaders must make explicit connections between shared values and the actions that exemplify those values. Celebrations are magnificent opportunities for leaders to link principles to practices in a memorable, motivating, and uplifting way.

What leaders preach and what leaders celebrate must be the same. If they aren't, the event will come off as insincere and phony—and the leader's credibility will suffer. The celebration must be an honest expression of commitment to certain key values and the hard work and dedication of those who have lived the values. Authenticity is what makes conscious celebrations work.

Some people are reluctant to recognize others in public, fearing that it might cause jealousy or resentment. Forget these fears. All winning teams have MVPs (Most Valuable Players), usually selected by their teammates. Public celebrations are meaningful opportunities to reinforce shared values and recognize individuals for their contributions. They give you a chance to say thanks to specific individuals for their outstanding performance and to remind everyone around of exactly what the organization stands for and the significance of the work or service they provide.

Private rewards may work fine to motivate individuals, but they have little impact on the team. Researchers have shown that people tend to pick up on the mood and attitudes of those around them, called "emotional contagion," and often in ways they don't consciously realize.[10] Circuits in the brain are activated when people see others act in a particular manner, and watching someone else can impact the brain in ways that mirror experiencing it directly.[11] People not only imitate the particulars of positive actions but also the spirit underlying them. This was precisely what Brian Dalton, finance manager with an ad technology company, observed: "In publicly acknowledging someone for doing a good job, you help to set a standard of what is judged to be good work. You want the recipient of the praise to feel valued and recognized for their contributions, but you also want to publicly celebrate those values and victories so that others can see and replicate them." Brian's experience is borne out in the data. The extent to which direct reports feel valued by their organizations, as shown in Figure 11.1, is directly related to the frequency that their leaders "publicly recognize people who exemplify commitment to shared values."

To generate community-wide energy and commitment for the common cause, you need to celebrate successes in public. Ceremonies and celebrations are opportunities to build healthier groups and enable members of the organization to know and care about each other. Celebrations provide concrete evidence that individuals aren't alone in their efforts, that other people care about them, and that they can count on others. They reinforce the fact that people need each other and that it takes a group of individuals with a common purpose working together in an atmosphere of trust and collaboration to get extraordinary things done. By making achievements public, leaders build a culture in which people know that their actions and decisions are not taken for granted. They see that their contributions are recognized, appreciated, and valued. They also serve to reduce we–they demarcations between leaders and constituents.

**Provide Social Support** Supportive relationships at work—relationships characterized by a genuine belief in and advocacy for the

**Figure 11.1 Direct Reports Feel Valued by Their Organization as a Result of Their Leader's Public Recognition**

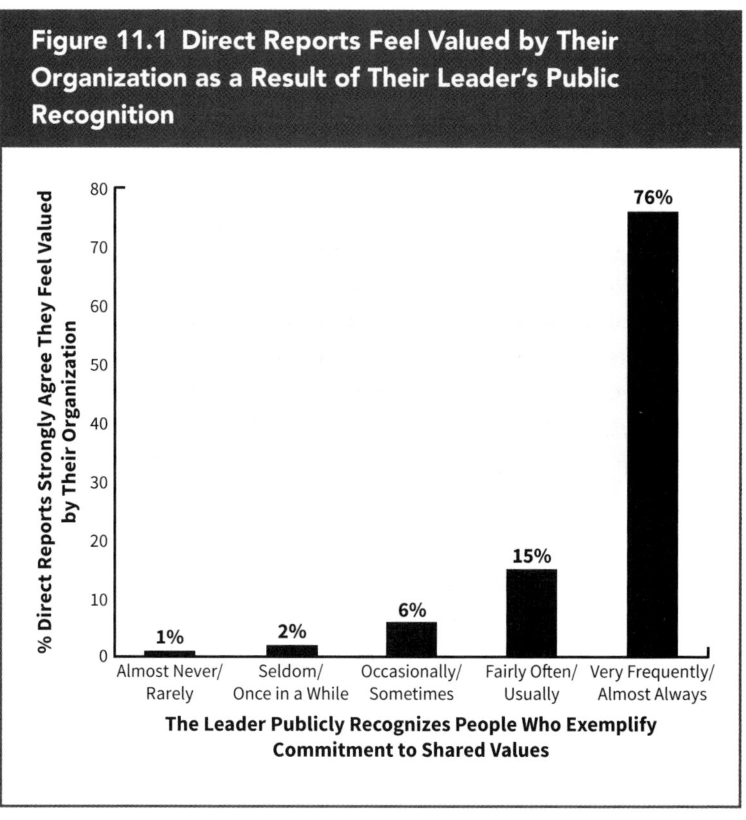


interests of others—are essential in maintaining personal and organizational vitality.[12] Individuals who don't like the people they're working with don't do their best work or remain with the organization for very long. Consider what studies have found about the differences between the task performances of groups of friends versus acquaintances. In groups composed of acquaintances, individuals prefer to work alone and speak with others in the group only when necessary. Consequently, they are reluctant to seek help or point out mistakes being made by others. Groups made up of friends, on the other hand, talk with one another right from the project's get-go. They evaluate ideas more critically, give timely feedback when others are veering off course, and offer teammates positive encouragement every step of the way.[13] Feeling a sense of connection with co-workers fosters greater accountability, engagement, and commitment to the organization.

Employees with a best friend at work are seven times more likely to engage fully in their work than those reporting no such friendships.[14] And there are plenty of prospects for strengthening these relationships, because less than one in five people indicate that they work for organizations that provide opportunities to develop friendships in their workplace.[15] Longitudinal studies in the United States and Europe also revealed that people who make use of social support have higher incomes than those who don't tap into the power of a social network. This was true two and nine years after the study's baseline period.[16] Lacking social support, individuals regularly ignored cooperative opportunities, distrusting other people and their motives. Studies involving more than three million people around the world show that social isolation has more serious consequences for people's health than obesity, smoking, or alcoholism.[17]

Research across a broad variety of disciplines consistently demonstrates that social support enhances productivity, psychological well-being, and even physical health.[18] Social support not only improves wellness but also buffers against disease, particularly during times of high stress. This finding is true irrespective of an individual's age, gender, or ethnic group. For example, even after adjusting for such factors as smoking and histories of major illness, people with few close contacts were two to three times more likely to die than those who had friends to turn to regularly.[19]

The various lockdowns associated with the coronavirus pandemic have definitely increased feelings of social isolation and exacerbated their accompanying problems. Remote work has a potentially similar isolating impact. You need to recognize the importance of social interaction and take the initiative to provide social support. Doing so increases peoples' feelings that they are valued and strengthens their commitment to the organization. Regardless of your choice of videoconferencing and social connection platforms, these tools can be used to interact and engage people more frequently in conversation and collaborative efforts.

Our files are full of personal-best leadership cases in which strong human connections produced spectacular results. When people feel a strong sense of affiliation and attachment to their colleagues, they're much more likely to have a higher sense of personal well-being, to feel more committed to the organization, and to perform at higher levels. When people feel distant and detached, they're unlikely to accomplish much of anything.[20] When everyone gets personally involved with the task and connected with their colleagues, they can enjoy achieving extraordinary feats.

**Have Fun Together** Leaders are on the lookout for every possible opportunity to inculcate fun into the work environment because fun isn't a luxury at work.[21] Every personal-best leadership experience was a combination of hard work *and* fun. In fact, most people agreed that without the enjoyment and the pleasure they experienced interacting with others on the team, they would have been unable to sustain the level of intensity and hard work required to achieve their personal best.

Shifts in the psychological contract between employers and employees, workforce demographics, and the work itself are necessitating that people experience their organizations as places where they can do more than just work.[22] A fun work environment "intentionally encourages, initiates, and supports a variety of enjoyable and pleasurable activities that positively impact the attitude and productivity of individuals and groups."[23] Having fun sustains productivity, creating what researchers refer to as "subjective well-being" and contributing positively to employees' affective, cognitive, and behavioral functioning. In addition, studies demonstrate that having fun enhances people's problem-solving skills because fun makes them more creative and productive—which in turn fosters lower turnover, higher morale, and a stronger bottom line.[24]

Mike Sawyer, vice president of marketing with a software security company, explained that his personal-best leadership experience involved ensuring that his team had fun with one another. To change the character of department-wide planning meetings, they "set up an informal meeting area in the marketing department with couches, a TV, and other things that allowed both standing and ad-hoc meetings to seem more like a friendly environment. This area was in the middle of where everyone sat, so even if just a few people were meeting, it let everyone know what was going on, and they could freely join others if they wanted."

People feel better about their work when they enjoy a supportive network of close relationships. The importance of fostering a sense of connection in even everyday mundane affairs is apparent in the experience of one of our colleagues. He simply brought a box of candy suckers (lollipops) to the office and placed them out in a common area. In no time at all, "everyone had a sucker sticking out of their mouth and a smile on their face," he told us. Later that afternoon, during the break in a particularly tedious and combative meeting, he put another bunch of suckers in the middle of the table. Before he knew it, he said, people were reaching for their favorite flavors and smiling at one another, and the tone of the meeting got noticeably friendlier. As he told us, with a smile on his face, "It's hard to be too combative or in a bad mood, when you and everyone around you has a sucker in their mouth!"

Moreover, it's not all about parties, games, festivities, and laughter. Research demonstrates that having fun enhances problem-solving skills. People are more creative and productive, fostering lower turnover, higher morale, and a stronger bottom line. Employees from *Fortune*'s 100 Best Companies to Work For list overwhelmingly—an average of 81 percent—agree that they are working in a "fun" environment.[25] Furthermore, according to neuroscientists, "laughter is not primarily about humor, but about social relationships. In fact, the health benefits of laughter may result from the social support it stimulates."[26] Researchers examining humor in the workplace offer additional evidence that laughing together strengthens the bonds between people. They report, "Shared laughter quickens the path to candor and vulnerability," and because candor and vulnerability help to increase trust, it follows that laughing together is a way to build more cohesive teams.[27]

Leaders set the tone. When you openly demonstrate the joy and passion you have for your organization, team members, clients, and even challenges, you send a very powerful message to others that it's perfectly acceptable for people to make public displays of playfulness. Leaders know that work in today's organizations is demanding, and consequently, people need to have a sense of personal well-being to sustain their commitment. It works for everyone when leaders show enthusiasm and excitement about the work performed.

Elizabeth James, chief information officer and the vice chair of a southwestern financial services company, came up with a fun way to launch a massive information-technology conversion at more than forty bank branches. Their new system was called TIPS (Technology Improving Personal Service) and a TIPS troupe traveled to every site and recruited employees at each bank to play roles in a skit designed to teach everyone about the conversion, its timeline, and the reasons for doing it. There were executives in miniskirts, grandmas with pompoms, and employees dancing in the aisles. By eliciting laughs and spreading goodwill, Elizabeth and the TIPS team made a challenging assignment, and the hard work that followed, easier for them as well as for the people learning the new system.

Sonya Lopes, a public elementary school reform coordinator, started putting the word "fun" in a few places. For example, she hung it as a sign by her office door so she could see it whenever she walked out, and she put it in her daily planner as a bookmark. These and other reminders helped her "become more proactive in the search for 'fun' opportunities." One week she had people turn in their "regular old staff meeting questionnaires" by making them into paper airplanes and flying them into her office. That was the first time, Sonya remarked, "everyone turned in the questionnaires."

Sonya started talking to everyone about having more fun at work. For instance, during Teacher Appreciation Week, she got the PTA involved in creating a more fun school environment by decorating the staff bathrooms with tables, potpourri, wall hangings, and color, color, color. "Teachers," she said, "talked about it for days!" She witnessed the organization's environment change, but most importantly Sonya learned a lesson that everyone who begins this journey realizes: "Encouraging the heart of others encouraged *my* heart. As I was going around smiling, looking at people, and saying their names, I became uplifted! I felt *excited* while making muffins and attaching notes to them as spirit-lifters for teachers."

# Be Personally Involved

*It's important that you get involved in these celebrations so that people know that you can be counted as part of the team.*

*Bob Branchi*

Sonya's experience illustrates what we said at the start of this book: leadership is a relationship. People are much more likely to enlist in initiatives led by those with whom they feel a personal attachment. It's precisely the human connection between leaders and constituents that ensures more commitment and more support. Saying thank you—and genuinely meaning it—and joining others to celebrate accomplishments are very concrete ways of showing respect and enhancing personal credibility. If you want others to believe in something and behave according to those beliefs, you must set the example by being personally involved. You have to practice what you preach.

When it comes to sending a message throughout the organization, nothing communicates more clearly than what leaders do. You're sending a positive signal by directly and visibly showing others that you're there to cheer them along. When you set an example through your actions that "around here we say thanks, show appreciation, and have fun," others will follow your lead. The organization will develop a culture of celebration and recognition.

Russell Singleton, project leader with a capital equipment company, recalled that he spent most of his time during his personal-best leadership experience wandering around, making sure that the different pieces of the project were moving along and that people "knew I cared about their part." He held meetings with the project team at the start of each workday, generally before the rest of the office and operating staff arrived. "We broke bread (sometimes doughnuts, or fruit) together each day," Russ recalled, and "everyone gave a status report of their progress and problems. Everyone had a personal goal for each day. The goals were short-range and very visible. Everybody knew what everyone else was doing. . .and when we achieved good results, we would gather together and demo the result to the whole team. And cheer."

Cheerleading was an important element in people's personal-best leadership experiences. (And please note that "cheer-managing" is not an actual word.) Ted Avery, general manager for a major winery in Western Australia, described his personal-best this way: "I was a cheerleader. I would see the great things that were going on in marketing, for example, and I'd tell them 'Way to go!' I'd hear about a new development in operations, and I'd go into the plant and tell them 'fantastic.' They figured out a more efficient process in the fields, I'd go out and find those responsible and let them know how much we appreciated their hard work."

If there's any doubt that being personally involved in celebrations impacts others or their assessment of your leadership, look at what we consistently find in our research. More than four out of every five direct reports who strongly agree that they are "committed to the organization's success" work for leaders who get personally involved in recognizing people and celebrating accomplishments almost all the time, as shown in Figure 11.2. The degree to which direct reports feel valued by their organization—and how they rate the trustworthiness and effectiveness of their leaders—traces directly to the extent that their leader gets personally involved in recognizing people and celebrating accomplishments. Wherever you find a strong culture built around strong values, you'll also find endless examples of leaders who live its values.

**Show You Care** Make sure that you pay attention to people and do not take them for granted. Not only does Judith Wiencke, engineering manager with an Australian telecom, understand that people "appreciate knowing that I care about them," but she experiences that "they seem to care more about what they're doing as a result." Peter Birgbauer remembers, when he was working as an investment banking analyst, how their CEO made "everyone he interacted with feel important and valued, regardless of their title or role in the company." Many years later, he still recalls the impact that receiving a handwritten note of appreciation from the CEO had on him: "It would have been very easy for him to send me

**Figure 11.2 Leaders Who Get Personally Involved in Recognizing People and Celebrating Accomplishments Have Direct Reports Who Feel Committed to the Organization's Success**

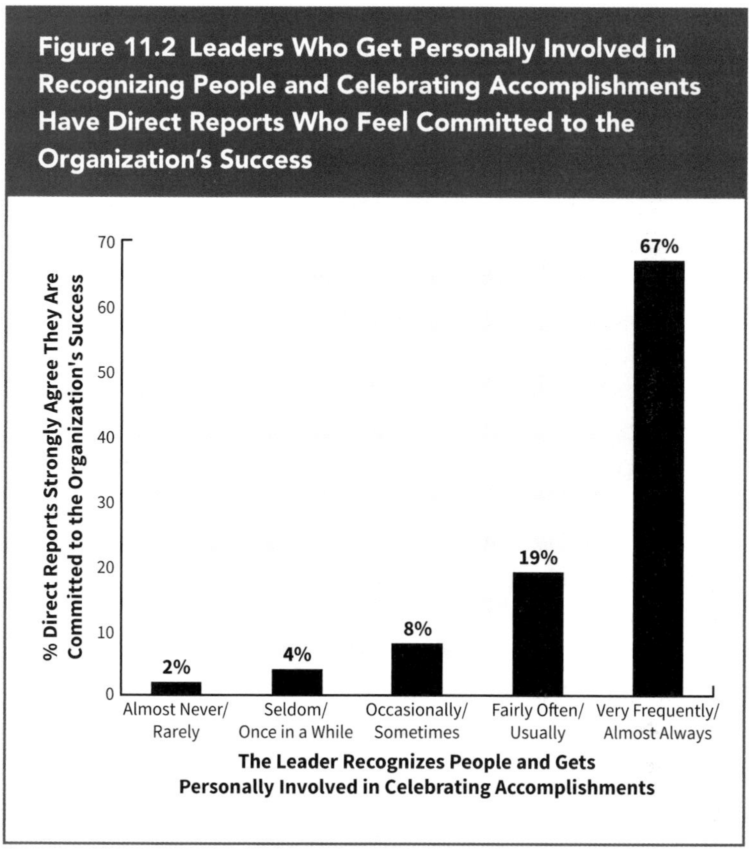


an email or thank me in person when we ran into one another, but he personalized his gratitude, showing that he cared, and this made a significant impression on me. I felt valued, and it made me want to work harder for the company."

People don't care how much you know until they know how much you care about them and what they do, demonstrating this isn't rocket science. For example, Jane Binger, responsible for leadership development and education for years with a large university-based healthcare system, found that most medical and administrative staff just desired simple gestures showing that she and others cared about how they were doing. This usually took the form of a personal note or email, a comment during a meeting or in the corridor, or just a quick stop by their office. “They want to know that I value them,” Jane said. “That I think they are doing a great job. That I am not taking them or their contributions for granted. This doesn’t require any grand over-the-top actions.” Our data backs up Jane’s experience. It shows a statistically significant correlation between the frequency to which a leader “praises people for a job well done” and the extent that their direct reports feel valued.

Showing someone that you care about them makes them feel that you have their best interests at heart. Research indicates that when people feel that others care about them, they work harder. But when they feel they’re being treated uncaringly or rudely at work, they respond by deliberately decreasing their effort or lowering the quality of their work.[28] Our data reveals that the extent to which direct reports feel their leader has “the best interests of other people at work” relates directly to their level of team spirit and pride. It’s also directly related to how favorably they evaluate the leader’s effectiveness and the likelihood that they would recommend that individual to a colleague as a good leader.

As the chief nursing officer with a large urban hospital, Lori Armstrong was in charge of leading more than 3000 RNs. Having been a frontline nurse for nearly a decade before progressing to higher levels of leadership, she told us:

> Losing a patient unexpectedly is traumatic. Of course, the family is devastated, and you always wonder and wish that you could have done that one more thing to change the outcome. Losing a patient is also profoundly lonely. As much as those around want to help, it is hard to welcome the support, hear the words, and accept the encouragement. As a nurse you also know the policies and procedures that follow an unexpected death. They should be there for safety purposes, but they are hard. During the safety review you recount each moment that occurred.

Lori vowed never to forget the experience of the frontline. One day, when she found out that a pediatric patient died unexpectedly, she was taken back to a time when that happened to her, the sadness, the feeling of helplessness, and the profound sorrow. She immediately visited the clinical unit where the death occurred and found out the nurse involved was in a conference room alone, distraught over what had transpired.

> When I walked in the room, I said nothing and just sat down next to the nurse. I touched her hand and said, "I have been where you are. You are not alone." She asked whether I came there just to be with her. I said yes: "We do not have to talk unless you want to; we can sit and be here for each other or we can cry together for all of the patients we have cared for and lost." She said that sitting there in silence was best for her, and she asked me how long I could stay. I answered, "As long as you need me."

At that moment, Lori did not fully realize how impactful her action was. She later received a note from that nurse, who told Lori it shaped her ability to process the trauma of losing a patient and made her feel supported as she went through the requisite regulatory review of what happened. She also wrote that she had shared with her colleagues what Lori had done. "Your actions showed the truth of your values, and as you have so often said, 'Never forget, first and foremost, we are skilled and compassionate caregivers for our patients, their families, and for each other.'" By the way, Lori told us that this nurse was so inspired by her actions and words that day that she decided to go back to school and become a nurse leader so that she, in her words, could "have the opportunity to impact others in the same way."

Through her actions and not just through her words, Lori showed that she cared. She did something to demonstrate how nurses in the hospital also needed to care for each other. Sending an email or scheduling a conference call would not have had the same impact in demonstrating her values as being personally involved.

Being *visible* in day-to-day undertakings is another way for leaders to demonstrate that they care. Attending important meetings, visiting customers, touring the plants or service centers, dropping in on the labs, making presentations at association gatherings, being at organizational events (even when you're not on the program), holding roundtable discussions, speaking with analysts, or just stopping by your constituents' cubicles to say hello—all are instances that show people that you are interested in them, the work they do, and the contributions they make. Being where they are helps you stay in touch, literally and figuratively, with what's going on. It shows that you walk the talk regarding the values you and your constituents share.

**Spread the Stories** Getting personally involved in showing that they care allows leaders to find and convey stories that put a human face on values. First-person examples are always more powerful and striking than third-party examples. It's that critical difference between "I saw it for myself" and "Someone told me about it." After many hours and struggles on developing their business plan, Dilpreet Singh, technical program manager with a global retailer, could sense that the team was getting frustrated and discouraged, losing energy, and willing to settle for mediocracy. He invited everyone over to his home, and made it clear that they would not talk about next steps, but rather "break bread together and enjoy each other's company." He asked each of them to bring along someone close to them (e.g., spouse, partner, kids). While sitting around enjoying pizza, Dilpreet said:

> I told the twelve-year-old daughter of one of my colleagues about how brave her mom is and what challenges she has taken on top of her job and taking care of her family. Everyone in the room was listening. I told them how much this business venture has gained because of her marketing knowledge. There was a shout-out of cheers in the room. I went around the room and shared a story about the contributions of each person on the team in front of people who matter most to them. This was a moment I will never forget. We were pumped up about our achievements and roaring to go to the finish line victorious.

He was a witness to the stories he told and he made the recognition personal. As Dilpreet realized, "As leaders, it is our job to show appreciation openly. When we appreciate people, it's acknowledging that what they are doing is meaningful. Their time, energy, and efforts matter!" He said that from that evening onwards, the team worked tirelessly to perfect their business plan.

You must constantly be on the lookout for whatever is being done well so that you can let that person know to keep up the good work and also be able to tell others about it. That way, you can give, as Dilpreet did, "up close and personal" accounts of what it means to put shared values and aspirations into practice. In the process, you create organizational role models to whom everyone can relate. You put behavior into a real context, and values become more than simply rules; they come alive. Through the stories that you tell, you dramatically and memorably illustrate how people should act and make decisions.

Lidia Kwiatkowska, personal banking area manager with a Canadian multinational investment and financial services company, shares stories at weekly staff meetings about how team members have demonstrated what it means to "build lasting relationships with customers through exceptional service." The stories celebrated these small wins but also challenged people. As we discussed in Chapter 3, storytelling is how people pass along lessons from generation to generation, culture to culture. Stories aren't meant to be kept private; they're meant to be told. And because they're public, they're tailor-made for celebrations. You can even think of stories as celebrations—celebrations of adventure and accomplishment, courage and perseverance, and being true to deeply held values and beliefs. Taking an intentional approach to sharing positive stories has been shown to boost employee morale.[29] Stories by their nature are public forms of communication. Much about an organization's culture can be gleaned from listening to and understanding the stories being told. For example, are they about whether people are rewarded or punished for asking questions, giving their opinions, challenging traditions, helping (or not) others, and so on? The data shows that leaders who most often "tell stories of encouragement about the good work of others" have direct reports who feel most personally valued, strongly believe that their leader brings out the best of people's talents and abilities, and care about the long-term success of their organization. In addition, the extent to which people would give a strong recommendation about their leader to a colleague relates directly to how frequently that leader tells stories of encouragement. Less than one in twenty-five would recommend a leader who seldom tells stories, while sixteen more times that number would favorably recommend a leader who most always tells stories of encouragement about the good work being done by others.

By telling stories, you more effectively accomplish the objectives of teaching, mobilizing, and motivating than you can through bullet points in a PowerPoint presentation or tweets on a mobile device. Listening to and understanding the stories leaders tell more effectively informs people about the values and culture of an organization than do company policies or the employee manual. Likewise, well-told stories are much more effective in reaching people's emotions and pulling them along. They make the message stick. They simulate the experience of actually being there and give people a compelling way of learning what is most important about the experience. Reinforcing stories through celebrations deepens the connections.

**Make Celebrations Part of Organizational Life** You need to put celebrations on the organization's calendar. These scheduled events serve as opportunities to get people together so that you can show people how they are part of the larger vision and a shared destiny. They are highly visible ways for you to affirm shared values, mark meaningful progress, and create a sense of community.

You probably already calendar birthdays, holidays, and anniversaries. You also should do it for the significant milestones in the life of your team and organization. Giving them a date, time, and place announces to everyone that these things matter. It also creates a sense of anticipation. Scheduling celebrations doesn't rule out spontaneous events; it just means that certain occasions are of such significance that everyone needs to pay particular attention to them.

In setting up celebrations, you first need to decide which organizational values, events of historical significance, or singular successes are of such importance that they warrant a special ritual, ceremony, or festivity. Perhaps you want to honor the group or team of people who created the year's breakthrough innovations, praise those who gave extraordinary customer service, or thank the families of your constituents for their support. Whatever you wish to celebrate, you need to formalize it, announce it, and tell people how they become eligible to participate. At a minimum, you ought to have at least one celebration each year that involves everyone and draws attention to each of your organization's core values.

Leaders make celebrations as much a part of their organization's life as possible. Here are examples of reasons for organizational celebrations.[30] Think about what might work for your organization.

- *Cyclical celebrations* (e.g., seasonal themes, key milestones, corporate anniversaries, opening day)
- *Success* (e.g., financial success, promotions, awards, expansions to new markets)
- *Loss* (e.g., of old procedures, financial opportunities, contracts, a job, status; death of a colleague; an experiment that failed)
- *Recognition ceremonies* (public applause and acknowledgment for a job well done)
- *Celebrations of triumph* (e.g., special occasions for accentuating collective accomplishments, such as launching a new product or strategy, and opening a new office, plant, or store)
- *Stages of organizational change* (e.g., expansions, reorganizations, closings, mergers, the end of an old technology and the introduction of a new one, moves to new locations)
- *Rituals for comfort and letting go* (e.g., loss of a contract, layoffs of employees, death of a colleague, entrances and exits)
- *People* (e.g., teamwork, team successes, founders, winners of sales contests, employee awards, individual birthdays, marriages, reunions)
- *Workplace altruism* (doing good for others, promoting social change)
- *Play* (e.g., games and sporting events, spoofing and poking fun)

Of course, celebrations don't have to be about a single achievement or for one person. Justin Brocato, senior manager of marketing operations with a multinational networking organization, told us how their annual awards banquet was a "wonderful way to celebrate our accomplishments and spread that sense of community." People brought their spouses, partners, and significant others to the event. He found this was "a nice way to get to know people outside of an office setting and further build upon existing relationships." Justin found that the banquet was a perfect forum to publicly recognize all of the contributions of the team and reflect on what they had accomplished.

In reflecting on this experience, Justin pondered, "What if management had just sent out an email to announce and congratulate the winners?" He concluded that people would have appreciated it, but the email would have paled compared to the roar of applause and whistles when someone goes on stage to accept their award and hears their manager tell that person and an audience full of their peers why these accomplishments were worthy of recognition. "Celebrating in public is so much more memorable," Justin decided, "and the impact that it has on the recipient and the team is longer lasting. People get energized, and suddenly they have a renewed sense of commitment for the year to come."

Justin has nailed it—whether they're to honor an individual, group, or organizational achievement or to encourage team learning and relationship building, celebrations, ceremonies, and similar events offer leaders the perfect opportunity to explicitly communicate and reinforce the actions and behaviors that are important in realizing shared values and mutual goals. Exemplary leaders know that promoting a culture of celebration fuels the sense of unity essential for retaining and motivating today's workforce. Celebrations, the data shows, significantly affect how people feel about their organization and their leader. The more often direct reports indicate that their leaders find ways to celebrate accomplishments, the more they feel effective in meeting their own work objectives and the more highly they rate the overall effectiveness of their leader. Research also finds that group rituals enhance the meaningfulness of work and increase the likelihood of prosocial behaviors among team members.[31]

There is no shortage of opportunities to bring people together to celebrate your organization's values and victories. In good times or bad, gathering together to acknowledge those who've contributed and the actions that have led to success signals to everyone that their efforts made a difference. Their energy, enthusiasm, and well-being—and yours—will be all the better for it.

## TAKE ACTION:

### Celebrate the Values and Victories

Celebrating together reinforces the fact that extraordinary performance results from many people's efforts. Visibly and publicly celebrating accomplishments creates community and sustains team spirit. By basing celebrations on acting congruently with fundamental values and attaining critical milestones, leaders reinforce and maintain people's focus.

Social interaction increases individuals' commitments to the group's standards and profoundly affects their well-being. When people are asked to go beyond their comfort zones, the support and encouragement of their colleagues boost their resistance to the possible debilitating effects of stress. It creates a sense of "we're all in this together." Make sure that people do not regard your organization as the place where "fun goes to die."

Leaders set the example by being personally involved in celebration and recognition, demonstrating that encouraging the heart is something everyone should do. Telling stories about individuals who have made exceptional efforts and achieved phenomenal successes allows leaders to showcase role models for others to emulate. Stories make people's experiences memorable, often even profound in ways they hadn't envisioned, and serve as a marker for future behaviors. Making personal connections with people in a culture of celebration also builds and sustains credibility. Adding vitality and a sincere sense of appreciation to the workplace is essential.

To Encourage the Heart, you must *celebrate the values and victories by creating a spirit of community.* These suggestions will help you more effectively make use of this important leadership behavior:

- Keep track of your positive-to-negative ratio. People need to experience three times the positive to negative in order to be fully engaged in their work. Never pass up an opportunity to relate publicly true stories about how people in your organization went above and beyond the call of duty.
- Give people tools that they can use to recognize one another. Create a culture in which peers look for opportunities to recognize the good work and accomplishments of their colleagues.
- Plan a festive celebration for each significant milestone that your team reaches. Don't wait until the whole project is finished to celebrate. Be personally involved.

Make the most of every opportunity to have regular conversations with people about leadership, so that they know it's important. Every interaction gives you the chance to direct people's attention to aspects of leadership that you think are important to focus on. Talk with others about:

- What are we doing to create a spirit of community among the team? Is it enough? How can we more effectively generate this spirit when working remotely?
- What ways can we bring people together with one another in other than a work context? What would be something fun that we could be doing with one another?

# CHAPTER 12

# Treat Challenge as an Opportunity

*What I learned from this pandemic moment is that The Five Practices of Exemplary Leadership are not meant just for good times. The practices strengthen our abilities to be stronger, bolder leaders during times of uncertainty, unpredictability, and precariousness.*

*Jonathan Reyes*

**NORMAL IS NOT** anymore. Or at best you can think about the "new" normal or the "next" normal, but there is little that is normal these days if normal means you can predict what is going to happen tomorrow based on what happened yesterday. Normal now means ambiguity, uncertainty, and disruption. Normal means having to be able to adapt quickly to changing circumstances. Normal means having to act before knowing all the facts or options.

Yet it is precisely words such as *turbulent*, *disruptive*, *chaotic*, *unexpected*, and *unpredictable* that describe the circumstances that demand leadership. Challenge is the defining context for leadership. Leadership has always been essential in getting through tough times. That's when leaders are most needed to mobilize, energize, and take people and organizations to places they have never been before.

It has been evident that leadership has played an essential part in dealing with the uncertainties and discontinuities associated with the coronavirus pandemic, social and political unrest, and global conflict. Both strong and weak examples abound, but leadership has been an influential part of every story. History tells the same tale. Leadership is not a fad that goes out of fashion next season. And neither do challenges. No one knows for sure which adversities are just over the horizon. Times change, problems change, technologies change, and throughout all the future challenges leadership will continue to be of enduring importance.

It is the work of leaders to inspire people to do things differently, to struggle against uncertain odds, and to persevere toward a misty image of a better future. Without leadership there would not be the extraordinary efforts necessary to solve existing problems and realize unimagined opportunities. We have today, at best, only faint clues of what the future may hold, but without leadership the possibilities will neither be envisioned nor attained.[1]

Let's revisit something we said in the introduction to this book. We noted that *The Leadership Challenge* has its origins in a research project we began over forty years ago. We wanted to know what people did when they were at their "personal best" in leading others. These personal bests were experiences in which people set their individual leadership standards of excellence. They were, so to speak, their Olympic gold medal–winning performances.

When we reviewed the Personal-Best Leadership Experiences, it became evident that every single case involved some kind of challenge. We didn't ask people to tell us about challenging times. We asked them to tell us about times when they did their best. It just turned out that whatever the situation, all the cases we've studied involved overcoming great adversity. It was the context in which people said they did their best. In other words, *challenge is the common denominator* in all the stories about personal-best leadership.

It is for that reason we opened this book with a core proposition that we repeat in this closing chapter: *Challenge is the crucible for leadership and the opportunity for greatness*. This is *the* critical lesson we have learned from reviewing thousands of Personal-Best Leadership Experiences over forty years. Challenge inspires us, shapes us, and requires us to open doors and chart new paths.

The challenges during the last few years have created opportunities for all of us to reexamine who we are and what we believe, reimagine what we aspire to achieve, invent new ways of doing things, reach out in ways we hadn't yet experienced to form and strengthen relationships, show more gratitude for the role others play in our lives, and reconsider the kind of leaders we want to become and align with. The challenges you face now—and inevitably will confront in the future—are opportunities to demonstrate more frequently and intentionally The Five Practices of Exemplary Leadership. They call out to you to renew your commitment to become the best leader you can be, and not just for yourself, but for others who are inevitably counting on you, sometimes quite explicitly but nearly always implicitly.

As you continue your learning journey, we want to reinforce a few lessons that will underscore why exemplary leadership is vitally important to turning current and future adversities into exciting opportunities for innovation and transformation.

# Your Leadership Matters

*Regardless of your position, you can always make a difference in this world.*

*Prashanth Thandavamurthy*

At the end of the day, what's expected of you as a leader? Is it to improve engagement and performance, keep them the same, or make them worse? Okay, this is a rhetorical question. Clearly, you're expected to have a positive impact on results. That's why, in every chapter of this book, we've provided case studies, examples, and empirical data that show how exemplary leadership makes a significant difference in people's levels of well-being, commitment, motivation, work performance, and the success of their organizations. We want you to know that your leadership matters.

You don't have to *look up* for leadership. Nor do you need to *look out* for leadership. You only have to *look inward*. You have the potential to lead others to places they have never been.

Before you can lead others, however, you have to believe that you can have a positive impact on others. You have to believe that your values are worthy and that what you do matters. You have to believe that your words can inspire and your actions can move others. Moreover, you have to be able to convince others that the same is true for them. In these turbulent times, there is no shortage of opportunities to lead, and our organizations and the world need more people who believe they can make a difference *and* who are willing to act on that belief.

Let's look at still another bit of data that should convince you that your leadership also matters *to you*. In our studies, we ask the leader's direct reports, upon completing the observer version of the *Leadership Practices Inventory (LPI)*, to indicate the likelihood they would recommend this individual "to their colleagues as a good leader." As shown in Figure 12.1, the more frequently, by decile, that they report that their leader engages in The Five Practices, the more strongly they agree that this individual is a leader they would recommend to others. The fact is those leaders in the top 20 percent of the frequency distribution are likely to be recommended more than ten times more often by their direct reports than their counterparts in the bottom 20 percent.

The bottom line empirically is that the more frequently the people who work with you observe you engaging in the behaviors associated with The Five Practices of Exemplary Leadership, the more likely it is that you'll have a positive influence on them and the organization. The more likely it is that *people will want to work with you*. That's what all our data and the hundreds of research studies conducted by independent scholars[2] add up to: if you want to have a significant impact on the

**Figure 12.1 Likelihood of Being Recommended as a Good Leader Increases with Greater Frequency of The Five Practices of Exemplary Leadership by Leaders**

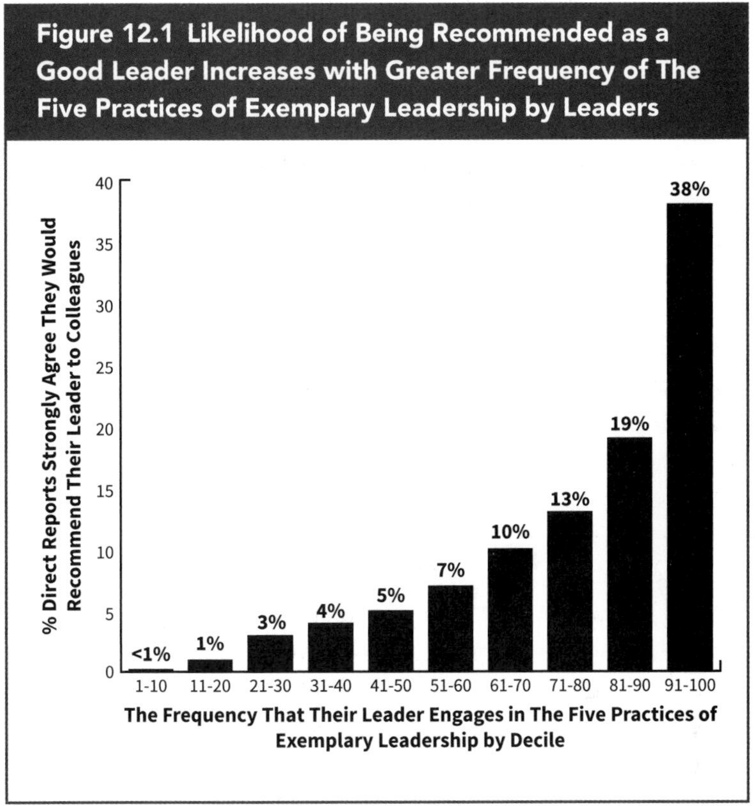


people around you, the organizations you are involved with, and on your professional and career options, you'd be wise to invest in learning and demonstrating the behaviors that enable you to become the very best leader you can.

Do you wonder if engagement and performance levels could be better explained by something other than leadership? Could it be that what matters is really more about the sort of person you are dealing with (for example, their age, gender, ethnicity), the type of job they have (e.g., accounting, engineering, sales), the industry they work in (e.g., manufacturing, healthcare, government, high technology), or some other variable? What do you think about these alternative hypotheses to leadership making the difference?

In the research, we find that such potentially significant and interesting variables as people's age, educational level, gender, functional area, hierarchical level, industry, length of time with the company, size of the organization, or nationality *together* account for only three-tenths of one percent (0.3 percent) in the variation around individuals' levels of engagement. Individually, the impact of any single one of these factors is negligible (zero). Demographics do not explain why leaders are effective and why people are engaged at work. Your leadership behaviors are a hundred times more important in influencing how people feel about their workplace, as expressed in terms of engagement, retention, and motivation and in how your direct reports evaluate your effectiveness.

It certainly makes sense that how leaders behave explains how engaged their direct reports are in the workplace, but what you might not expect is that the leaders' own behavior also explains how *they* feel about the workplace. Using the same measurements that we used with direct reports, we asked leaders to indicate their own levels of workplace engagement. The data revealed a direct positive relationship; as leaders reported themselves engaging in more and more of the behaviors associated with The Five Practices of Exemplary Leadership, they correspondingly indicated great degrees of engagement. For example, they felt more positive about their workplace, more committed to the organization's long-term success, more personally valued, and more strongly that they were making a meaningful contribution. This finding should not be surprising because the more you invest in making something special happen for others, the more attachment you feel to what you are doing and the organization you are involved with.

How you behave as a leader matters, and it matters a lot. *You* have the potential to make a meaningful and significant difference in the lives of those you lead. It's now up to you to determine the kind of difference you want to make and strengthen your capacity to have a positive impact on those you lead.

# Liberate the Leader Within Everyone

*Leadership is not accidental, bestowed, or inherited. Leadership is a deliberate, thoughtful process that is about lifting the people around you.*

*Mark Hary*

When challenge is greatest, so is the need for everyone to step up. While compelling stories are often told of the lone hero who overcomes impossible odds, when you dig deep into cases of extraordinary performance you discover that no one ever achieved greatness without the involvement, support, and encouragement of others. This is another one of the lasting truths about leadership, and a lesson repeated over and over again in people's personal-best leadership experiences. "You can't do it alone," as we noted in Chapter 8, is the mantra of exemplary leaders. None of the critical problems teams and organizations encounter can ever be solved by one leader. The most serious challenges require leadership at all levels and in all places. We can't just rely on those with formal titles to demonstrate the practices of exemplary leadership. It's especially important in challenging times to recognize that everyone has leadership ability and that a key responsibility of leaders is to liberate the leader within the people they work and interact with.

After all, over the past four decades, which have seen considerable technological, cultural, economic, and geopolitical turbulence, and through these most recent unprecedented times we've continued to find that exemplary leadership comes from many sources. This is even more true when people are working from anywhere and leaders and their constituents are more remote from one another. The data from millions of respondents clearly shows that 99.967 percent report that they do indeed engage in the 30 leadership behaviors on the Leadership Practices Inventory at least more than "almost never/rarely." And the responses from their managers, direct reports, and colleagues back up this percentage. Behaving as a leader is clearly within the capacity of everyone. Leadership is ultimately about what you *do,* and everyone can "do" these leadership behaviors.

No matter where people are in an organization, they have the potential to have a positive influence on other people's desire to stay or leave, the trajectory of their careers, their ethical choices, their ability and desire to perform at their best, and their motivation to share and serve the organization's vision and values.[3] Since everyone is capable of engaging in the leadership behaviors associated with The Five Practices, then leadership is essentially everyone's business, and this means that everyone becomes responsible for the quality of leadership in their organization, and each person becomes accountable for the leadership they demonstrate. The only decision anyone really has, then, is whether they want to become the *best* leader they can be. Accordingly, the objective is about bringing out the best in others, as well as in yourself, and not about finding and selecting the "right" people.

From the beginning of our research studies, as part of learning about their personal-best leadership experiences, we asked people to indicate how they learned to lead. One predominant theme was the importance of role models. In one study, we asked over 32,000 people around the world to think about the individuals in their lives who were their role models for learning how to lead.[4] Who comes to mind when you think about a role model? Table 12 indicates the percentage of respondents, by generation (age groups), who selected various categories of role models.

When thinking back over their lives and selecting their most important leadership role models, people overwhelmingly nominated a family member more often than anyone else. The next most important overall was an immediate supervisor; although for the youngest age group, it was a teacher/coach (probably because they haven't had much workplace experience). For those in the workplace, one's immediate supervisor/manager is often described in terms akin to a teacher/coach. Seven percent indicated a co-worker or colleague. Altogether these four categories—family member, teacher/coach, immediate supervisor, and colleague—accounted for more than four out of every five responses (84 percent). This response pattern was consistent across genders, ethnic groups, educational levels, industries, professions, and even hierarchical levels.[5]

**Table 12 Percentage of People Selecting Category as Their Most Important Role Model for Learning How to Lead by Generation (Respondent Ages)**

| Role Model Category | Gen Z (>26) | Gen Y (26–40) | Gen X (41–55) | Baby Boomers (>56) | Total |
|---|---|---|---|---|---|
| Family Member | 65 | 51 | 45 | 48 | 51 |
| Immediate Supervisor/ Manager | 6 | 16 | 19 | 17 | 16 |
| Business Leader | 6 | 9 | 12 | 11 | 10 |
| Teacher/Coach | 12 | 10 | 9 | 9 | 10 |
| Co-worker/ Colleague | 4 | 7 | 8 | 7 | 7 |
| Religious Leader | 2 | 2 | 3 | 4 | 3 |
| Entertainer/Actor/ Athlete | 3 | 2 | 1 | 0 | 1 |
| Political Leader | 1 | 2 | 2 | 2 | 2 |
| Community Leader | 1 | 1 | 1 | 1 | 1 |

The data clearly show that the people selected as role models are those individuals to whom respondents are closest, and having the most frequent contact with. It's not hip-hop artists, movie stars, professional athletes, politicians, or others generally reported about in the news, on TV, or through social media. In other words, leadership role models are *local*. While famous folks may capture the headlines, those with whom people have personal contact were most likely to become their role models for learning what it means to lead. The people you are closest to, in turn, are most likely going to look to *you* for the example of how a leader responds to competitive situations, handles crises, deals with loss, or resolves ethical dilemmas.

Further evidence of just how important *you* are comes from appreciating that people often turn to colleagues for guidance on decisions and actions, especially in unprecedented circumstances. As shown in Figure 12.2, the more frequently a peer is reported engaging in The Five Practices, the more strongly one's colleagues and co-workers agree that they would recommend this individual as a good leader to their colleagues. Notice that the pattern of these results is nearly identical to what was found from the direct reports of leaders (Figure 12.1), and

**Figure 12.2 Likelihood of Being Recommended as a Good Leader *by Peers* Increases with Greater Frequent Use of The Five Practices of Exemplary Leadership**

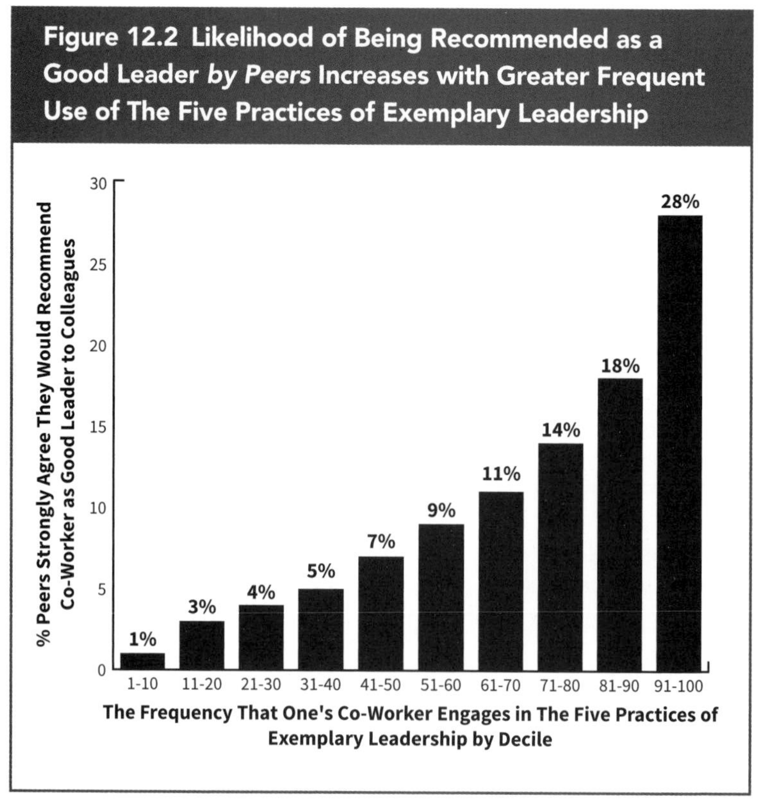

underscores how, whether as a leader, individual contributor, or colleague, you make a difference in liberating the leader in everyone.

# Everyone Can Learn to Lead

*True leaders have a growth mindset, not one that is fixed in believing that they were either born a leader or they weren't destined to lead.*

*Chrystine Lawson Villarreal*

Nearly every time we give a speech or conduct a workshop, someone will ask, "Are leaders born or made?" Whenever we're asked this question, our answer, always offered with a smile, is this: "We've never met a leader who wasn't born. We've also never met an accountant, artist, athlete, engineer, lawyer, physician, writer, or zoologist who wasn't born. We're all born. That's a given."

You might be thinking, "Well, that's not fair. That's a trick answer. Of course, everyone is born." That's precisely our point. Every one of us is born, and every one of us has the necessary material to become a leader. The question you and others should be asking yourselves is not "Am I born to be a leader?" In becoming a better leader, the more demanding and significant question you should be asking is: "Can I become a better leader tomorrow than I am today?" To that question, our answer is a resounding "Yes!"

Again, let's get something straight. Leadership is not some mystical quality that only a few people have and everyone else doesn't. Leadership is not preordained. It is not a gene, and it is not a trait. There is no hard evidence to support the assertion that leadership is imprinted in the DNA of only some individuals, and that everyone else missed out and is doomed to be clueless.

We've collected assessment data from millions of people around the world. We can tell you without a doubt that there are leaders in every profession and function, every type of organization, every religion, every country, and from every age, gender, and race. It's a myth that leadership can't be learned—that you either have it or you don't. There is leadership potential everywhere we look.

In fact, more than likely most everyone you work with is *already leading, just not frequently enough*. In over forty years of collecting data using the *Leadership Practices Inventory* to assess leader behavior, practically *no one* who completed the self-version of the LPI has scored a zero across all five leadership practices. To be precise, less than 0.033 percent gave themselves a response score of "*almost never*" in terms of engaging in *all* thirty of the essential leadership behaviors. In a more positive light, this means that approximately 99.967 percent of all the people who have taken the LPI-Self have frequency scores above zero (that is, above "almost never"). The percentage *above* "almost never" is even higher from their direct reports (99.983 percent), co-workers/peers (99.988 percent), and managers (99.994 percent).

Do the math. You'll discover that the chance of finding someone with a score of zero in a 100-person organization is zero. In a 1,000-person organization, the probability of finding someone with a score of zero is zero. In a 10,000-person organization, the chance of finding someone with a score of zero is still nearly zero. These results underscore our earlier assertion that everyone is capable of engaging in the leadership behaviors identified as essential to achieving record-setting standards of excellence.

Leadership is an *observable pattern of practices and behaviors*, and *a definable set of skills and abilities*. And any skill can be learned, strengthened, honed, and enhanced, given the motivation and desire, along with practice, feedback, role models, and coaching. When researchers track the progress of people who participate in leadership development programs, for example, the research demonstrates that they improve over time.[6] They learn to be more comfortable in using The Five Practices more frequently and become better leaders.

In challenging times, continuous learning has to be a priority for everyone. Learning leadership needs to be at the top of the agenda. Why? Very simply it's this: In our research, we find that people who are most actively involved in learning are also the ones who engage most often in The Five Practices of Exemplary Leadership.[7] It has also been reported that those leaders who engage in learning for five or more hours per week, compared to those who spend an hour or less per week, are 74 percent more likely to have more direction in their careers and 48 percent more likely to find purpose in their work. They are also happier in the work.[8] The more you seek to learn, the better you will become at leadership (or at anything, for that matter). What's clear is that you have to approach each new and unfamiliar experience with a willingness to learn and an appreciation of the importance of learning.

Building your and others' capacity to be an active learner requires a growth mindset, which is the belief that people's basic qualities can be improved and strengthened through their efforts, in contrast to a fixed mindset that presumes one's qualities are inherent and carved in stone. With a growth mindset you believe that you (as well as other people) can learn to be better leaders. Holding a fixed mindset means that you think that no amount of training or experience is going to make people better than they already are.[9] In our research, we've found that those with a growth mindset were more willing than those with a fixed mindset to embrace challenges, persist when facing obstacles, and sustain efforts, even when confronted with resistance. Believing that people can change and develop, growth-minded individuals were willing to foster innovation and focus on learning from setbacks. They showed a greater propensity to support experimentation by others. People with a fixed mindset avoided challenging situations and were unlikely to open themselves up to feedback of any sort.[10] Mindsets, and not just skill sets, make the critical difference in deciding to take on challenging situations.

You can create opportunities for yourself and others to continuously learn to lead in three important ways: through experience, observing others, and training and coursework. Of the three, the most often utilized by more than a two-to-one margin is learning-by-doing. Make available, or take advantage of, opportunities for everyone, for example, to facilitate a meeting, or lead a special task force, or present an important proposal, or chair a professional association conference. Then, at the end of such experiences, ask, "What did we learn from this?" Unless you, and others, are provided the chance to explore, experiment, and even work outside of your comfort zone, learning is unlikely to take place. Only the most marginal of improvements can happen when you do the same things over and over again.

Role models are also critical to learning. Make sure you and others take the time to observe the best leaders inside and outside your organization. Ask someone you admire as a leader to come speak to your team about the lessons they've learned in their roles, how they've recovered from mistakes, or how they've handled challenges and setbacks. Also, find the time to attend classes, workshops, or seminars. They enable you to spend a concentrated period on one subject, to learn about and possibly practice some specific skills. This focused attention helps you to absorb something more quickly, with the benefit of having multiple chances to practice new behaviors and skills and obtain feedback in a safe environment. Increasingly, as many people discovered during the pandemic, you can do training on your own, through a plethora of online learning technologies featuring seminars, workshops, presentations, simulations, how-to sessions, threaded discussions, and the like.

The most meaningful and important way that you can take charge of becoming an exemplary leader is to make learning leadership a daily habit for yourself and others. Learning leadership is not something that you add to your already busy schedule when you get around to it. It's not something that you do on a weekend or at the annual company retreat. It's not something that gets cut from the calendar when times are tough. It's something you do as automatically and instinctively as your other important priorities in the day. It's something that happens as routinely as checking your email, texting a colleague, or conducting a Zoom meeting. It's something you must consider essential to your and others' success.

# Become Your Best Self

*Great leaders have the courage to unlearn, learn, and relearn what they thought they knew before.*

*Rachelle Mata*

Challenges—whether they're the ones faced in the past, are confronting us now, or may be encountered in the future—force us to examine our fundamental values and beliefs. They cause us to ask ourselves what's most important to us. What is it that I really want for my life, for my family, for my colleagues, and for my organization? They also can make us question our competence and our commitment. Do I have what it takes right now to lead others through these challenging times? Am I up to the job?

Challenge reminds us that the quest for exemplary leadership is first an inner quest to discover who you are, and it's through self-examination that you find the awareness to lead. In the end, you come to realize and appreciate that the instrument of leadership is the self, and how mastery of the art of leadership comes from mastery of the self. *Leadership development is self-development*, and self-development is not simply about stuffing in a whole bunch of new information or trying out the latest technique. It's about liberating the leader within.

Being true to yourself and leading with your best self means that you need to be clear and comfortable with the kind of leader you want to become. Authentic leadership comes from the inside out. And inside-out leadership means becoming the author of your own story and the maker of your own history. Before you take your next step as a leader, get clear about your leadership story—the one that you would like others to share when you are no longer around to tell it yourself.

Now, and not at some point in the future, is the time to pause and ask yourself, "What kind of a leader do *I* want to be?" Kick-start that conversation with yourself by imagining the following scenario.

It's ten years from today, and you are attending a ceremony honoring you as the "Leader of the Year." One after another, colleagues and co-workers, members of your family, and good friends take the stage and talk about your leadership and how you have made a positive difference in their lives.

To help you think about what you hope people will say about you that day and how you would hope to be remembered, record your responses to this L.I.F.E. paradigm:

**Lessons:** What vital *lessons* do you hope others will say you have passed on? (For example, I hope they will say: I taught others how to face adversity with grace and determination, and I inspired them about the importance of giving back to those who've given to you.)

**Ideals:** What *ideals*—values, principles, and ethical standards—do you hope people will say you stand for? (For example, I hope they will say: I stood for freedom and justice, and I believed in always telling the truth, even when it wasn't what people necessarily wanted to hear.)

**Feelings:** What *feelings* do you hope people will say they have or had when being with you or when thinking about you? (For example, I hope they will say: They always felt, when working with me, that they were capable of doing the impossible, and I made them feel that they mattered and that what they had to say was worthy of being listened to.)

**Evidence:** What is the *evidence* that you made a difference; what lasting *expressions* or contributions—tangible and intangible—will people say that you leave to them and to others yet to come? (For example, I hope they will say: Together we turned around this project/division/organization when others had lost hope, and that my dedication to others is evident in those homes that we designed and built to house the less fortunate in our community.)

After you've written down your responses, ask yourself: How am I doing right now in teaching these *lessons*, living up to these *ideals*, creating these *feelings*, and providing the *evidence* that I am contributing as a leader? Don't stop there! Ask yourself: What can I do to do even better?

In your efforts to make leadership everyone's business, you can also do this same exercise with others on your team. Supporting everyone in becoming their best selves is an ennobling and empowering act that will benefit them, the team, and the organization.

## You Won't Always Get It Right

*The more I think I know about leadership, the less I actually know. There's always room for growth and improvement, and it's a never-ending process.*

*Zach Chien*

A few words of caution, however. As you, and others, set out to become the best leader you can be, it won't be easy. Exemplary leadership is really hard work. You will make mistakes. You will fall down. You will not always get everyone on board or make everyone happy. You won't be able to solve every problem. You won't get all the praise and credit you deserve. You will get exhausted.

Yes, in our research, we learned that in performing at their personal bests, leaders Model the Way, Inspire a Shared Vision, Challenge the Process, Enable Others to Act, and Encourage the Heart. They realize, as Robert Pearl, head of a large network of physicians did, that "being a good leader is not something that casually occurs. It takes great thought, care, insight, commitment, and energy. . . . When it all comes together, it brings out the best of who you are." Moreover, those leaders who most frequently engage in The Five Practices are significantly more likely to achieve extraordinary results than leaders who don't make much use of these practices. But there's a catch. *You can learn to do all of this perfectly and people may still not follow you!*

Maybe we should have told you this sooner, but no doubt you knew it already. There's absolutely no way we can say that any of these leadership practices will always work all the time with all people. We know for certain that there's a much greater probability that they will, but there's no ironclad, money-back guarantee. And if anyone ever stands in front of you and claims that they have *the* three-, five-, seven-, or nine-factor theory that's 100 percent certain to get you results and rewards, then grab onto your wallet and run. There's no get-rich-quick, instant weight-loss program for leadership.

The best thing you can do for yourself is to remain humble. The word *human* and the word *humble* both share their origins in the Latin *humus,* meaning earth or ground.[11] To be human and humble is to be down-to-earth, with your feet planted firmly on the ground. Interesting, isn't it, how as you climb the ranks you often climb to a higher floor in the building, getting farther and farther away from the ground? Is it any wonder that the higher you go, the harder it gets to keep your footing?

You must have the courage to be human and the courage to be humble.[12] It takes a lot of courage to admit that you aren't always right, that you can't always anticipate every possibility, that you can't envision every future, that you can't solve every problem, that you can't control every variable, that you aren't always congenial, that you make mistakes, and that you are, in a word, human. It takes courage to admit all these things to others, but it may take even more courage to admit them to yourself. If you can find the humility to do that, you invite others into a courageous conversation. When you let down your guard and open yourself up to others, you invite them to join you in the creation of something that you alone could not create. When you become more modest and unpretentious, others have the chance themselves to become visible and noticed.[13]

Just as you would with others, you may also need to give yourself a break and exercise self-compassion. Psychologists have discovered that self-compassion is a useful tool for enhancing performance in a variety of settings. This means being kind rather than judgmental about your own mistakes and shortcomings, recognizing that failures are a shared human experience, and adopting a balanced approach to negative emotions when you stumble or fall short (that is, allowing yourself to feel bad but not letting those negative emotions take over).[14] Self-compassion triggers people to adopt a growth mindset, boosting their drive to improve and become more authentic in the process.[15]

This is not to say that you shouldn't aspire to become the best leader you can be. Exemplary leadership is something to aspire to. It is a noble and worthy pursuit. We just want to remind you that nothing in our research hints that leaders should, or even can, be perfect. Leaders aren't saints. They're human beings, full of the flaws and failings like everyone else. One compassionate thing you can do for yourself along your journey to exemplary leadership is to remain humble and unassuming—to always remain open to learning more about yourself and the world around you.

## Make Becoming a Better Leader a Daily Habit

*No one said being a leader was going to be easy. Leadership takes practice and is something that must be attended to daily.*

*Jennifer Lee*

So where do you begin your journey to becoming the best leader you can be? Where have others begun theirs? Here's a riddle to get you thinking about your answer to these questions:

*Twelve frogs were sitting on a log.*
*Seven of the frogs decided to jump into the pond.*
*Now, how many frogs remain on the log?*

What's your answer? Is it seven, five, twelve, or none? The correct answer is twelve. Why? Because the seven frogs only *decided* to jump, they didn't actually take the leap. There's an enormous difference between deciding and doing. It's like the old saying goes: "To know and not to do is not yet to know."

Learning about leadership is not the same as leading. Deciding to be an exemplary leader is not the same as being one. Leading is doing, and you have to *do* leadership to be a leader. You need to jump into the pond, demonstrate that you know how to stay afloat, and over time become a more capable swimmer.

Where do you start in becoming an even better leader? Make leadership development a daily habit. Make a plan for where and when you are going to practice leadership, put this on your calendar, and keep track of your progress. Do something every day to learn more about leading, and then put those lessons into practice every day. Researchers find that committing to a specific plan, including time and dates, makes people more likely to stick with it.[16]

In reflecting on her own leadership journey, Monika Salquist, finance director for a fintech firm, realized that every day is a new opportunity to become the best leader you can be. "We each have the opportunity to make a difference if we choose to do so," she said, and "it is up to us to decide whether we want to make a difference through the actions we choose to take every day and through the values and beliefs we live by every day." Monika recognized that there were countless opportunities every day to build and demonstrate her leadership skills. "Through simple conversations, daily routine emails and phone calls, chats in the hallway, or conversations with my children, the door suddenly became wide open for me to find the openings through which I could use The Five Practices of Exemplary Leadership. The first step was becoming more intentional and conscientious about taking advantage of these opportunities."

Monica discovered that it wasn't the every-once-in-a-while, transformational acts that demonstrated her leadership and contributed to her becoming better at leadership. It was the little things that she did, day in and day out. Her actions were exactly those things that enable people to experience a good day at work. That's how we recommend you continue along your leadership journey—finding opportunities every day to make a small difference and practice being the best leader you can be.

Leadership is in the moment. There are many moments each day when you can choose to lead. Each day you can choose to make a difference. Each of these moments serves up the prospect of contributing to a lasting legacy.

## Remember the Secret to Success in Life

There's one final leadership lesson that we'd like to pass along. And it's not insignificant that we've ended all of the editions of this book by sharing what we refer to as the secret to success in life.

When we began our study of leadership bests, we were fortunate to cross paths with U.S. Army Major General John H. Stanford. We knew that John had grown up poor, that he failed sixth grade but went on to graduate from Penn State University on an ROTC scholarship, that he survived multiple military tours in both Korea and Vietnam, that he was highly decorated, and that the loyalty of his troops was extraordinary. John headed up the Military Traffic Management Command for the U.S. Army during the Persian Gulf War. When he retired from the Army, he became county manager of Fulton County, Georgia, when Atlanta was gearing up to host the 1996 Summer Olympics. John then became superintendent of the Seattle public school system, where he sparked a revolution in public education, before untimely passing away from leukemia.

All that we learned of John's public service was impressive, but his answer to one of our interview questions significantly influenced our own appreciation of leadership. We asked John how he'd go about developing leaders, whether in colleges and universities, in the military, in government, in the nonprofit sector, or in private business. Here was his reply:

> When anyone asks me that question, I tell them I have the secret to success in life. The secret to success is to stay in love. Staying in love gives you the fire to ignite other people, to see inside other people, to have a greater desire to get things done than other people. A person

> who is not in love doesn't really feel the kind of excitement that helps them to get ahead and to lead others and to achieve. I don't know any other fire, any other thing in life that is more exhilarating and is more positive a feeling than love is.

"Staying in love" isn't the answer we expected to get—at least not when we began our study of leadership. But after studying leadership for over forty years and counting, through thousands of interviews and case analyses, we are constantly reminded about how many leaders use the word *love* freely when talking about their own motivations to lead.

Of all the things that sustain a leader over time, love is the most lasting. It's hard to imagine leaders getting up day after day, putting in the long hours and hard work it takes to get extraordinary things done, without having their hearts in it. The best-kept secret of successful leaders is love: staying in love with leading, with the people who do the work, with what their organizations provide, and with those who honor the organization by using its products and services.

Leadership is not an affair of the head. Leadership is an affair of the heart.

# ENDNOTES

## Introduction: Making Extraordinary Things Happen

1. The challenges we've enumerated here are not exhaustive, and no doubt others will arise between the time we finish this manuscript and the time you are reading it. This only strengthens our point that challenge defines the context for leadership.

## Chapter 1 When Leaders Are at Their Best

1. All of the quotations in this book are from real people: from a personal interview, Personal-Best Leadership Experience case study, or leadership reflective essay. We chose not to include titles or specific affiliations because the focus is on the individuals' experience and their comments generalize beyond any particular organization or setting. Another reason is that their titles and organizational affiliations are not static and are most

likely to be different now from what they were when the comment or experience was shared and when this edition was published.

2. More information about the myths that keep people from fully developing as leaders can be found in J. M. Kouzes and B. Z. Posner, *Learning Leadership: The Five Fundamentals of Becoming an Exemplary Leader* (San Francisco: The Leadership Challenge–A Wiley Brand, 2016).
3. More information about the research methodology and findings can be found in B. Z. Posner, "Bringing the Rigor of Research to the Art of Leadership: Evidence Behind The Five Practices of Exemplary Leadership and the LPI: Leadership Practices Inventory," https://www.leadershipchallenge.com/LeadershipChallenge/media/SiteFiles/research/TLC-Research-to-the-Art-of-Leadership.pdf, accessed May 7, 2022.
4. R. Roi, *Leadership Practices, Corporate Culture, and Company Financial Performance: 2005 Study Results* (Palo Alto, CA: Crawford & Associates International, 2006), http://www.hr.com/en?s=ldYUsXbBU1qzkTZI&t=/documentManager/sfdoc.file.supply&fileID=1168032065880. For information about hundreds of scholarly articles examining how The Five Practices impact engagement and performance, see Posner, "Bringing the Rigor."
5. For a more in-depth discussion about leadership being a relationship, what people look for in their leaders, and the actions leaders need to take to strengthen that relationship, see J. M. Kouzes and B. Z. Posner, *Credibility: How Leaders Gain and Lose It, Why People Demand It* (San Francisco: Jossey-Bass, 2011).
6. J. W. Gardner, *On Leadership* (New York: Free Press, 1990): 28–29.
7. For more information about the original studies, see B. Z. Posner and W. H. Schmidt, "Values and the American Manager: An Update," *California Management Review* 26, no. 3 (1984): 202–216; and B. Z. Posner and W. H. Schmidt, "Values and Expectations of Federal Service Executives," *Public Administration Review* 46, no. 5 (1986): 447–454.
8. B. Z. Posner, "The Influence of Demographic Factors on What People Want from Their Leaders," *Journal of Leadership Studies* 12, no. 2 (2018): 7–16.
9. H. Wang, K. S. Law, R. D. Hackett, D. Wang, and Z. X. Chan, "Leader-Member Exchange as a Mediator of the Relationship between Transformational Leadership and Followers' Performance and Organizational Citizenship Behavior," *Academy of Management Journal* 48 (2005): 420–432. See also B. Artz, A. H. Goodall, and A. J. Oswald

(December 29, 2016), "If Your Boss Could Do Your Job, You're More Likely to Be Happy at Work," *Harvard Business Review,* Reprint H03DTB; and B. Artz, A. H. Goodall, and A. J. Oswald, "Boss Competence and Worker Well-being," *ILR Review,* May 16, 2016.

10. The classic study on credibility goes back to C. I. Hovland, I. L. Janis, and H. H. Kelley, *Communication and Persuasion* (New Haven, CT: Yale University Press, 1953). Early measurement studies include J. C. McCroskey, "Scales for the Measurement of Ethos," *Speech Monographs* 33 (1966): 65–72; and D. K. Berlo, J. B. Lemert, and R. J. Mertz, "Dimensions for Evaluating the Acceptability of Message Sources," *Public Opinion Quarterly* 3 (1969): 563–576. A contemporary perspective is provided in R. Cialdini, *Influence: The Psychology of Persuasion* (New York: Collins, 2007).
11. B. Z. Posner and J. M. Kouzes, "Relating Leadership and Credibility," *Psychological Reports* 63 (1988): 527–530.
12. Frederick. F. Reichheld, *Loyalty Rules: How Today's Leaders Build Lasting Relationships* (Boston: Harvard Business Publishing, 2001), 6. See also J. Kaufman, R. Markey, S. D. Burton, and D. Azzarello, "Who's Responsible for Employee Engagement? Line Supervisors, Not HR, Must Lead the Charge," *Bain Brief* (2013), http://www.bain.com/Images/BAIN_BRIEF_Who's_responsible_for_employee_engagement.pdf, accessed February 26, 2022.

# Chapter 2
# Clarify Values

1. J. Smith, PhD, *Learning Curve: Lessons on Leadership, Education, and Personal Growth* (Self-published, 2021).
2. F. Kiel, *Return on Character: The Real Reason Leaders and Their Companies Win* (Boston: Harvard Business Publishing, 2015).
3. M. Rokeach, *The Nature of Human Values* (New York: Free Press, 1973).
4. L. Legault, T. Al-Khindi, and M. Inzlicht, "Preserving Integrity in the Face of Performance Threat: Self-affirmation Enhances Neurophysiological Responsiveness to Errors," *Psychological Science* 23(12) (2012): 1455–1460.
5. A. Lamott, *Bird by Bird: Some Instructions on Writing and Life* (New York: Pantheon, 1994): 199–200.

6. W. Zinsser, *On Writing Well: The Classic Guide to Writing Nonfiction* (New York: HarperCollins, 1998), 238.
7. B. Z. Posner and W. H. Schmidt, "Values Congruence and Differences Between the Interplay of Personal and Organizational Value Systems," *Journal of Business Ethics* 12 (1992): 171–177. See also B. Z. Posner, "Another Look at the Impact of Personal and Organizational Values Congruency," *Journal of Business Ethics* 97, no. 4 (2010): 535–541.
8. Posner, B. Z. "After All These Years, Personal Values Still Make a Difference," Working Paper (Santa Clara University), May 2022.
9. S. Houle and K. Campbell, "What High-Quality Job Candidates Look for in a Company, *Gallup Business Journal,* January 4, 2016, http://www.gallup.com/businessjournal/187964/high-quality-job-candidates-look-company.aspx, accessed February 26, 2022.
10. L. E. Paarlberg and J. L. Perry, "Values Management: Aligning Employee Values and Organization Goals," *American Review of Public Administration* 37, no. 4 (2007): 387–408. *Talent Pulse: New Research-Defining and Exemplifying Organizational Core Values*, Human Capital Institute, October 30, 2019, https://www.hci.org/research/talentpulse63, accessed March 7, 2022. H. D Cooper-Thomas, A. van Vianen and N. Anderson, "Changes in Person-Organization Fit: The Impact of Socialization Tactics on Perceived and Actual P–O Fit," *European Journal of Work and Organizational Psychology* 13, no. 1 (2004): 52–78.
11. N. Dvorak and B. Nelson, "Few Employees Believe in Their Company's Values," *Gallup Business Journal*, September 13, 2016, http://www.gallup.com/businessjournal/195491/few-employees-believe-company-values.aspx.
12. See, for example, S. A. Sackmann, "Culture and Performance," in N. Ashkanasy, C. Wilderom, and M. Peterson (eds.), *The Handbook of Organizational Culture and Climate,* 2nd ed. (Thousand Oaks, CA: Sage Publications, 2011), 188–224; A. S. Boyce, L. R. G. Nieminen, M. A. Gillespie, A. M. Ryan, and D. R. Denison (2015). "Which Comes First, Organizational Culture or Performance? A Longitudinal Study of Causal Priority with Automobile Dealerships," *Journal of Organizational Behavior* 36, no. 3 (2015): 339–359; *The Business Case for Purpose* (EY Beacon Institute, 2015). Available at https://assets.ey.com/content/dam/ey-sites/ey-com/en_gl/topics/digital/ey-the-business-case-for-purpose.pdf, accessed May 4, 2022; G. Caesens, G. Marique, D. Hanin, F. Stinglhamber, "The Relationship Between Perceived Organizational Support and Proactive Behaviour Directed Towards the Organization,"

*European Journal of Work and Organizational Psychology* 25, no. 3 (2016): 398–411; and C. M. Gartenberg, A. Prat, and G. Serafeim, "Corporate Purpose and Financial Performance," Columbia Business School Research Paper No. 16-69, June 30, 2016, available at SSRN, https://ssrn.com/abstract=2840005, accessed February 26, 2022.

13. As quoted in A. Carr, "The Inside Story of Starbucks's Race Together Campaign, No Foam," *Fast Company,* June 15, 2015, http://www.fastcompany.com/3046890/the-inside-story-of-starbuckss-race-together-campaign-no-foam, accessed February 26, 2022.
14. See, for example, A. Rhoads and N. Shepherdson, *Built on Values: Creating an Enviable Culture That Outperforms the Competition* (San Francisco: Jossey-Bass, 2011); R. C. Roi, "Leadership, Corporate Culture and Financial Performance" (doctoral dissertation, University of San Francisco, 2006); S. Lee, S. J. Yoon, S. Kim, and J. W. Kang, "The Integrated Effects of Market-Oriented Culture and Marketing Strategy on Firm Performance, *Journal of Strategic Marketing* 14 (2006): 245–261; and T. M Gunarajal, D. Venkatramaraju, and G. Brindha, "Impact of Organizational Culture in Public Sectors," *International Journal of Science and Research* 4, no. 10 (2015): 400–402.
15. P. G. Dominick, D. Iordanoglou, G. Prastacos, and R. R. Reilly, "Espoused Values of the 'Fortune 100 Best Companies to Work For': Essential Themes and Implementation Practices," *Journal of Business Ethics* 173, no. 1–2 (2021): 69–88.
16. B. Z. Posner and R. I. Westwood, "A Cross-Cultural Investigation of the Shared Values Relationship," *International Journal of Value-Based Management* 11, no. 4 (1995): 1–10.
17. L. Guiso, R. Sapienze, and L. Zingales, "The Value of Corporate Culture," *Journal of Financial Economics* 117, no. 1 (2015): 60–76.
18. See, for example, B. Z. Posner, W. H. Schmidt, and J. M. Kouzes, "Shared Values Make a Difference: An Empirical Test of Corporate Culture," *Human Resource Management* 24, no. 3 (1985): 293–310; B. Z. Posner, W. A. Randolph, and W. H. Schmidt, "Managerial Values Across Functions: A Source of Organizational Problems," *Group & Organization Management* 12, no. 4 (1987): 373–385; B. Z. Posner and W. H. Schmidt, "Demographic Characteristics and Shared Values," *International Journal of Value-Based Management* 5, no. 1 (1992): 77–87; B. Z. Posner, "Person-Organization Values Congruence: No Support for Individual Differences as a Moderating Influence," *Human Relations* 45, no. 2 (1992): 351–361; B. Z. Posner and R. I. Westwood, "A Cross-Cultural Investigation of

the Shared Values Relationship," *International Journal of Value-Based Management* 11, no. 4 (1995): 1–10; and B. Z. Posner, "Values and the American Manager: A Three-Decade Perspective," *Journal of Business Ethics* 91, no. 4 (2010): 457–465.

19. R. Roi, *Leadership Practices, Adaptive Corporate Culture & Company Financial Performance: 2005 Study Results*. Crawford International, 2005, http://www.hr.com/en?s=ldYUsXbBU1qzkTZI&t=/documentManager/sfdoc.file.supply&fileID=1168032065880, accessed February 26, 2022. See also S. Lee, S. J. Yoon, S. Kim, and J. W. Kang, "The Integrated Effects of Market-Oriented Culture and Marketing Strategy on Firm Performance, *Journal of Strategic Marketing* 14 (2006): 245–261; T. M. Gunarajal, D. Venkatramaraju, and G. Brindha, "Impact of Organizational Culture in Public Sectors," *International Journal of Science and Research* 4, no. 10 (2015): 400–402; J. Filipkowski, *Defining and Exemplifying Organizational Core Values* (Cincinnati: Human Capital Institute, 2019); and A. Nieto-Rodriquez, *Harvard Business Review Project Management Handbook: How to Launch, Lead, and Sponsor Successful Projects* (Boston: Harvard Business Publishing, 2021).
20. J. P. Kotter and J. L. Heskett, *Corporate Culture and Performance* (New York: Free Press, 1992).
21. B. Z. Posner and W. H. Schmidt, "Values and Expectations of Federal Service Executives," *Public Administration Review* 46, no. 5 (1986): 447–454.
22. C. A. O'Reilly and D. F. Caldwell, "The Power of Strong Corporate Cultures in Silicon Valley Firms," presentation to the Executive Seminar in Corporate Excellence, Santa Clara University, February 13, 1985. See also C. A. O'Reilly, "Corporations, Culture, and Commitment: Motivation and Social Control in Organizations," *California Management Review* 23 (1989): 9–17.
23. J. C. Collins and J. I. Porras, *Built to Last: Successful Habits of Visionary Companies* (New York: Harper-Collins, 1994).
24. C. A. O'Reilly and J. Pfeffer, *Hidden Value: How Great Companies Achieve Extraordinary Results with Ordinary People* (Boston: Harvard Business Publishing, 2000).
25. B. Z. Posner, "Values and the American Manager: A Three-Decade Perspective," *Journal of Business Ethics* 91, no. 4 (2010): 457–465.
26. R. A. Stevenson, "Clarifying Behavioral Expectations Associated with Espoused Organizational Values" (doctoral dissertation, Fielding Institute, 1995).

# Chapter 3
# Set the Example

1. T. Yaffe and R. Kark, "Leading by Example: The Case of Leader OCB," *Journal of Applied Psychology* 96, no. 4 (July 2011): 806–826; and R. Qu, O. Janssen, and K. Shi, "Transformation Leadership and Follower Creativity: The Mediating Role of Follower Relational Identification and the Moderating Role of Leader Creativity," *Leadership Quarterly* 26, no. 2 (2015): 286–299.
2. T. Simons, H. Leroy, V. Collewaert, and S. Masschelein, "How Leader Alignment of Words and Deeds Affects Followers: A Meta-Analysis of Behavioral Integrity Research," *Journal of Business Ethics* 132 (2014): 831–844. M. Palanski and F. J. Yammarino, "Impact of Behavioral Integrity on Follower Job Performance: A Three-Study Examination," *Leadership Quarterly* 22 (2011): 765–786. H. Leroy, M. Palanski, and T. Simons, "How Being True to the Self Helps Leadership Walk the Talk: Authentic Leader and Leader Behavioral Integrity as Drivers of Follower Affective Organizational Commitment and Work Role Performance," *Journal of Business Ethics* 107 (2012): 255–264.
3. "Talent Pulse: New Research-Defining and Exemplifying Organizational Core Values," Human Capital Institute, October 30, 2019, 12, https://www.hci.org/research/talentpulse63, accessed March 7, 2022.
4. E. Schein, *Organizational Culture and Leadership*, 4th ed. (San Francisco: Jossey-Bass, 2010).
5. S. Zuboff, *In the Age of the Smart Machine: The Future of Work and Power* (New York: Basic Books, 1988).
6. K. Allen, *Hidden Agenda: A Proven Way to Win Business and Create a Following* (Brookline, MA: Bibliomotion, 2012).
7. G. Hamel, "Moon Shots for Management," *Harvard Business Review*, February 2009, 91.
8. A. Newberg and M. R. Waldman, *Words Can Change Your Brain: 12 Conversation Strategies to Build Trust, Resolve Conflict, and Increase Intimacy* (New York: Penguin, 2012), 7.
9. M. Adams, *Change Your Questions, Change Your Life: 12 Powerful Tools for Leadership, Coaching, and Life,* 3rd ed. (Oakland, CA: Berrett-Koehler, 2016). A. W. Brooks and L. K. John, "The Surprising Power of Questions," *Harvard Business Review* 96, no. 2 (2018): 61–67.

J. Hagel, "Good Leadership Is About Asking Good Questions," *Harvard Business Review*, January 8, 2021, https://hbr.org/2021/01/good-leadership-is-about-asking-good-questions.

10. D. Stone and S. Heen, *Thanks for the Feedback: The Science and Art of Receiving Feedback Well* (New York: Penguin, 2015).
11. F. Gino, "Research: We Drop People Who Give Us Critical Feedback," *Harvard Business Review*, September 16, 2016, https://hbr.org/2016/09/research-we-drop-people-who-give-us-critical-feedback, accessed February 26, 2022. See also P. Green, F. Gino, and B. Staats, "Shopping for Confirmation: How Threatening Feedback Leads People to Reshape Their Social Networks" (working paper, Harvard Business School, 2016).
12. Robert. W. Eichinger, Michael M. Lombardo, and Dave Ulrich, *100 Things* You *Need to Know: Best Practices for Managers and HR* (Minneapolis: Lominger, 2004), 492.
13. J. Zenger, "There Is No Feedback Fallacy: Understanding the Value of Feedback," *Forbes* (May 13, 2019), https://www.forbes.com/sites/jackzenger/2019/05/13/there-is-no-feedback-fallacy-understanding-the-value-of-feedback/?sh=7402d3853682.
14. J. Yoon, H. Blunden, A. Kristal, and A. Whillans, "Why Asking for Advice Is More Effective Than Asking for Feedback," *Harvard Business Review*, September 20, 2019. See https://hbr.org/2019/09/why-asking-for-advice-is-more-effective-than-asking-for-feedback, accessed February 26, 2022.
15. H. N. Schwarzkopf with P. Pietre, *It Doesn't Take a Hero* (New York: Bantam Books, 1992), 240–241.
16. Haesung Jung, Eunjin Seo, E., Eunjoo Han, Marlone D. Henderson, and Erika A. Patall, "Prosocial Modeling: A Meta-analytic Review and Synthesis," *Psychological Bulletin*, 146, no. 8 (2020): 635–663, https://doi.org/10.1037/bul0000235
17. S. Callahan, *Putting Stories to Work: Mastering Business Storytelling* (Melbourne: Pepperberg Press, 2016). To learn about research into the physiology of why stories are so persuasive, see J. A. Barraza, V. Alexander, L. E. Beavin, E. T. Terris, and P. J. Zak, "The Heart of the Story: Peripheral Physiology During Narrative Exposure Predicts Charitable Giving," *Biological Psychology* 105 (2015): 138–143.
18. As quoted in D. Schawbel, "How to Use Storytelling as a Leadership Tool," *Forbes*, April 13, 2012, http://www.forbes.com/sites/danschawbel/2012/08/13/how-to-use-storytelling-as-a-leadership-tool/#3fdcf5277ac9, accessed February 26, 2022. For more on how to write, tell, and use stories to convey important organizational lessons, see

P. Smith, *Lead with a Story: A Guide to Crafting Business Narratives that Captivate, Convince, and Inspire* (New York: AMACOM, 2012).

19. S. Denning, *The Springboard: How Storytelling Ignites Action in Knowledge-Era Organizations* (Boston: Butterworth-Heinemann, 2001), xiii. For some of the best ways to tell and use stories to communicate vision and values, see S. Denning, *The Secret Language of Leadership: How Leaders Inspire Action Through Narrative* (San Francisco: Jossey-Bass, 2007).
20. See, for example, C. Wortmann, *What's Your Story? Using Stories to Ignite Performance and Be More Successful* (Chicago: Kaplan, 2006); H. Monarth, "The Irresistible Power of Storytelling as a Strategic Business Tool," *Harvard Business Review*, March 11, 2014, https://hbr.org/2014/03/the-irresistible-power-of-storytelling-as-a-strategic-business-tool; P. J. Zak, "Why Your Brain Loves Good Storytelling," *Harvard Business Review*, October 28, 2014, https://hbr.org/2014/10/why-your-brain-loves-good-storytelling, accessed February 26, 2022; and S. R. Martin, "Stories about Values and Valuable Stories: A Field Experiment of the Power of Narratives to Shape Newcomers' Actions," *Academy of Management Journal* 59, no. 5 (2016): 1707–1724.

# Chapter 4
# Envision the Future

1. W. Bennis and B. Nanus, *Leaders: The Strategies for Taking Charge* (New York: Harper Business Essentials, 2007), 89.
2. P. Schuster, *The Power of Your Past: The Art of Recalling, Recasting, and Reclaiming* (San Francisco: Berrett-Koehler, 2011).
3. J. T. Seaman, Jr., and G. D. Smith, "Your Company's History as a Leadership Tool," *Harvard Business Review*, December 2012.
4. M. D. Watkins, *The First 90 Days: Proven Strategies for Getting Up to Speed Faster and Smarter, Updated and Expanded* (Boston: Harvard Business Publishing, 2013).
5. G. Hamel, *Leading the Revolution* (Boston: Harvard Business Publishing, 2000), 128.
6. J. Naisbett, *Mindset: Reset Your Thinking and Set the Future* (New York: HarperCollins, 2006), 20.

7. See, for example, P. Thoms, *Driven by Time: Time Orientation and Leadership* (Westport, CT: Praeger Publishers, 2004); N. Halevy, Y. Berson, and A. D. Galinsky, "The Mainstream Is Not Electable: When Vision Trumps Over Representativeness in Leader Emergence and Effectiveness," *Personality and Social Psychology Bulletin* 37, no. 7 (2011): 893–904; D. P. Moynihan, S. K. Pandey, and B. E. Wright. "Setting the Table: How Transformational Leadership Fosters Performance Information Use," *Journal of Public Administration Research and Theory* 22, no. 1 (2012): 143–164; W. Zhang, H. Wang, and C. L. Pearce, "Consideration for Future Consequences as an Antecedent of Transformational Leadership Behavior: The Moderating Effects of Perceived Dynamic Work Environment," *Leadership Quarterly* 25, no. 2 (2013): 329–343; and S. Sokoll, "The Relationship between GLOBE's Future Orientation Cultural Dimension and Servant Leadership Endorsement," *Emerging Leadership Journeys* 4, no. 1 (2011): 141–153.
8. A. Grant, "These Two Questions Predict Your Ability to Predict the Future," *Adam Grant Bulletin*, January 29, 2022, https://adamgrant.bulletin.com/these-two-questions-predict-your-ability-to-predict-the-future/, accessed March 10, 2022. A. Grant, *Think Again: The Power of Knowing What You Don't Know* (New York: Viking, 2021), 55–76. For useful suggestions on how to strengthen your ability to look further into the future, see Jane McGonigal, *Imaginable: How to See the Future Coming and Feel Ready for Anything—Even Things That Seem Impossible Today* (New York: Spiegel & Grau, 2022).
9. K. M. Sheldon and S. Lyubomirsky, "How to Increase and Sustain Positive Emotion: The Effects of Expressing Gratitude and Visualizing Best Possible Selves," *Journal of Positive Psychology* 1, no. 2 (2006): 73–82. See also, V. Costin and V. L. Vignoles, "Meaning Is About Mattering: Evaluating Coherence, Purpose, and Existential Mattering as Precursors of Meaning in Life Judgments," *Journal of Personality and Social Psychology* 118, no. 4 (2020): 864–884.
10. D. S. Yeager, M. D. Henderson, D. Paunesku, G. M. Walton, S. D'Mello, B. J. Spitzer, and A. L. Duckworth, "Boring but Important: A Self-Transcendent Purpose for Learning Fosters Academic Self-Regulation," *Journal of Personal and Social Psychology* 107, no. 4 (2014): 559–580.
11. B. D. Rosso, K. H. Dekas, and A. Wrzesniewski, "On the Meaning of Work: A Theoretical Integration and Review," *Research in Organizational Behavior* 30 (2010): 91–127. See also R. F. Baumeister, K. D. Vohs, J. Aaker, and E. N. Garbinsky, "Some Key Differences between a Happy Life and a Meaningful Life," *Journal of Positive Psychology* 8, no. 6

(2013): 505–516; and E. E. Smith and J. L. Aaker, "Millennial Searchers," *New York Times Sunday Review*, November 30, 2013, http://www.nytimes.com/2013/12/01/opinion/sunday/millennial-searchers.html?_r=0.

12. Deloitte, "Culture of Purpose: A Business Imperative. 2013 Core Beliefs & Culture Survey," http://www2.deloitte.com/content/dam/Deloitte/us/Documents/about-deloitte/us-leadership-2013-core-beliefs-culture-survey-051613.pdf, accessed February 26, 2022.
13. J. M. Kouzes and B. Z. Posner, "To Lead, Create a Shared Vision," *Harvard Business Review*, January 2009, 20–21.
14. J. Selby, *Listening with Empathy: Creating Genuine Connections with Customers and Colleagues* (Charlottesville, VA: Hampton Roads, 2007). D. Patnaik, *Wired to Care: How Companies Prosper When They Create Widespread Empathy* (Upper Saddle River, NJ: FT Press, 2009). P. Zak, *Trust Factor: The Science of Creating High-Performance* (New York: American Management Association, 2017).
15. S. Coats, "Leadership on the River," August 1, 2016, http://i-lead.com/uncategorized/2036/, accessed February 26, 2022.
16. B. L. Kaye and S. Jordon-Evans, *Love 'em or Lose 'em: Getting Good People to Stay*, 5th ed. (Oakland, CA: Berrett-Koehler, 2014).
17. See, for example, S. E. Humphrey, J. D. Nahrgang, and F. P. Morgeson, "Integrating Motivational, Social, and Contextual Design Features: A Meta-Analytic Summary and Theoretical Extension of the Work Design Literature," *Journal of Applied Psychology*, 90, no. 5 (2007): 1332–1356; D. Ulrich and W. Ulrich, *The Why of Work: How Great Leaders Build Abundant Organizations That Win* (New York: McGraw-Hill, 2010); D. Pontefract, *The Purpose Effect: Building Meaning in Yourself, Your Role, and Your Organization* (Boise, ID: Elevate Publishing, 2016); and Universum, "Millennials: Understanding a Misunderstood Generation," 2015, http://universumglobal.com/millennials.
18. See, for example, "Rethink: 2022 Global Culture Report," O. C. Tanner Institute, https://www.octanner.com/content/dam/oc-tanner/images/v2/culture-report/2022/home/INT-GCR2022.pdf, accessed February 29, 2022; C. Romero, "What We Know About Purpose & Relevance from Scientific Research," Mindset Scholars Network, http://studentexperiencenetwork.org/wp-content/uploads/2015/09/What-We-Know-About-Purpose-and-Relevance-.pdf, accessed February 29, 2022; D. Goleman, "Millennials: The Purpose Generation," July 22, 2019, https://www.kornferry.com/insights/this-week-in-leadership/millennials-purpose-generation, accessed February 29, 2022; J. J. Deal

and A. Levenson, *What Millennials Want from Work: How to Maximize Engagement in Today's Workforce* (New York: McGraw-Hill, 2016); R. J. Leider, *The Power of Purpose: Find Meaning, Live Longer, Better* (Oakland, CA: Berrett-Koehler, 2015); P. L. Hill, N. A. Turiano, D. K. Mroczek, and A. L. Burrow, "The Value of a Purposeful Life: Sense of Purpose Predicts Greater Income and Net Worth," *Journal of Research in Personality* 65, NO. 5 (2016): 38–42; C. M. Christensen, J. Allworth, and K. Dillon, *How Will You Measure Your Life* (New York: Harper Business, 2012); and D. Pink, *Drive: The Surprising Truth About What Motivates Us* (New York: Riverhead Books, 2009).

19 McKinsey & Company, "The Search for Purpose at Work," McKinsey Quarterly, June 2021, accessed March 10, 2022, https://www.mckinsey.com/business-functions/people-and-organizational-performance/our-insights/the-search-for-purpose-at-work.

20. A. De Smet, B. Dowling, M. Mugayar-Baldocchi, and B. Schaninger, "Gone for Now, or Gone for Good? How to Play the New Talent Game and Win Back Workers," *McKinsey Quarterly*, March 2022, https://www.mckinsey.com/business-functions/people-and-organizational-performance/our-insights/gone-for-now-or-gone-for-good-how-to-play-the-new-talent-game-and-win-back-workers, accessed March 10, 2022.

21. N. Doshi and L. McGregor, *Primed to Perform: How to Build the Highest Performing Cultures Through the Science of Total Motivation* (New York: Harper Business, 2015), xiii.

22. S. L. Lopez, *Making Hope Happen: Create the Future for Yourself and Others* (New York: Atria Books, 2013).

# Chapter 5 Enlist Others

1. In a similar way, Simon Sinek talks about how people can be inspired by starting with "why." See S. Sinek, *Start with Why: How Great Leaders Inspire Everyone to Take Action* (New York: Portfolio, 2010).
2. See, for example, R. M. Spence, *It's Not What You Sell, It's What You Stand For: Why Every Extraordinary Business Is Driven by Purpose* (New York: Portfolio, 2010); D. Ulrich and W. Ulrich, *The Why of Work: How Great Leaders Build Abundant Organizations That Win*

(New York: McGraw-Hill, 2010); B. D. Rosso,, K. H. Dekas, and A. Wrzesniewski, "On the Meaning of Work: A Theoretical Integration and Review," *Research in Organizational Behavior* 31 (2011): 91–127; D. Ariely, *Payoff: The Hidden Logic That Shapes Our Motivations* (New York: Simon & Schuster, 2016); and A. M. Carton, "'I'm Not Mopping the Floors—I'm Putting a Man on the Moon': How NASA Leaders Enhanced the Meaningfulness of Work by Changing the Meaning of Work," *Administrative Science Quarterly*, 63, no. 2 (2018): 323–369.

3. V. Stretcher and R. E. Quinn, "Can Purpose Help Us in Hard Times?" *Greater Good Magazine,* March 3, 2022, https://positiveorgs.bus.umich.edu/news/can-purpose-help-us-in-hard-times/, accessed March 10, 2022.
4. 2016 Workforce Purpose Index, "Purpose at Work: The Largest Global Study on the Role of Purpose in the Workforce," https://cdn.imperative.com/media/public/Global_Purpose_Index_2016.pdf, accessed February 26, 2022.
5. R. F. Baumeister, K. D. Vohs, J. L. Aaker, and E. N. Garbinsky, "Some Key Differences between a Happy Life and a Meaningful Life," *Journal of Positive Psychology* 8, no. 6 (2013): 505–516.
6. E. E. Smith and J. L. Aaker, "Millennial Searchers," *New York Times,* November 30, 2013, http://nyti.ms/1dHVKid. 2016 Workforce Purpose Index, "Purpose at Work." S. M. Schaefer, J. M. Boylan, C. M. van Reekum, R. C. Lapate, C. J. Norris, C. D. Ryff, and R. J. Davidson, "Purpose in Life Predicts Better Emotional Recovery from Negative Stimuli," *PLOS ONE* 8, no. 11 (2013), https://journals.plos.org/plosone/article?id=10.1371/journal.pone.0080329. *Meaning and Purpose at Work*, BetterUp (2017), https://grow.betterup.com/resources/meaning-and-purpose-report. J. Emmett, G. Schrah, M. Schrimper, and A. Wood, "COVID-19 and the Employee Experience: How Leaders Can Seize the Moment," June 2020, McKinsey.com, https://www.mckinsey.com/business-functions/people-and-organizational-performance/our-insights/covid-19-and-the-employee-experience-how-leaders-can-seize-the-moment. N. Dhingra, J. Emmett, A. Sarno, and B. Schaninger, "Igniting Individual Purpose in Times of Crisis," April 18, 2020, McKinsey.com, https://www.mckinsey.com/business-functions/people-and-organizational-performance/our-insights/igniting-individual-purpose-in-times-of-crisis.
7. J. Newton and J. Davis, "Three Secrets of Organizational Effectiveness," *strategy+business* 76, August (2014), reprint 00271.
8. M. Burchell and J. Robin, *The Great Workplace: How to Build It, How to Keep It, and Why It Matters* (San Francisco: Jossey-Bass, 2011), 127–128.

9. D. Hall, *Jump Start Your Business Brain: Win More, Lose Less, and Make More Money with Your New Products, Services, Sales and Advertising* (Cincinnati: Clerisy Books, 2005), 126.
10. Pride is one of the five dimensions of a great workplace, and scoring high on this variable qualifies a company as a *Fortune* magazine 100 Best Companies to Work For (M. Burchell and J. Robin, *The Great Workplace: How to Build It, How to Keep It, and Why It Matters* [San Francisco: Jossey-Bass, 2011], 127–154). Pride has also been postulated as a primary intrinsic motivation (e.g., J. Tracy, *Take Pride: Why the Deadliest Sin Holds the Secret to Human Success* [New York: Houghton Mifflin Harcourt, 2016]).
11. "'I Have a Dream' Leads Top 100 Speeches of the Century," press release, University of Wisconsin, December 15, 1999, www.news.wisc.edu/releases/3504.html or at http://www.americanrhetoric.com/top100speechesall.html. See also S. E. Lucas and M. J. Medhurst, *Words of a Century: The Top 100 American Speeches, 1900–1999* (New York: Oxford University Press, 2008).
12. The audio version of the "I Have a Dream" speech can be downloaded from http://www.amazon.com/Greatest-Speeches-All-Time-Vol/dp/B001L0RONE/ref=sr_1_cc_3?ie=UTF8&qid=1301516046&sr=1-3-catcorr, accessed February 26, 2022.
13. A. M. Carton, "People Remember What You Say When You Paint a Picture," *Harvard Business Review*, June 12, 2015, https://hbr.org/2015/06/employees-perform-better-when-they-can-literally-see-what-youre-saying, accessed February 26, 2022.
14. A. M. Carton, C. Murphy, and J. R. Clark. "A (Blurry) Vision of the Future: How Leader Rhetoric about Ultimate Goals Influences Performance," *Academy of Management Journal* 57, no. 6 (2014): 1544–1570.
15. J. Geary, *I Is an Other: The Secret Life of Metaphor and How It Shapes the Way We See the World* (New York: Harper, 2011), 5.
16. V. Lieberman, S. M. Samuels, and L. Ross, "The Name of the Game: Predictive Power of Reputations Versus Situational Labels in Determining Prisoner's Dilemma Game Moves," *Personality and Social Psychology Bulletin* 30 (2004): 1175–1185. See also Y. Benkler, "The Unselfish Gene," *Harvard Business Review*, July–August 2011, 78.
17. C. Heath and D. Heath, *Made to Stick: Why Some Ideas Survive and Others Die* (New York: Random House, 2007).
18. B. L. Fredrickson, *Positivity: Groundbreaking Research Reveals How to Embrace the Hidden Strengths of Positive Emotions, Overcome Negativity, and Thrive* (New York: Crown, 2008).

19. D. T. Hsu, B. J. Sanford, K. K. Meyers, T. M. Love, K. E. Hazlett, H. Wang, L. Ni, S. J. Walker, B. J. Mickey, S. T. Korycinski, R. A. Koeppe, J. K. Crocker, S. A. Langenecker, and J-K. Zubieta, "Response of the μ-Opioid System to Social Rejection and Acceptance," *Molecular Psychiatry* 18 (2013): 1211–1217. See also D. Goleman, *Social Intelligence: The New Science of Human Relationships* (New York: Bantam, 2006).
20. See, for example, H. S. Friedman, L. M. Prince, R. E. Riggio, and M. R. DiMatteo, "Understanding and Assessing Nonverbal Expressiveness: The Affective Communication Test," *Journal of Personality and Social Psychology* 39, no. 2 (1980): 333–351; J. Conger, *Winning 'em Over: A New Model for Management in the Age of Persuasion* (New York: Simon & Schuster, 1998); D. Goleman, R. Boyatzis, and A. McKee, *Primal Leadership: Realizing the Power of Emotional Intelligence* (Boston: Harvard Business Publishing, 2002); J. Conger, "Charismatic Leadership," in M. G. Rumsey (ed.) *The Oxford Handbook of Leadership* (New York: Oxford University Press, 2013), 376–391; and G. A. Sparks, "Charismatic Leadership: Findings of an Exploratory Investigation of the Techniques of Influence," *Journal of Behavioral Studies in Business* 7 (2014): 1–11.
21. J. L. McGaugh, *Memory and Emotion* (New York: Columbia University Press, 2003), 90. See also R. Maxwell and R. Dickman, *The Elements of Persuasion: Use Storytelling to Pitch Better Ideas, Sell Faster, & Win More Business* (New York: HarperCollins, 2007), especially "Sticky Stories: Memory, Emotions and Markets," 122–150.
22. McGaugh, *Memory and Emotion*, 93.
23. D. A. Small, G. Loewenstein, and P. Slovic. "Sympathy and Callousness: The Impact of Deliberative Thought on Donations to Identifiable and Statistical Victims," *Organizational Behavior and Human Decision Processes* 102, no. 2 (2007): 143–153.
24. Health and Health, *Made to Stick*, 101–123.

# Chapter 6
# Search for Opportunities

1. R. M. Kanter, *The Change Masters: Innovation for Productivity in the American Corporation* (New York: Simon & Schuster, 1983).

2. "The Committed Innovator: A Conversation with Amy Brooks of the NBA," podcast, McKinsey & Company Insights, July 20, 2021, https://www.mckinsey.com/business-functions/strategy-and-corporate-finance/our-insights/the-committed-innovator-a-conversation-with-amy-brooks-of-the-nba, accessed April 5, 2022.
3. W. Berger, *A More Beautiful Question* (New York: Bloomsbury, 2014).
4. H. Schultz and D. J. Yang, *Pour Your Heart into It* (New York: Hachette, 1999), 205–210.
5. See, for example, J. M. Crant and T. S. Bateman, "Charismatic Leadership Viewed from Above: The Impact of Proactive Personality," *Journal of Organizational Behavior* 21, no. 1 (2000): 63–75; and M. Spitzmuller, H-P. Sin, M. Howe, and S. Fatimah. "Investigating the Uniqueness and Usefulness of Proactive Personality in Organizational Research: A Meta-Analytic Review," *Human Performance* 28, no. 4 (2015): 351–379.
6. See, for example, T. S. Bateman and J. M. Crant, "The Proactive Component of Organizational Behavior: Measures and Correlates," *Journal of Organizational Behavior* 14 (1993): 103–118; T-Y. Kim, A. H. Y. Hon, and J. M. Crant, "Proactive Personality, Employee Creativity, and Newcomer Outcomes: A Longitudinal Study," *Journal of Business and Psychology* 24, no. 1 (2009): 93–103; N. Li, J. Liang, and J. M. Crant, "The Role of Proactive Personality in Job Satisfaction and Organizational Citizenship Behavior: A Relational Perspective," *Journal of Applied Psychology* 95, no. 2 (2010): 395–404.
7. See, for example, J. A. Thompson, "Proactive Personality and Job Performance: A Social Capital Perspective," *Journal of Applied Psychology* 90, no. 5 (2005): 1011–1017. See also S. E. Seibert and M. L. Braimer, "What Do Proactive People Do? A Longitudinal Model Linking Proactive Personality and Career Success," *Personnel Psychology* 54 (2001): 845–875; D. J. Brown, R. T. Cober, K. Kane, P. E. Levy, and J. Shalhoop, "Proactive Personality and the Successful Job Search: A Field Investigation of College Graduates," *Journal of Applied Psychology* 91, no. 3 (2006): 717–726; C-H. Wu, Y. Want, and W. H. Mobley, "Understanding Leaders' Proactivity from a Goal-Process View and Multisource Ratings," in W. H. Mobley, M. Li, and Y. Wang (eds.), *Advances in Global Leadership,* vol. 7 (Bingley, UK: Emerald Group Publishing, 2012); and V. P. Prabhu, S. J. McGuire, E. A. Drost, K. K. Kwong, "Proactive Personality and Entrepreneurial Intent: Is Entrepreneurial Self-Efficacy a Mediator or Moderator?" *International Journal of Entrepreneurial Behavior & Research* 18, no. 5 (2012): 559–586.

8. B. Z. Posner and J. W. Harder, "The Proactive Personality, Leadership, Gender and National Culture" (paper presented to the Western Academy of Management Conference, Santa Fe, New Mexico, April 2002).
9. A. Duckworth, *Grit: The Power of Passion and Perseverance* (New York: Scribner, 2016).
10. Victor Frankl provides dramatic examples that how people deal with challenge comes from inside them. See V. E. Frankl, *Man's Search for Meaning: An Introduction to Logotherapy* (New York: Touchstone, 1984; originally published 1946).
11. See, for example, D. Ariely, *Predictably Irrational: The Hidden Forces That Shape Our Decisions* (New York: HarperCollins, 2009); "LSE: When Performance-Related Pay Backfires," *Financial*, June 25, 2009; and F. Ederer and G. Manso, "Is Pay for Performance Detrimental to Innovation? *Management Science* 59, no. 7 (2013): 1496–1513.
12. E. L. Deci with R. Flaste, *Why We Do What We Do: Understanding Self-Motivation* (New York: Penguin, 1995). See also K. W. Thomas, *Intrinsic Motivation at Work: What Really Drives Employee Engagement,* 2nd ed. (Oakland, CA: Berrett-Koehler, 2009); and D. Pink, Drive: *The Surprising Truth About What Motivates You* (New York: Riverhead Press, 2011).
13. As quoted in P. LaBarre, "How to Make It to the Top," Fast Company, September 1998, 72. See also A. Blum, *Annapurna: A Woman's Place* (Berkeley, CA: Counterpoint Press, 2015).
14. A. De Smet, B. Dowling, M. Mugayar-Baldocchi, and B. Schaninger, "'Great Attrition or 'Great Attraction'? The Choice is Yours," *McKinsey Quarterly,* September 2021, https://www.mckinsey.com/business-functions/people-and-organizational-performance/our-insights/great-attrition-or-great-attraction-the-choice-is-yours, accessed February 1, 2020. See also E. Field, D. Mendelsohn, N. Rainone, and B. Schaninger, "The Great Attrition: Same Turnover, but the "Why" Differs by Industry," *McKinsey Quarterly,* November 8, 2021, https://www.mckinsey.com/business-functions/people-and-organizational-performance/our-insights/the-organization-blog/the-great-attrition-same-turnover-but-the-why-differs-by-industry, accessed February 29, 2022; and N. Dhingra, A. Samo, B. Schaninger, and M. Schrimper, "Help Your Employees Find Purpose—or Watch Them Leave," *McKinsey Quarterly,* April 2021, https://www.mckinsey.com/business-functions/people-and-organizational-performance/our-insights/help-your-employees-find-purpose-or-watch-them-leave#, accessed February 29, 2022.

15. See, for example, J. Ettlie, Managing Innovation, 2nd ed. (Abingdon, UK: Taylor & Francis, 2006); S. Johnson, *Where Good Ideas Come From: The Natural History of Innovation* (New York: Riverhead, 2010); E. Ries, *The Lean Startup: How Constant Innovation Creates Radically Successful Businesses* (New York: Penguin Group, 2011); T. Davila, M. J. Epstein, and R. Shelton, *Making Innovation Work: How to Manage It, Measure It, and Profit from It,* rev. ed. (Upper Saddle River, NJ: FT Press, 2012); S. Kelman, "Innovation in Government Can Come from Anywhere," FCW blog, September 20, 2016, https://fcw.com/blogs/lectern/2016/09/kelman-micro-innovation-pianos.aspx, accessed February 26, 2022; I. Asimov, "How Do People Get New Ideas?" *MIT Technology Review,* October 20, 2014, https://www.technologyreview.com/s/531911/isaac-asimov-asks-how-do-people-get-new-ideas/, accessed February 26, 2022.
16. IBM, "Expanding the Innovation Horizons: The Global CEO Study" 2006 (Somers, NY: IBM Global Services, 2006).
17. D. Nicolini, M. Korica, and K. Ruddle, "Staying in the Know," *Sloan Management Review* 56, no. 4 (Summer 2015): 57–65. See also S. Bahcall, *Loonshots: How to Nurture the Crazy Ideas that Win Wars, Cure Diseases, and Transform Industries* (New York St. Martin's Press, 2019); and O. Varol, *Think Like a Rocket Scientist: Simple Strategies You Can Use to Make Giant Leaps in Work and Life* (New York: Hachette Book Group, 2020).
18. G. Berns, *Iconoclast: A Neuroscientist Reveals How to Think Differently* (Boston: Harvard Business Publishing, 2008).
19. M. M. Capozzi, R. Dye, and A. Howe, "Sparking Creativity in Teams: An Executive's Guide," *McKinsey Quarterly,* April 2011.
20. R. Katz, "The Influence of Group Longevity: High Performance Research Teams," *Wharton Magazine* 6, no. 3 (1982): 28–34. R. Katz and T. J. Allen, "Investigating the Not Invented Here (NIH) Syndrome: A Look at the Performance, Tenure, and Communication Patterns of 50 R&D Project Groups," in M. L. Tushman and W. L. Moore (eds.), *Readings in the Management of Innovation,* 2nd ed. (Cambridge, MA: Ballinger, 1988), 293–309.
21. Katz, "The Influence of Group Longevity," 31.
22. A. W. Brooks, F. Gino, and M. E. Schweitzer, "Smart People Ask for (My) Advice: Seeking Advice Boosts Perceptions of Competence," *Management Science* 61, no. 6 (June 2015): 1421–1435.
23. Z. Achi and J. G. Berger, "Delighting in the Possible," *McKinsey Quarterly,* March 2016, 5.

# Chapter 7
# Experiment and Take Risks

1. K. E. Weick, "Small Wins: Redefining the Scale of Social Problems," *American Psychologist* 39, no. 1 (1984): 43.
2. L. A. Barroso, "The Roofshot Manifesto," re:Work, July 13, 2016, https://rework.withgoogle.com/blog/the-roofshot-manifesto/?utm_source=newsletter&utm_medium=email&utm_campaign=august_newsletter, accessed February 26, 2022.
3. P. Sims, *Little Bets: How Breakthrough Ideas Emerge from Small Discoveries* (New York: Free Press, 2011), 141–152; and A. Grant, *Think Again: The Power of Knowing What You Don't Know* (New York, Viking, 2021).
4. K. M. Eisenstadt and B. N. Tabrizi, "Accelerating Adaptive Processes: Product Innovation in the Global Computer Industry," *Administrative Science Quarterly* 40 (1995): 84–110. E. Williams and A. R. Shaffer. "The Defense Innovation Initiative: The Importance of Capability Prototyping," *Joint Force Quarterly* (2015, 2nd Quarterly): 34–43.
5. B. J. Lucas and L. Nordgren, "People Underestimate the Value of Persistence for Creative Performance," *Journal of Personality and Social Psychology* 109, no. 2 (2015): 232–243.
6. T. A. Amabile and S. J. Kramer, "The Power of Small Wins," *Harvard Business Review*, May 2011, 75. See also their book *The Progress Principle: Using Small Wins to Ignite Joy, Engagement, and Creativity at Work* (Boston: Harvard Business Publishing, 2011).
7. See S. R. Maddi, *Hardiness: Turning Stressful Circumstances into Resilient Growth* (New York: Springer, 2013).
8. See, for example, P. T. Bartone, "Resilience Under Military Operational Stress: Can Leaders Influence Hardiness?" *Military Psychology* 18 (2006): S141–S148; P. T. Bartone, R. R. Roland, J. J. Picano, and T. J. Williams, "Psychological Hardiness Predicts Success in US Army Special Forces Candidates," *International Journal of Selection and Assessment* 16, no. 1 (2008): 78–81; R. A. Bruce and R. F. Sinclair, "Exploring the Psychological Hardiness of Entrepreneurs," *Frontiers of Entrepreneurship Research* 29, no. 6 (2009): 5; P. T. Bartone, "Social and Organizational Influences on Psychological Hardiness: How Leaders Can Increase Stress Resilience," *Security Informatics* 1 (2012): 1–10; B. Hasanvand, M. Khaledian, A. R. Merati, "The Relationship between Psychological Hardiness and

Attachment Styles with the University Student's Creativity," *European Journal of Experimental Biology* 3, no. 3 (2013): 656–660; and A. M. Sandvik, A. L. Hansena, S. W. Hystada, B. H. Johnsena, and P. T. Barton, "Psychopathy, Anxiety, and Resiliency: Psychological Hardiness as a Mediator of the Psychopathy–Anxiety Relationship in a Prison Setting," *Personality and Individual Differences* 72 (2015): 30–34.

9. As quoted in C. Dahle, "Natural Leader," *Fast Company,* November 30, 2000, https://www.fastcompany.com/41857/natural-leader.
10. B. L. Frederickson, *Positivity: Groundbreaking Research Reveals How to Embrace the Hidden Strengths of Positive Emotions Over Negativity, and Thrive* (New York: Crown, 2009). A. Sood, *The Mayo Clinic Guide to Stress-Free Living* (Boston: Da Capo Press, 2013). K. S. Cameron and G. M. Spreitzer (eds.), *The Oxford Handbook of Positive Organizational Scholarship* (New York: Oxford University Press, 2013).
11. J. M. Kouzes and B. Z. Posner, *Turning Adversity into Opportunity* (San Francisco: The Leadership Challenge–A Wiley Brand, 2014).
12. D. Bayles and T. Orland, *Art and Fear: Observations on the Perils (and Rewards) of Artmaking* (Eugene, OR: Image Continuum Press, 2001).
13. P. M. Madsen, "Failing to Learn? The Effects of Failure and Success on Organizational Learning in the Global Orbital Launch Vehicle Industry, *Academy of Management Journal* 53, no. 3 (2010): 451–476. Studies of organizational learning reach some similar conclusions; for example, R. Khannal, I. Guler, and A. Nerkar, "Fail Often, Fail Big, and Fail Fast? Learning from Small Failures and R&D Performance in the Pharmaceutical Industry," *Academy of Management Journal* 59, no. 2 (2016): 436–459.
14. L. M. Brown and B. Z. Posner, "Exploring the Relationship Between Learning and Leadership," *Leadership & Organization Development Journal* 22, no. 6 (2001): 274–280. See also J. M. Kouzes and B. Z. Posner, *The Truth about Leadership: The No-Fads, Heart-of-the-Matter Facts You Need to Know* (San Francisco: Jossey-Bass, 2010), 119–135.
15. P. A. Heslin and L. A. Keating, "In Learning Mode? The Role of Mindsets in Derailing and Enabling Experiential Leadership Development," *Leadership Quarterly* 28, no. 3 (2017): 362–384. S. J. Ashford and D. S. DeRue, "Developing as a Leader: The Power of Mindful Engagement," *Organizational Dynamics* 41, no. 2 (2012): 146–154.
16. N. Doshi and L. McGregor, *Primed to Perform: How to Build the Highest Performing Cultures Through the Science of Total Motivation* (New York, Harper Business, 2015).

17. As quoted in https://www.brainyquote.com/quotes/hank_aaron_125240.
18. J. K. Rowling, *Very Good Lives: The Fringe Benefits of Failure and the Importance of Imagination* (New York: Little, Brown, and Company, 2015), 34.
19. G. Manso, "Experimentation and the Returns to Entrepreneurship," *Review of Financial Studies* 29, no. 9 (2016): 2319–2340.
20 P. J. Schoemaker and R. E. Cunther, "The Wisdom of Deliberate Mistakes," *Harvard Business Review,* June 2006, 108–115. *Harvard Business Review* devoted the entire April 2011 issue to a discussion of failure and its role in business, http://hbr.org/archive-toc/BR1104?conversationId=1855599, accessed February 26, 2022.
21. C. S. Dweck, *Mindset: The New Psychology of Success* (New York: Random House, 2006), 6–7. See also C. Dweck, "Carol Dweck Revisits the 'Growth Mindset," *Education Week,* September 22, 2016, http://www.edweek.org/ew/articles/2015/09/23/carol-dweck-revisits-the-growth-mindset.html, accessed February 26, 2022.
22. A. Bandura and R. E. Wood, "Effects of Perceived Controllability and Performance Standards on Self-Regulation of Complex Decision Making," *Journal of Personality and Social Psychology* 56, no. 5 (1989): 805–814. See also Dweck, *Mindset.*
23. T. K. Kouzes and B. Z. Posner, "Influence of Mindset on Leadership Behavior," *Leadership & Organization Development Journal* 40, no. 8 (2019), 829–844.
24. A. Ericsson and R. Pool, *Peak: Secrets from the New Science of Expertise* (New York: Houghton Mifflin Harcourt, 2016).
25. For an extensive review of the origins of psychological safety, its impact, and practices, see A. C. Edmondson, *The Fearless Organization: Creating Psychological Safety in the Workplace for Learning, Innovation, and Growth* (Hoboken, NJ: Wiley, 2019). See also D. Brueller and A. Carmeli, "Linking Capacities of High-Quality Relationships to Team Learning and Performance in Service Organizations," *Human Resource Management* 50, no. 4 (2011): 455–77; M. L. Frazier, S. Fainshmidt, R. L. Klinger, A. Pezeshkan, and V. Vracheva, "Psychological Safety: A Meta-Analytic Review and Extension," *Personnel Psychology* 70, no. 1 (2017): 113–65; O. S. Jung, P. Kundu, A. C. Edmondson, J. Hegde, N. Agazaryan, M. Steinberg, and A. Raldow, "Resilience vs. Vulnerability: Psychological Safety and Reporting of Near Misses with Varying Proximity to Harm in Radiation Oncology," *Joint Commission Journal on Quality and Patient Safety* 47, no. 1 (January 2021): 15–22; T. R. Clark, "Agile Doesn't Work

Without Psychological Safety," *Harvard Business Review*, February 21, 2022, https://hbr.org/2022/02/agile-doesnt-work-without-psychological-safety, accessed March 13, 2022; A. C. Edmondson and G. Daley, "How to Foster Psychological Safety in Virtual Meetings," *Harvard Business Review*, August 25, 2020, https://hbr.org/2020/08/how-to-foster-psychological-safety-in-virtual-meetings, accessed March 13, 2022; A. C. Edmondson and M. Mortensen, "What Psychological Safety Looks Like in a Hybrid Workplace," *Harvard Business Review* April 19, 2021, https://hbr.org/2021/04/what-psychological-safety-looks-like-in-a-hybrid-workplace, accessed March 13, 2022.

26. A. C. Edmondson, "Learning from Mistakes Is Easier Said Than Done: Group and Organizational Influences on the Detection and Correction of Human Error," *Journal of Applied Behavioral Science* 32, no. 1 (1996): 5–28. A. C. Edmondson, "Psychological Safety and Learning Behavior in Work Teams," *Administrative Science Quarterly* 44, no. 2 (June 1999): 350–383.
27. C. Duhigg, "What Google Learned from its Quest to Build the Perfect Team," *The New York Times Magazine* (February 25, 2016), https://www.nytimes.com/2016/02/28/magazine/what-google-learned-from-its-quest-to-build-the-perfect-team.html, accessed March 1, 2022.
28. O. C. Tanner Institute, *2020 Global Culture Report* (Salt Lake City, 2020), 2.
29. R. Friedman, *The Best Place to Work: The Art and Science of Creating an Extraordinary Workplace* (New York: Penguin, 2014).
30. A. C. Edmondson, "Learning from Mistakes Is Easier Said Than Done: Group and Organizational Influences on the Detection and Correction of Human Error," *Journal of Applied Behavioral Science* 32, no. 1 (1996): 5–28. See also A. Edmondson and S. S. Reynolds, *Building the Future: Big Teaming for Audacious Innovation* (Oakland, CA: Berrett-Koehler, 2016).
31. O. C. Tanner Institute, *2021 Global Culture Report*, 7.
32. M. J. Guber, B. D. Gelman, and C. Ranganath, "States of Curiosity Modulate Hippocampus-Dependent Learning via the Dopaminergic Circuit," *Neuron* 84, no. 2 (2014): 486–496.
33. B. Grazer and C. Fishman, *A Curious Mind: The Secret to a Bigger Life* (New York: Simon & Schuster, 2015).
34. M. Warrell, *Stop Playing Safe* (Melbourne: John Wiley & Sons, 2013).
35. S. R. Maddi and D. M. Khoshaba, *Resilience at Work: How to Succeed No Matter What Life Throws at You* (New York: MJF Books, 2005). M. E. P. Seligman, *Learned Optimism: How to Change Your Mind and Your Life*

(New York: Random House, 2006). J. D. Margolis and P. G. Stoltz, "How to Bounce Back from Adversity," *Harvard Business Review,* January–February 2010, 86–92. A. Graham, K. Cuthbert, and K. Sloan, *Lemonade: The Leader's Guide to Resilience at Work* (Lancaster, PA: Veritae Press, 2012).

36. E. S. Smith, "On Coronavirus Lockdown? Look for Meaning, Not Happiness," *New York Times* (April 7, 2020), https://www.nytimes.com/2020/04/07/opinion/coronavirus-mental-health.html, accessed February 26, 2022.
37. While this example comes from our interview, you can learn much more about his perspective in P. Williams with J. Denney, *Leadership Excellence: The Seven Sides of Leadership for the 21st Century* (Uhrichsville, OH: Barbour Books, 2012); and *Lead Like Walt: Discover Walt Disney's Magical Approach to Building Successful Organizations* (Deerfield Beach, FL: Health Communications, 2019).
38. A. L. Duckworth, C. Peterson, M. D. Matthews, and D. R. Kelly, "Grit: Perseverance and Passion for Long-Term Goals," *Journal of Personality and Social Psychology* 92, no. 6 (2007): 1087–1101.
39. A. Duckworth, *Grit: The Power of Passion and Perseverance* (New York: Simon & Schuster, 2016).
40. M. E. P. Seligman, "Building Resilience," *Harvard Business Review*, April 2011, 101–106 (p 102). For a more complete discussion of this subject, see M. E. P. Seligman, *Flourish: A Visionary New Understanding of Happiness and Well-Being* (New York: Free Press, 2011).

# Chapter 8 Foster Collaboration

1. We use *cooperate* and *collaborate* synonymously. Their dictionary definitions are very similar. In the *Merriam-Webster Unabridged* online dictionary, the first definition of *cooperate* is "To act or work with another or others to a common end: operate jointly," https://www.merriam-webster.com/dictionary/cooperate. The first definition of *collaborate* is, "To work jointly with others or together especially in an intellectual endeavor," https://www.merriam-webster.com/dictionary/collaborate, accessed February 26, 2022.
2. K. T. Dirks, "Trust in Leadership and Team Performance: Evidence from NCAA Basketball," *Journal of Applied Psychology* 85, no. 6

(2000): 1004–1012. J. A. Colquitt and S. C. Salam, "Foster Trust through Ability, Benevolence, and Integrity," in J. Locke (ed.), *Handbook of Principles of Organizational Behavior: Indispensable Knowledge for Evidence-Based Management,* 2nd ed. (Hoboken, NJ: Wiley, 2009) 389–404. R. S. Sloyman and J. D. Ludema, "That's Not How I See It: How Trust in the Organization, Leadership, Process, and Outcome Influence Individual Responses to Organizational Change," *Organizational Change and Development* 18 (2010): 233–276. M. Mach, S. Dolan, and S. Tzafrir, "The Differential Effect of Team Members' Trust on Team Performance: The Mediation Role of Team Cohesion," *Journal of Occupational and Organizational Psychology* 83, no. 3 (2010): 771–794. R. F. Hurley, *The Decision to Trust: How Leaders Create High-Trust Organizations* (San Francisco: Jossey-Bass, 2012). S. Brown, D. Gray, J. McHardy, and K. Taylor, "Employee Trust and Workplace Performance," *Journal of Economic Behavior & Organization* 116 (2015): 361–378.

3. K. M. Newman, "Why Cynicism Can Hold You Back," Greater Good, June 11, 2015, http://greatergood.berkeley.edu/article/item/why_cynicism_can_hold_you_back. See also G. D. Grace and T. Schill, "Social Support and Coping Style Differences in Subjects High and Low in Interpersonal Trust," *Psychological Reports* 59, no. 2 (1986): 584–586; M. B. Gurtman, "Trust, Distrust, and Interpersonal Problems: A Circumplex Analysis," *Journal of Personality and Social Psychology* 62, no. 6 (1992): 989–1002; and O. Stavrova and D. Ehlebracht, "Cynical Beliefs About Human Nature and Income: Longitudinal and Cross-Cultural Analyses," *Journal of Personality and Social Psychology* 110, no. 1 (2016): 116–132.
4. B. A. De-Jong, K. T. Dirks, and N. Gillespie, "Trust and Team Performance: A Meta-analysis of Main Effects, Moderators, and Covariates," *Journal of Applied Psychology* 101, no. 8 (2016): 1134–1150.
5. K. Twaronite, "A Global Survey on the Ambiguous State of Employee Trust," *Harvard Business Review*, July 22, 2016, https://hbr.org/2016/07/a-global-survey-on-the-ambiguous-state-of-employee-trust, accessed February 26, 2022. See also M. Javidan and A. Zaheer, "How Leaders Around the World Build Trust Across Cultures," *Harvard Business Review,* May 27, 2019, https://hbr.org/2019/05/how-leaders-around-the-world-build-trust-across-cultures.
6. J. F. Helliwell, H. Huang, S. Wang, and M. Norton, "Happiness, Trust, and Deaths Under COVID-19," in J. F. Helliwell, R. Layard, K. D. Sachs, Jan-Emmanuel De Neve, L. B. Aknin, and S. Wang, "2021 World Happiness

Report," Sustainable Development Solutions Network (2021), 13–56, 51, https://worldhappiness.report/ed/2021/, accessed March 7, 2022.

7. T. Neeley, *Remote Work Revolution: Succeeding from Anywhere* (New York: HarperCollins, 2021). See also N. S. Hill and K. M. Bartol, "Five Ways to Improve Communication in Virtual Teams," *MIT Sloan Management Review,* June 13, 2018, https://sloanreview.mit.edu/article/five-ways-to-improve-communication-in-virtual-teams/.
8. A. Atkins, *Building Workplace Trust* (Boston and San Francisco: Interaction Associates, 2014). O. Faleye and E. A. Trahan, "Labor-Friendly Corporate Practices: Is What Is Good for Employees Good for Stakeholders?" *Journal of Business Ethics* 101, no. 1 (2011): 1–27. A. Harary, "Trust Is Tangible," Edelman, January 22, 2019, https://www.edelman.com/research/trust-is-tangible.
9. B. B. Kimmel, "Most Trustworthy Public Companies 2021," June 24, 2021, http://www.trustacrossamerica.com/blog/?cat=400.
10. L. P. Willcocks and S. Cullen, "The Power of Relationships The Outsourcing Enterprise," 2. Logica, in association with the London School of Economics, https://www.researchgate.net/publication/270573256_The_Outsourcing_Enterprise_The_Power_of_Relationships, accessed February 26, 2022.
11. M. Burchell and J. Robin, *No Excuses: How You Can Turn Any Workplace into a Great One* (San Francisco: Jossey-Bass, 2013), 5. See also "Defining the World's Best Workplaces" (2019), Great Places to Work, https://www.greatplacetowork.com/resources/reports/defining-the-worlds-best-workplaces, accessed March 6, 2022.
12. Edelman, 2017 Edelman Trust Barometer: Global Report, http://www.edelman.com/trust2017/. See also 2022 Edelman Trust Barometer: The Cycle of Distrust, https://www.edelman.com/trust/2022-trust-barometer, accessed March 1, 2022.
13 W. R. Boss, "Trust and Managerial Problem Solving Revisited," *Group & Organization Studies* 3, no. 3 (1978): 331–342.
14. Boss, "Trust and Managerial Problem Solving Revisited," 338.
15. K. Thomas, "Get It On! What It Means to Lead the Way," Keynote presentation at the Leadership Challenge Forum, Nashville, TN, June 16, 2016.
16. See, for example, P. Zak, *Trust Factor: The Science of Creating High-Performance Organizations* (New York: AMACOM, 2017); F. Fukuyama, *Trust: The Social Virtues and the Creation of Prosperity* (New York: Free

Press, 1996); and Y. Benkler, "The Unselfish Gene," *Harvard Business Review*, July-August 2011, 77–85.

17. See P. S. Shockley-Zalabak, S. Morreale, and M. Hackman, *Building the High-Trust Organization: Strategies for Supporting Five Key Dimensions of Trust* (San Francisco: Jossey-Bass, 2010); M. Hernandez, C. P. Long, and S. B. Sitkin, "Cultivating Follower Trust: Are All Leader Behaviors Equally Influential?" *Organization Studies* 35, no. 12 (2014): 1867–1892; L. Fosslien and W. W. Duffy, *No Hard Feelings: The Secret Power of Embracing Emotions at Work* (New York: Random House, 2019); S. J. Sucher and S. Gupta, *The Power of Trust: How Companies Build It, Lose It, Regain It* (New York: Public Affairs, 2021); and B. Ho, *Why Trust Matters: An Economist's Guide to the Ties That Bind Us* (New York: Columbia University Press, 2021).

18. J. Zenger and J. Folkman, "What Great Listeners Actually Do," *Harvard Business Review*, July 14, 2016, https://hbr.org/2016/07/what-great-listeners-actually-do, accessed March 6, 2022. K. Cameron, *Positively Energizing Leadership: Virtuous Actions and Relationships that Create High Performance* (Oakland, CA: Berrett-Koehler Publishers, 2021). B. Gorman, "Finding the Dynamic Balance Between Empathy and Accountability," *Forbes*, March 6, 2020, https://www.forbes.com/sites/forbescoachescouncil/2020/03/06/finding-the-dynamic-balance-between-empathy-and-accountability/?sh=22edab944ff6, accessed March 6, 2022. E. Seppälä and K. Cameron, "The Best Leaders Have a Contagious Positive Energy," *Harvard Business Review*, April 18, 2022, https://hbr.org/2022/04/the-best-leaders-have-a-contagious-positive-energy, accessed May 9, 2022.

19. R. Krznaric, *Empathy: Why It Matters, and How to Get It* (New York: Perigee Random House, 2015). For a discussion of the application of empathy, see J. Love, "Take 5: Cultivating Empathy in the Workplace," *KelloggInsight*, April 8, 2019, https://insight.kellogg.northwestern.edu/article/cultivating-empathy-workplace, accessed March 8, 2022. For an extensive discussion of the evidence that compassion impacts outcomes and performance in healthcare, see S. Trzeciak and A. Mazzarelli, *Compassionomics: The Revolutionary Scientific Evidence that Caring Makes a Difference* (Pensacola, FL: Synder Group Publishing, 2019).

20. DDI, "High-Resolution Leadership: A Synthesis of 15,000 Assessments into How Leaders Shape the Business Landscape," 2016, page 21, https://media.ddiworld.com/research/high-resolution-leadership-2015-2016_tr_ddi.pdf, accessed March 6, 2022. W. A. Gentry, T. J. Weber, and G. Sadri, *Empathy in the Workplace: A Tool for Effective Leadership* (Greensboro,

NC: Center for Creative Leadership, 2007), http://insights.ccl.org/wp-content/uploads/2015/04/EmpathyInTheWorkplace.pdf. G. Whitelaw, *The Zen Leader: 10 Ways to Go from Barely Managing to Leading Fearlessly* (Pompton Plains, NJ: Career Press, 2012).

21. G. Sadri, T. J. Weber, and W. A. Gentry, "Empathic Emotion and Leadership Performance; An Empirical Analysis Across 38 Countries," *Leadership Quarterly* 22, no. 5 (2011): 818–830.
22. S. A. Morelli, I. A. Lee, M. E. Arnn, and J. Zaki, "Emotional and Instrumental Support Provision Interact to Predict Well-Being," *Emotion* 15, no. 4 (2015): 484–493.
23. See, for example, M. Mortensen and T. Neeley, "Reflected Knowledge and Trust in Global Collaboration," *Management Science* 58, no. 12 (December 2012): 2207–2224; S. Sinek, *Leaders Eat Last: Why Some Teams Pull Together and Others Don't* (New York: Penguin, 2014); E. J. Wilson III, "Empathy Is Still Lacking in the Leaders Who Need It Most," *Harvard Business Review,* September 21, 2015, https://hbr.org/2015/09/empathy-is-still-lacking-in-the-leaders-who-need-it-most; and J. Zaki, *The War for Kindness: Building Empathy in a Fractured World* (New York: Crown Publishing Group, 2019).
24. C. A. O'Reilly and K. H. Roberts, "Information Filtration in Organizations: Three Experiments," *Organizational Behavior and Human Performance* 11, no. 2 (1974). P. J. Sweeney, "Do Soldiers Reevaluate Trust in Their Leaders Prior to Combat Operations?" *Military Psychology* 22, suppl. 1 (2010): S70–S88. O. Özer, Y. Zheng, and Y. Ren, "Trust, Trustworthiness, and Information Sharing in Supply Chains Bridging China and the United States," *Management Science* 60, no. 10 (2014): 2435–2460.
25. R. Axelrod, *The Evolution of Cooperation: Revised Edition* (New York: Basic Books, 2006).
26. Axelrod, *The Evolution of Cooperation,* 20, 190.
27. See, for example, R. B. Cialdini, "Harnessing the Science of Persuasion," *Harvard Business Review,* October 2001, 72–79; J. K. Butler Jr., "Behaviors, Trust, and Goal Achievement in a Win-Win Negotiating Role Play," *Group & Organization Management* 20, no. 4 (1995): 486–501; R. B. Cialdini, *Influence: Science and Practice,* 5th ed. (Boston: Pearson/Allyn & Bacon, 2009), 19–51; A. Grant, *Give and Take: Why Helping Others Drives Our Success* (New York: Penguin Group, 2013); D. Melamed, B. Simpson, and J. Abernathy, "The Science of Reciprocity: Experimental Evidence That Each Form of Reciprocity Is Robust to the Presence of Other Forms of

Reciprocity," *Science Advances* 6, no. 23 (2020): 656–662; and H. Jung, E. Seo, E. Han, M. D. Henderson, and E. A. Patall, "Prosocial Modeling: A Meta-Analytic Review and Synthesis," *Psychological Bulletin* 146, no. 8 (2020): 635–663.

28. R. Putnam, *Bowling Alone: The Collapse and Revival of American Community* (New York: Touchstone by Simon & Schuster, 2001), 134.
29. See, for example, H. Ibarra and Mt. T. Hansen, "Are You a Collaborative Leader?" *Harvard Business Review*, July–August 2011, 69–74; "Secrets of Greatness: Teamwork!" *Fortune*, June 12, 2006, 64–152; A. M. Brandenburger and B. J. Nalebuff, *Co-Opetition: A Revolution Mindset That Combines Competition and Cooperation: The Game Theory Strategy That's Changing the Game of Business* (New York: Currency, 1997); P. Hallinger and R. H. Heck, "Leadership for Learning: Does Collaborative Leadership Make a Difference in School Improvement?" *Educational Management Administration & Leadership* 38, no. 6 (2010): 654–678; W. C. Kim and R. Mauborgne, *Blue Ocean Strategy, Expanded Edition: How to Create Uncontested Market Space and Make the Competition Irrelevant* (Boston: Harvard Business Publishing, 2015); and D. Tjosvold and M. M. Tjosvold, *Building the Team Organization: How to Open Minds, Resolve Conflict, and Ensure Cooperation* (New York: Palgrave Macmillan, 2015).
30. J. Vesterman, "From Wharton to War," *Fortune*, June 12, 2006, 106.
31. A. Grant, *Give and Take: Why Helping Others Drives Our Success* (New York: Penguin Books, 2014).
32. M. D. Johnson, J. R. Hollenbeck, S. E. Humphrey, D. R. Ilgen, D. Jundt, and C. J. Meyer, "Cutthroat Cooperation: Asymmetrical Adaptation to Changes in Team Reward Structures," *Academy of Management Journal* 49, no. 1 (2006): 103–119.
33. See, for example, W. Baker, *Achieving Success Through Social Capital: Tapping the Hidden Resources in Your Personal and Business Networks* (San Francisco: Jossey-Bass, 2000); J. F. Helliwell, and R. D. Putnam, "The Social Context of Well-Being," *Philosophical Transactions of the Royal Society B: Biological Sciences* 359, no. 1449 (2004): 1435–1446; and N. Powdthavve, "Putting a Price Tag on Friends, Relatives, and Neighbours: Using Surveys of Life Satisfaction to Value Social Relationships," *Journal of Socio-Economics* 37, no. 4 (2008): 1459–1480.
34. See, for example, V. K. Bohns and F. J. Flynn, "'Why Didn't You Just Ask?' Understanding the Discomfort of Help-Seeking," *Journal of Experimental Social Psychology* 46, no. 2 (2020): 402–409; and B. M. DePaulo and

J. D. Fisher, "The Costs of Asking for Help," *Basic and Applied Social Psychology* 1, no. 1 (2010): 23–35.

35. See, for example, J. E. Dutton, "Building High-Quality Connections", in J. E. Dutton and G. Spreitzer (eds.), *How to Be a Positive Leader: Small Actions, Big Impact* (Oakland: Berrett-Koehler Publishers, 2014) 11–21; T. Clausen, , K. B. Christensen, and K. Nielsen, "Does Group-Level Commitment Predict Employee Well-Being?" *Journal of Occupational and Environmental Medicine* 57, no. 11 (2015): 1141–1146; and S. Pinker, *The Village Effect: How Face-to-Face Contact Can Make Us Healthier and Happier* (New York: Random House, 2015).
36. R. Jenkins, "This Is How Generation Z Will Communicate at Work," *Inc.*, https://www.inc.com/ryan-jenkins/72-percent-of-generation-z-want-this-communication-at-work.html, accessed January 31, 2022.
37. P. A. Gloor, F. Grippa, J. Putzke, C. Lassenius, H. Fuehres, K. Fischbach, and D. Schoder, "Measuring Social Capital in Creative Teams Through Sociometric Sensors," *International Journal of Organizational Design and Engineering* 2, no. 4 (2012): 380–401. G. Colvin, "The Hidden—But Very Real—Cost of Working from Home," *Fortune* (August 10, 2020): 19–21, https://fortune.com/2020/08/10/remote-work-from-home-cost-zoom-innovation-google-goldman-sachs/.

# Chapter 9
# Strengthen Others

1. See, for example, R. M. Kanter, *The Change Masters: Innovation for Productivity in the American Corporation* (New York: Simon & Schuster, 1983); R. B. Cialdini, *Influence: The Psychology of Persuasion,* rev. ed. (New York: William Morrow, 2006); and J. A. Simpson, A. K. Farrell, M. M. Orina, and A. J. Rothman, "Power and Social Influence in Relationships," in M. Mikulincer and P. R. Shaver (eds.), *APA Handbook of Personality and Social Psychology,* vol. 3, Interpersonal Relations (Washington, DC: American Psychological Association, 2015), 393–420.
2. T. Allas and B. Schaninger, "The Boss Factor: Making the World a Better Place Through Workplace Relationships," *McKinsey Quarterly* (September 22, 2020), https://www.mckinsey.com/business-functions/people-and-organizational-performance/our-insights/the-boss-factor-making-the-world-a-better-place-through-workplace-relationships.

3. A. Bandura, *Self-Efficacy: The Exercise of Control* (New York: Freeman, 1997). C. M. Shea and J. M. Howell, "Charismatic Leadership and Task Feedback: A Laboratory Study of Their Effects on Self-Efficacy and Task Performance," *Leadership Quarterly* 10, no. 3 (1999): 375–396. M. J. McCormick, J. Tanguma, and A. S. Lopez-Forment, "Extending Self-Efficacy Theory to Leadership: A Review and Empirical Test," *Journal of Leadership Education* 1, no. 2 (2002): 34–49. D. L. Feltz, S. E. Short, and P. J. Sullivan, *Self-Efficacy in Sport* (Champaign, IL: Human Kinetics, 2007). J. Hagel and J. S. Brown, "Do You Have a Growth Mindset?" *Harvard Business Review*, November 23, 2010, http://blogs.hbr.org/bigshift/2010/11/do-you-have-a-growth-mindset.html. F. C. Lunenburg, "Self-Efficacy in the Workplace: Implications for Motivation and Performance," *International Journal of Management, Business, and Administration* 14, no. 1 (2011): 1–6. J. E. Maddux, "Self-Efficacy: The Power of Believing You Can," in S. J. Lopez, and C. B. Synder (eds.), *The Oxford Handbook of Positive Psychology*, 2nd ed. (New York: Oxford University Press, 2011), 335–344.
4. M. R. Delgado, "Reward-Related Responses in the Human Striatum," *Annals of the New York Academy of Science* 1104 (2007): 70–88. D. S. Fareri, L. N. Martin, and M. R. Delgado, "Reward-Related Processing in the Human Brain: Developmental Considerations," *Development & Psychopathology* 20, no. 4 (2008): 1191–1211. M. R. Delgado, M. M. Carson, and E. A. Phelps, "Regulating the Expectation of Reward," *Nature Neuroscience* 11, no. 8 (2008): 880–881. M. R. Delgado and J. G. Dilmore, "Social and Emotional Influences on Decision-Making and the Brian," *Minnesota Journal of Law, Science & Technology* 9, no. 2 (2008): 899–912. B. W. Balleine, M. R. Delgado, and O. Hikosaka, "The Role of Dorsal Striatum in Reward and Decision-Making, *Journal of Neuroscience* 27, no. 31 (2007): 8159–8160.
5. A. Wrzeniewski, and J. Dutton, "Crafting a Job: Revisioning Employees as Active Crafters of Their Work," *Academy of Management Review* 26, no. 2 (2001): 179–201. M. S. Christian, A. S. Garza, and J. E. Slaugher, "Work Engagement: A Quantitative Review and Test of Its Relations with Task and Conceptual Performance," *Personnel Psychology* 64, no. 1 (2011): 89–136.
6. See, for example, G. Spagnolo, D. Coviello, and A. Guglielmo, "The Effects of Discretion on Procurement Performance," *Management Science* 64, no. 2 (February 2018), 715–738; and D. N. Ammons and D. J. Roenigk, "Exploring Devolved Decision Authority in Performance Management Regimes: The Relevance of Perceived and Actual Decision Authority as

Elements of Performance Management Success," *Public Performance & Management Review* 43, no. 1 (2020), 28–52.

7. M. I. Norton, D. Mochon, and D. Ariely, "The IKEA Effect: When Labor Leads to Love," *Journal of Consumer Psychology* 22, no. 3 (2012), 453–460, https://doi.org/10.1016/j.jcps.2011.08.002.
8. M. G. Mayhew, N. M. Ashkanasay, T. Bramble, and J. Gardner, "A Study of the Antecedents and Consequences of Psychological Ownership in Organizational Settings," *Journal of Social Psychology* 147, no. 5 (2007): 477–500. H. Peng and J. Pierce, "Job- and Organization-Based Psychological Ownership: Relationship and Outcomes," *Journal of Managerial Psychology* 30, no. 2 (2015): 151–168. S. Dawkins, S. W. Tian, A. Newman, and A. Martin, "Psychological Ownership: A Review and Research Agenda," *Journal of Organizational Behavior* 38, no. 2 (2017): 163–183.
9. Evolutionary psychology demonstrates that in ecosystems, collaboration is what assists species to survive rather than become extinct; the group ends up eradicating bad or inefficient behavior. See R. Wright, *The Moral Animal: Why We Are the Way We Are: The New Science of Evolutionary Psychology* (New York: Vintage, 1995); and A. Fields, *Altruistically Inclined? The Behavioral Sciences, Evolutionary Theory, and the Origins of Reciprocity* (Ann Arbor, MI: University of Michigan Press, 2004).
10. M. Csikszentmilhalyi, *Finding Flow: The Power of Optimal Experience* (New York: HarperCollins, 2008).
11. S. Kotler, *The Rise of Superman: Decoding the Science of Ultimate Human Performance* (New York: New Harvest, 2014).
12. M. Burchell and J. Robin, *The Great Workplace: How to Build It, How to Keep It, and Why It Matters* (San Francisco: Jossey-Bass, 2011), 66. See also "Defining the World's Best Workplaces" (2019), Great Places to Work, https://www.greatplacetowork.com/resources/reports/defining-the-worlds-best-workplaces, accessed March 6, 2022.
13. L. J. Bassi and M. E. Van Buren, "The 1998 ASTD State of the Industry Report," *Training & Development,* January 1998, 21ff. B. Sugrue and R. J. Rivera, *2005 State of the Industry Report* (Alexandria, VA: ASTD Press, 2005). E. Rizkalla, "Not Investing in Employee Training Is Risky Business," *Huffington Post,* August 30, 2014, http://www.huffingtonpost.com/emad-rizkalla/not-investing-in-employee_b_5545222.html, accessed February 26, 2022.
14. "Employee Training Is Worth the Investment," May 11, 2016, https://www.go2hr.ca/articles/employee-training-worth-investment, accessed March 1, 2022.

15. N. Merchant, *The New How: Creating Business Solutions Through Collaborative Strategy* (San Francisco: O'Reilly Media, 2010), 63.
16. A. Bryant, *The Corner Office: Indispensable and Unexpected Lessons from CEOS on How to Lead and Succeed* (New York, Times Books, 2011).
17. R. E. Wood and A. Bandura, "Impact of Conceptions of Ability on Self-Regulatory Mechanisms and Complex Decision Making," *Journal of Personality and Social Psychology* 56 (1989): 407–415.
18. A. Bandura and R. E. Wood, "Effects of Perceived Controllability and Performance Standards on Self-Regulation of Complex Decision Making," *Journal of Personality and Social Psychology* 56, no. 3 (1989): 805–814.
19. A. M. Saks, "Longitudinal Field Investigation of the Moderating and Mediating Effects of Self-Efficacy on the Relationship Between Training and Newcomer Adjustment," *Journal of Applied Psychology* 80, no. 2 (1995): 211–225.
20. H. Sari, S. Ekici, F. Soyer, and E. Eskiller, "Does Self-Confidence Link to Motivation? A Study in Field Hockey Athletes," *Journal of Human Sport & Exercise* 10, no. 1 (2015): 24–35.
21. J. M. Kouzes and B. Z. Posner, *Learning Leadership: The Five Fundamentals of Becoming an Exemplary Leader* (San Francisco: The Leadership Challenge–A Wiley Brand, 2016). M. Reynolds, *Coach the Person, Not the Problem: A Guide to Using Reflective Inquiry* (Oakland, CA: Berrett-Koehler, 2020).
22. F. Colon and D. Clifford, "Measuring Enabling Others to Act: The Travelers Coaching Questionnaire" (presentation at the 8th Annual Leadership Challenge Forum San Francisco, June 18, 2015).
23. P. Leone, "Was It Worth It? Measuring the Impact and ROI of Leadership Training," *Training Industry Magazine,* 20, no. 19 (2019), 33–35, https://www.nxtbook.com/nxtbooks/trainingindustry/tiq_20190708/index.php?startid=33#/p/34, accessed March 13, 2022.

# Chapter 10 Recognize Contributions

1. J. Harter, "The Fifth Element of Great Managing," Gallup, September 13, 2007, https://news.gallup.com/businessjournal/28561/Fifth-Element-Great-Managing.aspx?version=print, accessed January 31, 2022.

See also D. LaGree, B. Houston, M. Duffy, and H. Shin, "The Effect of Respect: Respectful Communication at Work Drives Resiliency, Engagement, and Job Satisfaction Among Early Career Employees," *International Journal of Business Communications* 2021, 232948842110165, DOI: 10.1177/23294884211016529.

2. See, for example, S. Madon, J. Willard, M. Guyll, and K. C. Scherr, "Self-Fulfilling Prophecies: Mechanisms, Power, and Links to Social Problems," *Social and Personality Psychology Compass* 5, no. 8 (2011): 578–590; D. Eden, "Self-fulfilling Prophecy and the Pygmalion Effect in Management," in R. W. Griffin (ed.), *Oxford Bibliographies in Management* (New York: Oxford University Press) 2014); and D. Eden, "Self-Fulfilling Prophecy: The Pygmalion Effect," in S. G. Rogelberg (ed.), *Encyclopedia of Industrial and Organizational Psychology*, 2nd ed. (Thousand Oaks, CA: SAGE Publications, 2016), 711–712.
3. D. S. Yeager, V. Purdie-Vaughns, J. Garcia, N. Apfel, P. Brzustoski, A. Master, W. T. Hessert, M. E. Williams, and G. L. Cohen, "Breaking the Cycle of Mistrust: Wide Interventions to Provide Critical Feedback across the Racial Divide," *Journal of Experimental Psychology* 143, no. 2 (2014): 804–824.
4. D. Whitney and A. Trosten-Bloom, *The Power of Appreciative Inquiry: A Practical Guide to Positive Change*, 2nd ed. (San Francisco: Berrett-Koehler, 2010). M. E. Seligman, *Flourish: A Visionary New Understanding of Happiness and Well-Being* (New York: Free Press, 2011). A. Gostick and C. Elton, *All In: How the Best Managers Create a Culture of Belief and Drive Big Results* (New York: Free Press, 2012).
5. H. G. Halvorson, *Succeed: How We Can Reach Our Goals* (New York: Hudson Street Press, 2010).
6. J. E. Sawyer, W. R. Latham, R. D. Pritchard, and W. R. Bennett Jr., "Analysis of Work Group Productivity in an Applied Setting: Application of a Time Series Panel Design," *Personnel Psychology* 52, no. 4 (1999): 927–967. A. Gostick and C. Elton, *Managing with Carrots: Using Recognition to Attract and Retain the Best People* (Layton, UT: Gibbs Smith, 2001). A. Fishbach and S. R. Finkelstein, "How Feedback Influences Persistence, Disengagement, and Change in Goal Pursuit," in H. Aarts and A. J. Elliot (eds.), *Goal-Directed Behavior* (New York: Psychology Press, 2012): 203–230.
7. P. A. McCarty, "Effects of Feedback on the Self-Confidence of Men and Women," *Academy of Management Journal* 29, no. 4 (1986): 840–847. See also J. Hattie and H. Timperley, "The Power of Feedback," *Review of*

*Educational Research* 77, no. 1 (2007): 81–112; Halvorson, *Succeed*; and Fishbach and Finkelstein, "How Feedback Influences."

8. K. A. Ericsson, M. J. Prietula, and E. T. Cokely, "The Making of an Expert," *Harvard Business Review*, July–August 2007, 114–121.
9. A. Grant, "Stop Serving the Feedback Sandwich," https://medium.com/@AdamMGrant/stop-serving-the-feedback-sandwich-bc1202686f4e#.7p94arriu, accessed February 26, 2022.
10. K. Scott, First Round Review, "Radical Candor: The Surprising Secret to Being a Good Boss," http://firstround.com/review/radical-candor-the-surprising-secret-to-being-a-good-boss/, accessed February 26, 2022.
11. J. M. Kouzes and B. Z. Posner, *The Truth about Leadership: The No-Fads, Heart-of-the-Matter Facts You Need to Know* (San Francisco: Jossey-Bass, 2010), especially Truth Nine: "The Best Leaders Are the Best Learners."
12. B. Nelson, *1001 Ways to Reward Employees*, 2nd ed. (New York: Workman, 2005).
13. C. Hastwell, "Creating a Culture of Recognition," Great Place to Work, September 9, 2021, https://www.greatplacetowork.com/resources/blog/creating-a-culture-of-recognition, accessed March 13, 2022.
14. J. M. Kouzes and B. Z. Posner, *A Leader's Legacy* (San Francisco: Jossey-Bass, 2006), especially Chapter 7, "Leaders *Should* Want to Be Liked," 56–61.
15. J. A. Ross, "Does Friendship Improve Job Performance?" *Harvard Business Review,* March–April 1977, 8–9. K. A. Jehn and P. P. Shah, "Interpersonal Relationships and Task Performance: An Examination of Mediating Processes in Friendship and Acquaintance Groups," *Journal of Personality and Social Psychology* 72, no. 4 (1997): 775–790. D. H. Francis and W. R. Sandberg, "Friendship within Entrepreneurial Teams and Its Association with Team and Venture Performance," *Entrepreneurship: Theory and Practice* 25, no. 2 (Winter 2000): 5–15.
16. T. Rath, *Vital Friends: The People You Cannot Afford to Live Without* (New York: Gallup Press, 2006).
17. J. Heyman and D. Ariely, "Effort for Payment: A Tale of Two Markets," *Psychological Science* 15, no. 1 (2004): 787–793. K. R. Gibson, K. O'Leary, and J. R. Weinstraub, "The Little Things That Make Employees Feel Appreciated," *Harvard Business Review*, January 23, 2020, https://hbr.org/2020/01/the-little-things-that-make-employees-feel-appreciated, accessed May 5, 2022.
18. J. Shriar, "The State of Employee Engagement in 2016," November 1, 2016, https://www.officevibe.com/blog/employee-engagement-2016.

19. J. Pfeffer and R. I. Sutton, *Hard Facts, Dangerous Half-Truths, and Total Nonsense: Profiting from Evidence-Based Management* (Boston: Harvard Business Publishing, 2006).
20. See, for example, E. Harvey, *180 Ways to Walk the Recognition Talk* (Dallas: Walk the Talk Company, 2000); B. Nelson, op. cit.; L. Yerkes, *Fun Works: Creative Places Where People Love to Work* (San Francisco: Berrett-Koehler, 2007); C. Ventrice, *Make Their Day! Employee Recognition That Works,* 2nd ed. (San Francisco: Berrett-Koehler, 2009); J. W. Umlas, *Grateful Leadership: Using the Power of Acknowledgment to Engage All Your People and Achieve Superior Results* (New York: McGraw-Hill, 2013); and B. Kaye and S. Jordan-Evans, *Love 'em or Lose 'em: Getting Good People to Stay*, 5th ed. (San Francisco: Berrett-Koehler, 2014).
21. K. Thomas, *Intrinsic Motivation at Work: What Really Drives Employee Engagement*, 2nd ed. (Oakland, CA: Berrett-Koehler, 2009); A. B. Thompson, "The Intangible Things Employees Want from Employers," *Harvard Business Review,* December 3, 2015, https://hbr.org/2015/12/the-intangible-things-employees-want-from-employers, accessed February 26, 2022. T. Smith, "5 Things People Who Love Their Jobs Have in Common," *Fast Company,* November 3, 2015, https://www.fastcompany.com/3052985/5-things-people-who-love-their-jobs-have-in-common. J. Stringer, "7 Common Misconceptions Employers Have About Employees," National Business Research Institute, https://www.nbrii.com/employee-survey-white-papers/7-common-misconceptions-employers-have-about-their-employees/, accessed February 26, 2022. See also L. K. Thaler and R. Koval, *The Power of Small: Why Little Things Make All the Difference* (New York: Broadway Books, 2009), 36–37.
22. A. Achor. *Big Potential: How Transforming the Pursuit of Success Raises Our Achievement, Happiness, and Well-Being* (New York: Currency, 2018).
23. *People Management Survey 2018* (October), https://predictiveindex.pixieset.com/people-management-survey2018/, accessed May 7, 2022.
24. A. M. Grant and F. Gino, "A Little Thanks Goes a Long Way: Explaining Why Gratitude Expressions Motivate Prosocial Behavior," *Journal of Personality and Social Psychology* 98, no. 6 (June 2010): 946–955. For some practical advice, see C. Littlefield, "How to Give and Receive Compliments at Work," *Harvard Business Review*, October 12, 2019, https://hbr.org/2019/10/how-to-give-and-receive-compliments-at-work, accessed May 8, 2022.
25. O. C. Tanner Learning Group White Paper, "Performance: Accelerated: A New Benchmark for Initiating Employee Engagement, Retention and Results," https://www.octanner.com/content/dam/oc-tanner/documents/

global-research/White_Paper_Performance_Accelerated.pdf, accessed March 17, 2022.

26. *The ROI of Effective Recognition*, O. C. Tanner Institute, 2014, at www.octanner.com/content/dam/oc-tanner/documents/white-papers/O.C.-Tanner_Effective-Recognition-White-Paper.pdf, accessed February 26, 2022. See also C. Chen, Y. Chen, P. Hsu, and E. J. Podolski, "Be Nice to Your Innovators: Employee Treatment and Corporate Innovation Performance," *Journal of Corporate Finance*, June 7, 2016. Available at SSRN, https://ssrn.com/abstract=2461021 or http://dx.doi.org/10.2139/ssrn.2461021, accessed February 26, 2022.
27. M. Losada and E. Heaphy, "The Role of Positivity and Connectivity in the Performance of Business Teams: A Nonlinear Dynamics Model," *American Behavioral Scientist* 47, no. 6 (2004): 740–765. See also T. Rath and D. O. Clifton, *How Full Is Your Bucket? Positive Strategies for Work and Life* (New York: Gallup Press, 2004), and B. Fredrickson, *Positivity: To-Notch Research Reveals the 3-to-1 Ratio That Will Change Your Life* (New York: Three Rivers Press, 2009).
28. R. A. Emmons, *Thanks! How Practicing Gratitude Makes You* Happier (New York: Houghton Mifflin, 2008); N. Lesowitz, *Living Life as a Thank You: The Transformative Power of Daily Gratitude* (New York: Metro Books, 2009); and A. R. Starkey, C. D. Mohr, D. M. Cadiz, and R. R. Sinclair, "Gratitude Reception and Physical Health: Examining the Mediating Role of Satisfaction with Patient Care in a Sample of Acute Care Nurses," *Journal of Positive Psychology* 14, no. 6 (2019): 779–788.

# Chapter 11 Celebrate the Values and Victories

1. D. Campbell, *If I'm in Charge Here, Why Is Everybody Laughing?* (Greensboro, NC: Center for Creative Leadership, 1984), 64.
2. D. Brooks, *The Social Animal: The Hidden Sources of Love, Character, and Achievement* (New York: Random House, 2011).
3. W. Baker, *Achieving Success Through Social Capital: Tapping the Hidden Resources in Your Personal and Business Networks* (San Francisco: Jossey-Bass, 2000); R. Putnam, *Bowling Alone: The Collapse and Revival*

*of American Community* (New York: Touchstone, 2001); W. Bolander, C. B. Satornino, D. E. Hughes, and G. R. Ferris, "Social Networks Within Sales Organizations: Their Development and Importance for Salesperson Performance," *Journal of Marketing* 79, no. 6 (2015): 1–16; and J. Pfeffer, *Drying for a Paycheck: How Modern Management Harms Employee Health and Company Performance—and What We Can Do About It* (New York: harper/Collins, 2018).

4. Source: "List of Social Networking Websites," *Wikipedia*, http://en.wikipedia.org/wiki/List_of_social_networking_websites, accessed February 26, 2022.
5. K. N. Hampton, L. S. Goulet, L. Rainie, and K. Purcell, "Social Networking Sites and Our Lives," *Pew Internet & American Life Project*, June 16, 2011, http://pewinternet.org/Reports/2011/Technology-and-social-networks.aspx.
6. T. Deal and M. K. Key, *Corporate Celebration: Play, Purpose, and Profit at Work* (Oakland, CA: Berrett-Koehler, 1998), 5.
7. W. Johnson, *Smart Growth: How to Grow Your People to Grow Your Company* (Boston: Harvard Business Publishing, 2022).
8. As quoted by D. Novak, "What I've Learned After 20 Years on the Job," May 20, 2016, http://www.cnbc.com/2016/05/20/yum-chair-what-ive-learned-after-20-years-on-the-job-commentary.html, accessed February 26, 2022.
9. S. O'Flaherty, M. T. Sanders, and A. Whillans, "Research: A Little Recognition Can Provide a Big Morale Boost," *Harvard Business Review*, March 29, 2021, https://hbr.org/2021/03/research-a-little-recognition-can-provide-a-big-morale-boost.
10. C. von Scheve and M. Salmela, *Collective Emotions: Perspectives from Psychology, Philosophy, and Sociology* (Oxford, UK: Oxford University Press, 2014).
11. A. Olsson and E. A. Phelps, "Social Learning of Fear," *Nature Neuroscience* 10, no. 9 (2007): 1095–1102. J. Zaki, "Kindness Contagion: Witnessing Kindness Inspires Kindness, Causing It to Spread Like a Virus" *Scientific America* (July 26, 2016), https://www.scientificamerican.com/article/kindness-contagion/. J. Zaki, *The War for Kindness: Building Empathy in a Fractured World* (New York: Crown Publishing Group, 2019).
12. J. S. Mulbert, "Social Networks, Social Circles, and Job Satisfaction," *Work & Occupations* 18, no. 4 (1991): 415–430. K. J. Fenlason and T. A. Beehr, "Social Support and Occupational Stress: Effects of Talking to Others," *Journal of Organizational Behavior* 15, no. 2 (1994): 157–175. H. A.

Tindle, Y. Chang, L. H. Kuller, J. E. Manson, J. G. Robinson, M. C. Rosal, G. J. Siegle, and K. A. Matthews, "Optimism, Cynical Hostility, and Incident Coronary Heart Disease and Mortality in the Women's Health Initiative," *Circulation* 120, no. 8 (2009): 656–662. V. Dagenais-Desmarais, J. Forest, S. Girouard, and L. Crevier-Braud, "The Important of Need-Supportive Relationships for Motivation and Psychological Health at Work," in N. Weinstein (ed.), *Human Motivation and Interpersonal Relationships: Theory, Research, and Applications* (New York: Springer Science+Business Media, 2014), 263–297. A. J. Smith, K. Shoji, B. J. Griffin, L. M. Sippel, E. R. Dworkin, H. M. Wright, E. Morrow, A. Locke, T. M. Love, J. I. Harris, K. Kaniasty, S. A. Langenecker, and C. C. Benight, "Social Cognitive Mechanisms in Healthcare Worker Resilience Across Time During the Pandemic," *Social Psychiatry and Psychiatric Epidemiology* (March 2022): 1–12.

13. R. Friedman, *The Best Place to Work: The Art and Science of Creating an Extraordinary Workplace* (New York: Penguin Random House, 2014).
14. Gallup, *State of the American Workplace 2014*, www.gallup.com/services/178514/state-american-workplace.aspx, accessed February 26, 2022. See also A. Mann, "Why We Need Best Friends at Work," January 15, 2018, https://www.gallup.com/workplace/236213/why-need-best-friends-work.aspx.
15. T. Rath, *Vital Friends: The People You Cannot Afford to Live Without* (New York: Gallup Press, 2006).
16. O. Stavrova and D. Ehlebracht, "Cynical Beliefs about Human Nature and Income: Longitudinal and Cross-Cultural Analyses," *Journal of Personality and Social Psychology* 110, no. 1: 116–132.
17. J. Holt-Lunstad, T. B. Smith, M. Baker, T. Harris, and D. Stephenson, "Loneliness and Social Isolation as Risk Factors for Mortality: A Meta-Analytic Review," *Perspectives on Psychological Science* 10, no. 2 (March 2015): 227–237.
18. S. Achor, *The Happiness Advantage: The Seven Principles of Positive Psychology That Fuel Success and Performance at Work* (New York: Crown, 2010).
19. J. Holt-Lunstad, T. B. Smith, and J. B. Layton, "Social Relationships and Mortality Risk: A Meta-analytic Review," *PLoS Medicine* 7, no. 7 (2010). D. Umberson and J. K. Montez, "Social Relationships and Health: A Flashpoint for Health Policy," *Journal of Health and Social Behavior* 51, no. 1 (2010 suppl): S54–S66.

20. See, for example, R. F. Baumeister and M. R. Leary, "The Need to Belong: Desire for Interpersonal Attachment as a Fundamental Human Motivation," *Psychological Bulletin* 117, no. 3 (1995): 497–529; D. G. Myers, "The Funds, Friends, and Faith of Happy People," *American Psychologist* 55, no. 1 (2000): 56–67; S. Crabtree, "Getting Personal in the Workplace: Are Negative Relationships Squelching Productivity in Your Company?" *Gallup Management Journal*, June 10, 2004, http://www.gallup.com/businessjournal/11956/getting-personal-workplace.aspx; J. Baek-Kyoo and S. Park, "Career Satisfaction, Organizational Commitment, and Turnover Intention," *Leadership & Organization Development Journal* 31, no. 6 (2010),482–500; O. Zeynep, "Managing Emotions in the Workplace: Its Mediating Effect on the Relationship between Organizational Trust and Occupational Stress, *International Business Research* 6, no. 4 (2013): 81–88; and T. Clausen, K. B. Christensen, and K. Nielsen, "Does Group-Level Commitment Predict Employee Well-Being?", *Journal of Occupational and Environmental Medicine* 57, no. 11: 1141–146.
21. T. McDowell, S. Ehteshami, and K. Sandell, "Are You Having Fun Yet?" *Deloitte Review* 24 (2019): 133–44.
22. S. Achor, *Happiness Advantage: The Seven Principles that Fuel Success and Performance at Work* (New York: Crown Business, 2010). Y. G. Choi, J. Kwon, and W. Kim, "Effects of Attitudes vs. Experience of Workplace Fun on Employee Behaviors," *International Journal of Contemporary Hospitality Management* 25, no. 1 (2013): 410–27. K. Georganta and A. J. Montgomery, "Exploring Fun as a Job Resource: The Enhancing and Protecting Role of a Key Modern Workplace Factor," *International Journal of Applied Positive Psychology* 1 (2016): 107–31.
23. R. C. Ford, F. S. McLaughlin, and J. W. Newstrom, "Questions and Answers about Fun at Work," *Human Resource Planning* 26, no. 4 (2003): 18–33, at 22.
24. See, for example, D. Sgroi, "Happiness and Productivity: Understanding the Happy-Productive Worker," Social Market Foundation, October 2015, https://www.ciphr.com/wp-content/uploads/2016/11/Social-Market-Foundation-Publication-Briefing-CAGE-4-Are-happy-workers-more-productive-281015.pdf; B. Chignell, "Six Reasons Why Fun in the Office is the Future of Work," *CIPHR*, May 22, 2018, https://www.ciphr.com/advice/fun-in-the-office/; Greg Winteregg, *Fun at Work: More Time, Freedom, Profit and More of What You Love to Do* (Clearwater, FL: Matterhorn Business Development, 2019).

25. A. Gostick and S. Christopher, *The Levity Effect: Why It Pays to Lighten Up* (New York: Wiley, 2008).
26. R. Provine, *Laughter: A Scientific Investigation* (New York: Penguin, 2001). See also A. W. Gray, B. Parkinson, and R. I. Dunbar. "Laughter's Influence on the Intimacy of Self-Disclosure," *Motivation and Emotion* 31, no. 1 (2007): 28–43.
27. J. Aaker and N. Bagdonas, *Humor, Seriously: Why Humor Is a Secret Weapon in Business and Life* (New York: Random House, 2021): 51–55.
28. C. L. Porath, A. Gerbasi, and S. L. Schorch, "The Effects of Civility on Advice, Leadership, and Performance," *Journal of Applied Psychology* 100, no. 5 (2015): 1527–1541. See also C. L. Porath and A. Gerbasi, "Does Civility Pay?" *Organizational Dynamics* 44, no. 4 (2015): 281–286.
29. P. Cecchi-Dimeglio, "Why Sharing Good News Matters, *MIT Sloan Management Review*, June 17, 2020; https://sloanreview.mit.edu/article/why-sharing-good-news-matters/.
30. Deal and Key, *Corporate Celebration,* 28.
31. T. Kim, O. Sezer, J. Schroeder, J. Risen, F. Gino, and M. I. Norton, "Work Group Rituals Enhance the Meaning of Work," *Organizational Behavior and Human Decision Processes* 165, no. 4 (2021): 197–212.

# Chapter 12
# Treat Challenge as an Opportunity

1. For perspective and specific considerations on how leaders deal with adversity, see J. M. Kouzes and B. Z. Posner, *Turning Adversity into Opportunity* (Hoboken, NJ: Wiley, 2014).
2. For more information about these studies, see our website, http://www.leadershipchallenge.com/research/others-research.aspx, accessed February 28, 2022.
3. J. M. Kouzes and B. Z. Posner, *Everyday People, Extraordinary Leadership: How to Make a Difference Regardless of Your Title, Position or Authority* (Hoboken, NJ: Wiley, 2020).
4. B. Z. Posner, "When Learning How to Lead, An Exploratory Look at the Role Models," *Leadership & Organization Development Journal* 42, no. 5 (2021), 802–818.

5. Posner, ibid.
6. J. M. Kouzes and B. Z. Posner, "Learning to Lead," in L. Ukens (ed.), *What Smart Trainers Know* (San Francisco: Jossey-Bass, 2001), 339–351; B. Z. Posner, "A Longitudinal Study Examining Changes in Students' Leadership Behavior," *Journal of College Student Development* 50, no. 5 (2009), 551–563; R. J. Jones, S. A. Woods, and Yves R. R. Guillaume, "The Effectiveness of Workplace Coaching: A Meta-Analysis of Learning and Performance Outcomes from Coaching," *Journal of Occupational and Organizational Psychology* 89, no. 2 (June 2016): 249–277, https://doi.org/10.1111/joop.12119, accessed February 28, 2022.
7. L. M. Brown and B. Z. Posner, "Exploring the Relationship Between Learning and Leadership," *Leadership & Organization Development Journal* 22, no. 6 (2001), 274–280; B. Z. Posner, "Understanding the Learning Tactics of College Students and Their Relationship to Leadership," *Leadership & Organization Development Journal* 30, no. 4 (2009), 386–395; and S. Konuk and B. Z. Posner, "The Effectiveness of a Student Leadership Program in Turkey," *Journal of Leadership Education* 20, no. 1 (2021), 10.12806/V20/I1/R6.
8. J. Bersin, "New Research Shows 'Heavy Learners' More Confident, Successful, and Happy at Work," November 9, 2018, https://www.linkedin.com/pulse/want-happy-work-spend-time-learning-josh-bersin/, accessed February 26, 2022.
9. C. S. Dweck, *Mindset: The New Psychology of Success* (New York: Random House, 2006), 6–7. See also C. Dweck, "Carol Dweck Revisits the 'Growth Mindset,'" Education Week, September 22, 2016, http://www.edweek.org/ew/articles/2015/09/23/carol-dweck-revisits-the-growth-mindset.html, accessed February 26, 2022.
10. T. K. Kouzes and B. Z. Posner, "Influence of Mindset on Leadership Behavior," *Leadership & Organization Development Journal* 40, no. 8 (2019): 829–844.
11. Eric Partridge, *Origins: A Short Etymological Dictionary of Modern Language* (New York: Macmillan Publishing Co., 1977), 292–293, 299.
12. J. M. Kouzes and B. Z. Posner, *A Leader's Legacy* (San Francisco: Jossey-Bass, 2006).
13. For more on the importance of humility in leadership and organizational success, see J. Collins, *Good to Great: Why Some Companies Make the Leap . . . and Others Don't* (New York: Harper Business, 2001): 17–40; A. L. Delbecq, "The Spiritual Challenges of Power: Humility and Love as Offsets to Leadership Hubris," *Journal of Management, Spirituality*

*& Religion* 3, no. 1–2 (2006): 141–154; H. M. Kraemer, *From Values to Action: The Four Principles of Value-Based Leadership* (San Francisco: Jossey-Bass, 2011): 59–76; B. P. Owens and D. R. Hackman, "How Does Leader Humility Influence Team Performance? Exploring the Mechanisms of Contagion and Collective Promotion Focus," *Academy of Management Journal* 59, no. 3 (2016): 1088–1111; A. Y. Ou, D. A. Waldman, and S. J. Peterson, "Do Humble CEOs Matter? An Examination of CEO Humility and Firm Outcomes," *Journal of Management* 44, no. 3 (2015): 1147–1173; D. Brooks, *The Road to Character* (New York: Random House, 2015), 8–13; and E. H. Schein, *Humble Inquiry: The Gentle Art of Asking Instead of Telling* (Oakland, CA: Berrett-Koehler, 2018).

14. S. Chen, "Give Yourself a Break: The Power of Self-Compassion," *Harvard Business Review* 96, no. 5 (2018): 116–123.
15. J. G. Breines and S. Chen, "Self-Compassion Increases Self-Improvement Motivation," *Personality and Social Psychology Bulletin* 38, no. 9 (2012): 1133–1143.
16. S. Milne, S. Orbell, and P. Sheeran, "Combining Motivational and Volitional Interventions to Promote Exercise Participation: Protection Motivation Theory and Implementation Intentions," *British Journal of Health Psychology* 7 (May 2002): 163–184. E. Schultz and M. Schultz, *Not Today: The 9 Habits of Extreme Productivity* (Dallas, TX: Matt Holt, 2021).

# ACKNOWLEDGMENTS

**TRADITIONALLY, AUTHORS EXPRESS** their appreciation as acknowledgments. But acknowledgment doesn't adequately express our sentiments—especially after over 40 years of researching and writing and now seven editions of *The Leadership Challenge*. Gratitude better captures the spirit of how we feel as we reflect on all those who have been part of this undertaking. We have had the opportunity to collaborate with hundreds of talented, hardworking, and inspiring people along the way. They've encouraged, enlightened, supported, challenged, and coached us. Because of them, we keep relearning a fundamental lesson about leadership, and life: *You can't do it alone.*

We begin by sending our gratitude to the thousands of everyday leaders we've met over the years. We wouldn't ever have been able to begin this journey without their willingness to share their inspiring stories with us. They are the heartbeat of *The Leadership Challenge*. Their experiences bring the text to life. They make it breathe and give it real-world relevance. We are honored, humbled, and thankful that they have made themselves available to us and to our readers.

We continue to be grateful to the gifted people at John Wiley & Sons. Jeanenne Ray, our acquisitions editor and associate publisher, has guided this manuscript, among many others of ours, from the editorial process through to production. We appreciate her confidence, expertise, and perseverance. And without her initial nudge, new editions would never happen. Kezia Endsley was our developmental editor on this edition, and her craftsmanship and guidance brought clarity and focus to our writing. Michelle Hacker, managing editor, insured that the book made it from Word files to printed pages. Our copy editor, Amy Handy, applied her acumen, making sure that the narratives flowed smoothly. A shoutout to Jozette Moses, editorial assistant, for the important part she played in keeping us connected and on schedule. Without Michael Friedberg and Alyssa Benigno, marketing managers, and Amy Ladicano, publicity manager, you wouldn't know about this book. Both do an awesome job of getting the word out about the book and its contributions. Thanks to art director Chris Wallace and graphic designer Jon Bolan for creating the attractive and eye-catching jacket and getting the interior look and feel just right. We are blessed to be working with a passionate team of professionals who make our work better every day.

We also want to express our gratitude to Tricia Weinhold, senior brand manager, The Leadership Challenge with Wiley, for her ongoing support in expanding the global reach and practical application of The Leadership Challenge. We offer special thanks to William Hull, Bradley Sallmen, and Ginger Weil and the entire Leadership Challenge Team at Wiley for their roles in bringing our work to the people who continue to want to become the best leaders they can be and make extraordinary things happen.

Our immediate families are our constant companions in all our books, and this one is no exception. They have been there through the highs and lows, deadlines and long hours, frustrations, and exhilarations. They have been our champions, cheerleaders, coaches, teachers, and best friends. We most definitely could not have done it without them. To our spouses, Tae Kyung Kouzes and Jackie Schmidt-Posner, we publicly express our deepest gratitude for their love, encouragement, sacrifices, and graciousness. And big hugs to Nicholas and Kimberly Lopez, and to Amanda Posner and Darryl Collins, for continuing to inspire our quest to develop new generations of leaders.

Last, and certainly not least, we express our gratitude to you, our readers. Without you, we'd never be able to contribute beyond the perimeter of our immediate friends and family. We greatly appreciate how you have accepted us into your organizations and communities. Thank you for the opportunity to collaborate in leaving this world a little bit better than we found it.

Jim Kouzes
Orinda, California

Barry Posner
Berkeley, California

January 2023

# ABOUT THE AUTHORS

**JIM KOUZES AND BARRY POSNER** have been working together for over forty years, studying leaders, researching leadership, conducting leadership development seminars, and providing leadership, with and without titles, in various capacities. They are coauthors of the award-winning, best-selling book *The Leadership Challenge*. Since its first edition in 1987, *The Leadership Challenge* has sold over nearly three million copies worldwide and is available in more than twenty-two languages. It has won numerous awards, including the Critics' Choice Award from the nation's book review editors and book-of-the-year awards from both the American Council of Healthcare Executives and *Fast Company*. *The Leadership Challenge* is listed in *The Top 100 Business Books of All Time*, as one of the Top 10 books on leadership.

Jim and Barry have co-authored more than a dozen other award-winning leadership books, including *Everyday People, Extraordinary Leadership; Leadership in Higher Education; Stop Selling & Start Leading; Learning Leadership: The Five Fundamentals for Becoming an Exemplary Leader; Turning Adversity into Opportunity; Finding the Courage to Lead; Great Leadership Creates Great Workplaces; Credibility: How Leaders Gain and Lose It, Why People Demand It; The Truth About*

*Leadership: The No-Fads, Heart-of-the Matter Facts You Need to Know; Encouraging the Heart: A Leader's Guide to Recognizing and Rewarding Others; A Leader's Legacy; Extraordinary Leadership in Australia and New Zealand; Making Extraordinary Things Happen in Asia;* and *The Student Leadership Challenge.*

Jim and Barry developed the widely used and highly acclaimed Leadership Practices Inventory (LPI), a 360-degree questionnaire assessing leadership behavior. The LPI has been completed by over five million people around the globe. Over 900 doctoral dissertations and academic research projects have been based on their The Five Practices of Exemplary Leadership® framework. More information about their publications and research is available at www.leadershipchallenge.com. You can also sign up on the website for their monthly newsletter.

Among the honors and awards that Jim and Barry have received are the Association for Talent and Development's (ATD) highest award for their *Distinguished Contribution to Workplace Learning and Performance*; named Management/Leadership Educators of the Year by the International Management Council; ranked by *Leadership Excellence* magazine in the top 20 on their list of the Top 100 Thought Leaders; named by *Coaching for Leadership* in the Top 50 Leadership Coaches in the nation; considered by *HR Magazine* as one of the Most Influential International Thinkers; and listed among the Top 75 Management Experts in the World by *Inc.* magazine.

Jim and Barry are frequent keynote speakers, and each has conducted leadership development programs for hundreds of organizations, including Apple, Applied Materials, ARCO, AT&T, Australia Institute of Management, Australia Post, Bank of America, Bose, Charles Schwab, Cisco Systems, Clorox, Community Leadership Association, Conference Board of Canada, Consumers Energy, Deloitte Touche, Dow Chemical, Egon Zehnder International, Federal Express, Genentech, Google, Gymboree, HP, IBM, Jobs DR-Singapore, Johnson & Johnson, Kaiser Foundation Health Plans and Hospitals, Intel, Itaú Unibanco, L.L. Bean, Lawrence Livermore National Labs, Lucile Packard Children's Hospital, Merck, Motorola, NetApp, Northrop Grumman, Novartis, Oakwood Housing, Oracle, Petronas, Roche Bioscience, Siemens, 3M, Toyota, the

U.S. Postal Service, United Way, USAA, Verizon, VISA, Westpac, and the Walt Disney Company. In addition, they have presented seminars and lectures at over 100 college and university campuses.

**Jim Kouzes** is a fellow at the Doerr Institute for New Leaders at Rice University and has been the Dean's Executive Fellow of Leadership, Leavey School of Business, at Santa Clara University. He lectures on leadership around the world to corporations, governments, and nonprofits. He is a highly regarded leadership scholar, an experienced executive, and the *Wall Street Journal* cited him as one of the twelve best executive educators in the United States. Jim has received the Thought Leadership Award from the Instructional Systems Association, the most prestigious award given by the trade association of training and development industry providers, and the Golden Gavel, the highest honor awarded by Toastmasters International.

Jim served as president, CEO, and chairman of the Tom Peters Company for eleven years, and led the Executive Development Center at Santa Clara University for seven years. He was the founder and executive director for eight years of the Joint Center for Human Services Development at San Jose State University and was on the staff of the School of Social Work, University of Texas. His career in training and development began in 1969 when he conducted seminars for Community Action Agency staff and volunteers in the war on poverty. Following graduation from Michigan State University (BA with honors in political science), he served as a Peace Corps volunteer (1967–1969). You can reach Jim directly at jim@kouzes.com.

**Barry Posner** holds the Michael J. Accolti, S.J., Chair at Santa Clara University and is Professor of Leadership with the Leavey School of Business, and chair of the Department of Management and Entrepreneurship. He previously served for six years as Associate Dean for Graduate Education, six years as Associate Dean for Executive Education, and twelve years as dean of the school. He has been a distinguished visiting professor around the globe: Hong Kong University of Science and Technology, Sabanci University (Istanbul), University of Western Australia, and University of Auckland. At Santa Clara he has received the President's Distinguished Faculty Award, the School's Extraordinary Faculty Award, and several other outstanding teaching and academic honors. An internationally renowned scholar and educator, Barry is author or coauthor of more than 100 research and practitioner-focused articles. He currently serves on the editorial review boards for *Leadership & Organizational Development Journal* and *The International Journal of Servant-Leadership*, and is a recipient of the *Journal of Management Inquiry*'s Outstanding Scholar Award for Career Achievement.

Barry received his baccalaureate degree with honors in political science from the University of California, Santa Barbara; his master's degree in public administration from the Ohio State University; and his doctoral degree in organizational behavior and administrative theory from the University of Massachusetts, Amherst. Having consulted worldwide with many public and private sector organizations, he also works at a strategic level with a number of community-based and professional organizations. He has served previously on the board of the American Institute of Architects (AIA), Big Brothers/Big Sisters of Santa Clara County, Center for Excellence in Nonprofits, Junior Achievement of Silicon Valley and Monterey Bay, Public Allies, San Jose Repertory Theater, SVCreates, Sigma Phi Epsilon Fraternity, Uplift Family Services, and several startup companies. Barry can be reached directly at bposner@scu.edu.

# INDEX


*1001 Ways to Reward Employees* (Nelson), 262

## A

Aaron, Hank (learning), 180
Abilities, leader confidence (importance/expression), 253, 254f
Accomplishments, public celebrations, 280–283
Accountability, fostering, 230–233
Achievements, increase, 270
Action, enabling, 4, 10–11, 145–148, 319
Active learner, 178–181
  capacity, building, 315
Active listening, importance, 202
Adventure, 160–162, 167
Advice/input, asking (fear), 159
Aho, Brenda (time/attention, spending), 64–66
*Alice's Adventures in Wonderland* (Carroll), 256
Appreciations, creativity, 265–269
Appreciativeness, 269–272
Armstrong, Lori (care, display), 292–293
Astafev, Alexey (recognition), 262
Attentiveness, 115, 264

## B

Baer, Brian (coaching), 242–243
Ballagh, Courtney (voice/shared values/outsight), 37, 51, 156–157
Barsi, Joe (leadership experience), 145
Basu, Radha (values, clarity), 38

Baxter, Louise (lives, brightening), 132
Behaviors, reinforcement, 78–79
Bennhold, Florian (trust/ payoff), 211
Best, expectation, 251–260
Binger, Jane (care, display), 291–292
Bjorkman, Sarah (feedback), 70–71
Blum, Arlene (purpose), 153
Brainstorming, 116, 144–145, 158
Brocato, Justin (celebrations), 298
Brown, Vince (example, setting), 5
Business goals, achievement, 197–198

## C

Campbell, David, 277
Campion, Dina (opportunity), 146–147
Caring
  display, 290–294
  reasons, supply, 51–52
Carroll, Lewis, 256
Carter, Joan (attitude/communication style), 129–130
Celebrate the values and victories, 275, 300–301
Celebrations, usage, 278–283, 296–299
Challenges, 317
  crucible/importance, 304–305
  opportunity, treatment, 303
  purpose, usage, 151–153
Challenge the Process, 4, 8–10, 142, 319
Chandrasekhar, Preethi (vision/ brainstorming), 116–117
Changes
  coping, 173
  forward-looking action, 106–108
Chan, Grace (jobs, structuring), 230
Chan, Maurice (recognition, personalization), 261–262
Characteristics of Admired Leaders (CAL) checklist, 19–20, 21t
Charisma, impact, 130–131
Cheerleading, importance, 290
Cheng, Andy (empathy, display), 204
Choices, providing, 225–228
Christen, Pat (shared values, importance), 53–54
Christensen, Kent (V-S-E-M), 123
Clarify values, 5, 31, 43–45, 56–57, 107
Clark, Sonia (recognition), 267–268
Cleveland, Jill (employee trust), 193–195
Coaching/mentoring, 241–243
Cole, Amy (metaphor, usage), 126
Coleman, Brian (behavior reinforcement), 78
Collaboration
  fostering, 10–11, 193, 195, 217–218
  occurrence, 207

Collins, Maureen (hardiness principles), 172–173
Commitment, 104–106
  finding, values clarification (usage), 43–45, 44f
Commitment, control, challenge (psychological hardiness factors), 172
Common ideals, appeal, 113–124
Common purpose, identification, 90, 101–108
Community, spirit (creation), 12–13, 277–288
Competence, development/ building, 11, 221, 233–243
  work, organization (impact), 238–239
Concern, display, 201–204
Confidence, development, 221, 233–243
Connectedness, increase, 214–215
Constituents, knowledge, 263–265
Content, learning (question), 177f
Contributions, recognition, 249, 272–273
Cooperation/competition strategies, 210
Cooperative goals/roles, development, 208–210
Cooperative relationships, 209f
Corporate celebrations, usage, 278
COVID-19
  impact, 9, 62, 106, 158, 172–173, 197, 228
  lockdowns, impact, 285
  uncertainties/discontinuities, leadership (impact), 304
Creativity, importance, 266
Credibility, 65
  behavioral definition, 70
  behavioral perception, 26–27
  exemplary practices, link, 27
  importance, 23–27
Critical incidents, confrontation, 75–76
Curiosity
  conversations, 183–184
  nurturing, 183
Customer retention/engagement, improvement, 66

## D

Dalton, Brian (public acknowledgments, value), 283
Davidson, Megon (past, reflection), 93
Denning, Steve (storytelling), 77
Diemer, Ryan (risk-taking), 184
Dilpreet, Singh (storytelling), 294–295
Direct reports
  engagement, 308
  organizational valuation, 284f
Distinctiveness, levels, 118–119
Diversity, equity, and inclusion, xiv, 64, 127
Dokiparthi, Venkat (task breakdown), 174
Donahue, Robin (initiative), 143–145

Do What You Say You Will Do (DWYSYWD), 27
Doyle, John (goals, achievement), 208
Dreams, alignment, 121–124
Durable social connections, maintenance, 213–216

## E

Emotional arousal, impact, 131–132
Emotional trust, 197
Emotions, expression, 130–133
Empathy, demonstration, 204
Employees
  engagement, 118, 270, 285
  fun, enjoyment, 286–288
Empowerment, 224–225
Enable Others to Act, 4, 10–11, 145–148, 319
Encourage the Heart, 4, 11–13, 251, 319
Engagement
  employee engagement, 118, 270, 285
  explanation, 307
  factors, 169
  Five Practices, impact, 13
  fostering, 285
  improvement, 66, 305
  increase, 100, 116
  leaders, impact, xiv
  levels
    elevation, 195, 221
    variation, 308
  measures, 3
  variance, 17
  weakening, 35
Enlisting, importance, 111, 135–136
Enlist others, 7, 99, 104, 111
Envision the future, 87–100, 109–110
Equity, xiv, 64, 127
Ernst, Jennifer (celebrations), 275–276
Evans, Larry (process, challenge), 142
Evidence-based practices operating system, xvi
Example, setting, 5, 59–61, 65, 82–83
Exemplary leaders
  celebration culture, benefits, 277
  experimentation/risk-taking, 167–168
  focus, 19
  forward-looking characteristic, 90
  reality, acceptance, 175–176
Exemplary leadership
  examples, 2–3
  practices, 4–5, 14t, 15, 178, 305–307
    increase, 16f
    usage, increase (benefit/financial impact), 17–18
Experience
  examination, 155–157
  learning/knowledge acquisition, 167, 176–187
Experiment and take risks, 9, 165, 184, 188–190

## F

Fakharzadeh, Masood (trust), 200
Feedback, 78–79, 272
  absence, 263
  asking/providing, 70–73, 76, 258–260
  sandwich, serving (avoidance), 260
  sessions, 145
Feelings, attention, 202
Fernandes, Shandon Lee (personal-best leadership experience), 43
Field, Rob (values, examination), 39–40
Fixed mindset, 181, 315
Flow, experience, 234, 257
Foster collaboration, 10–11, 193, 195, 217–218
Fradenburg, Joshua (questions, focus), 69–70
Freedom, feeling, 226
Fundraising event, experimentation, 165–167
Fun, inculcation, 286–288
Future
  envisioning, 87–100, 109–110
  images, creation, 127–129
  prospecting, 96–98

## G

Gad, Sachin (goals/values, clarity), 257
Gardner, John, 19
Generalized reciprocity, norm, 211
Genuine speech, usage, 133–134
Gere, Andy (accountability), 232
Ghimire, Bhupendra (plans), 87–88
Givers/takers, contrast, 213
Goals/rules, clarity, 256–258
Goals/values, impact, 257–258
Golden Rule, 211
Grant, Adam (predicting), 98
Greatness
  challenge, impact, 8–10
  team effort, requirement, 10–11
Great Resignation, xiii
Grimm, Diann (dreams/ambitions), 87–89
Growth mindset, 180–181, 186, 315, 321
Guidance, importance, 260
Guiding vision, creation, 101–102

## H

Hage, Joe (learning), 180
Hall, Doug, 118
Hall, Hilary (learning experience), 260
Hamel, Gary, 95
Harvey, Kyle (vision, development), 108
Heart, encouragement/giving, 4, 11–13, 251, 319
Hodson, Celia (information sharing), 236–237, 241
Ho, Suk Yee (questions), 155
Humility, importance, 320

**I**

Ideas/aspirations, sharing, 52, 239
IKEA effect, 231
Image-based words,
usage, 122–123
Inclusion, xiv, 64, 127, 216
consideration, 69
Individuals
appreciation, 12–13
values, organizational values (congruence), 49
Information
education/sharing, 204–205, 235–238
processing, 156
Initiative
encouragement, 148–151
seizing, 9, 141–153
Innovation
leadership, relationship, 142
mistakes, experience (learning), 179
Insight, 154
Inspire a Shared Vision, 4, 7–8, 13, 152, 319
Institutional trust, 197

**J**

Jaiswal, Ankur (work environment support), 11
James, Elizabeth (employee fun), 288
Jamieson, Gary(small wins), 168
Jiang, Kevin (appreciative emails), 270–271
Jobs
adventures, equivalence, 160–162
structuring, 228–230
Johnson, Paul (credo/vision statement creation), 101–102
Joint effort, promotion, 211–213

**K**

Klotzach, Darrell (vision, non-limitation), 96
Klotzbach, Darrell (knowledge/information, sharing), 204–205
Knowledge, sharing, 204–206
Kozlovsky, Patti (abilities, belief), 254–255

**L**

Lai, Olivia (appreciation, display), 270
Lamott, Anne (experience, truth), 40–41
Language, communication, 67–68
LaSalandra, Jim (artist life, periods), 41
Law, Charles (shared values, agreement), 54–55
Leaders
behavior, multivariate analyses, 17
celebrations, usage, 297–299
cooperative relationships, 209f
effectiveness, 169, 226

engagement/performance levels, explanation, 307–308
futures department role, 97
ideals, 115
image-based words, usage, 122–123
improvement, habit, 321–323
initiative, 144f
job performance, evaluations, 150f
joy/passion, demonstration, 287–288
liberation, 309–313
listening, results, 104
personal example, power, 61–62
personal involvement, impact, 291f
positive expectations, impact, 254–256
questions, 33–34
recommendation, likelihood, 307f, 312f
search/admiration, 19–23
trust, increase, 63f
values, clarity, 48
Leadership, 143
behavior, 178, 309–310
competence, 22
credibility (foundation), 24
development, 317
direct report effectiveness ratings, 169, 170f
experience, 1, 19
forward-looking approach, 23
Golden Rule, 66
honesty, 20–21
importance, 305–308
inspiration, 22–23
learning, 41–42, 313–316
mistakes, 319–321
philosophy, articulation/clarity, 35–37, 36f
relationship, 18–23
skills, identification, 3
Leadership Practices Inventory (LPI)
behaviors, 309–310, 314
creation/development, 3
feedback, 70–71
usage/completion, 15, 306, 314
*Leading the Revolution* (Hamel), 95
*Lead with a Story* (Smith), 77
Learning, 259
climate, creation, 181–185
skill, 10
Lee, Seang Wee (feedback, usage), 71
Lessons, learning, 74–75
L.I.F.E. paradigm, responses (recording), 318
Life, success (secret), 323–324
Life/work, beliefs/assumptions, 91
Lim, Anita (best, expectation), 252–253
Limaye, Raj (competence building), 238–239
Lin, Anita (recognition), 268
Lin, Michael (values, expression), 52–53

Lin, Tsung-Chieh (praise, effectiveness), 269–270
Listening, depth (importance), 102–104, 157–160
Long, Erika (information sharing), 237–238
Long-term interests, impact, 119f
Lopes, Sonya (employee fun), 288
Lu, Hong (team focus), 171
Lukach, Jerry (ceremonies, usage), 282

## M

Maartense, Jacqueline (company creation), 139–141
MacIntyre, Janet (symbolic language, usage), 125
Malik, Eakta (team spirit), 12
Managers, credibility (perception), 25–26
McCale, Dawn, 187
McLaughlin, Sean (concern, display), 200–202
McNeil, Nathalie (attention), 261
Meaningfulness, connection, 116–118
Merchant, Nilofer, 237
Messenger, belief (importance), 24
Metaphors, usage, 126
Micromanagement, 220
Mistakes, 182–183, 319–321
Model the Way, 4, 5–7, 60, 65, 319
Molina, Sebastian (celebrations), 278
Moreno-Ramirez, Juliana (leadership direction), 35
Moser, Anne (team/individual celebration/recognition), 11–12
Most Valuable Players (MVPs), selection, 282

## N

Nagaraj, Srinath Thurthahalli (risk-taking), 9
Naisbitt, John, 95
Needs, attention, 201
Nelson, Bob, 262
Nicolo, Joan (contribution recognition), 249–251

## O

Ojakian, David, 9
O'Leary, Patrick (values, trust), 32
O'Neill, Tyrone (example, leading), 66
Opportunities
  creation, 315–316
  search, 139, 163–164
Organizational effectiveness, shared values (importance), 50
Organizational life, celebrations (usage), 296–299
Organizational values, absence, 35
Organizations
  direct reports, perception, 203f
  pride, increase, 227f
Others
  action, enabling, 4, 10–11, 145–148, 319
  appreciation, 264

belief, 255–256
strengthening, 219, 237, 244–245
Outcomes, experience, 117
Outside the box thinking, 183
Outsight
exercising, 141, 154–162
importance, 156–157

## P

Pacas, Jan (celebrations), 281
Panuccio, Anthony (job roles, playbook), 219–221
Pari, Divya (relationship, facilitation), 205–206
Passion, expression, 98–101
Past, reflection, 93–94
Pearl, Robert (leadership, understanding), 319
Peer-nominated awards, usage, 281
Perepelitsky, Leon (collaboration), 207
Performance
improvement/enhancement, 203–204, 320–321
motivation, 170–171
self-confidence, impact, 140
Personal-Best Leadership Experience, 123–124, 175, 206, 270, 304
cases/stories, 32, 187
questionnaire, usage, 1–2
understanding, 310
Personal-best leadership, story, 3
Personal-best projects, distinction, 6
Personal expression, 40–43
Personal history, importance, 93–94
Personal involvement, importance, 277, 289–299
Personal values, clarity, 44
Perspectives, diversity (promotion), 157–160
Physical distance, maintenance, 214
Pickett, Siobhan (leadership experience), 206–207
Positive communication, practice, 129–130
Positive workplace attitude (PWA), 92
Possibilities, imagining, 90–101
Power, feeling, 224–225
Powerlessness, problem, 222–223
Prabhu, Santosh, 81
Present, attention, 94–96
Prisoners' Dilemma paradigm, 210
Private rewards, limitations, 283
Process, challenge, 4, 8–10, 142, 319
Productivity (enhancement), social support (impact), 285
Progress, accentuation, 173–176
Projects, structuring, 212–214
Promises/commitments, follow-through, 63f

Psychological hardiness
building, 171–173
factors, 172
Psychological ownership, 231–232
Psychological safety, feeling, 181–182
Purposeful questions, asking, 68–70
Purpose, power, 151–153
Pygmalion Effect, 252

R

Rajamani, Srini (lunch and learn sessions), 234–235
Ravizza, Stephen (positive outlook), 149
Razouk, Laila (beliefs), 133–134
Reciprocity, norms (support), 210–211
Recognition
frequency, impact, 281–282
personalization, 251, 261–272
specificity, effectiveness, 268
Recognize contributions, 249, 272–273
Relationships
building, 298
facilitation, 10–11, 195, 205–216, 265
Relevant language, usage, 67–68
Remote environments, recognition (importance), 251
Remote work
isolating impact, 285
setting, 200
Remote-work environments, trust (building), 197
Remote workplaces, challenges, 268
Remote Zoom meetings, usage, xiii–xiv
Resilience/grit, strengthening, 185–187
Rewards, cost/responses, 267–268
Rickerson, Wilson (trust/payoff), 211
Risk-taking, 9, 165, 184, 189–190
Role models
importance, 316
selection, percentage, 311t
Rowling, J.K. (learning), 180
Ryan, Michael (company core values, importance), 47

S

Salquist, Monika (leader opportunities), 322
Sasser, Richard (values, display), 48
Sawyer, Mike (employee fun), 286–287
Schwab, Dan, 96
Schwappach, Jim (vision, defining), 103
Schwarzkopf, H. Norman (shared values, teaching), 73–74, 76
Schweizer, Carol, 253
Search for opportunities, 139, 163–164
Sedlock, Julie (company values, sharing), 45

Selden, Robin, 143
Self-compassion, triggers, 321
Self-confidence, fostering, 239–241
Self-determination, increase/enhancement, 11, 221–233
Self-development, 317–319
Self-disclosure, usage, 200
Self-reflection, usage, 71–72
Set the example, 5, 59–61, 65, 82–83
Shah, Kinjal (empowerment), 224–225
Shakir, Sumaya (self-questions), 34
Shared aspirations
  practice, 295
  struggle, 18–19
Shared values
  affirmation, 6, 32, 45
  basis, benefits, 47–48
  impact, 48–51
  living, 61–73
  management support, 53
  practice, 295
Shared vision
  delivery, 112
  inspiration, 4, 7–8, 13, 152, 319
Sharma, Akansha (feedback), 259
Sharp, Debbie (future, seeing), 128–129
Sharpnack, Rayona (task breakdown), 174–175
Shukla, Prashant (action/inventiveness), 147
Siegel, John (values, discussion), 39
Silberman, Blaze, 266
Singh, Emily (critical incident), 76
Singleton, Russell (personal involvement), 289–290
Skarke, Steve (example, setting), 59–60
Small wins
  generation, 167–176
  process, usage, 170f
Smith, Jared (leadership principles, focus/sharing), 36–37
Smith, Paul, 77
Social capital, 213–214, 216
Social support, providing, 283–286
Social trust, 197
Sones, Eric B. (teamwork), 111–113
Staff, development, 241–242
Standard operating procedure (SOP), 158
Standing Ovations, usage, 279
Stanford, John H. (life success, secret), 323–324
Storytelling, 76–78
  spreading, 294–296
Strengthen others, 219, 237, 244–245
Stress, coping, 173
Symbolic language, usage, 125–127

**T**

Tai, Eddie (feedback), 258–259
Tasks
  breakdown, 173–176
  success/failure, allowance, 194

Teaching/reinforcement, informal methods (usage), 79–81
Team
  celebration/appreciation, 11–13
  confidence, 255
  differentiation, 8–9
  spirit, increase, 236f
Thank-you, usage/expression, 269–271
Time/attention, spending, 64–66
Tiwari, Arpana (values, clarification), 6
Tolmare, Amit (present, understanding), 94–95
Tomlinson, Amy (feedback), 72
Tran, Jennifer (shared values), 75, 76
Triage methodology, 197
Trust
  absence, problems, 198–199
  benefits, 198
  building, 10–11, 199–200, 217
  climate, creation, 195–206
  increase, 264
  investment, 197–199
Turner, Phil (actions), 147–148

## U

Undertakings, leader visibility, 293–294
Uniqueness, pride, 118–121
Unity, forging, 52–55

## V

Values
  celebration, 275, 300–301
  clarification/clarity, 5, 31, 43–45, 56–57, 107
  discussions/conversations, 37–39, 51–52
  empowerment ability, 39
  examination, 39–40
  guidance, 37–40
  modeling, teaching, 61, 73
  reinforcement, rewards/recognition (usage), 79
Van Sant, Emma (celebrations), 279
Vesterman, Jim (collaboration), 212
Victories, celebration, 275, 300–301
Virtual connections, quality (debate), 215
Virtual reality/trust, problem, 215–216
Virtual workplace, 52, 127
Vision
  animation, 113, 124–134
  collaborative process, 112–113
  declarations, 114
  knowledge, importance, 91
  projection, 92
Vision, Strategy, Execution, and Metrics (V-S-E-M), 123
Vision, usage, 38, 89
Voice, finding, 32, 33

Volatile, uncertain, complex, and ambiguous (VUCA) world, 213
Vu, M.T. (award, receiving), 280

**W**

Wang, Barbara (abilities, belief), 255–256
Wang, Cathy (personal/work values, impact), 48
Watkins, Michael (historical perspective), 93–94
Watson, Matthew (trust issues), 196–197
Wiencke, Judith (care, display), 290–291
Williams, Imani (shared values), 62–63
Williams, Pat (leadership study), 185–186
Wingate, Jenna (risk-taking), 165–167
Wong, Anne (questions), 155
Work (meaning/purpose), conviction (speaking), 99f
Work/life, meaning (themes), 105
Work, motivation, 212

**Y**

Yamunan, Anu (appreciations), 265–266
Yu, Raymond (voice, discovery), 41

**Z**

Zaveleta, Luis (training/job encouragement), 157–158, 263–264
Zaveri, Azmeena (pride/tradition), 120, 148
Zhang, John (choices, providing), 225
Zinsser, William (imitation), 42